The Schengen acquis

integrated into the European Union

1 May 1999

Notice

This booklet, which has been prepared by the General Secretariat of the Council, does not commit either the Community institutions or the governments of the Member States.

Please note that only the text that shall be published in the *Official Journal of the European Communities* L 239, 22 September 2000, is deemed authentic.

For further information, please contact the Information Policy, Transparency and Public Relations Division at the following address:

General Secretariat of the Council
Rue de la Loi 175
B-1048 Brussels
Fax 32 (0)2 285 5332
E-mail: public.info@consilium.eu.int

Internet: http://ue.eu.int

A great deal of additional information on the European Union is available on the Internet. It can be accessed through the Europa server (http://europa.eu.int).

Cataloguing data can be found at the end of this publication.

Luxembourg: Office for Official Publications of the European Communities, 2001

ISBN 92-824-1776-X

Printed in Belgium

FOREWORD

When the Amsterdam Treaty entered into force on 1 May 1999, cooperation measures hitherto in the Schengen framework were integrated into the European Union framework.

The Schengen Protocol annexed to the Amsterdam Treaty lays down detailed arrangements for that integration process. An annex to the protocol specifies what is meant by 'Schengen *acquis*'.

The decisions and declarations adopted within the Schengen institutional framework by the Executive Committee have never before been published.

The General Secretariat of the Council has decided to produce for those interested a collection of the Executive Committee decisions and declarations integrated by the Council decision of 20 May 1999 (1999/435/EC).

The Schengen *acquis* will be published in the Official Journal in all language versions as soon as all translations are available.

This collection presents the Schengen *acquis* chronologically and according to topic.

I trust that this publication will serve to ensure greater transparency.

Charles Elsen
Director-General
Justice and Home Affairs

CONTENTS

ABBREVIATIONS USED

OJ	Agenda
PV	Minutes
REV	Revision
CORR	Correction
CM	Common manual
CCI	Common consular instructions
SCH	Schengen
SCH/M	Ministers and State secretaries (until October 1993)
SCH/COM-EX	Executive Committee
SCH/C	Central Group
SCH/I	Working Group I 'Police and Security'
SCH/I-AR	Working Group I 'Police and Security' — Subgroup on 'Arms and ammunition'
SCH/I-FRONT	Working Group I 'Police and Security' — Subgroup on 'Frontiers'
SCH/I-TELECOM	Working Group I 'Police and Security' — Subgroup on 'Telecommunications'
SCH/GEM-HANDB	Working Group I 'Police and Security' — Subgroup on 'Common manual'
SCH/STUP	Working Group 'Drugs' (Article 70)
SCH/II	Working Group II 'Movement of persons'
SCH/II-READ	Working Group II 'Movement of persons' — Subgroup on 'Readmission'
SCH/II-VISA	Working Group II 'Movement of persons' — Subgroup on 'Visas'
SCH/II-VISION	Working Group II 'Movement of persons' — 'Vision' Subgroup (Visa Inquiry Open-border Network)
SCH/III	Working Group III 'Judicial cooperation'
SCH/OR.SIS	Working Group 'SIS steering committee'

SCH/OR.SIS/SIS	Working Group 'SIS steering committee' — Subgroup 'Schengen information system'
SCH/OR.SIS/SIRENE	Working Group 'SIS steering committee' — Subgroup 'Sirene'
SCH/SG	Note Schengen 'General Secretariat'
SIS	Schengen information system
C.SIS	Schengen information system 'Central section'
N.SIS	Schengen information system 'National section'

INTRODUCTORY NOTE

1. Article 1(2) of Council Decision 1999/435/EC of 20 May 1999 [1] provides that the Schengen *acquis*, as referred to in paragraph 1 of that same article, is to be published in the *Official Journal of the European Communities*, with the exception of those of its provisions listed in Article 2 and those provisions which at the time of adoption are classified as 'confidential' by the Schengen Executive Committee.

Article 2 of the same Council decision states that it will not be necessary for the Council to determine, in conformity with the provisions of the Treaties, a legal basis for the provisions and decisions constituting part of the Schengen *acquis* and listed in Annex B to the decision.

This unofficial publication, prepared pending the publication of the Schengen *acquis* in the Official Journal in all official languages of the Community institutions, therefore contains the provisions and decisions constituting part of the *acquis* for which the Council, in its Decision 1999/436/EC of 20 May 1999 [2], has determined the legal basis in conformity with the relevant provisions of the Treaties.

2. This publication also lists the provisions and decisions forming part of the Schengen *acquis* which concern the Schengen information system (SIS); they are annotated with 'for the record' in the Council decision determining the legal basis in conformity with the relevant provisions of the Treaties.

3. This publication sets out the Schengen *acquis* as it stood when it was integrated into the European Union on the entry into force of the Treaty of Amsterdam (1 May 1999). Since the Schengen *acquis* comprises information provided by the States concerned, for example regarding their visa policy towards nationals of third States that do not figure on the common list of third States whose nationals must hold a visa in order to cross the external borders, information should be sought from the appropriate Commission departments or the General Secretariat of the Council as to any changes since 1 May 1999.

(1) Council decision concerning the definition of the Schengen *acquis* for the purpose of determining, in conformity with the relevant provisions of the Treaty establishing the European Community and the Treaty on European Union, the legal basis for each of the provisions or decisions which constitute the *acquis*, OJ L 176, 10.7.1999, p. 1.

(2) Council decision determining, in conformity with the relevant provisions of the Treaty establishing the European Community and the Treaty on European Union, the legal basis for each of the provisions or decisions which constitute the Schengen *acquis*, OJ L 176, 10.7.1999, p. 17.

4. For the sake of the broad picture, this publication contains all of the provisions of the convention of 19 June 1990 implementing the Schengen Agreement of 14 June 1985 on the gradual abolition of checks at the common borders. However, the Council has decided that a legal basis does not need to be determined in conformity with the relevant provisions of the Treaties for the provisions printed in italics.

5. In order to facilitate access to the part of the Schengen *acquis* consisting of the decisions and declarations of the Executive Committee of Schengen, they have been grouped according to subject matter in this publication. To that end, the decisions and declarations have been classified as follows:

— 'horizontal' issues;

— the abolition of checks at internal borders and the free movement of persons;

— police cooperation;

— judicial cooperation in criminal matters;

— the SIS.

The decisions are given in chronological order within each heading. The same applies for the declarations of the Executive Committee.

6. Some of the Executive Committee decisions refer to documents drawn up within the framework of Schengen cooperation which, according to the Council decision on the definition of the Schengen *acquis*, do indeed form part of the Schengen *acquis* but for which the Council has decided there is no need to determine a legal basis in conformity with the relevant provisions of the Treaties. As a result, these documents do not figure in this publication.

7. The same is true of documents referred to in the preamble to certain Executive Committee decisions, but to which no reference is made in the enacting terms of the decisions themselves.

8. Lastly, there are some Executive Committee decisions adopting documents in annex which the Secretary-General of the Council, by virtue of the responsibility incumbent upon him in accordance with Article 20(2) of the rules of procedure of the Council, has decided should be classified as *confidentiel* or *restreint* Council documents. These annexes have therefore deliberately not been published either.

1. AGREEMENT + CONVENTION + ACCESSIONS

AGREEMENT
BETWEEN THE GOVERNMENTS
OF THE STATES OF THE BENELUX ECONOMIC UNION,
THE FEDERAL REPUBLIC OF GERMANY
AND THE FRENCH REPUBLIC
ON THE GRADUAL ABOLITION OF CHECKS
AT THEIR COMMON BORDERS

The Governments of the Kingdom of Belgium, the Federal Republic of Germany, the French Republic, the Grand Duchy of Luxembourg and the Kingdom of the Netherlands,

hereinafter referred to as 'the Parties',

Aware that the ever closer union of the peoples of the Member States of the European Communities should find its expression in the freedom to cross internal borders for all nationals of the Member States and in the free movement of goods and services,

Anxious to strengthen the solidarity between their peoples by removing the obstacles to free movement at the common borders between the States of the Benelux Economic Union, the Federal Republic of Germany and the French Republic,

Considering the progress already achieved within the European Communities with a view to ensuring the free movement of persons, goods and services,

Prompted by the resolve to achieve the abolition of checks at their common borders on the movement of nationals of the Member States of the European Communities and to facilitate the movement of goods and services at those borders,

Considering that application of this agreement may require legislative measures which will have to be submitted to the parliaments of the Signatory States in accordance with their constitutions,

Having regard to the statement by the Fontainebleau European Council on 25 and 26 June 1984 on the abolition of police and customs formalities for people and goods crossing intra-Community frontiers,

Having regard to the agreement concluded at Saarbrücken on 13 July 1984 between the Federal Republic of Germany and the French Republic,

Having regard to the conclusions adopted on 31 May 1984 following the meeting of the transport ministers of the Benelux States and the Federal Republic of Germany at Neustadt/Aisch,

Having regard to the memorandum of the Governments of the Benelux Economic Union of 12 December 1984 forwarded to the Governments of the Federal Republic of Germany and the French Republic,

HAVE AGREED AS FOLLOWS:

TITLE I

MEASURES APPLICABLE IN THE SHORT TERM

Article 1

As soon as this agreement enters into force and until all checks are abolished completely, the formalities for nationals of the Member States of the European Communities at the common borders between the States of the Benelux Economic Union, the Federal Republic of Germany and the French Republic shall be carried out in accordance with the conditions laid down below.

Article 2

With regard to the movement of persons, from 15 June 1985 the police and customs authorities shall as a general rule carry out simple visual surveillance of private vehicles crossing the common border at reduced speed, without requiring such vehicles to stop.

However, they may carry out more thorough controls by means of spot checks. These shall be performed where possible off the main road, so as not to interrupt the flow of other vehicles crossing the border.

Article 3

To facilitate visual surveillance, nationals of the Member States of the European Communities wishing to cross the common border in a motor vehicle may affix to the windscreen a green disc measuring at least 8 centimetres in diameter. This disc shall indicate that they have complied with border police rules, are carrying only goods permitted under the duty-free arrangements and have complied with exchange regulations.

Article 4

The Parties shall endeavour to keep to a minimum the time spent at common borders in connection with checks on the carriage of passengers by road for hire or reward.

The Parties shall seek solutions enabling them by 1 January 1986 to waive systematic checks at their common borders on passenger waybills and licences for the carriage of passengers by road for hire or reward.

Article 5

By 1 January 1986, common checks shall be put in place at adjacent national control posts insofar as that is not already the case and insofar as physical conditions so permit. Consideration shall subsequently be given to the possibility of introducing common checks at other border crossing points, taking account of local conditions.

Article 6

Without prejudice to the application of more favourable arrangements between the Parties, the latter shall take the measures required to facilitate the movement of nationals of the Member States of the European Communities resident in the local administrative areas along their common borders with a view to allowing them to cross those borders at places other than authorised crossing points and outside checkpoint opening hours.

The persons concerned may benefit from these advantages provided that they transport only goods permitted under the duty-free arrangements and comply with exchange regulations.

Article 7

The Parties shall endeavour to approximate their visa policies as soon as possible in order to avoid the adverse consequences in the field of immigration and security that may result from easing checks at the common borders. They shall take, if possible by 1 January 1986, the necessary steps in order to apply their procedures for the issue of visas and admission to their territories, taking into account the need to ensure the protection of the entire territory of the five States against illegal immigration and activities which could jeopardise security.

Article 8

With a view to easing checks at their common borders and taking into account the significant differences in the laws of the States of the Benelux Economic Union, the Federal Republic of Germany and the French Republic, the Parties undertake to combat vigorously illicit drug trafficking on their territories and to coordinate their action effectively in this area.

Article 9

The Parties shall reinforce cooperation between their customs and police authorities, notably in combating crime, particularly illicit trafficking in narcotic drugs and arms, the unauthorised entry and residence of persons, customs and tax fraud and smuggling. To that end and in accordance with their national laws, the Parties shall endeavour to improve the exchange of information and to reinforce that exchange where information which could be useful to the other Parties in combating crime is concerned.

Within the framework of their national laws the Parties shall reinforce mutual assistance in respect of unauthorised movements of capital.

Article 10

With a view to ensuring the cooperation provided for in Articles 6 to 9, meetings between the Parties' competent authorities shall be held at regular intervals.

Article 11

With regard to the cross-border carriage of goods by road, the Parties shall waive, as from 1 July 1985, systematic performance of the following checks at their common borders:

— control of driving and rest periods (Council Regulation (EEC) No 543/69 of 25 March 1969 on the harmonisation of certain social legislation relating to road transport and AETR);

— control of the weights and dimensions of commercial vehicles; this provision shall not prevent the introduction of automatic weighing systems for spot checks on weight;

— controls on the vehicles' technical state.

Measures shall be taken to avoid checks being duplicated within the territories of the Parties.

Article 12

From 1 July 1985 checks on documents detailing transport operations not carried out under licence or quota pursuant to Community or bilateral rules shall be replaced at the common borders by spot checks. Vehicles carrying out transport operations under such arrangements shall display a visual symbol to that effect when crossing the border.

The Parties' competent authorities shall determine the features of this symbol by common agreement.

Article 13

The Parties shall endeavour to harmonise by 1 January 1986 the systems applying among them to the licensing of commercial road transport with regard to cross-border traffic, with the aim of simplifying, easing and possibly replacing licences for journeys by licences for a period of time, with a visual check when vehicles cross common borders.

The procedures for converting licences for journeys into licences for periods of time shall be agreed on a bilateral basis, account being taken of the road haulage requirements in the different countries concerned.

Article 14

The Parties shall seek solutions to reduce the waiting times of rail transport at the common borders caused by the completion of border formalities.

Article 15

The Parties shall recommend to their respective rail companies:

— to adapt technical procedures in order to minimise stopping times at the common borders;

— to do their utmost to apply to certain types of carriage of goods by rail, to be defined by the rail companies, a special routing system whereby the common borders can be crossed rapidly without any appreciable stops (goods trains with reduced stopping times at borders).

Article 16

The Parties shall harmonise the opening dates and opening hours of customs posts for inland waterway traffic at the common borders.

TITLE II

MEASURES APPLICABLE IN THE LONG TERM

Article 17

With regard to the movement of persons, the Parties shall endeavour to abolish checks at common borders and transfer them to their external borders. To that end they shall endeavour first to harmonise, where necessary, the laws, regulations and administrative provisions concerning the prohibitions and restrictions on which the checks are based and to take complementary measures to safeguard internal security and prevent illegal immigration by nationals of States that are not members of the European Communities.

Article 18

The Parties shall open discussions, in particular on the following matters, account being taken of the results of the short-term measures:

(a) drawing up arrangements for police cooperation on crime prevention and investigation;

(b) examining any difficulties that may arise in applying agreements on international judicial assistance and extradition, in order to determine the most appropriate solutions for improving cooperation between the Parties in those fields;

(c) seeking means to combat crime jointly, *inter alia* by studying the possibility of introducing a right of hot pursuit for police officers, taking into account existing means of communication and international judicial assistance.

Article 19

The Parties shall seek to harmonise laws and regulations, in particular on:

— narcotic drugs;

— arms and explosives;

— the registration of travellers in hotels.

Article 20

The Parties shall endeavour to harmonise their visa policies and the conditions for entry to their territories. Insofar as is necessary, they shall also prepare the harmonisation of their rules governing certain aspects of the law on aliens in regard to nationals of States that are not members of the European Communities.

Article 21

The Parties shall take common initiatives within the European Communities:

(a) to achieve an increase in the duty-free allowances granted to travellers;

(b) in the context of Community allowances to remove any remaining restrictions on entry to the Member States of goods possession of which is not prohibited for their nationals.

The Parties shall take initiatives within the European Communities so that VAT on tourist transport services within the European Communities is collected in the country of departure on a harmonised basis.

Article 22

The Parties shall endeavour both among themselves and within the European Communities:

— to increase the duty-free allowance for fuel in order to bring it into line with the normal contents of bus and coach fuel tanks (600 litres);

— to approximate the tax rates on diesel fuel and to increase the duty-free allowances for the normal contents of lorry fuel tanks.

Article 23

In the field of goods transport the Parties shall also endeavour to reduce stopping times and the number of stopping points at adjacent national control posts.

Article 24

With regard to the movement of goods, the Parties shall seek means of transferring the checks currently carried out at the common borders to the external borders or to within their own territories.

To that end they shall take, where necessary, common initiatives among themselves and within the European Communities to harmonise the provisions on which checks on goods at the common borders are based. They shall ensure that these measures do not adversely affect the necessary protection of the health of humans, animals and plants.

Article 25

The Parties shall develop their cooperation with a view to facilitating customs clearance of goods crossing a common border, through a systematic, automatic exchange of the necessary data collected by means of the single document.

Article 26

The Parties shall examine how indirect taxes (VAT and excise duties) may be harmonised in the framework of the European Communities. To that end they shall support the initiatives undertaken by the European Communities.

Article 27

The Parties shall examine whether, on a reciprocal basis, the limits on the duty-free allowances granted at the common borders to frontier-zone residents, as authorised under Community law, may be abolished.

Article 28

Before the conclusion of any bilateral or multilateral arrangements similar to this agreement with States that are not Parties thereto, the Parties shall consult among themselves.

Article 29

This agreement shall also apply to Berlin, unless a declaration to the contrary is made by the Government of the Federal Republic of Germany to the Governments of the States of the Benelux Economic Union and the Government of the French Republic within three months of entry into force of this agreement.

Article 30

The measures provided for in this agreement which are not applicable as soon as it enters into force shall be applied by 1 January 1986 as regards the measures provided for in Title I and if possible by 1 January 1990 as regards the measures provided for in Title II, unless other deadlines are laid down in this agreement.

Article 31

This agreement shall apply subject to the provisions of Articles 5 and 6 and 8 to 16 of the agreement concluded at Saarbrücken on 13 July 1984 between the Federal Republic of Germany and the French Republic.

Article 32

This agreement shall be signed without being subject to ratification or approval, or subject to ratification or approval, followed by ratification or approval.

This agreement shall apply provisionally from the day following that of its signature.

This agreement shall enter into force 30 days after deposit of the last instrument of ratification or approval.

Article 33

This agreement shall be deposited with the Government of the Grand Duchy of Luxembourg, which shall transmit a certified copy to each of the governments of the other Signatory States.

ZU URKUND DESSEN haben die unterzeichneten Bevollmächtigten ihre Unterschriften unter dieses Übereinkommen gesetzt.

EN FOI DE QUOI, les représentants des Gouvernements dûment habilités à cet effet ont signé le présent Accord.

TEN BLIJKE WAARVAN de daartoe naar behoren gemachtigde vertegenwoordigers van de Regeringen dit Akkoord hebben ondertekend.

GESCHEHEN ZU SCHENGEN (Grossherzogtum Luxemburg) am vierzehnten Juni neunzehnhundertfünfundachtzig in deutscher, französischer und niederländischer Sprache abgefasst, wobei jeder Wortlaut gleichermassen verbindlich ist.

FAIT à SCHENGEN (Grand-Duché de Luxembourg), le quatorze juin mil neuf cent quatre-vingt-cinq, les textes du présent Accord en langues allemande, française et néerlandaise, faisant également foi.

GEDAAN te SCHENGEN (Groothertogdom Luxemburg), de veertiende juni negentienhonderdvijfentachtig, zijnde te teksten van dit Akkoord in de Duitse, de Franse en de Nederlandse taal gelijkelijk authentiek.

Pour le Gouvernement du Royaume de Belgique
Voor de Regering van het Koninkrijk België

P. DE KEERSMAEKER
Secrétaire d'Etat aux Affaires européennes
Staatssecretaris voor Europese Zaken

Für die Regierung der Bundesrepublik Deutschland

Waldemar Schreckenberger

Prof.Dr. W. SCHRECKENBERGER
Staatssekretär im Bundeskanzleramt

Pour le Gouvernement de la République française

C. LALUMIERE
Secrétaire d'Etat aux Affaires européennes

Sous réserve de ratification

Pour le Gouvernement du Grand-Duché de Luxembourg

R. GOEBBELS
Secrétaire d'Etat aux Affaires étrangères

Voor de Regering van het Koninkrijk der Nederlanden

sous réserve d'approbation

W.F. van EEKELEN
Staatssecretaris van Buitenlandse Zaken

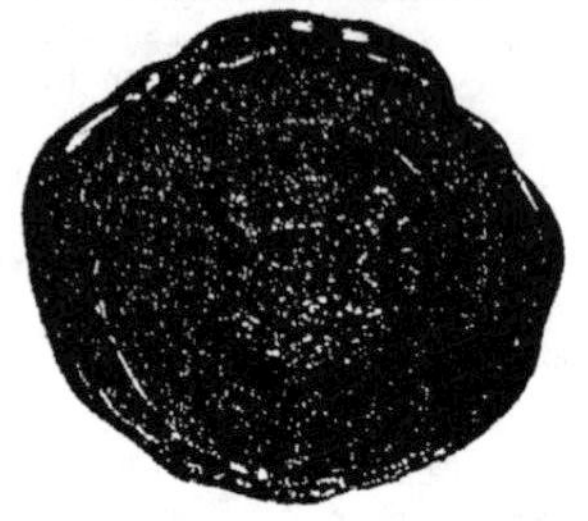

CONVENTION
IMPLEMENTING THE SCHENGEN AGREEMENT OF 14 JUNE 1985 BETWEEN THE GOVERNMENTS OF THE STATES OF THE BENELUX ECONOMIC UNION, THE FEDERAL REPUBLIC OF GERMANY AND THE FRENCH REPUBLIC ON THE GRADUAL ABOLITION OF CHECKS AT THEIR COMMON BORDERS

The Kingdom of Belgium, the Federal Republic of Germany, the French Republic, the Grand Duchy of Luxembourg and the Kingdom of the Netherlands, hereinafter referred to as 'the contracting parties',

Taking as their basis the Schengen Agreement of 14 June 1985 on the gradual abolition of checks at their common borders,

Having decided to fulfil the resolve expressed in that agreement to abolish checks at their common borders on the movement of persons and facilitate the transport and movement of goods at those borders,

Whereas the Treaty establishing the European Communities, supplemented by the Single European Act, provides that the internal market shall comprise an area without internal frontiers,

Whereas the aim pursued by the contracting parties is in keeping with that objective, without prejudice to the measures to be taken to implement the provisions of the Treaty,

Whereas the fulfilment of that resolve requires a series of appropriate measures and close cooperation between the contracting parties,

HAVE AGREED AS FOLLOWS:

TITLE I

Definitions

Article 1

For the purposes of this convention:

Internal borders	shall mean the common land borders of the contracting parties, their airports for internal flights and their sea ports for regular ferry connections exclusively from or to other ports within the territories of the contracting parties and not calling at any ports outside those territories;
External borders	shall mean the contracting parties' land and sea borders and their airports and sea ports, provided that they are not internal borders;
Internal flight	shall mean any flight exclusively to or from the territories of the contracting parties and not landing in the territory of a third State;
Third State	shall mean any State other than the contracting parties;
Alien	shall mean any person other than a national of a Member State of the European Communities;
Alien for whom an alert has been issued for the purposes of refusing entry	shall mean an alien for whom an alert has been introduced into the Schengen information system in accordance with Article 96 with a view to that person being refused entry;
Border crossing point	shall mean any crossing point authorised by the competent authorities for crossing external borders;
Border check	shall mean a check carried out at a border in response exclusively to an intention to cross that border, regardless of any other consideration;
Carrier	shall mean any natural or legal person whose occupation it is to provide passenger transport by air, sea or land;

Residence permit	shall mean an authorisation of whatever type issued by a contracting party which grants right of residence within its territory. This definition shall not include temporary permission to reside in the territory of a contracting party for the purposes of processing an application for asylum or a residence permit;
Application for asylum	shall mean any application submitted in writing, orally or otherwise by an alien at an external border or within the territory of a contracting party with a view to obtaining recognition as a refugee in accordance with the Geneva Convention relating to the Status of Refugees of 28 July 1951, as amended by the New York Protocol of 31 January 1967, and as such obtaining the right of residence;
Asylum seeker	shall mean any alien who has lodged an application for asylum within the meaning of this convention and in respect of which a final decision has not yet been taken;
Processing applications for asylum	shall mean all the procedures for examining and taking a decision on applications for asylum, including measures taken under a final decision thereon, with the exception of the determination of the contracting party responsible for processing applications for asylum pursuant to this convention.

TITLE II

Abolition of checks at internal borders and movement of persons

CHAPTER 1

Crossing internal borders

Article 2

1. Internal borders may be crossed at any point without any checks on persons being carried out.

2. However, where public policy or national security so require a contracting party may, after consulting the other contracting parties, decide that for a limited period national border checks appropriate to the situation shall be carried out at internal borders. If public policy or national security require immediate action, the contracting party concerned shall take the necessary measures and at the earliest opportunity shall inform the other contracting parties thereof.

3. The abolition of checks on persons at internal borders shall not affect the provisions laid down in Article 22, or the exercise of police powers throughout a contracting party's territory by the competent authorities under that Party's law, or the requirement to hold, carry and produce permits and documents provided for in that Party's law.

4. Checks on goods shall be carried out in accordance with the relevant provisions of this convention.

CHAPTER 2

Crossing external borders

Article 3

1. External borders may in principle only be crossed at border crossing points and during the fixed opening hours. More detailed provisions, exceptions and arrangements for local border traffic, and rules governing special categories of maritime traffic such as pleasure boating and coastal fishing, shall be adopted by the Executive Committee.

2. The contracting parties undertake to introduce penalties for the unauthorised crossing of external borders at places other than crossing points or at times other than the fixed opening hours.

Article 4

1. The contracting parties shall ensure that, as from 1993, passengers on flights from third States who transfer onto internal flights will be subject to an entry check, together with their hand baggage, at the airport at which the external flight arrives. Passengers on internal flights who transfer onto flights bound for third States will be subject to a departure check, together with their hand baggage, at the airport from which the external flight departs.

2. The contracting parties shall take the necessary measures to ensure that checks are carried out in accordance with paragraph 1.

3. Neither paragraph 1 nor paragraph 2 shall affect checks on registered baggage; such checks shall be carried out either in the airport of final destination or in the airport of initial departure.

4. Until the date laid down in paragraph 1, airports shall, by way of derogation from the definition of internal borders, be considered as external borders for internal flights.

Article 5

1. For stays not exceeding three months, aliens fulfilling the following conditions may be granted entry into the territories of the contracting parties:

(a) that the aliens possess a valid document or documents, as defined by the Executive Committee, authorising them to cross the border;

(b) that the aliens are in possession of a valid visa if required;

(c) that the aliens produce, if necessary, documents justifying the purpose and conditions of the intended stay and that they have sufficient means of subsistence, both for the period of the intended stay and for the return to their country of origin or transit to a third State into which they are certain to be admitted, or are in a position to acquire such means lawfully;

(d) that the aliens shall not be persons for whom an alert has been issued for the purposes of refusing entry;

(e) that the aliens shall not be considered to be a threat to public policy, national security or the international relations of any of the contracting parties.

2. An alien who does not fulfil all the above conditions must be refused entry into the territories of the contracting parties unless a contracting party considers it necessary to derogate from that principle on humanitarian grounds, on grounds of national interest or because of international obligations. In such cases authorisation to enter will be restricted to the territory of the contracting party concerned, which must inform the other contracting parties accordingly.

These rules shall not preclude the application of special provisions concerning the right of asylum or of the provisions laid down in Article 18.

3. Aliens who hold residence permits or re-entry visas issued by one of the contracting parties or, where required, both documents, shall be authorised entry for transit purposes, unless their names are on the national list of alerts of the contracting party whose external borders they are seeking to cross.

Article 6

1. Cross-border movement at external borders shall be subject to checks by the competent authorities. Checks shall be carried out for the contracting parties'

territories, in accordance with uniform principles, within the scope of national powers and national law and taking account of the interests of all contracting parties.

2. The uniform principles referred to in paragraph 1 shall be as follows.

(a) Checks on persons shall include not only the verification of travel documents and the other conditions governing entry, residence, work and exit but also checks to detect and prevent threats to the national security and public policy of the contracting parties. Such checks shall also be carried out on vehicles and objects in the possession of persons crossing the border. They shall be carried out by each contracting party in accordance with its national law, in particular where searches are involved.

(b) All persons shall undergo at least one such check in order to establish their identities on the basis of the production or presentation of their travel documents.

(c) On entry, aliens shall be subject to a thorough check, as defined in (a).

(d) On exit, the checks shall be carried out as required in the interest of all contracting parties under the law on aliens in order to detect and prevent threats to the national security and public policy of the contracting parties. Such checks shall always be carried out on aliens.

(e) If in certain circumstances such checks cannot be carried out, priorities must be set. In that case, entry checks shall as a rule take priority over exit checks.

3. The competent authorities shall use mobile units to carry out external border surveillance between crossing points; the same shall apply to border crossing points outside normal opening hours. This surveillance shall be carried out in such a way as to discourage people from circumventing the checks at crossing points. The surveillance procedures shall, where appropriate, be established by the Executive Committee.

4. The contracting parties undertake to deploy enough suitably qualified officers to carry out checks and surveillance along external borders.

5. An equal degree of control shall be exercised at external borders.

Article 7

The contracting parties shall assist each other and shall maintain constant, close cooperation with a view to the effective implementation of checks and surveillance. They shall, in particular, exchange all relevant, important information, with the exception of personal data, unless otherwise provided for in this convention. They shall as far as possible harmonise the instructions given to the authorities responsible for checks and shall promote standard basic and further training of officers manning checkpoints. Such cooperation may take the form of an exchange of liaison officers.

Article 8

The Executive Committee shall take the necessary decisions on the practical procedures for carrying out border checks and surveillance.

CHAPTER 3

Visas

SECTION 1

Short-stay visas

Article 9

1. The contracting parties undertake to adopt a common policy on the movement of persons and, in particular, on the arrangements for visas. They shall assist each other to that end. The contracting parties undertake to pursue through common consent the harmonisation of their policies on visas.

2. The visa arrangements relating to third States whose nationals are subject to visa arrangements common to all the contracting parties at the time of signing this convention or at a later date may be amended only by common consent of all the contracting parties. A contracting party may in exceptional cases derogate from the common visa arrangements relating to a third State where overriding reasons of national policy require an urgent decision. It shall first consult the other contracting parties and, in its decision, take account of their interests and the consequences of that decision.

Article 10

1. A uniform visa valid for the entire territory of the contracting parties shall be introduced. This visa, the period of validity of which shall be determined by Article 11, may be issued for visits not exceeding three months.

2. Pending the introduction of such a visa, the contracting parties shall recognise their respective national visas, provided that these are issued in accordance with common conditions and criteria determined in the context of the relevant provisions of this chapter.

3. By way of derogation from paragraphs 1 and 2, each contracting party shall reserve the right to restrict the territorial validity of the visa in accordance with common arrangements determined in the context of the relevant provisions of this chapter.

Article 11

1. The visa provided for in Article 10 may be:

(a) a travel visa valid for one or more entries, provided that neither the length of a continuous visit nor the total length of successive visits exceeds three months in any half-year, from the date of first entry;

(b) a transit visa authorising its holder to pass through the territories of the contracting parties once, twice or exceptionally several times en route to the territory of a third State, provided that no transit shall exceed five days.

2. Paragraph 1 shall not preclude a contracting party from issuing a new visa, the validity of which is limited to its own territory, within the half-year in question if necessary.

Article 12

1. The uniform visa provided for in Article 10(1) shall be issued by the diplomatic and consular authorities of the contracting parties and, where appropriate, by the authorities of the contracting parties designated under Article 17.

2. The contracting party responsible for issuing such a visa shall in principle be that of the main destination. If this cannot be determined, the visa shall in principle be issued by the diplomatic or consular post of the contracting party of first entry.

3. The Executive Committee shall specify the implementing arrangements and, in particular, the criteria for determining the main destination.

Article 13

1. No visa shall be affixed to a travel document that has expired.

2. The period of validity of a travel document must exceed that of the visa, taking account of the period of use of the visa. It must enable aliens to return to their country of origin or to enter a third country.

Article 14

1. No visa shall be affixed to a travel document if that travel document is not valid for any of the contracting parties. If a travel document is only valid for one contracting party or for a number of contracting parties, the visa to be affixed shall be limited to the contracting party or Parties in question.

2. If a travel document is not recognised as valid by one or more of the contracting parties, an authorisation valid as a visa may be issued in place of a visa.

Article 15

In principle the visas referred to in Article 10 may be issued only if an alien fulfils the entry conditions laid down in Article 5(1)(a), (c), (d) and (e).

Article 16

If a contracting party considers it necessary to derogate on one of the grounds listed in Article 5(2) from the principle laid down in Article 15, by issuing a visa to an alien who does not fulfil all the entry conditions referred to in Article 5(1), the validity of this visa shall be restricted to the territory of that contracting party, which must inform the other contracting parties accordingly.

Article 17

1. The Executive Committee shall adopt common rules for the examination of visa applications, shall ensure their correct implementation and shall adapt them to new situations and circumstances.

2. The Executive Committee shall also specify the cases in which the issue of a visa shall be subject to consultation with the central authority of the contracting party

with which the application is lodged and, where appropriate, the central authorities of other contracting parties.

3. The Executive Committee shall also take the necessary decisions on the following:

(a) the travel documents to which a visa may be affixed;

(b) the visa-issuing authorities;

(c) the conditions governing the issue of visas at borders;

(d) the form, content, and period of validity of visas and the fees to be charged for their issue;

(e) the conditions for the extension and refusal of the visas referred to in (c) and (d), in accordance with the interests of all the contracting parties;

(f) the procedures for limiting the territorial validity of visas;

(g) the principles governing the drawing-up of a common list of aliens for whom an alert has been issued for the purposes of refusing entry, without prejudice to Article 96.

SECTION 2

Long-stay visas

Article 18

Visas for stays exceeding three months shall be national visas issued by one of the contracting parties in accordance with its national law. Such visas shall enable their holders to transit through the territories of the other contracting parties in order to reach the territory of the contracting party which issued the visa, unless they fail to fulfil the entry conditions referred to in Article 5(1)(a), (d) and (e) or they are on the national list of alerts of the contracting party through the territory of which they seek to transit.

CHAPTER 4

Conditions governing the movement of aliens

Article 19

1. Aliens who hold uniform visas and who have legally entered the territory of a contracting party may move freely within the territories of all the contracting parties during the period of validity of their visas, provided that they fulfil the entry conditions referred to in Article 5(1)(a), (c), (d) and (e).

2. Pending the introduction of a uniform visa, aliens who hold visas issued by one of the contracting parties and who have legally entered the territory of one contracting party may move freely within the territories of all the contracting parties during the period of validity of their visas up to a maximum of three months from the date of first entry, provided that they fulfil the entry conditions referred to in Article 5(1)(a), (c), (d) and (e).

3. Paragraphs 1 and 2 shall not apply to visas whose validity is subject to territorial limitation in accordance with Chapter 3 of this title.

4. This article shall apply without prejudice to Article 22.

Article 20

1. Aliens not subject to a visa requirement may move freely within the territories of the contracting parties for a maximum period of three months during the six months following the date of first entry, provided that they fulfil the entry conditions referred to in Article 5(1)(a), (c), (d) and (e).

2. Paragraph 1 shall not affect each contracting party's right to extend beyond three months an alien's stay in its territory in exceptional circumstances or in accordance with a bilateral agreement concluded before the entry into force of this convention.

3. This article shall apply without prejudice to Article 22.

Article 21

1. Aliens who hold valid residence permits issued by one of the contracting parties may, on the basis of that permit and a valid travel document, move freely for up to three months within the territories of the other contracting parties, provided that they fulfil the entry conditions referred to in Article 5(1)(a), (c) and (e) and are not on the national list of alerts of the contracting party concerned.

2. Paragraph 1 shall also apply to aliens who hold provisional residence permits issued by one of the contracting parties and travel documents issued by that contracting party.

3. The contracting parties shall send the Executive Committee a list of the documents that they issue as valid travel documents, residence permits or provisional residence permits within the meaning of this article.

4. This article shall apply without prejudice to Article 22.

Article 22

1. Aliens who have legally entered the territory of one of the contracting parties shall be obliged to report, in accordance with the conditions laid down by each contracting party, to the competent authorities of the contracting party whose territory they enter. Such aliens may report either on entry or within three working days of entry, at the discretion of the contracting party whose territory they enter.

2. Aliens resident in the territory of one of the contracting parties who enter the territory of another contracting party shall be required to report to the authorities, as laid down in paragraph 1.

3. Each contracting party shall lay down its exemptions from paragraphs 1 and 2 and shall communicate them to the Executive Committee.

Article 23

1. Aliens who do not fulfil or who no longer fulfil the short-stay conditions applicable within the territory of a contracting party shall normally be required to leave the territories of the contracting parties immediately.

2. Aliens who hold valid residence permits or provisional residence permits issued by another contracting party shall be required

to go to the territory of that contracting party immediately.

3. Where such aliens have not left voluntarily or where it may be assumed that they will not do so or where their immediate departure is required for reasons of national security or public policy, they must be expelled from the territory of the contracting party in which they were apprehended, in accordance with the national law of that contracting party. If under that law expulsion is not authorised, the contracting party concerned may allow the persons concerned to remain within its territory.

4. Such aliens may be expelled from the territory of that Party to their countries of origin or any other State to which they may be admitted, in particular under the relevant provisions of the readmission agreements concluded by the contracting parties.

5. Paragraph 4 shall not preclude the application of national provisions on the right of asylum, the Geneva Convention relating to the Status of Refugees of 28 July 1951, as amended by the New York Protocol of 31 January 1967, paragraph 2 of this article or Article 33(1) of this convention.

Article 24

Subject to the Executive Committee's definition of the appropriate criteria and practical arrangements, the contracting parties shall compensate each other for any financial imbalances which may result from the obligation to expel as provided for in Article 23 where such expulsion cannot be effected at the alien's expense.

CHAPTER 5

Residence permits and alerts for the purposes of refusing entry

Article 25

1. Where a contracting party considers issuing a residence permit to an alien for whom an alert has been issued for the purposes of refusing entry, it shall first consult the contracting party issuing the alert and shall take account of its interests; the residence permit shall be issued for substantive reasons only, notably on humanitarian grounds or by reason of international commitments.

If a residence permit is issued, the contracting party issuing the alert shall withdraw the alert but may put the alien concerned on its national list of alerts.

2. Where it emerges that an alert for the purposes of refusing entry has been issued for an alien who holds a valid residence permit issued by one of the contracting parties, the contracting party issuing the alert shall consult the Party which issued the residence permit in order to determine whether there are sufficient reasons for withdrawing the residence permit.

If the residence permit is not withdrawn, the contracting party issuing the alert shall withdraw the alert but may nevertheless put the alien in question on its national list of alerts.

CHAPTER 6

Accompanying measures

Article 26

1. The contracting parties undertake, subject to the obligations resulting from their accession to the Geneva Convention relating to the Status of Refugees of 28 July 1951, as amended by the New York Protocol of 31 January 1967, to incorporate the following rules into their national law.

(a) If aliens are refused entry into the territory of one of the contracting parties, the carrier which brought them to the external border by air, sea or land shall be obliged immediately to assume responsibility for them again. At the request of the border surveillance authorities the carrier shall be obliged to return the aliens to the third State from which they were transported or to the third State which issued the travel document on which they travelled or to any other third State to which they are certain to be admitted.

(b) The carrier shall be obliged to take all the necessary measures to ensure that an alien carried by air or sea is in possession of the travel documents required for entry into the territories of the contracting parties.

2. The contracting parties undertake, subject to the obligations resulting from their accession to the Geneva Convention relating to the Status of Refugees of 28 July 1951, as amended by the New York Protocol of 31 January 1967, and in accordance with their constitutional law, to impose penalties on carriers which transport aliens who do not possess the necessary travel documents by air or sea from a third State to their territories.

3. Paragraphs 1(b) and 2 shall also apply to international carriers transporting groups overland by coach, with the exception of border traffic.

Article 27

1. The contracting parties undertake to impose appropriate penalties on any person who, for financial gain, assists or tries to assist an alien to enter or reside within the territory of one of the contracting parties in breach of that contracting party's laws on the entry and residence of aliens.

2. If a contracting party is informed of actions as referred to in paragraph 1 which are in breach of the law of another contracting party, it shall inform the latter accordingly.

3. Any contracting party which requests another contracting party to prosecute, on the grounds of a breach of its own laws, actions as referred to in paragraph 1 must specify, by means of an official report or a certificate from the competent authorities, the provisions of law that have been breached.

CHAPTER 7

Responsibility for processing applications for asylum

Article 28

The contracting parties reaffirm their obligations under the Geneva Convention relating to the Status of Refugees of 28 July 1951, as amended by the New York Protocol of 31 January 1967, with no geographic restriction on the scope of those instruments, and their commitment to cooperating with the United Nations High Commissioner for Refugees in the implementation of those instruments.

Article 29

1. The contracting parties undertake to process any application for asylum lodged by an alien within any one of their territories.

2. This obligation shall not bind a contracting party to authorising all asylum seekers to enter or remain within its territory.

Every contracting party shall retain the right to refuse entry or to expel asylum seekers to a third State on the basis of its national provisions and in accordance with its international commitments.

3. Regardless of the contracting party with which an alien lodges an application for asylum, only one contracting party shall be responsible for processing that application. This shall be determined on the basis of the criteria laid down in Article 30.

4. Notwithstanding paragraph 3, every contracting party shall retain the right, for special reasons connected in particular with national law, to process an application for asylum even if, under this convention, the responsibility for so doing lies with another contracting party.

Article 30

1. The contracting party responsible for processing an application for asylum shall be determined as follows.

(a) If a contracting party has issued an asylum seeker with a visa, of whatever type, or a residence permit, it shall be responsible for processing the application. If the visa was issued on the authorisation of another contracting party, the contracting party which gave the authorisation shall be responsible.

(b) If two or more contracting parties have issued an asylum seeker with a visa, of whatever type, or a residence permit, the contracting party responsible shall be the one which issued the visa or the residence permit that will expire last.

(c) As long as the asylum seeker has not left the territories of the contracting parties, the responsibility defined in (a) and (b) shall remain even if the period of validity of the visa, of whatever type, or of the residence permit has expired. If the asylum seeker has left the territories of the contracting parties after the visa or the residence permit has been issued, these documents shall be the

basis for the responsibility as defined in (a) and (b), unless they have expired in the meantime under national provisions.

(d) If the contracting parties exempt the asylum seeker from the visa requirement, the contracting party across whose external borders the asylum seeker entered the territories of the contracting parties shall be responsible.

Until the harmonisation of visa policies is fully achieved, and if the asylum seeker is exempted from the visa requirement by some contracting parties only, the contracting party across whose external border the asylum seeker, through exemption from the visa requirement, has entered the territories of the contracting parties shall be responsible, subject to (a), (b) and (c).

If the application for asylum is lodged with a contracting party which has issued a transit visa to the asylum seeker — whether the asylum seeker has passed through passport control or not — and if the transit visa was issued after the country of transit had ascertained from the consular or diplomatic authorities of the contracting party of destination that the asylum seeker fulfilled the entry conditions for the contracting party of destination, the contracting party of destination shall be responsible for processing the application.

(e) If the asylum seeker has entered the territory of the contracting parties without being in possession of one or more documents, to be defined by the Executive Committee, authorising the crossing of the border, the contracting party across whose external borders the asylum seeker entered the territories of the contracting parties shall be responsible.

(f) If an alien whose application for asylum is already being processed by one of the contracting parties lodges a new application, the contracting party responsible shall be the one processing the first application.

(g) If an alien on whose previous application for asylum a contracting party has already taken a final decision lodges a new application, the contracting party responsible shall be the one that processed the previous application unless the asylum seeker has left the territory of the contracting parties.

2. If a contracting party has undertaken to process an application for asylum in accordance with Article 29(4), the contracting party responsible under paragraph 1 of this article shall be relieved of its obligations.

3. Where no contracting party responsible can be determined on the basis of the criteria laid down in paragraphs 1 and 2, the contracting party with which the application for asylum was lodged shall be responsible.

Article 31

1. The contracting parties shall endeavour to determine as quickly as possible which Party is responsible for processing an application for asylum.

2. If an application for asylum is lodged with a contracting party which is not responsible under Article 30 by an alien residing within its territory, that contracting party may request the contracting party responsible to take charge of the asylum seeker in order to process the application for asylum.

3. The contracting party responsible shall be obliged to take charge of the asylum seeker referred to in paragraph 2 if the request is made within six months of the application for asylum being lodged. If the request is not made within that time, the contracting party with whom the application for asylum was lodged shall be responsible for processing the application.

Article 32

The contracting party responsible for processing an application for asylum shall process it in accordance with its national law.

Article 33

1. If an asylum seeker is illegally within the territory of another contracting party while the asylum procedure is in progress, the contracting party responsible shall be obliged to take the asylum seeker back.

2. Paragraph 1 shall not apply where the other contracting party has issued an asylum seeker with a residence permit valid for one year or more. In that case, responsibility for processing the application shall be transferred to the other contracting party.

Article 34

1. The contracting party responsible shall be obliged to take back an alien whose application for asylum has been definitively rejected and who has entered the territory of another contracting party without being authorised to reside there.

2. Paragraph 1 shall not, however, apply where the contracting party responsible expelled the alien from the territories of the contracting parties.

Article 35

1. The contracting party which granted an alien the status of refugee and right of residence shall be obliged to take responsibility for processing any application for asylum made by a member of the alien's family provided that the persons concerned agree.

2. For the purposes of paragraph 1, a family member shall be the refugee's spouse or unmarried child who is less than 18 years old or, if the refugee is an unmarried child who is less than 18 years old, the refugee's father or mother.

Article 36

Any contracting party responsible for processing an application for asylum may, for humanitarian reasons, based in particular family or cultural grounds, ask another contracting party to assume that responsibility provided that the asylum seeker so desires. The contracting party to which such a request is made shall consider whether it can be granted.

Article 37

1. The competent authorities of the contracting parties shall at the earliest opportunity send each other details of:

(a) any new rules or measures adopted in the field of asylum law or the treatment of asylum seekers no later than their entry into force;

(b) statistical data on the monthly arrivals of asylum seekers, indicating the main countries of origin and decisions on applications for asylum where available;

(c) the emergence of, or significant increases in, certain categories of asylum seekers and any information available on this subject;

(d) any fundamental decisions in the field of asylum law.

2. The contracting parties shall also ensure close cooperation in gathering information on the situation in the asylum seekers' countries of origin with a view to a joint assessment.

3. Any instruction given by a contracting party concerning the confidential processing of the information that it communicates must be complied with by the other contracting parties.

Article 38

1. Every contracting party shall send every other contracting party at their request any information it has on an asylum seeker which is necessary for the purposes of:

— determining the contracting party responsible for processing the application for asylum;

— processing the application for asylum;

— implementing the obligations arising under this chapter.

2. Such information may concern only:

(a) identity (surname and forename, any previous names, nicknames or aliases, date and place of birth, present nationality and any previous nationalities of the asylum seeker and, where appropriate, of the asylum seeker's family members);

(b) identity and travel documents (references, periods of validity, dates of issue, issuing authorities, place of issue, etc.);

(c) any other details needed to establish the asylum seeker's identity;

(d) places of residence and routes travelled;

(e) residence permits or visas issued by a contracting party:

(f) the place where the application for asylum was lodged;

(g) where appropriate, the date any previous application for asylum was lodged, the date on which the present application was lodged, the stage reached in the procedure and the decision taken.

3. In addition, a contracting party may ask another contracting party to inform it of the grounds invoked by an asylum seeker in support of an application and, where appropriate, the grounds for the decision taken on the asylum seeker. The contracting party requested shall consider whether it can comply with such a request. In all events the communication of such information shall be subject to the asylum seeker's consent.

4. Information shall be exchanged at the request of a contracting party and may only be exchanged between the authorities designated by each contracting party, once the Executive Committee has been informed thereof.

5. The information exchanged may only be used for the purposes laid down in paragraph 1. Such information may only be communicated to the authorities and courts and tribunals responsible for:

— determining the contracting party responsible for processing the application for asylum;

— processing the application for asylum;

— implementing obligations arising under this chapter.

6. The contracting party that forwards the information shall ensure it is accurate and up-to-date.

If it appears that a contracting party has supplied information that is inaccurate or should not have been forwarded, the recipient contracting parties shall be informed immediately thereof. They shall be obliged to correct such information or delete it.

7. Asylum seekers shall have the right to receive on request the information exchanged which concerns them as long as it remains available.

If they establish that such information is inaccurate or should not have been forwarded, they shall have the right to demand its correction or deletion. Corrections shall be made in accordance with paragraph 6.

8. Each contracting party concerned shall record the forwarding and receipt of information exchanged.

9. Information forwarded shall be held no longer than necessary for the purposes for which it was exchanged. The contracting party concerned shall assess in due course whether it is necessary for it to be held.

10. In any case, information thus forwarded shall enjoy at least the same protection as is provided for similar information in the law of the recipient contracting party.

11. If information is not processed automatically but is handled in some other form, each contracting party shall take the appropriate measures to ensure compliance with this article by means of effective controls. If a contracting party has a body of the type referred to in paragraph 12, it may assign the control task to it.

12 If one or more contracting parties wishes to computerise all or part of the information referred to in paragraphs 2 and 3, such computerisation shall only be authorised if the contracting parties concerned have adopted laws applicable to such processing which implement the principles of the Council of Europe Convention for the Protection of Individuals with regard to Automatic Processing of Personal Data of 28 January 1981 and if they have entrusted an appropriate national body with the independent monitoring of the processing and use of data forwarded pursuant to this convention.

TITLE III

Police and security

CHAPTER 1

Police cooperation

Article 39

1. The contracting parties undertake to ensure that their police authorities shall, in compliance with national law and within the scope of their powers, assist each other for the purposes of preventing and detecting criminal offences, insofar as national law does not stipulate that the request has to be made and channelled via the judicial authorities and provided that the request or the implementation thereof does not involve the application of measures of constraint by the requested contracting party. Where the requested police authorities do not have the power to deal with a request, they shall forward it to the competent authorities.

2. Written information provided by the requested contracting party under paragraph 1 may not be used by the requesting contracting party as evidence of the offence charged other than with the consent of the competent judicial authorities of the requested contracting party.

3. Requests for assistance referred to in paragraph 1 and the replies to such requests may be exchanged between the central bodies responsible in each contracting party for international police cooperation. Where the request cannot be made in good time using the above procedure, the police authorities of the requesting contracting party may address it directly to the competent authorities of the requested Party, which may reply directly. In such cases, the requesting police authority shall at the earliest opportunity inform the central body responsible for international police cooperation in the requested contracting party of its direct request.

4. In border areas, cooperation may be covered by arrangements between the competent Ministers of the contracting parties.

5. The provisions of this article shall not preclude more detailed present or future bilateral agreements between contracting parties with a common border. The contracting parties shall inform each other of such agreements.

Article 40

1. Officers of one of the contracting parties who, as part of a criminal investigation, are keeping under surveillance in their country a person who is presumed to have participated in an extraditable criminal offence shall be authorised to continue their surveillance in the territory of another contracting party where the latter has

authorised cross-border surveillance in response to a request for assistance made in advance. Conditions may be attached to the authorisation.

On request, the surveillance will be entrusted to officers of the contracting party in whose territory this is carried out.

The request for assistance referred to in the first subparagraph must be sent to an authority designated by each of the contracting parties and empowered to grant or to pass on the requested authorisation.

2. Where, for particularly urgent reasons, prior authorisation cannot be requested from the other contracting party, the officers carrying out the surveillance shall be authorised to continue beyond the border the surveillance of a person presumed to have committed criminal offences listed in paragraph 7, provided that the following conditions are met.

(a) The authority of the contracting party designated under paragraph 5, in whose territory the surveillance is to be continued, must be notified immediately, during the surveillance, that the border has been crossed;

(b) A request for assistance submitted in accordance with paragraph 1 and outlining the grounds for crossing the border without prior authorisation shall be submitted immediately.

Surveillance shall cease as soon as the contracting party in whose territory it is taking place so requests, following the notification referred to in (a) or the request referred to in (b) or, where authorisation has not been obtained, five hours after the border was crossed.

3. The surveillance referred to in paragraphs 1 and 2 shall be carried out only under the following general conditions.

(a) The officers carrying out the surveillance must comply with the provisions of this article and with the law of the contracting party in whose territory they are operating; they must obey the instructions of the competent local authorities.

(b) Except in the situations outlined in paragraph 2, the officers shall, during the surveillance, carry a document certifying that authorisation has been granted.

(c) The officers carrying out the surveillance must at all times be able to prove that they are acting in an official capacity.

(d) The officers carrying out the surveillance may carry their service weapons during the surveillance save where specifically otherwise decided by the requested Party; their use shall be prohibited save in cases of legitimate self-defence.

(e) Entry into private homes and places not accessible to the public shall be prohibited.

(f) The officers carrying out the surveillance may neither challenge nor arrest the person under surveillance.

(g) All operations shall be the subject of a report to the authorities of the contracting party in whose territory they took place; the officers carrying out the surveillance may be required to appear in person.

(h) The authorities of the contracting party from which the surveillance officers have come shall, when requested by the authorities of the contracting party in whose territory the surveillance took place, assist the enquiry subsequent to the operation in which they took part, including judicial proceedings.

4. The officers referred to in paragraphs 1 and 2 shall be:

— as regards the Kingdom of Belgium: members of the *police judiciaire près les Parquets* (criminal police attached to the Public Prosecutor's Office), the gendarmerie and the *police communale* (municipal police), as well as customs officers, under the conditions laid down in appropriate bilateral agreements referred to in paragraph 6, with respect to their powers regarding illicit trafficking in narcotic drugs and psychotropic substances, trafficking in arms and explosives, and the illicit transportation of toxic and hazardous waste;

— as regards the Federal Republic of Germany: officers of the *Polizeien des Bundes und der Länder* (federal police and federal State police), as well as, with respect only to illicit trafficking in narcotic drugs and psychotropic substances and arms trafficking, officers of the *Zollfahndungsdienst* (customs investigation service) in their capacity as auxiliary officers of the Public Prosecutor's Office;

— as regards the French Republic: criminal police officers of the national police and national gendarmerie, as well as customs officers, under the conditions laid down in appropriate bilateral agreements referred to in paragraph 6, with respect to their powers regarding illicit trafficking in narcotic drugs and psychotropic substances, trafficking in arms and explosives, and the illicit transportation of toxic and hazardous waste;

— as regards the Grand Duchy of Luxembourg: officers of the gendarmerie and the police, as well as customs officers, under the conditions laid down in appropriate bilateral agreements referred to in paragraph 6, with respect to their powers regarding illicit trafficking in narcotic drugs and psychotropic substances, trafficking in arms and explosives, and the illicit transportation of toxic and hazardous waste;

— as regards the Kingdom of the Netherlands: officers of the *Rijkspolitie* (national police) and the *Gemeentepolitie* (municipal police), as well as, under the conditions laid down in appropriate bilateral agreements referred to in paragraph 6, with respect to their powers regarding illicit trafficking in narcotic drugs and psychotropic substances, trafficking in arms and explosives and the illicit transportation of toxic and hazardous waste, officers of the tax inspection and investigation authorities responsible for import and excise duties.

5. The authority referred to in paragraphs 1 and 2 shall be:

— as regards the Kingdom of Belgium: the *Commissariat général de la Police judiciaire* (Criminal Investigation Department);

— as regards the Federal Republic of Germany: the *Bundeskriminalamt* (Federal Crime Office);

— as regards the French Republic: the *Direction centrale de la Police judiciaire* (central headquarters of the criminal police);

— as regards the Grand Duchy of Luxembourg: the *Procureur général d'Etat* (Principal State Prosecutor);

— as regards the Kingdom of the Netherlands: the *Landelijk Officier van Justitie* (National Public Prosecutor) responsible for cross-border surveillance.

6. The contracting parties may, at bilateral level, extend the scope of this article and adopt additional measures in application thereof.

7. The surveillance referred to in paragraph 2 may only be carried out where one of the following criminal offences is involved:

— murder,

— manslaughter,

— rape,

— arson,

— forgery of money,

— aggravated burglary and robbery and receiving stolen goods,

— extortion,

— kidnapping and hostage taking,

— trafficking in human beings,

— illicit trafficking in narcotic drugs and psychotropic substances,

— breach of the laws on arms and explosives,

— wilful damage through the use of explosives,

— illicit transportation of toxic and hazardous waste.

Article 41

1. Officers of one of the contracting parties who are pursuing in their country an individual caught in the act of committing or of participating in one of the offences referred to in paragraph 4 shall be authorised to continue pursuit in the territory of another contracting party without the latter's prior authorisation where, given the particular urgency of the situation, it is not possible to notify the competent authorities of the other contracting party by one of the means provided for in Article 44 prior to entry into that territory or where these authorities are unable to reach the scene in time to take over the pursuit.

The same shall apply where the person being pursued has escaped from provisional custody or while serving a sentence involving deprivation of liberty.

The pursuing officers shall, not later than when they cross the border, contact the competent authorities of the contracting party in whose territory the hot pursuit is to take place. The hot pursuit will cease as soon as the contracting party in whose territory the pursuit is taking place so requests. At the request of the pursuing officers, the competent local authorities shall challenge the pursued person in order to establish the person's identity or to make an arrest.

2. Hot pursuit shall be carried out in accordance with one of the following procedures, defined by the declaration laid down in paragraph 9.

(a) The pursuing officers shall not have the right to apprehend the pursued person.

(b) If no request to cease the hot pursuit is made and if the competent local authorities are unable to intervene quickly enough, the pursuing officers may detain the person pursued until the officers of the contracting party in whose territory the pursuit is taking place, who must be informed immediately, are able to establish the person's identity or make an arrest.

3. Hot pursuit shall be carried out in accordance with paragraphs 1 and 2 and in one of the following ways as defined by the declaration provided for in paragraph 9:

(a) in an area or during a period as from the crossing of the border, to be established in the declaration;

(b) without limit in space or time.

4. In the declaration referred to in paragraph 9, the contracting parties shall define the offences referred to in paragraph 1 in accordance with one of the following procedures.

(a) The following criminal offences:

- murder,
- manslaughter,
- rape,
- arson,
- forgery of money,
- aggravated burglary and robbery and receiving stolen goods,
- extortion,
- kidnapping and hostage taking,
- trafficking in human beings,
- illicit trafficking in narcotic drugs and psychotropic substances,
- breach of the laws on arms and explosives,
- wilful damage through the use of explosives,
- illicit transportation of toxic and hazardous waste,
- failure to stop and give particulars after an accident which has resulted in death or serious injury.

(b) Extraditable offences.

5. Hot pursuit shall be carried out only under the following general conditions.

(a) The pursuing officers must comply with the provisions of this article and with the law of the contracting party in whose territory they are operating; they must obey the instructions issued by the competent local authorities.

(b) Pursuit shall be solely over land borders.

(c) Entry into private homes and places not accessible to the public shall be prohibited.

(d) The pursuing officers shall be easily identifiable, either by their uniform, by means of an armband or by accessories fitted to their vehicles; the use of civilian clothes combined with the use of unmarked vehicles without the aforementioned identification is prohibited; the pursuing officers must at all times be able to prove that they are acting in an official capacity.

(e) The pursuing officers may carry their service weapons; their use shall be prohibited save in cases of legitimate self-defence.

(f) Once the pursued person has been apprehended as provided for in paragraph 2(b), for the purpose of being brought before the competent local authorities that person may only be subjected to a security search; handcuffs may be used during the transfer; objects carried by the pursued person may be seized.

(g) After each operation referred to in paragraphs 1, 2 and 3, the pursuing officers shall appear before the competent local authorities of the contracting party in whose territory they were operating and shall report on their mission; at the request of those authorities, they shall remain at their disposal until the circumstances surrounding their action have been sufficiently clarified; this condition shall apply even where the hot pursuit has not resulted in the arrest of the person pursued.

(h) The authorities of the contracting party from which the pursuing officers have come shall, when requested by the authorities of the contracting party in whose territory the hot pursuit took place, assist the enquiry subsequent to the operation in which they took part, including judicial proceedings.

6. A person who, following the action provided for in paragraph 2, has been arrested by the competent local authorities may, whatever that person's nationality, be held for questioning. The relevant rules of national law shall apply *mutatis mutandis*.

If the person is not a national of the contracting party in whose territory the person was arrested, that person shall be released no later than six hours after the arrest was made, not including the hours between midnight and 9 a.m., unless the competent local authorities have previously received a request for that person's provisional arrest for the purposes of extradition in any form whatsoever.

7. The officers referred to in the previous paragraphs shall be:

— as regards the Kingdom of Belgium: members of the *police judiciaire près les Parquets* (criminal police attached to the Public Prosecutor's Office), the gendarmerie and the *police communale* (municipal police), as well as customs officers, under the conditions laid down in appropriate bilateral agreements referred to in paragraph 10, with respect to their powers regarding illicit trafficking in narcotic drugs and psychotropic substances, trafficking in arms and explosives, and the illicit transportation of toxic and hazardous waste;

— as regards the Federal Republic of Germany: officers of the *Polizeien des Bundes und der Länder* (federal and federal State police), as well as, with respect only to illegal trafficking in narcotic drugs and psychotropic substances and arms trafficking, officers of the *Zollfahndungsdienst* (customs investigation service) in their capacity as auxiliary officers of the Public Prosecutor's Office;

— as regards the French Republic: criminal police officers of the national police and national gendarmerie, as well as customs officers, under the conditions laid down in the appropriate bilateral agreements referred to in paragraph 10, with respect to their powers regarding illicit trafficking in narcotic drugs and psychotropic substances, trafficking in arms and explosives, and the illicit transportation of toxic and hazardous waste;

— as regards the Grand Duchy of Luxembourg: officers of the gendarmerie and the police, as well as customs officers, under the conditions laid down in the appropriate bilateral agreements referred to in paragraph 10, with respect to their powers regarding illicit trafficking in narcotic drugs and psychotropic substances, trafficking in arms and explosives, and the illicit transportation of toxic and hazardous waste:

— as regards the Kingdom of the Netherlands: officers of the *Rijkspolitie* (national police) and the *Gemeentepolitie* (municipal police) as well as, under the conditions laid down in the appropriate bilateral agreements referred to in paragraph 10, with respect to their powers regarding the illicit trafficking in narcotic drugs and psychotropic substances, trafficking in arms and explosives and the illicit transportation of toxic and hazardous waste, officers of the tax inspection and investigation authorities responsible for import and excise duties.

8. For the contracting parties concerned this article shall apply without prejudice to Article 27 of the Benelux Treaty concerning Extradition and Mutual Assistance in Criminal Matters of 27 June 1962, as amended by the protocol of 11 May 1974.

9. At the time of signing this convention, each contracting party shall make a declaration in which it shall define for each of the contracting parties with which it has a common border, on the basis of paragraphs 2, 3 and 4, the procedures for carrying out a hot pursuit in its territory.

A contracting party may at any time replace its declaration by another declaration provided the latter does not restrict the scope of the former.

Each declaration shall be made after consultation with each of the contracting parties concerned and with a view to obtaining equivalent arrangements on both sides of internal borders.

10. The contracting parties may, on a bilateral basis, extend the scope of paragraph 1 and adopt additional provisions in implementation of this article.

Article 42

During the operations referred to in Articles 40 and 41, officers operating in the territory of another contracting party shall be regarded as officers of that Party with respect to offences committed against them or by them.

Article 43

1. Where, in accordance with Articles 40 and 41 of this convention, officers of a contracting party are operating in the territory of another contracting party, the first contracting party shall be liable for any damage caused by them during their operations, in accordance with the law of the contracting party in whose territory they are operating.

2. The contracting party in whose territory the damage referred to in paragraph 1 was caused shall make good such damage under the conditions applicable to damage caused by its own officers.

3. The contracting party whose officers have caused damage to any person in the territory of another contracting party shall reimburse the latter in full any sums it has paid to the victims or persons entitled on their behalf.

4. Without prejudice to the exercise of its rights vis-à-vis third parties and with the exception of paragraph 3, each contracting party shall refrain in the case provided for in paragraph 1 from requesting reimbursement of damages it has sustained from another contracting party.

Article 44

1. In accordance with the relevant international agreements and account being taken of local circumstances and technical possibilities, the contracting parties shall install, in particular in border areas, telephone, radio, and telex lines and other direct links to facilitate police and customs cooperation, in particular for the timely transmission of information for the purposes of cross-border surveillance and hot pursuit.

2. In addition to these short-term measures, they will in particular consider the following options:

(a) exchanging equipment or posting liaison offers provided with appropriate radio equipment;

(b) widening the frequency bands used in border areas;

(c) establishing common links for police and customs services operating in these same areas;

(d) coordinating their programmes for the procurement of communications equipment, with a view to installing standardised and compatible communications systems.

Article 45

1. The contracting parties undertake to adopt the necessary measures in order to ensure that:

(a) the managers of establishments providing accommodation or their agents see to it that aliens accommodated therein, including nationals of the other contracting parties and those of other Member States of the European Communities, with the exception of accompanying spouses or accompanying minors or members of travel groups, personally complete and sign registration forms and confirm their identity by producing a valid identity document;

(b) the completed registration forms will be kept for the competent authorities or forwarded to them where such authorities deem this necessary for the prevention of threats, for criminal investigations or for clarifying the circumstances of missing persons or accident victims, save where national law provides otherwise.

2. Paragraph 1 shall apply *mutatis mutandis* to persons staying in any commercially rented accommodation, in particular tents, caravans and boats.

Article 46

1. In specific cases, each contracting party may, in compliance with its national law and without being so requested, send the contracting party concerned any information which may be important in helping it combat future crime and prevent offences against or threats to public policy and public security.

2. Information shall be exchanged, without prejudice to the arrangements for cooperation in border areas referred to in Article 39(4), via a central body to be designated. In particularly urgent cases, the exchange of information within the meaning of this article may take place directly between the police authorities concerned, unless na-

tional provisions stipulate otherwise. The central body shall be informed of this as soon as possible.

Article 47

1. The contracting parties may conclude bilateral agreements providing for the secondment, for a specified or unspecified period, of liaison officers from one contracting party to the police authorities of another contracting party.

2. The secondment of liaison officers for a specified or unspecified period is intended to further and accelerate cooperation between the contracting parties, particularly by providing assistance:

(a) in the form of the exchange of information for the purposes of combating crime by means of both prevention and law enforcement;

(b) in executing requests for mutual police and judicial assistance in criminal matters;

(c) with the tasks carried out by the authorities responsible for external border surveillance.

3. Liaison officers shall have the task of providing advice and assistance. They shall not be empowered to take independent police action. They shall supply information and perform their duties in accordance with the instructions given to them by the seconding contracting party and by the contracting party to which they are seconded. They shall report regularly to the head of the police department to which they are seconded.

4. The contracting parties may agree within a bilateral or multilateral framework that liaison officers from a contracting party seconded to third States shall also represent the interests of one or more other contracting parties. Under such agreements, liaison officers seconded to third States shall supply information to other contracting parties when requested to do so or on their own initiative and shall, within the limits of their powers, perform duties on behalf of such Parties. The contracting parties shall inform one another of their intentions with regard to the secondment of liaison officers to third States.

CHAPTER 2

Mutual assistance in criminal matters

Article 48

1. The provisions of this chapter are intended to supplement the European Convention on Mutual Assistance in Criminal Matters of 20 April 1959 as well as, in relations between the contracting parties which are members of the Benelux Economic Union, Chapter II of the Benelux Treaty concerning Extradition and Mutual Assistance in Criminal Matters of 27 June 1962, as amended by the protocol of 11 May 1974, and to facilitate the implementation of those agreements.

2. Paragraph 1 shall not affect the application of the broader provisions of the bilateral agreements in force between the contracting parties.

Article 49

Mutual assistance shall also be afforded:

(a) in proceedings brought by the administrative authorities in respect of acts which are punishable under the national law of one of the two contracting parties, or of both, by virtue of being infringements of the rules of law, and where the decision may give rise to proceedings before a court having jurisdiction in particular in criminal matters;

(b) in proceedings for claims for damages arising from wrongful prosecution or conviction;

(c) in clemency proceedings;

(d) in civil actions joined to criminal proceedings, as long as the criminal court has not yet taken a final decision in the criminal proceedings;

(e) in the service of judicial documents relating to the enforcement of a sentence or a preventive measure, the imposition of a fine or the payment of costs for proceedings;

(f) in respect of measures relating to the deferral of delivery or suspension of enforcement of a sentence or a preventive measure, to conditional release or to a stay or interruption of enforcement of a sentence or a preventive measure.

Article 50

1. The contracting parties undertake to afford each other, in accordance with the convention and the Treaty referred to in Article 48, mutual assistance as regards infringements of their laws and regulations on excise duties, value added tax and customs duties. Customs provisions shall mean the rules laid down in Article 2 of the convention of 7 September 1967 between Belgium, the Federal Republic of Germany, France, Italy, Luxembourg and the Netherlands on Mutual Assistance between Customs Administrations, and Article 2 of Council Regulation (EEC) No 1468/81 of 19 May 1981.

2. Requests regarding evasion of excise duties may not be rejected on the grounds that the requested country does not levy excise duties on the goods referred to in the request.

3. The requesting contracting party shall not forward or use information or evidence obtained from the requested contracting party for investigations, prosecutions or proceedings other than those referred to in its request without the prior consent of the requested contracting party.

4. The mutual assistance provided for in this article may be refused where the alleged amount of duty underpaid or evaded does not exceed ECU 25 000 or where the presumed value of the goods exported or imported without authorisation does not exceed ECU 100 000, unless, given the circumstances or the identity of the accused, the case is deemed to be extremely serious by the requesting contracting party.

5. The provisions of this article shall also apply when the mutual assistance requested concerns acts punishable only by a fine by virtue of being infringements of the rules of law in proceedings brought by the administrative authorities, where the request for assistance was made by a judicial authority.

Article 51

The contracting parties may not make the admissibility of letters rogatory for search or seizure dependent on conditions other than the following:

(a) The act giving rise to the letters rogatory is punishable under the law of both contracting parties by a penalty involving deprivation of liberty or a detention order of a maximum period of at least six months, or is punishable under the law of one of the two contracting parties by an equivalent penalty and under the law of the other contracting party by virtue of being an infringement of the rules of law which is being prosecuted by the administrative authorities, and where the decision may give rise to proceedings before a court having jurisdiction in particular in criminal matters;

(b) Execution of the letters rogatory is consistent with the law of the requested contracting party.

Article 52

1. Each contracting party may send procedural documents directly by post to persons who are in the territory of another contracting party. The contracting parties shall send the Executive Committee a list of the documents which may be forwarded in this way.

2. Where there is reason to believe that the addressee does not understand the language in which the document is written, the document — or at least the important passages thereof — must be translated into (one of) the language(s) of the contracting party in whose territory the addressee is staying. If the authority forwarding the document knows that the addressee understands only some other language, the document — or at least the important passages thereof — must be translated into that other language.

3. Experts or witnesses who have failed to answer a summons to appear sent to them by post shall not, even if the summons contains a notice of penalty, be subjected to any punishment or measure of constraint, unless subsequently they voluntarily enter into the territory of the requesting Party and are there again duly summoned. Authorities sending a postal summons to appear shall ensure that this does not involve a notice of penalty. This provision shall be without prejudice to Article 34 of the Benelux Treaty concerning Extradition and Mutual Assistance in Criminal Matters of 27 June 1962, as amended by the protocol of 11 May 1974.

4. If the act on which the request for assistance is based is punishable under the law of both contracting parties by virtue of being an infringement of the rules of law which is being prosecuted by the administrative authorities, and where the decision may give rise to proceedings before a court having jurisdiction in particular in criminal matters, the procedure outlined in paragraph 1 must in principle be used for the forwarding of procedural documents.

5. Notwithstanding paragraph 1, procedural documents may be forwarded via the judicial authorities of the requested contracting party where the addressee's address is unknown or where the requesting contracting party requires a document to be served in person.

Article 53

1. Requests for assistance may be made directly between judicial authorities and returned via the same channels.

2. Paragraph 1 shall not prejudice the possibility of requests being sent and returned between Ministries of Justice or through national central bureaux of the International Criminal Police Organisation.

3. Requests for the temporary transfer or transit of persons who are under provisional arrest, being detained or who are the subject of a penalty involving depriva-

tion of liberty, and the periodic or occasional exchange of information from the judicial records must be effected through the ministries of justice.

4. Within the meaning of the European Convention on Mutual Assistance in Criminal Matters of 20 April 1959, where the Federal Republic of Germany is concerned, Ministry of Justice shall mean the Federal Minister for Justice and the justice ministers or senators in the federal States (*Länder*).

5. Information laid in connection with proceedings against infringement of the legislation on driving and rest periods, in accordance with Article 21 of the European Convention on Mutual Assistance in Criminal Matters of 20 April 1959 or Article 42 of the Benelux Treaty on Extradition and Mutual Assistance in Criminal Matters of 27 June 1962, as amended by the protocol of 11 May 1974, may be sent by the judicial authorities of the requesting contracting party directly to the judicial authorities of the requested contracting party.

CHAPTER 3

Application of the *ne bis in idem* principle

Article 54

A person whose trial has been finally disposed of in one contracting party may not be prosecuted in another contracting party for the same acts provided that, if a penalty has been imposed, it has been enforced, is actually in the process of being enforced or can no longer be enforced under the laws of the sentencing contracting party.

Article 55

1. A contracting party may, when ratifying, accepting or approving this convention, declare that it is not bound by Article 54 in one or more of the following cases:

(a) where the acts to which the foreign judgment relates took place in whole or in part in its own territory; in the latter case, however, this exception shall not apply if the acts took place in part in the territory of the contracting party where the judgment was delivered;

(b) where the acts to which the foreign judgment relates constitute an offence against national security or other equally essential interests of that contracting party;

(c) where the acts to which the foreign judgment relates were committed by officials of that contracting party in violation of the duties of their office.

2. A contracting party which has made a declaration regarding the exception referred to in paragraph 1(b) shall specify the categories of offences to which this exception may apply.

3. A contracting party may at any time withdraw a declaration relating to one or more of the exceptions referred to in paragraph 1.

4. The exceptions which were the subject of a declaration under paragraph 1 shall not apply where the contracting party concerned has, in connection with the

same acts, requested the other contracting party to bring the prosecution or has granted extradition of the person concerned.

Article 56

If a further prosecution is brought in a contracting party against a person whose trial, in respect of the same acts, has been finally disposed of in another contracting party, any period of deprivation of liberty served in the latter contracting party arising from those acts shall be deducted from any penalty imposed. To the extent permitted by national law, penalties not involving deprivation of liberty shall also be taken into account.

Article 57

1. Where a contracting party charges a person with an offence and the competent authorities of that contracting party have reason to believe that the charge relates to the same acts as those in respect of which the person's trial has been finally disposed of in another contracting party, those authorities shall, if they deem it necessary, request the relevant information from the competent authorities of the contracting party in whose territory judgment has already been delivered.

2. The information requested shall be provided as soon as possible and shall be taken into consideration as regards further action to be taken in the proceedings under way.

3. Each contracting party shall, when ratifying, accepting or approving this convention, nominate the authorities authorised to request and receive the information provided for in this article.

Article 58

The above provisions shall not preclude the application of broader national provisions on the *ne bis in idem* principle with regard to judicial decisions taken abroad.

CHAPTER 4

Extradition

Article 59

1. The provisions of this chapter are intended to supplement the European Convention on Extradition of 13 September 1957 as well as, in relations between the contracting parties which are members of the Benelux Economic Union, Chapter I of the Benelux Treaty concerning Extradition and Mutual Assistance in Criminal Matters of 27 June 1962, as amended by the protocol of 11 May 1974, and to facilitate the implementation of those agreements.

2. Paragraph 1 shall not affect the application of the broader provisions of the bilateral agreements in force between the contracting parties.

Article 60

In relations between two contracting parties, one of which is not a Party to the European Convention on Extradition of 13 September 1957, the provisions of the said convention shall apply, subject to the reservations and declarations made at the time of ratifying that convention or, for contracting parties which are not Parties to the convention, at the time of ratifying, approving or accepting this convention.

Article 61

The French Republic undertakes to extradite, at the request of one of the contracting parties, persons against whom proceedings are being brought for acts punishable under French law by a penalty involving deprivation of liberty or a detention order of a maximum period of at least two years and under the law of the requesting contracting party by a penalty involving deprivation of liberty or a detention order of a maximum period of at least one year.

Article 62

1. As regards interruption of limitation of actions, only the provisions of the requesting contracting party shall apply.

2. An amnesty granted by the requested contracting party shall not prevent extradition unless the offence falls within the jurisdiction of that contracting party.

3. The absence of a charge or an official notice authorising proceedings, necessary only under the law of the requested contracting party, shall not affect the obligation to extradite.

Article 63

The contracting parties undertake, in accordance with the convention and the Treaty referred to in Article 59, to extradite between themselves persons being prosecuted by the judicial authorities of the requesting contracting party for one of the offences referred to in Article 50(1), or sought by the requesting contracting party for the purposes of enforcing a sentence or preventive measure imposed in respect of such an offence.

Article 64

An alert entered into the Schengen information system in accordance with Article 95 shall have the same force as a request for provisional arrest under Article 16 of the European Convention on Extradition of 13 September 1957 or Article 15 of the Benelux Treaty concerning Extradition and Mutual Assistance in Criminal Matters of 27 June 1962, as amended by the protocol of 11 May 1974.

Article 65

1. Without prejudice to the option of using the diplomatic channel, requests for extradition and transit shall be sent by the relevant ministry of the requesting contracting party to the competent ministry of the requested contracting party.

2. The competent Ministries shall be:

— as regards the Kingdom of Belgium: the Ministry of Justice;

— as regards the Federal Republic of Germany: the Federal Ministry of Justice and the justice ministers or senators in the federal States (*Länder*);

— as regards the French Republic: the Ministry of Foreign Affairs;

— as regards the Grand Duchy of Luxembourg: the Ministry of Justice;

— as regards the Kingdom of the Netherlands: the Ministry of Justice.

Article 66

1. If the extradition of a wanted person is not clearly prohibited under the laws of the requested contracting party, that contracting party may authorise extradition without formal extradition proceedings, provided that the wanted person agrees thereto in a statement made before a member of the

judiciary after being heard by the latter and informed of the right to formal extradition proceedings. The wanted person may be assisted by a lawyer during the hearing.

2. In cases of extradition under paragraph 1, wanted persons who explicitly state that they will relinquish the protection offered by the principle of speciality may not revoke that statement.

CHAPTER 5

Transfer of the enforcement of criminal judgments

Article 67

The following provisions shall apply between the contracting parties which are Parties to the Council of Europe Convention on the Transfer of Sentenced Persons of 21 March 1983, for the purposes of supplementing that convention.

Article 68

1. The contracting party in whose territory a penalty involving deprivation of liberty or a detention order has been imposed by a judgment which has obtained the force of *res judicata* in respect of a national of another contracting party who, by escaping to the national's own country, has avoided the enforcement of that penalty or detention order may request the latter contracting party, if the escaped person is within its territory, to take over the enforcement of the penalty or detention order.

2. The requested contracting party may, at the request of the requesting contracting party, prior to the arrival of the documents supporting the request that the enforcement of the penalty or detention order or part thereof remaining to be served be taken over, and prior to the decision on that request, take the sentenced person into police custody or take other measures to ensure that the person remains within the territory of the requested contracting party.

Article 69

The transfer of enforcement under Article 68 shall not require the consent of the person on whom the penalty or the detention order has been imposed. The other provisions of the Council of Europe Convention on the Transfer of Sentenced Persons of 21 March 1983 shall apply *mutatis mutandis*.

CHAPTER 6

Narcotic drugs

Article 70

1. The contracting parties shall set up a permanent working party to examine common problems relating to combating crime involving narcotic drugs and to draw up proposals, where necessary, to improve the practical and technical aspects of cooperation between the contracting parties. The working party shall submit its proposals to the Executive Committee.

2. The working party referred to in paragraph 1, whose members shall be nominated by the competent national authorities, shall include representatives of the police and customs authorities.

Article 71

1. The contracting parties undertake as regards the direct or indirect sale of narcotic drugs and psychotropic substances of whatever type, including cannabis, and the possession of such products and substances for sale or export, to adopt in accordance with the existing United Nations conventions ([1]), all necessary measures to prevent and punish the illicit trafficking in narcotic drugs and psychotropic substances.

2. The contracting parties undertake to prevent and punish by administrative and penal measures the illegal export of narcotic drugs and psychotropic substances, including cannabis, as well as the sale, supply and handing over of such products and substances, without prejudice to the relevant provisions of Articles 74, 75 and 76.

3. To combat the illegal import of narcotic drugs and psychotropic substances, including cannabis, the contracting parties shall step up their checks on the movement of persons, goods and means of transport at their external borders. Such measures shall be drawn up by the working party provided for in Article 70. This working party shall consider *inter alia* transferring some of the police and customs staff released from internal border duty and the use of modern drug-detection methods and sniffer dogs.

4. To ensure compliance with this article, the contracting parties shall specifically carry out surveillance of places known to be used for drug trafficking.

5. The contracting parties shall do their utmost to prevent and combat the negative effects arising from the illicit demand for narcotic drugs and psychotropic substances of whatever type, including cannabis. Each contracting party shall be responsible for the measures adopted to this end.

Article 72

The contracting parties shall, in accordance with their constitutions and their national legal systems, ensure that legislation is enacted to enable the seizure and confiscation of the proceeds of the illicit trafficking in narcotic drugs and psychotropic substances.

Article 73

1. The contracting parties undertake, in accordance with their constitutions and their national legal systems, to adopt measures to allow controlled deliveries to be made in the context of the illicit trafficking in narcotic drugs and psychotropic substances.

2. In each individual case, a decision to allow controlled deliveries will be taken on the basis of prior authorisation from each contracting party concerned.

3. Each contracting party shall retain responsibility for and control over any operation carried out in its own territory and shall be entitled to intervene.

([1]) Single Convention on Narcotic Drugs of 1961, as amended by the 1972 protocol amending the 1961 Single Convention on Narcotic Drugs; the 1971 Convention on Psychotropic Substances; the United Nations Convention against Illicit Traffic in Narcotic Drugs and Psychotropic Substances of 20 December 1988.

Article 74

As regards the legal trade in narcotic drugs and psychotropic substances, the contracting parties agree that the checks arising from obligations under the United Nations conventions listed in Article 71 and which are carried out at internal borders shall, wherever possible, be transferred to within the country.

Article 75

1. As regards the movement of travellers to the territories of the contracting parties or their movement within these territories, persons may carry the narcotic drugs and psychotropic substances that are necessary for their medical treatment provided that, at any check, they produce a certificate issued or authenticated by a competent authority of their State of residence.

2. The Executive Committee shall lay down the form and content of the certificate referred to in paragraph 1 and issued by one of the contracting parties, with particular reference to details on the nature and quantity of the products and substances and the duration of the journey.

3. The contracting parties shall notify each other of the authorities responsible for the issue and authentication of the certificate referred to in paragraph 2.

Article 76

1. The contracting parties shall, where necessary, and in accordance with their medical, ethical and practical usage, adopt appropriate measures for the control of narcotic drugs and psychotropic substances which in the territory of one or more contracting parties are subject to more rigorous controls than in their own territory, so as not to jeopardise the effectiveness of such controls.

2. Paragraph 1 shall also apply to substances frequently used in the manufacture of narcotic drugs and psychotropic substances.

3. The contracting parties shall notify each other of the measures taken in order to monitor the legal trade of the substances referred to in paragraphs 1 and 2.

4. Problems experienced in this area shall be raised regularly in the Executive Committee.

CHAPTER 7

Firearms and ammunition

Article 77

1. The contracting parties undertake to adapt their national laws, regulations and administrative provisions relating to the acquisition, possession, trade in and handing over of firearms and ammunition to the provisions of this chapter.

2. This chapter covers the acquisition, possession, trade in and handing over of firearms and ammunition by natural and legal persons; it does not cover the supply of firearms or ammunition to, or their acquisition or possession by, the central and territorial authorities, the armed forces or the police or the manufacture of firearms and ammunition by public undertakings.

Article 78

1. For the purposes of this chapter, firearms shall be classified as follows:

(a) prohibited firearms;

(b) firearms subject to authorisation;

(c) firearms subject to declaration.

2 The breach-closing mechanism, the magazine and the barrel of firearms shall be subject mutatis mutandis *to the regulations governing the weapon of which they are, or are intended to be, mounted.*

3. For the purposes of this convention, 'short firearms' shall mean firearms with a barrel not exceeding 30 cm or whose overall length does not exceed 60 cm; 'long firearms' shall mean all other firearms.

Article 79

1. The list of prohibited firearms and ammunition shall include the following:

(a) firearms normally used as weapons of war;

(b) automatic firearms, even if they are not weapons of war;

(c) firearms disguised as other objects;

(d) ammunition with penetrating, explosive or incendiary projectiles and the projectiles for such ammunition;

(e) ammunition for pistols and revolvers with dumdum or hollow-pointed projectiles and projectiles for such ammunition.

2. In special cases the competent authorities may grant authorisations for the firearms and ammunition referred to in paragraph 1 if this is not contrary to public policy or public security.

Article 80

1. The list of firearms the acquisition and possession of which is subject to authorisation shall include at least the following if they are not prohibited:

(a) semi-automatic or repeating short firearms;

(b) single-shot short firearms with centrefire percussion;

(c) single-shot short firearms with rimfire percussion, with an overall length of less than 28 cm;

(d) semi-automatic long firearms whose magazine and chamber can together hold more than three rounds;

(e) repeating semi-automatic long firearms with smoothbore barrels not exceeding 60 cm in length;

(f) semi-automatic firearms for civilian use which resemble weapons of war with automatic mechanisms.

2. The list of firearms subject to authorisation shall not include:

(a) arms used as warning devices or alarms or to fire non-lethal incapacitants, provided that it is guaranteed by technical means that such arms cannot be converted, using ordinary tools, to fire ammunition with projectiles and provided that the firing of an irritant substance does not cause permanent injury to persons;

(b) semi-automatic long firearms whose magazine and chamber cannot hold more than three rounds without being reloaded, provided that the loading device is non-removable or that it is

certain that the firearms cannot be converted, using ordinary tools, into firearms whose magazine and chamber can together hold more than three rounds.

Article 81

The list of firearms subject to declaration shall include, if such arms are neither prohibited nor subject to authorisation:

(a) repeating long firearms;

(b) long firearms with single-shot rifled barrel or barrels;

(c) single-shot short firearms with rimfire percussion whose overall length exceeds 28 cm;

(d) the arms listed in Article 80(2)(b).

Article 82

The list of arms referred to in Articles 79, 80 and 81 shall not include:

(a) firearms whose model or year of manufacture, save in exceptional cases, predates 1 January 1870, provided that they cannot fire ammunition intended for prohibited arms or arms subject to authorisation;

(b) reproductions of arms listed under (a), provided that they cannot be used to fire metal-case cartridges;

(c) firearms which by technical procedures guaranteed by the stamp of an official body or recognised by such a body have been rendered unfit to fire any kind of ammunition.

Article 83

Authorisation to acquire and to possess a firearm listed in Article 80 may be issued only:

(a) if the person concerned is over 18 years of age, with the exception of dispensations for hunting or sporting purposes;

(b) if the person concerned is not unfit, as a result of mental illness or any other mental or physical disability, to acquire or possess a firearm;

(c) if the person concerned has not been convicted of an offence, or if there are no other indications that the person might be a danger to public policy or public security;

(d) if the reasons given by the person concerned for acquiring or possessing firearms can be considered legitimate.

Article 84

1. Declarations in respect of the firearms mentioned in Article 81 shall be entered in a register kept by the persons referred to in Article 85.

2. If a firearm is transferred by a person not referred to in Article 85, a declaration of transfer must be made in accordance with procedures to be laid down by each contracting party.

3. The declarations referred to in this article shall contain the details necessary in order to identify the persons and the arms concerned.

Article 85

1. The contracting parties undertake to impose an authorisation requirement on manufacturers of and on dealers in firearms subject to authorisation and to impose a declaration requirement on manufacturers of and on dealers in firearms subject to declaration. Authorisation for firearms subject to authorisation shall also cover firearms subject to declaration. The contracting parties shall carry out checks on arms manufacturers and arms dealers, thereby guaranteeing effective control.

2. The contracting parties undertake to adopt measures to ensure that, as a minimum requirement, all firearms are permanently marked with a serial number enabling identification and that they carry the manufacturer's mark.

3. The contracting parties shall require manufacturers and dealers to keep a register of all firearms subject to authorisation or declaration; the register shall enable rapid identification of the type and origin of the firearms and the persons acquiring them.

4. As regards firearms subject to authorisation under Articles 79 and 80, the contracting parties undertake to adopt measures to ensure that the serial number and the manufacturer's mark on the firearm are entered in the authorisation issued to its holder.

Article 86

1. The contracting parties undertake to adopt measures prohibiting legitimate holders of firearms subject to authorisation or declaration from handing such arms over to persons who do not hold either an authorisation to acquire them or a declaration certificate.

2. The contracting parties may authorise the temporary handing over of such firearms in accordance with procedures that they shall lay down.

Article 87

1. The contracting parties shall incorporate in their national law provisions enabling authorisation to be withdrawn from persons who no longer satisfy the conditions for the issue of authorisations under Article 83.

2. The contracting parties undertake to adopt appropriate measures, including the seizure of firearms and withdrawal of authorisations, and to lay down appropriate penalties for any infringements of the laws and regulations on firearms. Such penalties may include the confiscation of firearms.

Article 88

1. A person who holds an authorisation to acquire a firearm shall not require an authorisation to acquire ammunition for that firearm.

2. The acquisition of ammunition by persons not holding an authorisation to acquire arms shall be subject to the arrangements governing the weapon for which the ammunition is intended. The authorisation may be issued for a single category or for all categories of ammunition.

Article 89

The lists of firearms which are prohibited, subject to authorisation or subject to declaration, may be amended or supplemented by the Executive Committee to take account of technical and economic developments and national security.

Article 90

The contracting parties may adopt more stringent laws and provisions on the acquisition and possession of firearms and ammunition.

Article 91

1. The contracting parties agree, on the basis of the European Convention on the Control of the Acquisition and Possession of Firearms by Individuals of 28 June 1978, to set up within the framework of their national laws an exchange of information on the acquisition of firearms by persons — whether private individuals or firearms dealers — habitually resident or established in the territory of another contracting party. A firearms dealer shall mean any person whose trade or business consists, in whole or in part, in the retailing of firearms.

2. The exchange of information shall concern:

(a) between two contracting parties having ratified the convention referred to in paragraph 1: the firearms listed in Appendix 1(A)(1)(a) to (h) of the said convention;

(b) between two contracting parties at least one of which has not ratified the convention referred to in paragraph 1: firearms which are subject to authorisation or declaration in each of the contracting parties.

3. Information on the acquisition of firearms shall be communicated without delay and shall include the following:

(a) the date of acquisition of the firearm and the identity of the person acquiring it, i.e.:

- in the case of a natural person: surname, forenames, date and place of birth, address and passport or identity card number, date of issue and details of the issuing authority, whether firearms dealer or not;

- in the case of a legal person: the name or business name and registered place of business and the surname, forenames, date and place of birth, address and passport or identity card number of the person authorised to represent the legal person;

(b) the model, manufacturer's number, calibre and other characteristics of the firearm in question and its serial number.

4. Each contracting party shall designate the national authority responsible for sending and receiving the information referred to in paragraphs 2 and 3 and shall immediately inform the other contracting parties of any change of designated authority.

5. The authority designated by each contracting party may forward the information it has received to the competent local police authorities and the authorities responsible for border surveillance, for the purposes of preventing or prosecuting criminal offences and infringements of rules of law.

TITLE IV

The Schengen information system

CHAPTER 1

Establishment of the Schengen information system

Article 92

1. The contracting parties shall set up and maintain a joint information system, hereinafter referred to as 'the Schengen information system', consisting of a national section in each of the contracting parties and a technical support function. The Schengen information system shall enable the authorities designated by the contracting parties, by means of an automated search procedure, to have access to alerts on persons and property for the purposes of border checks and other police and customs checks carried out within the country in accordance with national law and, in the case of the specific category of alerts referred to in Article 96, for the purposes of issuing visas, residence permits and the administration of legislation on aliens in the context of the application of the provisions of this convention relating to the movement of persons.

2. Each contracting party shall set up and maintain, for its own account and at its own risk, its national section of the Schengen information system, the data file of which shall be made materially identical to the data files of the national sections of each of the other contracting parties by means of the technical support function. To ensure the rapid and effective transmission of data as referred to in paragraph 3, each contracting party shall observe, when setting up its national section, the protocols and procedures which the contracting parties have jointly established for the technical support function. Each national section's data file shall be available for the purposes of carrying out automated searches in the territory of each of the contracting parties. It shall not be possible to search the data files of other contracting parties' national sections.

3. The contracting parties shall set up and maintain, on a common cost basis and bearing joint liability, the technical support function of the Schengen information system. The French Republic shall be responsible for the technical support function, which shall be located in Strasbourg. The technical support function shall comprise a data file which will ensure via on-line transmission that the data files of the national sections contain identical information. The data files of the technical support function shall contain alerts for persons and property insofar as these concern all the contracting parties. The data file of the technical support function shall contain no

data other than that referred to in this paragraph and in Article 113(2).

CHAPTER 2

Operation and use of the Schengen information system

Article 93

The purpose of the Schengen information system shall be in accordance with this convention to maintain public policy and public security, including national security, in the territories of the contracting parties and to apply the provisions of this convention relating to the movement of persons in those territories, using information communicated via this system.

Article 94

1. The Schengen information system shall contain only those categories of data which are supplied by each of the contracting parties, as required for the purposes laid down in Articles 95 to 100. The contracting party issuing an alert shall determine whether the case is important enough to warrant entry of the alert in the Schengen information system.

2. The categories of data shall be as follows:

(a) persons for whom an alert has been issued,

(b) objects referred to in Article 100 and vehicles referred to in Article 99.

3. For persons, the information shall be no more than the following:

(a) surname and forenames, any aliases possibly entered separately;

(b) any specific objective physical characteristics not subject to change;

(c) first letter of second forename;

(d) date and place of birth;

(e) sex;

(f) nationality;

(g) whether the persons concerned are armed;

(h) whether the persons concerned are violent;

(i) reason for the alert;

(j) action to be taken.

Other information, in particular the data listed in the first sentence of Article 6 of the Council of Europe Convention for the Protection of Individuals with regard to Automatic Processing of Personal Data of 28 January 1981, shall not be authorised.

4. Where a contracting party considers that an alert in accordance with Articles 95, 97 or 99 is incompatible with its national law, its international obligations or essential national interests, it may subsequently add to the alert contained in the data file of the national section of the Schengen information system a flag to the effect that the action to be taken on the basis of the alert will not be taken in its territory. Consultation must be held in this connection with the other contracting parties. If the contracting party issuing the alert does not withdraw the alert, it shall continue to apply in full for the other contracting parties.

Article 95

1. Data on persons wanted for arrest for extradition purposes shall be entered at the request of the judicial authority of the requesting contracting party.

2. Before issuing an alert, the contracting party shall check whether the arrest is authorised under the national law of the requested contracting parties. If the contracting party issuing the alert has any doubts, it must consult the other contracting parties concerned.

The contracting party issuing the alert shall send the requested contracting parties by the quickest means possible both the alert and the following essential information relating to the case:

(a) the authority which issued the request for arrest;

(b) whether there is an arrest warrant or other document having the same legal effect, or an enforceable judgment;

(c) the nature and legal classification of the offence;

(d) a description of the circumstances in which the offence was committed, including the time, place and the degree of participation in the offence by the person for whom the alert has been issued;

(e) insofar as is possible, the consequences of the offence.

3. A requested contracting party may add to the alert in the data file of its national section of the Schengen information system a flag prohibiting arrest on the basis of the alert until the flag is deleted. The flag must be deleted no later than 24 hours after the alert has been entered, unless the contracting party refuses to make the requested arrest on legal grounds or for special reasons of expediency. In particularly exceptional cases where this is justified by the complex nature of the facts behind the alert, the above time limit may be extended to one week. Without prejudice to a flag or a decision to refuse the arrest, the other contracting parties may make the arrest requested in the alert.

4. If, for particularly urgent reasons, a contracting party requests an immediate search, the requested contracting party shall examine whether it is able to withdraw its flag. The requested contracting party shall take the necessary steps to ensure that the action to be taken can be carried out immediately if the alert is validated.

5. If the arrest cannot be made because an investigation has not been completed or because a requested contracting party refuses, the latter must regard the alert as being an alert for the purposes of communicating the place of residence of the person concerned.

6. The requested contracting parties shall carry out the action as requested in the alert in accordance with extradition conventions in force and with national law. They shall not be obliged to carry out the action requested where one of their nationals is involved, without prejudice to the possibility of making the arrest in accordance with national law.

Article 96

1. Data on aliens for whom an alert has been issued for the purposes of refusing entry shall be entered on the basis of a national alert resulting from decisions taken

by the competent administrative authorities or courts in accordance with the rules of procedure laid down by national law.

2. Decisions may be based on a threat to public policy or public security or to national security which the presence of an alien in national territory may pose.

This situation may arise in particular in the case of:

(a) an alien who has been convicted of an offence carrying a penalty involving deprivation of liberty of at least one year;

(b) an alien in respect of whom there are serious grounds for believing that he has committed serious criminal offences, including those referred to in Article 71, or in respect of whom there is clear evidence of an intention to commit such offences in the territory of a contracting party.

3. Decisions may also be based on the fact that the alien has been subject to measures involving deportation, refusal of entry or removal which have not been rescinded or suspended, including or accompanied by a prohibition on entry or, where applicable, a prohibition on residence, based on a failure to comply with national regulations on the entry or residence of aliens.

Article 97

Data on missing persons or persons who, for their own protection or in order to prevent threats, need temporarily to be placed under police protection at the request of the competent authority or the competent judicial authority of the Party issuing the alert shall be entered, so that the police authorities may communicate their whereabouts to the Party issuing the alert or may move the persons to a safe place in order to prevent them from continuing their journey, if so authorised by national law. This shall apply in particular to minors and persons who must be interned following a decision by a competent authority. The communication of data on a missing person who is of age shall be subject to the person's consent.

Article 98

1. Data on witnesses, persons summoned to appear before the judicial authorities in connection with criminal proceedings in order to account for acts for which they are being prosecuted, or persons who are to be served with a criminal judgment or a summons to report in order to serve a penalty involving deprivation of liberty shall be entered, at the request of the competent judicial authorities, for the purposes of communicating their place of residence or domicile.

2. Information requested shall be communicated to the requesting Party in accordance with national law and the conventions in force on mutual assistance in criminal matters.

Article 99

1. Data on persons or vehicles shall be entered in accordance with the national law of the contracting party issuing the alert, for the purposes of discreet surveillance or of specific checks in accordance with paragraph 5.

2. Such an alert may be issued for the purposes of prosecuting criminal offences and for the prevention of threats to public security:

(a) where there is clear evidence that the person concerned intends to commit or is committing numerous and extremely serious criminal offences, or

(b) where an overall assessment of the person concerned, in particular on the basis of past criminal offences, gives reason to suppose that that person will also commit extremely serious criminal offences in the future.

3. In addition, the alert may be issued in accordance with national law, at the request of the authorities responsible for national security, where there is clear evidence that the information referred to in paragraph 4 is necessary in order to prevent a serious threat by the person concerned or other serious threats to internal or external national security. The contracting party issuing the alert shall be obliged to consult the other contracting parties beforehand.

4. For the purposes of discreet surveillance, all or some of the following information may be collected and communicated to the authority issuing the alert when border checks or other police and customs checks are carried out within the country:

(a) the fact that the person for whom or the vehicle for which an alert has been issued has been found;

(b) the place, time or reason for the check;

(c) the route and destination of the journey;

(d) persons accompanying the person concerned or occupants of the vehicle;

(e) the vehicle used;

(f) objects carried;

(g) the circumstances under which the person or the vehicle was found.

During the collection of this information steps must be taken not to jeopardise the discreet nature of the surveillance.

5. During the specific checks referred to in paragraph 1, persons, vehicles and objects carried may be searched in accordance with national law for the purposes referred to in paragraphs 2 and 3. If the specific check is not authorised under the law of a contracting party, it shall automatically be replaced, for that contracting party, by discreet surveillance.

6. A requested contracting party may add to the alert in the data file of its national section of the Schengen information system a flag prohibiting, until the flag is deleted, performance of the action to be taken on the basis of the alert for the purposes of discreet surveillance or specific checks. The flag must be deleted no later than 24 hours after the alert has been entered unless the contracting party refuses to take the action requested on legal grounds or for special reasons of expediency. Without prejudice to a flag or a refusal, the other contracting parties may carry out the action requested in the alert.

Article 100

1. Data on objects sought for the purposes of seizure or use as evidence in criminal proceedings shall be entered in the Schengen information system.

2. If a search brings to light an alert for an object which has been found, the authority which matched the two items of data shall contact the authority which issued the alert in order to agree on the measures to be taken. For this purpose, personal data may also be communicated in accordance with

this convention. The measures to be taken by the contracting party which found the object must be in accordance with its national law.

3. The following categories of objects shall be entered:

(a) motor vehicles with a cylinder capacity exceeding 50 cc which have been stolen, misappropriated or lost;

(b) trailers and caravans with an unladen weight exceeding 750 kg which have been stolen, misappropriated or lost;

(c) firearms which have been stolen, misappropriated or lost;

(d) blank official documents which have been stolen, misappropriated or lost;

(e) issued identity papers (passports, identity cards, driving licences) which have been stolen, misappropriated or lost;

(f) banknotes (suspect notes).

Article 101

1. Access to data entered in the Schengen information system and the right to search such data directly shall be reserved exclusively to the authorities responsible for:

(a) border checks;

(b) other police and customs checks carried out within the country, and the coordination of such checks.

2. In addition, access to data entered in accordance with Article 96 and the right to search such data directly may be exercised by the authorities responsible for issuing visas, the central authorities responsible for examining visa applications and the authorities responsible for issuing residence permits and for the administration of legislation on aliens in the context of the application of the provisions of this convention relating to the movement of persons. Access to data shall be governed by the national law of each contracting party.

3. Users may only search data which they require for the performance of their tasks.

4. Each contracting party shall send the Executive Committee a list of competent authorities which are authorised to search the data contained in the Schengen information system directly. That list shall specify, for each authority, which data it may search and for what purposes.

CHAPTER 3

Protection of personal data and security of data in the Schengen information system

Article 102

1. The contracting parties may use the data provided for in Articles 95 to 100 only for the purposes laid down for each category of alert referred to in those articles.

2. Data may only be copied for technical purposes, provided that such copying is necessary in order for the authorities referred to in Article 101 to carry out a direct search. Alerts issued by other contracting parties may not be copied from the national section of the Schengen information system into other national data files.

3. With regard to the alerts laid down in Articles 95 to 100 of this convention, any derogation from paragraph 1 in order to change from one category of alert to

another must be justified by the need to prevent an imminent serious threat to public policy and public security, on serious grounds of national security or for the purposes of preventing a serious criminal offence. Prior authorisation from the contracting party issuing the alert must be obtained for this purpose.

4. Data may not be used for administrative purposes. By way of derogation, data entered under to Article 96 may be used in accordance with the national law of each contracting party for the purposes of Article 101(2) only.

5. Any use of data which does not comply with paragraphs 1 to 4 shall be considered as misuse under the national law of each contracting party.

Article 103

Each contracting party shall ensure that, on average, every 10th transmission of personal data is recorded in the national section of the Schengen information system by the data file management authority for the purposes of checking whether the search is admissible or not. The record may only be used for this purpose and shall be deleted after six months.

Article 104

1. Alerts shall be governed by the national law of the contracting party issuing the alert unless more stringent conditions are laid down in this convention.

2. Insofar as this convention does not lay down specific provisions, the law of each contracting party shall apply to data entered in its national section of the Schengen information system.

3. Insofar as this convention does not lay down specific provisions concerning performance of the action requested in the alert, the national law of the requested contracting party performing the action shall apply. Insofar as this convention lays down specific provisions concerning performance of the action requested in the alert, responsibility for that action shall be governed by the national law of the requested contracting party. If the requested action cannot be performed, the requested contracting party shall immediately inform the contracting party issuing the alert.

Article 105

The contracting party issuing the alert shall be responsible for ensuring that the data entered into the Schengen information system is accurate, up-to-date and lawful.

Article 106

1. Only the contracting party issuing the alert shall be authorised to modify, add to, correct or delete data which it has entered.

2. If one of the contracting parties which has not issued the alert has evidence suggesting that an item of data is factually incorrect or has been unlawfully stored, it shall advise the contracting party issuing the alert thereof as soon as possible; the latter shall be obliged to check the communication and, if necessary, correct or delete the item in question immediately.

3. If the contracting parties are unable to reach agreement, the contracting party which did not issue the alert shall submit the case to the joint supervisory authority referred to in Article 115(1) for its opinion.

Article 107

Where a person is already the subject of an alert in the Schengen information system, a contracting party which enters a further alert shall reach agreement on the entry of the alert with the contracting party which entered the first alert. The contracting parties may also lay down general provisions to this end.

Article 108

1. Each contracting party shall designate an authority which shall have central responsibility for its national section of the Schengen information system.

2. Each contracting party shall issue its alerts via that authority.

3. The said authority shall be responsible for the smooth operation of the national section of the Schengen information system and shall take the necessary measures to ensure compliance with the provisions of this convention.

4. The contracting parties shall inform one another, via the depositary, of the authority referred to in paragraph 1.

Article 109

1. The right of persons to have access to data entered in the Schengen information system which relate to them shall be exercised in accordance with the law of the contracting party before which they invoke that right. If national law so provides, the national supervisory authority provided for in Article 114(1) shall decide whether information shall be communicated and by what procedures. A contracting party which has not issued the alert may communicate information concerning such data only if it has previously given the contracting party issuing the alert an opportunity to state its position.

2. Communication of information to the data subject shall be refused if this is indispensable for the performance of a lawful task in connection with the alert or for the protection of the rights and freedoms of third parties. In any event, it shall be refused throughout the period of validity of an alert for the purpose of discreet surveillance.

Article 110

Any person may have factually inaccurate data relating to them corrected or unlawfully stored data relating to them deleted.

Article 111

1. Any person may, in the territory of each contracting party, bring before the courts or the authority competent under national law an action to correct, delete or obtain information or to obtain compensation in connection with an alert involving them.

2. The contracting parties undertake mutually to enforce final decisions taken by the courts or authorities referred to in paragraph 1, without prejudice to the provisions of Article 116.

Article 112

1. Personal data entered into the Schengen information system for the purposes of tracing persons shall be kept only for the time required to meet the purposes for

which they were supplied. The contracting party which issued the alert must review the need for continued storage of such data not later than three years after they were entered. The period shall be one year in the case of the alerts referred to in Article 99.

2. Each contracting party shall, where appropriate, set shorter review periods in accordance with its national law.

3. The technical support function of the Schengen information system shall automatically inform the contracting parties of scheduled deletion of data from the system one month in advance.

4. The contracting party issuing the alert may, within the review period, decide to keep the alert should this prove necessary for the purposes for which the alert was issued. Any extension of the alert must be communicated to the technical support function. The provisions of paragraph 1 shall apply to the extended alert.

Article 113

1. Data other than that referred to in Article 112 shall be kept for a maximum of 10 years, data on issued identity papers and suspect banknotes for a maximum of five years and data on motor vehicles, trailers and caravans for a maximum of three years.

2. Data which have been deleted shall be kept for one year in the technical support function. During that period they may only be consulted for subsequent checking as to their accuracy and as to whether the data were entered lawfully. Afterwards they must be destroyed.

Article 114

1. Each contracting party shall designate a supervisory authority responsible in accordance with national law for carrying out independent supervision of the data file of the national section of the Schengen information system and for checking that the processing and use of data entered in the Schengen information system does not violate the rights of the data subject. For this purpose, the supervisory authority shall have access to the data file of the national section of the Schengen information system.

2. Any person shall have the right to ask the supervisory authorities to check data entered in the Schengen information system which concern them and the use made of such data. That right shall be governed by the national law of the contracting party to which the request is made. If the data have been entered by another contracting party, the check shall be carried out in close coordination with that contracting party's supervisory authority.

Article 115

1. A joint supervisory authority shall be set up and shall be responsible for supervising the technical support function of the Schengen information system. This authority shall consist of two representatives from each national supervisory authority. Each contracting party shall have one vote. Supervision shall be carried out in accordance with the provisions of this convention, the Council of Europe Convention of 28 January 1981 for the Protection of Individuals with regard to the Automatic Processing of Personal Data, taking into account Recommendation No R (87) 15 of 17 September 1987 of the Committee of Ministers of the Council of Europe regulating the use of personal data in the police

sector, and in accordance with the national law of the contracting party responsible for the technical support function.

2. As regards the technical support function of the Schengen information system, the joint supervisory authority shall have the task of checking that the provisions of this convention are properly implemented. For that purpose, it shall have access to the technical support function.

3. The joint supervisory authority shall also be responsible for examining any difficulties of application or interpretation that may arise during the operation of the Schengen information system, for studying any problems that may occur with the exercise of independent supervision by the national supervisory authorities of the contracting parties or in the exercise of the right of access to the system, and for drawing up harmonised proposals for joint solutions to existing problems.

4. Reports drawn up by the joint supervisory authority shall be submitted to the authorities to which the national supervisory authorities submit their reports.

Article 116

1. Each contracting party shall be liable in accordance with its national law for any injury caused to a person through the use of the national data file of the Schengen information system. This shall also apply to injury caused by the contracting party which issued the alert, where the latter entered factually inaccurate data or stored data unlawfully.

2. If the contracting party against which an action is brought is not the contracting party issuing the alert, the latter shall be required to reimburse, on request, the sums paid out as compensation unless the data were used by the requested contracting party in breach of this convention.

Article 117

1. As regards the automatic processing of personal data communicated pursuant to this title, each contracting party shall, no later than the date of entry into force of this convention, adopt the necessary national provisions in order to achieve a level of protection of personal data at least equal to that resulting from the principles laid down in the Council of Europe Convention for the Protection of Individuals with regard to Automatic Processing of Personal Data of 28 January 1981 and in accordance with Recommendation No R (87) 15 of 17 September 1987 of the Committee of Ministers of the Council of Europe regulating the use of personal data in the police sector.

2. The communication of personal data provided for in this title may not take place until the provisions for the protection of personal data as specified in paragraph 1 have entered into force in the territories of the contracting parties involved in such communication.

Article 118

1. Each contracting party undertakes, in relation to its national section of the Schengen information system, to adopt the necessary measures in order to:

(a) deny unauthorised persons access to data processing equipment used for processing personal data (equipment access control);

(b) prevent the unauthorised reading, copying, modification or removal of data media (data media control);

(c) prevent the unauthorised input of data and the unauthorised inspection, modification or deletion of stored personal data (storage control);

(d) prevent the use of automated data processing systems by unauthorised persons using data communication equipment (user control);

(e) ensure that persons authorised to use an automated data processing system only have access to the data covered by their access authorisation (data access control);

(f) ensure that it is possible to verify and establish to which bodies personal data may be transmitted using data communication equipment (communication control);

(g) ensure that it is subsequently possible to verify and establish which personal data have been input into automated data processing systems and when and by whom the data were input (input control);

(h) prevent the unauthorised reading, copying, modification or deletion of personal data during transfers of personal data or during transportation of data media (transport control).

2. Each contracting party must take special measures to ensure the security of data while they are being communicated to services located outside the territories of the contracting parties. Such measures must be notified to the joint supervisory authority.

3. For the processing of data in its national section of the Schengen information system each contracting party may appoint only specially qualified persons who have undergone security checks.

4. The contracting party responsible for the technical support function of the Schengen information system shall adopt the measures laid down in paragraphs 1 to 3 in respect of that function.

CHAPTER 4

Apportionment of the costs of the Schengen information system

Article 119

1. The costs of installing and operating the technical support function referred to in Article 92(3), including the cost of lines connecting the national sections of the Schengen information system to the technical support function, shall be borne jointly by the contracting parties. Each contracting party's share shall be determined on the basis of the rate for each contracting party applied to the uniform basis of assessment of value added tax within the meaning of Article 2(1)(c) of the decision of the Council of the European Communities of 24 June 1988 on the system of the Communities' own resources.

2. The costs of installing and operating the national section of the Schengen information system shall be borne by each contracting party individually.

TITLE V

Transport and movement of goods

Article 120

1. The contracting parties shall jointly ensure that their laws, regulations or administrative provisions do not unjustifiably impede the movement of goods at internal borders.

2. The contracting parties shall facilitate the movement of goods across internal borders by carrying out formalities relating to prohibitions and restrictions when goods are cleared through customs for home use. Such customs clearance may, at the discretion of the Party concerned, be conducted either within the country or at the internal borders. The contracting parties shall endeavour to encourage customs clearance within the country.

3. Insofar as it is not possible in certain fields to achieve the simplifications referred to in paragraph 2 in whole or in part, the contracting parties shall endeavour either to create the conditions therefor amongst themselves or to do so within the framework of the European Communities.

This paragraph shall apply in particular to monitoring compliance with rules on commercial transport permits, roadworthiness of means of transport, veterinary inspections and animal health checks, veterinary checks on health and hygiene, including meat inspections, plant health inspections and monitoring the transportation of dangerous goods and hazardous waste.

4. The contracting parties shall endeavour to harmonise formalities governing the movement of goods across external borders and to monitor compliance therewith according to uniform principles. The contracting parties shall, to this end, work closely together within the Executive Committee in the framework of the European Communities and other international forums.

Article 121

1. In accordance with Community law, the contracting parties shall waive, for certain types of plant and plant products, the plant health inspections and presentation of plant health certificates required under Community law.

The Executive Committee shall adopt the list of plants and plant products to which the simplification specified in the first subparagraph shall apply. It may amend this list and shall fix the date of entry into force for such amendments. The contracting parties shall inform each other of the measures taken.

2. Should there be a danger of harmful organisms being introduced or propagated, a contracting party may request the temporary reinstatement of the control measures laid down in Community law and may implement those measures. It shall immediately inform the other contracting parties thereof in writing, giving the reasons for its decision.

3. Plant health certificates may continue to be used as the certificate required under the law on the protection of species.

4. The competent authority shall, upon request, issue a plant health certificate when a consignment is intended in whole or in part for re-export insofar as plant health requirements are met for the plants or plant products concerned.

Article 122

1. The contracting parties shall step up their cooperation with a view to ensuring the safe transportation of hazardous goods and undertake to harmonise their national provisions adopted pursuant to international conventions in force. In addition, they undertake, particularly with a view to maintaining the existing level of safety, to:

(a) harmonise their requirements with regard to the vocational qualifications of drivers;

(b) harmonise the procedures for and the intensity of checks conducted during transportation and within undertakings;

(c) harmonise the classification of offences and the legal provisions concerning the relevant penalties;

(d) ensure a permanent exchange of information and experience with regard to the measures implemented and the checks carried out.

2. The contracting parties shall step up their cooperation with a view to conducting checks on transfers of hazardous and non-hazardous waste across internal borders.

To this end, they shall endeavour to adopt a common position regarding the amendment of Community directives on the monitoring and management of transfers of hazardous waste and regarding the introduction of Community acts on non–hazardous waste, with the aim of setting up an adequate infrastructure for its disposal and of introducing waste disposal standards harmonised at a high level.

Pending Community rules on non-hazardous waste, checks on transfers of such waste shall be conducted on the basis of a special procedure whereby transfers may be checked at the point of destination during clearance procedures.

The second sentence of paragraph 1 shall also apply to this paragraph.

Article 123

1. The contracting parties undertake to consult each other for the purposes of abolishing among themselves the current requirement to produce a licence for the export of strategic industrial products and technologies, and to replace such a licence, if necessary, by a flexible procedure in cases where the countries of first and final destination are contracting parties.

Subject to such consultations, and in order to guarantee the effectiveness of such checks as may prove necessary, the contracting parties shall, by cooperating clo-

sely through a coordinating mechanism, endeavour to exchange relevant information, while taking account of national law.

2. With regard to products other than the strategic industrial products and technologies referred to in paragraph 1, the contracting parties shall endeavour, on the one hand, to have export formalities carried out within the country and, on the other, to harmonise their control procedures.

3. In pursuit of the objectives set out in paragraphs 1 and 2, the contracting parties shall consult the other partners concerned.

Article 124

The number and intensity of checks on goods carried by travellers when crossing internal borders shall be reduced to the lowest level possible. Further reductions in and the final abolition of such checks will depend on the gradual increase in travellers' duty-free allowances and on future developments in the rules applicable to the cross-border movement of travellers.

Article 125

1. The contracting parties shall conclude arrangements on the secondment of liaison officers from their customs administrations.

2. The secondment of liaison officers shall have the general purposes of promoting and accelerating cooperation between the contracting parties, in particular under existing conventions and Community acts on mutual assistance.

3. The task of liaison officers shall be to advise and to provide assistance. They shall not be authorised to take customs administration measures on their own initiative. They shall provide information and shall perform their duties in accordance with the instructions given to them by the seconding contracting party.

TITLE VI

Protection of personal data

Article 126

1. As regards the automatic processing of personal data communicated pursuant to this convention, each contracting party shall, no later than the date of entry into force of this convention, adopt the necessary national provisions in order to achieve a level of protection of personal data at least equal to that resulting from the Council of Europe Convention for the Protection of Individuals with regard to Automatic Processing of Personal Data of 28 January 1981.

2. The communication of personal data provided for in this convention may not take place until the provisions for the protection of personal data as specified in paragraph 1 have entered into force in the territories of the contracting parties involved in such communication.

3. In addition, the following provisions shall apply to the automatic processing of personal data communicated pursuant to this convention.

(a) Such data may be used by the recipient contracting party solely for the purposes for which this convention stipulates that they may be communicated; such data may be used for other purposes only with the prior authorisation of the contracting party communicating the data and in accordance with the law of the recipient contracting party; such authorisation may be granted insofar as the national law of the contracting party communicating the data so permits;

(b) Such data may be used only by the judicial authorities and the departments and authorities carrying out tasks or performing duties in connection with the purposes referred to in paragraph (a);

(c) The contracting party communicating such data shall be obliged to ensure the accuracy thereof; should it establish, either on its own initiative or further to a request by the data subject, that data have been provided that are inaccurate or should not have been communicated, the recipient contracting party or Parties must be immediately informed thereof; the latter Party or Parties shall be obliged to correct or destroy the data, or to indicate that the data are inaccurate or were unlawfully communicated;

(d) A contracting party may not plead that another contracting party communicated inaccurate data, in order to avoid its liability under its national law vis-à-vis an injured party; if damages are awarded against the recipient contracting party because of its use of inaccurate communicated data, the contracting party which communicated the data shall refund in full to the recipient contracting party the amount paid in damages;

(e) The transmission and receipt of personal data must be recorded both in the source data file and in the data file in which they are entered;

(f) The joint supervisory authority referred to in Article 115 may, at the request of one of the contracting parties, deliver an opinion on the difficulties of implementing and interpreting this article.

4. This article shall not apply to the communication of data provided for under Chapter 7 of Title II and Title IV. Paragraph 3 shall not apply to the communication of data provided for under Chapters 2 to 5 of Title III.

Article 127

1. Where personal data are communicated to another contracting party pursuant to the provisions of this convention, Article 126 shall apply to the communication of the data from a non-automated data file and to their inclusion in another non-automated data file.

2. Where, in cases other than those governed by Article 126(1), or paragraph 1 of this article, personal data are communicated to another contracting party pursuant to this convention, Article 126(3), with the exception of subparagraph (e), shall apply. The following provisions shall also apply:

(a) a written record shall be kept of the transmission and receipt of personal data; this obligation shall not apply where such a record is not necessary given the use of the data, in particular if they are not used or are used only very briefly;

(b) the recipient contracting party shall ensure, in the use of communicated data, a level of protection at least equal to that laid down in its national law for the use of similar data;

(c) the decision concerning whether and under what conditions the data subject shall, at his request, be provided information concerning communicated data relating to him shall be governed by the national law of the contracting party to which the request was addressed.

3. This article shall not apply to the communication of data provided for under Chapter 7 of Title II, Chapters 2 to 5 of Title III, and Title IV.

Article 128

1. The communication of personal data provided for by this convention may not take place until the contracting parties involved in that communication have instructed a national supervisory authority to monitor independently that the processing of personal data in data files complies with Articles 126 and 127 and the provisions adopted for their implementation.

2. Where the contracting party has, in accordance with its national law, instructed a supervisory authority to monitor independently, in one or more areas, compliance with the provisions on the protection of personal data not entered in a data file, that contracting party shall instruct the same authority to supervise compliance with the provisions of this title in the areas concerned.

3. This article shall not apply to the communication of data provided for under Chapter 7 of Title II and Chapters 2 to 5 of Title III.

Article 129

As regards the communication of personal data pursuant to Chapter 1 of Title III, the contracting parties undertake, without prejudice to Articles 126 and 127, to achieve a level of protection of personal data which complies with the principles of Recommendation No R (87) 15 of 17 September 1987 of the Committee of Ministers of the Council of Europe regulating the use of personal data in the police sector. In addition, as regards the communication of data pursuant to Article 46, the following provisions shall apply:

(a) the data may be used by the recipient contracting party solely for the purposes indicated by the contracting party which provided the data and in compliance with the conditions laid down by that contracting party;

(b) the data may be communicated to police forces and authorities only; data may not be communicated to other authorities without the prior authorisation of the contracting party which provided them;

(c) the recipient contracting party shall, upon request, inform the contracting party which provided the data of the use made of the data and the results thus obtained.

Article 130

If personal data are communicated via a liaison officer as referred to in Article 47 or Article 125, the provisions of this title shall not apply unless the liaison officer communicates such data to the contracting party which seconded the officer to the territory of the other contracting party.

TITLE VII

Executive Committee

Article 131

1. An Executive Committee shall be set up for the purposes of implementing this convention.

2. Without prejudice to the special powers conferred upon it by this convention, the overall task of the Executive Committee shall be to ensure that this convention is implemented correctly.

Article 132

1. Each contracting party shall have one seat on the Executive Committee. The contracting parties shall be represented on the Committee by a minister responsible for the implementation of this convention; that minister may, if necessary, be assisted by experts, who may participate in the deliberations.

2. The Executive Committee shall take its decisions unanimously. It shall draw up its own rules of procedure; in this connection it may provide for a written decision-making procedure.

3. At the request of the representative of a contracting party, the final decision on a draft on which the Executive Committee has acted may be postponed for no more than two months from the date of submission of that draft.

4. The Executive Committee may set up working parties composed of representatives of the administrations of the contracting parties in order to prepare decisions or to carry out other tasks.

Article 133

The Executive Committee shall meet in the territory of each contracting party in turn. It shall meet as often as is necessary for it to discharge its duties properly.

TITLE VIII

Final provisions

Article 134

The provisions of this convention shall apply only insofar as they are compatible with Community law.

Article 135

The provisions of this convention shall apply subject to the provisions of the Geneva Convention relating to the Status of Refugees of 28 July 1951, as amended by the New York Protocol of 31 January 1967.

Article 136

1. A contracting party which envisages conducting negotiations on border checks with a third State shall inform the other contracting parties thereof in good time.

2. No contracting party shall conclude with one or more third States agreements simplifying or abolishing border checks without the prior agreement of the other contracting parties, subject to the right of the Member States of the European Communities to conclude such agreements jointly.

3. Paragraph 2 shall not apply to agreements on local border traffic insofar as those agreements comply with the exceptions and arrangements adopted under Article 3(1).

Article 137

This convention shall not be the subject of any reservations, save for those referred to in Article 60.

Article 138

As regards the French Republic, the provisions of this convention shall apply only to the European territory of the French Republic.

As regards the Kingdom of the Netherlands, the provisions of this convention shall apply only to the territory of the Kingdom in Europe.

Article 139

1. This convention shall be subject to ratification, acceptance or approval. The instruments of ratification, acceptance or approval shall be deposited with the Government of the Grand Duchy of Luxembourg, which shall notify all the contracting parties thereof.

2. This convention shall enter into force on the first day of the second month following the deposit of the final instrument of ratification, acceptance or approval. The provisions concerning the setting-up, activities and powers of the Executive Commit-

tee shall apply as from the entry into force of this convention. The other provisions shall apply as from the first day of the third month following the entry into force of this convention.

3. The Government of the Grand Duchy of Luxembourg shall notify all the contracting parties of the date of entry into force.

Article 140

1. Any Member State of the European Communities may become a Party to this convention. Accession shall be the subject of an agreement between that State and the contracting parties.

2. Such an agreement shall be subject to ratification, acceptance or approval by the acceding State and by each of the contracting parties. It shall enter into force on the first day of the second month following the deposit of the final instrument of ratification, acceptance or approval.

Article 141

1. Any contracting party may submit to the depositary a proposal to amend this convention. The depositary shall forward that proposal to the other contracting parties. At the request of one contracting party, the contracting parties shall re-examine the provisions of the convention if, in their opinion, there has been a fundamental change in the conditions obtaining when the convention entered into force.

2. The contracting parties shall adopt amendments to this convention by common consent.

3. Amendments shall enter into force on the first day of the second month following the date of deposit of the final instrument of ratification, acceptance or approval.

Article 142

1. When conventions are concluded between the Member States of the European Communities with a view to the completion of an area without internal frontiers, the contracting parties shall agree on the conditions under which the provisions of this convention are to be replaced or amended in the light of the corresponding provisions of such conventions.

The contracting parties shall, to that end, take account of the fact that the provisions of this convention may provide for more extensive cooperation than that resulting from the provisions of the said conventions.

Provisions which conflict with those agreed between the Member States of the European Communities shall in any case be adapted.

2. Amendments to this convention which are deemed necessary by the contracting parties shall be subject to ratification, acceptance or approval. The provision contained in Article 141(3) shall apply on the understanding that the amendments will not enter into force before the said conventions between the Member States of the European Communities enter into force.

In witness whereof, the undersigned, duly empowered to this effect, have hereunto set their hands.

Done at Schengen, on 19 June 1990, in a single original in the Dutch, French and German languages, all three texts being equally authentic, such original remaining deposited in the archives of the Government of the Grand Duchy of Luxembourg, which shall transmit a certified copy to each of the contracting parties.

For the Government of the Kingdom of Belgium,

For the Government of the Federal Republic of Germany,

For the Government of the French Republic,

For the Government of the Grand Duchy of Luxembourg,

For the Government of the Kingdom of the Netherlands.

FINAL ACT

At the time of signing the convention implementing the Schengen Agreement of 14 June 1985 between the Governments of the States of the Benelux Economic Union, the Federal Republic of Germany and the French Republic on the gradual abolition of checks at their common borders, the contracting parties have adopted the following declarations:

1. Joint declaration on Article 139

The Signatory States shall, prior to the entry into force of the convention, inform each other of all circumstances that could have a significant bearing on the areas covered by this convention and the bringing into force thereof.

The convention shall not be brought into force until the preconditions for its implementation have been fulfilled in the Signatory States and checks at external borders are effective.

2. Joint declaration on Article 4

The contracting parties undertake to make every effort to comply simultaneously with this deadline and to preclude any shortcomings in security. Before 31 December 1992, the Executive Committee shall examine what progress has been made. The Kingdom of the Netherlands stresses that difficulties in meeting the deadline in a particular airport cannot be excluded but that this will not give rise to any shortcomings in security. The other contracting parties will take account of this situation although this may not be allowed to entail difficulties for the internal market.

In the event of difficulties, the Executive Committee shall examine how best to achieve the simultaneous implementation of these measures at airports.

3. Joint declaration on Article 71(2)

Insofar as a contracting party departs from the principle referred to in Article 71(2) in connection with its national policy on the prevention and treatment of addiction to narcotic drugs and psychotropic substances, all contracting parties shall adopt the necessary administrative measures and penal measures to prevent and punish the illicit import and export of such products and substances, particularly towards the territories of the other contracting parties.

4. Joint declaration on Article 121

In accordance with Community law, the contracting parties shall waive the plant health inspections and presentation of plant health certificates required under Community law for the types of plant and plant products:

(a) listed under 1, or

(b) listed under 2 to 6 and originating in one of the contracting parties:

(1) Cut flowers and parts of plants suitable for ornamental purposes of
Castanea
Chrysanthemum
Dendranthema
Dianthus
Gladiolus
Gypsophila
Prunus
Quercus
Rosa
Salix
Syringa
Vitis

(2) Fresh fruit of
Citrus
Cydonia
Malus
Prunus
Pyrus

(3) Wood of
Castanea
Quercus

(4) Growing medium constituted wholly or in part of earth or solid organic matter such as parts of plants, turf and bark with humus, but not constituted entirely of turf.

(5) Seeds

(6) Live plants listed below and appearing under the CN codes listed below in the Customs Nomenclature published in the Official Journal of the European Communities *of 7 September 1987.*

CN code	***Description***
0601 20 30	*Bulbs, onions, tubers, tuberous roots and rhizomes, in growth or in flower: orchids, hyacinths, narcissi and tulips*
0601 20 90	*Bulbs, onions, tubers, tuberous roots and rhizomes, in growth or in flower: other*
0602 30 10	*Rhododendron simsii (Azalea indica)*
0602 99 51	*Outdoor plants: perennial plants*
0602 99 59	*Outdoor plants: other*
0602 99 91	*Indoor plants: flowering plants with buds or flowers, excluding cactis*
0602 99 99	*Indoor plants: other*

5. Joint declaration on national asylum policies

The contracting parties shall draw up an inventory of national asylum policies with a view to the harmonisation thereof.

6. Joint declaration on Article 132

The contracting parties shall inform their national parliaments of the implementation of this convention.

Done at Schengen, on 19 June 1990, in a single original, in the Dutch, French and German languages, all three texts being equally authentic, such original remaining deposited in the archives of the Government of the Grand Duchy of Luxembourg, which shall transmit a certified copy to each of the contracting parties.

For the Government of the Kingdom of Belgium,

For the Government of the Federal Republic of Germany,

For the Government of the French Republic,

For the Government of the Grand Duchy of Luxembourg,

For the Government of the Kingdom of the Netherlands.

Minutes

Further to the final act of the convention implementing the Schengen Agreement of 14 June 1985 between the Governments of the States of the Benelux Economic Union, the Federal Republic of Germany and the French Republic on the gradual abolition of checks at their common borders, the contracting parties have adopted the following joint statement and taken note of the following unilateral declarations made in respect of the said convention.

I. Declaration on the scope of the convention

The contracting parties note that, after the unification of the two German States, the scope of the convention shall under international law also extend to the current territory of the German Democratic Republic.

II. Declarations by the Federal Republic of Germany on the interpretation of the convention

1. *The convention has been concluded in the light of the prospective unification of the two German States.*

   The German Democratic Republic is not a foreign country in relation to the Federal Republic of Germany.

   Article 136 shall not apply in relations between the Federal Republic of Germany and the German Democratic Republic.

2. *This convention shall be without prejudice to the arrangements agreed in the Germano-Austrian exchange of letters of 20 August 1984 simplifying checks at their common borders for nationals of both States. Such arrangements will however have to be implemented in the light of the overriding security and immigration requirements of the Schengen contracting parties so that such facilities will in practice be restricted to Austrian nationals.*

III. Declaration by the Kingdom of Belgium on Article 67

The procedure which will be implemented internally for the transfer of the enforcement of foreign criminal judgments will not be that specified under Belgian law for the transfer of sentenced persons between States, but rather a special procedure which will be determined when this convention is ratified.

Done at Schengen, on 19 June 1990, in a single original, in the Dutch, French and German languages, all three texts being equally authentic, such original remaining deposited in the archives of the Government of the Grand Duchy of Luxembourg, which shall transmit a certified copy to each of the contracting parties.

For the Government of the Kingdom of Belgium,

For the Government of the Federal Republic of Germany,

For the Government of the French Republic,

For the Government of the Grand Duchy of Luxembourg,

For the Government of the Kingdom of the Netherlands.

JOINT DECLARATION by the ministers and State secretaries meeting in Schengen on 19 June 1990

The governments of the contracting parties to the Schengen Agreement will open or continue discussions in particular in the following areas:

- *improving and simplifying extradition practices;*
- *improving cooperation on bringing proceedings against road traffic offences;*
- *arrangements for the mutual recognition of disqualifications from driving motor vehicles;*
- *possibilities of reciprocal enforcement of fines;*
- *introduction of rules on reciprocal transfers of criminal proceedings including the possibility of transferring the accused person to that person's country of origin;;*
- *introduction of rules on the repatriation of minors who have been unlawfully removed from the authority of the person responsible for exercising parental authority;*
- *further simplification of checks on commercial movements of goods.*

Done at Schengen, 19 June 1990, in a single original, in the Dutch, French and German languages, all three texts being equally authentic, such original remaining deposited in the archives of the Government of the Grand Duchy of Luxembourg, which shall transmit a certified copy to each of the contracting parties.

For the Government of the Kingdom of Belgium,

For the Government of the Federal Republic of Germany,

For the Government of the French Republic,

For the Government of the Grand Duchy of Luxembourg,

For the Government of the Kingdom of the Netherlands.

DECLARATION BY THE MINISTERS AND STATE SECRETARIES

On 19 June 1990 representatives of the Governments of the Kingdom of Belgium, the Federal Republic of Germany, the French Republic, the Grand Duchy of Luxembourg and the Kingdom of the Netherlands signed at Schengen, in the Grand Duchy of Luxembourg, the convention implementing the Schengen Agreement of 14 June 1985 between the Governments of the Benelux Economic Union, the Federal Republic of Germany and the French Republic on the gradual abolition of checks at their common borders.

At the time of signing that convention, they adopted the following declarations.

- *The contracting parties consider that the convention constitutes an important step towards creating an area without internal borders and take it as a basis for further activities amongst the Member States of the European Communities.*

- *In view of the risks in the fields of security and illegal immigration, the ministers and State secretaries underline the need for effective external border controls in accordance with the uniform principles laid down in Article 6. With a view to implementing those uniform principles, the contracting parties must, in particular, promote the harmonisation of working methods for border control and surveillance.*

Moreover, the Executive Committee will examine all relevant measures with a view to establishing uniform and effective external border controls and the practical implementation thereof. Such measures will include measures making it possible to ascertain the circumstances under which a third-country national has entered the territories of the contracting parties, application of the same procedures for refusing entry, the drafting of a common manual for the officials responsible for border surveillance and encouragement of an equivalent level of external border control by means of exchanges and joint working visits.

At the time of signing that convention, they also confirmed the Central Negotiating Group's decision to set up a working party with the following mandate:

- *to inform the Central Negotiating Group before the entry into force of the convention of all circumstances that have a significant bearing on the areas covered by the convention and on its entry into force, in particular the progress achieved in harmonising legal provisions in connection with the unification of the two German States;*

— *to consult each other on any impact that that harmonisation and those circumstances may have on the implementation of the convention;*

— *with a view to the movement of aliens exempt from the visa requirement, to devise practical measures and put forward proposals before the entry into force of the convention for harmonising procedures for carrying out controls on persons at the future external borders.*

AGREEMENT ON THE ACCESSION OF THE ITALIAN REPUBLIC

TO THE CONVENTION IMPLEMENTING THE SCHENGEN AGREEMENT OF 14 JUNE 1985 BETWEEN THE GOVERNMENTS OF THE STATES OF THE BENELUX ECONOMIC UNION, THE FEDERAL REPUBLIC OF GERMANY AND THE FRENCH REPUBLIC ON THE GRADUAL ABOLITION OF CHECKS AT THEIR COMMON BORDERS SIGNED AT SCHENGEN ON 19 JUNE 1990

The Kingdom of Belgium, the Federal Republic of Germany, the French Republic, the Grand Duchy of Luxembourg and the Kingdom of the Netherlands, Parties to the convention implementing the Schengen Agreement of 14 June 1985 between the Governments of the States of the Benelux Economic Union, the Federal Republic of Germany and the French Republic on the gradual abolition of checks at their common borders signed at Schengen on 19 June 1990, hereinafter referred to as 'the 1990 Convention', of the one part,

and the Italian Republic, of the other part,

Having regard to the signature done at Paris on 27 November 1990 of the protocol on the accession of the Government of the Italian Republic to the Schengen Agreement of 14 June 1985 between the Governments of the States of the Benelux Economic Union, the Federal Republic of Germany and the French Republic on the gradual abolition of checks at their common borders,

On the basis of Article 140 of the 1990 Convention,

HAVE AGREED AS FOLLOWS:

Article 1

The Italian Republic hereby accedes to the 1990 Convention.

Article 2

1. The officers referred to in Article 40(4) of the 1990 Convention as regards the Italian Republic shall be: criminal police officers of the *Polizia di Stato* (national police) and the *Arma dei Carabinieri*, and, with respect to their powers regarding forgery of money, the illicit trafficking in narcotic drugs and psychotropic substances, trafficking in arms and explosives, and the illicit transportation of toxic and hazardous waste, criminal police officers of the *Guardia di Finanza* (fiscal police), as well as customs officials, under the conditions laid down in appropriate bilateral agreements referred to in Article 40(6) of the 1990 Convention, with respect to their powers regarding the illicit trafficking in narcotic drugs and psychotropic substances, trafficking in arms and explosives, and the illicit transportation of toxic and hazardous waste.

2. The authority referred to in Article 40(5) of the 1990 Convention as regards the Italian Republic shall be the *Direzione Centrale della Polizia Criminale* (Central Directorate of the Criminal Police) at the Ministry of the Interior.

Article 3

1. The officers referred to in Article 41(7) of the 1990 Convention as regards the Italian Republic shall be: criminal police officers of the *Polizia di Stato* (national police) and the *Arma dei Carabinieri*, and, with respect to their powers regarding forgery of money, the illicit trafficking in narcotic drugs and psychotropic substances, trafficking in arms and explosives, and the illicit transportation of toxic and hazardous waste, criminal police officers of the *Guardia di Finanza* (fiscal police), as well as customs officers, under the conditions laid down in appropriate bilateral agreements referred to in Article 41(10) of the 1990 Convention, with respect to their powers regarding the illicit trafficking in narcotic drugs and psychotropic substances, trafficking in arms and explosives, and the illicit transportation of toxic and hazardous waste.

2. At the time of signing this agreement, the Government of the French Republic and the Government of the Italian Republic shall each make a declaration defining, on the basis of Article 41(2), (3) and (4) of the 1990 Convention, the procedures for carrying out hot pursuit on their territory.

Article 4

The competent ministry referred to in Article 65(2) of the 1990 Convention as regards the Italian Republic shall be the Ministry of Justice.

Article 5

1. This agreement shall be subject to ratification, acceptance or approval. The instruments of ratification, acceptance or approval shall be deposited with the Government of the Grand Duchy of Luxembourg, which shall notify all the contracting parties thereof.

2. This agreement shall enter into force on the first day of the second month following the deposit of the last instrument of ratification, acceptance or approval, and at the earliest on the date on which the 1990 Convention enters into force.

3. The Government of the Grand Duchy of Luxembourg shall notify each of the contracting parties of the date of entry into force.

Article 6

1. The Government of the Grand Duchy of Luxembourg shall transmit to the Government of the Italian Republic a certified copy of the 1990 Convention in the Dutch, French and German languages.

2. The text of the 1990 Convention drawn up in the Italian language is annexed to this agreement and shall be authentic under the same conditions as the original texts of the 1990 Convention drawn up in the Dutch, French and German languages.

In witness whereof, the undersigned, duly authorised to this effect, have signed this agreement.

Done at Paris on 27 November 1990 in a single original in the Dutch, French, German and Italian languages, all four texts being equally authentic, such original remaining deposited in the archives of the Government of the Grand Duchy of Luxembourg, which shall transmit a certified copy to each of the contracting parties.

For the Government of the Kingdom of Belgium,

For the Government of the Federal Republic of Germany,

For the Government of the French Republic,

For the Government of the Italian Republic,

For the Government of the Grand Duchy of Luxembourg,

For the Government of the Kingdom of the Netherlands.

FINAL ACT

I. At the time of signing the agreement on the accession of the Italian Republic to the convention implementing the Schengen Agreement of 14 June 1985 between the Governments of the States of the Benelux Economic Union, the Federal Republic of Germany and the French Republic on the gradual abolition of checks at their common borders signed at Schengen on 19 June 1990, the Italian Republic has subscribed to the final act, the minutes and the joint declaration of the ministers and State secretaries which were signed at the same time as the 1990 Convention.

The Italian Republic has subscribed to the joint declarations and has taken note of the unilateral declarations contained therein.

The Government of the Grand Duchy of Luxembourg shall transmit to the Government of the Italian Republic a certified copy of the final act, the minutes and the joint declaration of the ministers and State secretaries which were signed at the time of signing the 1990 Convention, in the Dutch, French and German languages.

The texts of the final act, the minutes and the joint declaration of the ministers and State secretaries which were signed at the time of signing the 1990 Convention, drawn up in the Italian language, are annexed to this final act and shall be authentic under the same conditions as the original texts drawn up in the Dutch, French and German languages.

II. At the time of signing the agreement on the accession of the Italian Republic to the convention implementing the Schengen Agreement of 14 June 1985 between the Governments of the States of the Benelux Economic Union, the Federal Republic of Germany and the French Republic on the gradual abolition of checks at their common borders signed at Schengen on 19 June 1990, the contracting parties have adopted the following declarations:

1. Joint declaration on Article 5 of the accession agreement

The Signatory States shall, prior to the entry into force of the accession agreement, inform each other of all circumstances that could have a significant bearing on the areas covered by the 1990 Convention and on the bringing into force of the accession agreement.

This accession agreement shall not be brought into force until the preconditions for implementation of the 1990 Convention have been fulfilled in all the Signatory States to the accession agreement and checks at the external borders are effective.

2. Joint declaration on Article 9(2) of the 1990 Convention

The contracting parties specify that at the time of signing the agreement on the accession of the Italian Republic to the 1990 Convention, the common visa arrangements referred to in Article 9(2) of the

1990 Convention shall be taken to mean the common arrangements applied by the five Signatory Parties to the said convention since 19 June 1990.

3. Joint declaration on data protection

The contracting parties note that the Government of the Italian Republic undertakes to take all the necessary steps before the ratification of the agreement on accession to the 1990 Convention to ensure that Italian legislation is supplemented in accordance with the Council of Europe Convention for the Protection of Individuals with regard to the Automatic Processing of Personal Data of 28 January 1981 and in accordance with Recommendation No R (87) 15 of 17 September 1987 of the Committee of the Ministers of the Council of Europe regulating the use of personal data in the police sector so as to ensure the full application of the provisions of Articles 117 and 126 of the 1990 Convention and the other provisions of said convention relating to the protection of personal data, with the aim of achieving a level of protection compatible with the relevant provisions of the 1990 Convention.

Done at Paris 27 November 1990 in a single original in the Dutch, French, German and Italian languages, all four texts being equally authentic, such original remaining deposited in the archives of the Government of the Grand Duchy of Luxembourg, which shall transmit a certified copy to each of the contracting parties.

For the Government of the Kingdom of Belgium,

For the Government of the Federal Republic of Germany,

For the Government of the French Republic,

For the Government of the Italian Republic,

For the Government of the Grand Duchy of Luxembourg,

For the Government of the Kingdom of the Netherlands.

Joint declaration on Articles 2 and 3 of the agreement on the accession of the Italian Republic to the convention implementing the Schengen Agreement of 14 June 1985

At the time of signing the agreement on the accession of the Italian Republic to the convention implementing the Schengen Agreement of 14 June 1985 between the Governments of the States of the Benelux Economic Union, the Federal Republic of Germany and the French Republic on the gradual abolition of checks at their common borders signed at Schengen on 19 June 1990, the contracting parties declare that Article 2(1) and Article 3(1) of the said agreement shall be without prejudice to the powers which the *Guardia di Finanza* is granted by Italian law and exercises on Italian territory.

DECLARATION OF THE MINISTERS AND STATE SECRETARIES

On 27 November 1990, representatives of the Governments of the Kingdom of Belgium, the Federal Republic of Germany, the French Republic, the Italian Republic, the Grand Duchy of Luxembourg and the Kingdom of the Netherlands signed at Paris the agreement on the accession of the Italian Republic to the convention implementing the Schengen Agreement of 14 June 1985 between the Governments of the States of the Benelux Economic Union, the Federal Republic of Germany and the French Republic on the gradual abolition of checks at their common borders, signed at Schengen on 19 June 1990.

They noted that the representative of the Government of the Italian Republic declared support for the declaration made at Schengen on 19 June 1990 by the ministers and State secretaries representing the Governments of the Kingdom of Belgium, the Federal Republic of Germany, the French Republic, the Grand Duchy of Luxembourg and the Kingdom of the Netherlands and for the decision confirmed on the same date upon signature of the convention implementing the Schengen Agreement.

AGREEMENT ON THE ACCESSION OF THE KINGDOM OF SPAIN

TO THE CONVENTION IMPLEMENTING THE SCHENGEN AGREEMENT OF 14 JUNE 1985 BETWEEN THE GOVERNMENTS OF THE STATES OF THE BENELUX ECONOMIC UNION, THE FEDERAL REPUBLIC OF GERMANY AND THE FRENCH REPUBLIC ON THE GRADUAL ABOLITION OF CHECKS AT THEIR COMMON BORDERS SIGNED AT SCHENGEN ON 19 JUNE 1990, TO WHICH THE ITALIAN REPUBLIC ACCEDED BY THE AGREEMENT SIGNED AT PARIS ON 27 NOVEMBER 1990

The Kingdom of Belgium, the Federal Republic of Germany, the French Republic, the Grand Duchy of Luxembourg and the Kingdom of the Netherlands, Parties to the convention implementing the Schengen Agreement of 14 June 1985 between the Governments of the States of the Benelux Economic Union, the Federal Republic of Germany and the French Republic on the gradual abolition of checks at their common borders signed at Schengen on 19 June 1990, hereinafter referred to as 'the 1990 Convention', as well as the Italian Republic, which acceded to the 1990 Convention by the agreement signed at Paris on 27 November 1990, of the one part,

and the Kingdom of Spain, of the other part,

Having regard to the signature done at Bonn on 25 June 1991 of the protocol on the accession of the Government of the Kingdom of Spain to the Schengen Agreement of 14 June 1985 between the Governments of the States of the Benelux Economic Union, the Federal Republic of Germany and the French Republic on the gradual abolition of checks at their common borders, as amended by the protocol on the accession of the Government of the Italian Republic signed at Paris on 27 November 1990,

On the basis of Article 140 of the 1990 Convention,

HAVE AGREED AS FOLLOWS:

Article 1

The Kingdom of Spain hereby accedes to the 1990 Convention.

Article 2

1. The officers referred to in Article 40(4) of the 1990 Convention as regards the Kingdom of Spain shall be: officers of the *Cuerpo Nacional de Policía* (national police) and of the *Cuerpo de la Guardia Civil* in the exercise of their criminal police duties, as well as officials of the customs administration, under the conditions laid down in appropriate bilateral agreements referred to in Article 40(6) of the 1990 Convention, with respect to their powers regarding the illicit trafficking in narcotic

drugs and psychotropic substances, trafficking in arms and explosives, and the illicit transportation of toxic and hazardous waste.

2. The authority referred to in Article 40(5) of the 1990 Convention as regards the Kingdom of Spain shall be the *Dirección General de la Policía* (Directorate-General of Police).

Article 3

1. The officers referred to in Article 41(7) of the 1990 Convention as regards the Kingdom of Spain shall be: the officers of the *Cuerpo Nacional de Policía* and the *Cuerpo de la Guardia Civil* in the exercise of their criminal police duties, as well as officials of the customs administration, under the conditions laid down in appropriate bilateral agreements referred to in Article 41(10) of the 1990 Convention, with respect to their powers regarding the illicit trafficking in narcotic drugs and psychotropic substances, trafficking in arms and explosives, and the illicit transportation of toxic and hazardous waste.

2. At the time of signing this agreement, the Government of the French Republic and the Government of the Kingdom of Spain shall each make a declaration defining, on the basis of Article 41(2), (3) and (4) of the 1990 Convention, the procedures for carrying out hot pursuit on their territories.

3. At the time of signing this agreement, the Government of the Kingdom of Spain shall make a declaration with regard to the Government of the Portuguese Republic defining, on the basis of Article 41(2), (3) and (4) of the 1990 Convention, the procedures for carrying out hot pursuit on Spanish territory.

Article 4

The competent ministry referred to in Article 65(2) of the 1990 Convention as regards the Kingdom of Spain shall be the Ministry of Justice.

Article 5

1. This agreement shall be subject to ratification, acceptance or approval. The instruments of ratification, acceptance or approval shall be deposited with the Government of the Grand Duchy of Luxembourg, which shall notify all the contracting parties thereof.

2. This agreement shall enter into force on the first day of the second month following the deposit of the instruments of ratification, acceptance or approval by the five Signatory States to the 1990 Convention and by the Kingdom of Spain, and at the earliest on the day on which the 1990 Convention enters into force. With regard to the Italian Republic, this agreement shall enter into force on the first day of the second month following the deposit of its instrument of ratification, acceptance or approval, and at the earliest on the day on which this agreement enters into force between the other contracting parties.

3. The Government of the Grand Duchy of Luxembourg shall notify each of the contracting parties of the date of entry into force.

Article 6

1. The Government of the Grand Duchy of Luxembourg shall transmit to the Government of the Kingdom of Spain a certified copy of the 1990 Convention in the Dutch, French and German languages.

2. The text of the 1990 Convention drawn up in the Spanish language is annexed to this agreement and shall be authentic under the same conditions as the texts of the 1990 Convention drawn up in the Dutch, French, German and Italian languages.

In witness whereof, the undersigned, duly authorised to this effect, have signed this agreement.

Done at Bonn on 25 June 1991 in a single original in the Dutch, French, German, Italian and Spanish languages, all five texts being equally authentic, such original remaining deposited in the archives of the Government of the Grand Duchy of Luxembourg, which shall transmit a certified copy to each of the contracting parties.

For the Government of the Kingdom of Belgium,

For the Government of the Federal Republic of Germany,

For the Kingdom of Spain,

For the Government of the French Republic,

For the Government of the Italian Republic,

For the Government of the Grand Duchy of Luxembourg,

For the Government of the Kingdom of the Netherlands.

FINAL ACT

I. At the time of signing the agreement on the accession of the Kingdom of Spain to the convention implementing the Schengen Agreement of 14 June 1985 between the Governments of the States of the Benelux Economic Union, the Federal Republic of Germany and the French Republic on the gradual abolition of checks at their common borders signed at Schengen on 19 June 1990, to which the Italian Republic acceded by the agreement signed at Paris on 27 November 1990, the Kingdom of Spain has subscribed to the final act, the minutes and the joint declaration of the ministers and State secretaries which were signed at the same time as the 1990 Convention.

The Kingdom of Spain has subscribed to the joint declarations and has taken note of the unilateral declarations contained therein.

The Government of the Grand Duchy of Luxembourg shall transmit to the Government of the Kingdom of Spain a certified copy of the final act, the minutes and the joint declaration of the ministers and State secretaries, which were signed at the time of signing the 1990 Convention, in the Dutch, French, German and Italian languages.

The texts of the final act, the minutes and the joint declaration of the ministers and State secretaries which were signed at the time of signing the 1990 Convention, drawn up in the Spanish language, are annexed to this final act and shall be authentic under the same conditions as the texts drawn up in the Dutch, French, German and Italian languages.

II. At the time of signing the agreement on the accession of the Kingdom of Spain to the convention implementing the Schengen Agreement of 14 June 1985 between the Governments of the States of the Benelux Economic Union, the Federal Republic of Germany and the French Republic on the gradual abolition of checks at their common borders signed at Schengen on 19 June 1990, to which the Italian Republic acceded by the agreement signed at Paris on 27 November 1990, the contracting parties have adopted the following declarations.

1. Joint declaration on Article 5 of the accession agreement

The Signatory States shall, prior to the entry into force of the accession agreement, inform each other of all circumstances that could have a significant bearing on the areas covered by the 1990 Convention and on the bringing into force of the accession agreement.

This accession agreement shall not be brought into force between the five Signatory States to the 1990 Convention and the Kingdom of Spain until the preconditions for implementation of the 1990 Convention have been fulfilled in these six States and checks at the external borders are effective there. With regard to the Italian Republic, this accession agreement shall not be brought into force until the preconditions for the implementation of the 1990 Convention have been fulfilled in the Signatory States to the said agreement and checks at the external borders are effective there.

2. Joint declaration on Article 9(2) of the 1990 Convention

The contracting parties specify that at the time of signing the agreement on the accession of the Kingdom of Spain to the 1990 Convention, the common visa arrangements referred to in Article 9(2) of the 1990 Convention shall be taken to mean the common arrangements applied by the Signatory Parties to the said convention since 19 June 1990.

The contracting parties take note that the Government of the Kingdom of Spain undertakes to apply, at the latest at the time of the entry into force of this agreement, the common visa arrangements in the cases last examined during negotiations on accession to the 1990 Convention.

3. Joint declaration on data protection

The contracting parties note that the Government of the Kingdom of Spain undertakes to take all the necessary steps before the ratification of the agreement on the accession to the 1990 Convention to ensure that Spanish legislation is supplemented in accordance with the Council of Europe Convention for the Protection of Individuals with regard to the Automatic Processing of Personal Data of 28 January 1981 and in accordance with Recommendation No R (87) 15 of 17 September 1987 of the Committee of the Ministers of the Council of Europe regulating the use of personal data in the police sector, so as to ensure the full application of the provisions of Articles 117 and 126 of the 1990 Convention and the other provisions of said convention relating to the protection of personal data, with the aim of achieving a level of protection compatible with the relevant provisions of the 1990 Convention.

III. The contracting parties have taken note of the following declarations made by the Kingdom of Spain.

1. Declaration on the towns of Ceuta and Melilla

(a) The current controls on goods and travellers entering the customs territory of the European Economic Community from the towns of Ceuta and Melilla shall continue to be performed in accordance with the provisions of Protocol No 2 of the Act of Accession of Spain to the European Communities.

(b) The specific arrangements for visa exemptions for local border traffic between Ceuta and Melilla and the Moroccan provinces of Tetuan and Nador shall continue to apply.

*(c) Moroccan nationals who are not resident in the provinces of Tetuan or Nador and who wish to enter the territory of the towns of Ceuta and Melilla exclusively shall remain subject to the visa requirement. The validity of these visas shall be limited to these two towns and may permit multiple entries and exits (*visado limitado múltiple*) in accordance with the provisions of Article 10(3) and Article 11(1)(a) of the 1990 Convention.*

(d) The interests of the other contracting parties shall be taken into account when applying these arrangements.

(e) Pursuant to its national law and in order to verify whether passengers still satisfy the conditions laid down in Article 5 of the 1990 Convention on the basis which they were authorised to enter national territory upon passport control at the external border, Spain shall maintain checks (on identity and documents) on sea and air connections departing from Ceuta and Melilla and having as their sole destination any other place on Spanish territory.

To the same end, Spain shall maintain checks on internal flights and on regular ferry connections departing from the towns of Ceuta and Melilla to a destination in another State party to the convention.

2. Declaration on the application of the European Convention on Mutual Assistance in Criminal Matters and the European Convention on Extradition

The Kingdom of Spain undertakes to refrain from invoking its reservations and declarations made when ratifying the European Convention on Extradition of 13 December 1957 and the European Convention on Mutual Assistance in Criminal Matters of 20 April 1959 insofar as they are incompatible with the 1990 Convention.

3. Declaration on Article 121 of the 1990 Convention

The Government of the Kingdom of Spain declares that, except in respect of fresh citrus fruit and palms, it shall apply the simplification of plant health checks and requirements referred to in Article 121 of the 1990 Convention from the date of signature of the agreement on the accession to the 1990 Convention.

The Government of the Kingdom of Spain declares that it shall conduct a pest risk assessment on fresh citrus fruit and palms before 1 January 1992, which, if it reveals a risk of harmful organisms being introduced or propagated, may, where appropriate, justify the derogation provided for in Article 121(2) of the 1990 Convention after the entry into force of the said agreement on the accession of the Kingdom of Spain.

4. Declaration on the agreement on the accession of the Portuguese Republic to the 1990 Convention

At the time of signing this agreement, the Kingdom of Spain takes note of the contents of the agreement on the accession of the Portuguese Republic to the 1990 Convention and the related final act and declaration.

Done at Bonn on 25 June 1991 in a single original in the Dutch, French, German, Italian and Spanish languages, all five texts being equally authentic, such original remaining deposited in the archives of the Government of the Grand Duchy of Luxembourg, which shall transmit a certified copy to each of the contracting parties.

For the Government of the Kingdom of Belgium,

For the Government of the Federal Republic of Germany,

For the Government of the Kingdom of Spain,

For the Government of the French Republic,

For the Government of the Italian Republic,

For the Government of the Grand Duchy of Luxembourg,

For the Government of the Kingdom of the Netherlands.

DECLARATION OF THE MINISTERS AND STATE SECRETARIES

On 25 June 1991, the representatives of the Governments of the Kingdom of Belgium, the Federal Republic of Germany, the Kingdom of Spain, the French Republic, the Italian Republic, the Grand Duchy of Luxembourg and the Kingdom of the Netherlands signed at Bonn the agreement on the accession of the Kingdom of Spain to the convention implementing the Schengen Agreement of 14 June 1985 between the Governments of the States of the Benelux Economic Union, the Federal Republic of Germany and the French Republic on the gradual abolition of checks at their common borders, signed at Schengen on 19 June 1990, to which the Italian Republic acceded by the agreement signed at Paris on 27 November 1990.

They noted that the representative of the Government of the Kingdom of Spain declared support for the declaration made at Schengen on 19 June 1990 by the ministers and State secretaries representing the Governments of the Kingdom of Belgium, the Federal Republic of Germany, the French Republic, the Grand Duchy of Luxembourg and the Kingdom of the Netherlands and for the decision confirmed on the same date upon signature of the convention implementing the Schengen Agreement, which declaration and decision the Government of the Italian Republic has also supported.

AGREEMENT ON THE ACCESSION OF THE PORTUGUESE REPUBLIC

TO THE CONVENTION IMPLEMENTING THE SCHENGEN AGREEMENT OF 14 JUNE 1985 BETWEEN THE GOVERNMENTS OF THE STATES OF THE BENELUX ECONOMIC UNION, THE FEDERAL REPUBLIC OF GERMANY AND THE FRENCH REPUBLIC ON THE GRADUAL ABOLITION OF CHECKS AT THEIR COMMON BORDERS SIGNED AT SCHENGEN ON 19 JUNE 1990, TO WHICH THE ITALIAN REPUBLIC ACCEDED BY THE AGREEMENT SIGNED AT PARIS ON 27 NOVEMBER 1990

The Kingdom of Belgium, the Federal Republic of Germany, the French Republic, the Grand Duchy of Luxembourg and the Kingdom of the Netherlands, Parties to the convention implementing the Schengen Agreement of 14 June 1985 between the Governments of the States of the Benelux Economic Union, the Federal Republic of Germany and the French Republic on the gradual abolition of checks at their common borders signed at Schengen on 19 June 1990, hereinafter referred to as 'the 1990 Convention', as well as the Italian Republic, which acceded to the 1990 Convention by the agreement signed at Paris on 27 November 1990, of the one part,

and the Portuguese Republic, of the other part,

Having regard to the signature done at Bonn on 25 June 1991 of the protocol on the accession of the Government of the Portuguese Republic to the Schengen Agreement of 14 June 1985 between the Governments of the States of the Benelux Economic Union, the Federal Republic of Germany and the French Republic on the gradual abolition of checks at their common borders, as amended by the protocol on the accession of the Government of the Italian Republic signed at Paris on 27 November 1990,

On the basis of Article 140 of the 1990 Convention,

HAVE AGREED AS FOLLOWS:

Article 1

The Portuguese Republic hereby accedes to the 1990 Convention.

Article 2

1. The officers referred to in Article 40(4) of the 1990 Convention as regards the Portuguese Republic shall be: the members of the *Polícia Judiciária* (criminal police), as well as customs officers in their capacity as auxiliary officers of the Public Prosecutor's Office, under the conditions laid down in appropriate bilateral agreements referred to in Article 40(6) of the 1990 Convention, with respect to their powers regarding the

illicit trafficking in narcotic drugs and psychotropic substances, trafficking in arms and explosives, and the illicit transportation of toxic and hazardous waste.

2. The authority referred to in Article 40(5) of the 1990 Convention as regards the Portuguese Republic shall be the *Direccão geral de la Polícia Judiciária* (Directorate-General of the Criminal Police).

Article 3

1. The officers referred to in Article 41(7) of the 1990 Convention as regards the Portuguese Republic shall be: the members of the *Polícia Judiciária*, as well as customs officers in their capacity as auxiliary officers of the Public Prosecutor's Office, under the conditions laid down in appropriate bilateral agreements referred to in Article 41(10) of the 1990 Convention with respect to their powers regarding the illicit trafficking in narcotic drugs and psychotropic substances, trafficking in arms and explosives, and the illicit transportation of toxic and hazardous waste.

2. At the time of signing this agreement, the Government of the Portuguese Republic shall make a declaration with regard to the Government of the Kingdom of Spain defining, on the basis of Article 41(2), (3) and (4) of the 1990 Convention, the procedures for carrying out hot pursuit on Portuguese territory.

Article 4

The competent ministry referred to in Article 65(2) of the 1990 Convention as regards the Portuguese Republic shall be the Ministry of Justice.

Article 5

For the purposes of extradition between the contracting parties to the 1990 Convention, paragraph (c) of the declaration made by the Portuguese Republic concerning Article 1 of the European Convention on Extradition of 13 December 1957 shall be interpreted as follows.

The Portuguese Republic shall not grant the extradition of persons wanted for an offence punishable by a life sentence or detention order for life. Nevertheless, extradition will be granted where the requesting State gives assurances that it will encourage, in accordance with its law and practice regarding the carrying out of sentences, the application of any measures of clemency to which the person whose extradition is requested might be entitled.

Article 6

For the purposes of mutual assistance in criminal matters between the contracting parties to the 1990 Convention, the Portuguese Republic shall not refuse requests on the grounds that the offences giving rise to the request are punishable by a life sentence or detention order for life under the law of the requesting State.

Article 7

1. This agreement shall be subject to ratification, acceptance or approval. The instruments of ratification, acceptance or approval shall be deposited with the Government of the Grand Duchy of Luxembourg, which shall notify all the contracting parties thereof.

2. This agreement shall enter into force on the first day of the second month following the deposit of the instruments of ratification, acceptance or approval by the five Signatory States to the 1990 Convention and by the Portuguese Republic, and at the earliest on the day on which the 1990 Convention enters into force. With regard to the Italian Republic, this agreement shall enter into force on the first day of the second month following the deposit of its instrument of ratification, acceptance or approval, and at the earliest on the day on which this agreement enters into force between the other contracting parties.

3. The Government of the Grand Duchy of Luxembourg shall notify each of the contracting parties of the date of entry into force.

Article 8

1. The Government of the Grand Duchy of Luxembourg shall transmit to the Government of the Portuguese Republic a certified copy of the 1990 Convention in the Dutch, French, German and Italian languages.

2. The text of the 1990 Convention drawn up in the Portuguese language is annexed to this agreement and shall be authentic under the same conditions as the texts of the 1990 Convention drawn up in the Dutch, French, German and Italian languages.

In witness whereof, the undersigned, duly authorised to this effect, have signed this agreement.

Done at Bonn on 25 June 1991 in a single original in the Dutch, French, German, Italian and Portuguese languages, all five texts being equally authentic, such original remaining deposited in the archives of the Government of the Grand Duchy of Luxembourg, which shall transmit a certified copy to each of the contracting parties.

For the Government of the Kingdom of Belgium,

For the Government of the Federal Republic of Germany,

For the Government of the French Republic,

For the Government of the Italian Republic,

For the Government of the Grand Duchy of Luxembourg,

For the Government of the Kingdom of the Netherlands,

For the Government of the Portuguese Republic.

FINAL ACT

I. At the time of signing the agreement on the accession of the Portuguese Republic to the convention implementing the Schengen Agreement of 14 June 1985 between the Governments of the States of the Benelux Economic Union, the Federal Republic of Germany and the French Republic on the gradual abolition of checks at their common borders signed at Schengen on 19 June 1990, to which the Italian Republic acceded by the agreement signed at Paris on 27 November 1990, the Portuguese Republic has subscribed to the final act, the minutes and the joint declaration of the ministers and State secretaries which were signed at the same time as the 1990 Convention.

The Portuguese Republic has subscribed to the joint declarations and has taken note of the unilateral declarations contained therein.

The Government of the Grand Duchy of Luxembourg shall transmit to the Government of the Portuguese Republic a certified copy of the final act, the minutes and the joint declaration of the ministers and State secretaries, which were signed at the time of signing the 1990 Convention, in the Dutch, French, German and Italian languages.

The texts of the final act, the minutes and the joint declaration of the ministers and State secretaries which were signed at the time of signing the 1990 Convention, drawn up in the Portuguese language, are annexed to this final act and shall be authentic under the same conditions as the texts drawn up in the Dutch, French, German and Italian languages.

II. At the time of signing the agreement on the accession of the Portuguese Republic to the convention implementing the Schengen Agreement of 14 June 1985 between the Governments of the States of the Benelux Economic Union, the Federal Republic of Germany and the French Republic on the gradual abolition of checks at their common borders signed at Schengen on 19 June 1990, to which the Italian Republic acceded by the agreement signed at Paris on 27 November 1990, the contracting parties have adopted the following declarations.

1. Joint declaration on Article 7 of the accession agreement

The Signatory States shall, prior to the entry into force of the accession agreement, inform each other of all circumstances that could have a significant bearing on the areas covered by the 1990 Convention and on the bringing into force of the accession agreement.

This accession agreement shall not be brought into force between the five Signatory States to the 1990 Convention and the Portuguese Republic until the preconditions for implementation of the 1990 Convention have been fulfilled in these six States and checks at the external borders are effective there. With regard to the Italian Republic, this accession agreement shall not be brought into force until the preconditions for the implementation of the 1990 Convention have been fulfilled in the Signatory States to the said agreement and checks at the external borders are effective there.

2. Joint declaration on Article 9(2) of the 1990 Convention

The contracting parties specify that at the time of signing the agreement on the accession of the Portuguese Republic to the 1990 Convention, the common visa arrangements referred to in Article 9(2) of the 1990 Convention shall be taken to mean the common arrangements applied by the Signatory Parties to the said convention since 19 June 1990.

3. Joint declaration on data protection

The contracting parties take note that a law on the protection of personal data subject to automatic processing was published by the Portuguese Republic on 29 April 1991.

The contracting parties note that the Government of the Portuguese Republic undertakes to take all the necessary steps before the ratification of the agreement on the accession to the 1990 Convention to ensure that Portuguese legislation is supplemented so as to ensure the full application of all the provisions of the convention of 1990 relating to the protection of personal data.

III. The contracting parties have taken note of the following declarations made by the Portuguese Republic.

1. Declaration on Brazilian nationals entering Portugal under the Visa Waiver Agreement between Portugal and Brazil of 9 August 1960

The Government of the Portuguese Republic undertakes to readmit to its territory Brazilian nationals who, having entered the territories of the contracting parties via Portugal under the Visa Waiver Agreement between Portugal and Brazil, are intercepted in the territories of the contracting parties after the period referred to in Article 20(1) of the 1990 Convention has expired.

The Government of the Portuguese Republic undertakes to admit Brazilian nationals only insofar as they fulfil the conditions laid down in Article 5 of the 1990 Convention and to take all steps to ensure that their travel documents are stamped when they cross the external borders.

2. Declaration on the European Convention on Mutual Assistance in Criminal Matters

The Government of the Portuguese Republic undertakes to ratify the European Convention on Mutual Assistance in Criminal Matters of 20 April 1959 and the additional protocol thereto before the 1990 Convention enters into force for Portugal.

3. Declaration on the Missile Technology Control Regime

For the purposes of applying Article 123 of the 1990 Convention, the Government of the Portuguese Republic undertakes to join the Missile Technology Control Regime, as formulated on 16 April 1987, as soon as possible and at the latest upon the entry into force of the 1990 Convention for Portugal.

4. Declaration on Article 121 of the 1990 Convention

The Government of the Portuguese Republic declares that, except in respect of fresh citrus fruit, it shall apply the simplification of plant health checks and requirements referred to in Article 121 of the 1990 Convention from the date of signature of the agreement on the accession to the 1990 Convention.

The Government of the Portuguese Republic declares that it shall conduct a pest risk assessment on fresh citrus fruit before 1 January 1992, which, if it reveals a risk of harmful organisms being introduced or propagated, may, where appropriate, justify the derogation provided for in Article 121(2) of the 1990 Convention after the entry into force of the said agreement on the accession of the Portuguese Republic.

5. Declaration on the agreement on the accession of the Portuguese Republic to the 1990 Convention

At the time of signing this agreement, the Portuguese Republic takes note of the contents of the agreement on the accession of the Portuguese Republic to the 1990 Convention and the related final act and declaration.

Done at Bonn 25 June 1991 in a single original in the Dutch, French, German, Italian and Portuguese languages, all five texts being equally authentic, such original remaining deposited in the archives of the Government of the Grand Duchy of Luxembourg, which shall transmit a certified copy to each of the contracting parties.

For the Government of the Kingdom of Belgium,

For the Government of the Federal Republic of Germany,

For the Government of the French Republic,

For the Government of the Italian Republic,

For the Government of the Grand Duchy of Luxembourg,

For the Government of the Kingdom of the Netherlands,

For the Government of the Portuguese Republic.

DECLARATION OF THE MINISTERS AND STATE SECRETARIES

On 25 June 1991, the representatives of the Governments of the Kingdom of Belgium, the Federal Republic of Germany, the French Republic, the Italian Republic, the Grand Duchy of Luxembourg, the Kingdom of the Netherlands and the Portuguese Republic signed at Bonn the agreement on the accession of the Portuguese Republic to the convention implementing the Schengen Agreement of 14 June 1985 between the Governments of the States of the Benelux Economic Union, the Federal Republic of Germany and the French Republic on the gradual abolition of checks at their common borders, signed at Schengen on 19 June 1990, to which the Italian Republic acceded by the agreement signed at Paris on 27 November 1990.

They noted that the representative of the Government of the Portuguese Republic declared support for the declaration made at Schengen on 19 June 1990 by the ministers and State secretaries representing the Governments of the Kingdom of Belgium, the Federal Republic of Germany, the French Republic, the Grand Duchy of Luxembourg and the Kingdom of the Netherlands and for the decision confirmed on the same date upon signature of the convention implementing the Schengen Agreement, which declaration and decision the Government of the Italian Republic has also supported.

AGREEMENT ON THE ACCESSION OF THE HELLENIC REPUBLIC

TO THE CONVENTION IMPLEMENTING THE SCHENGEN AGREEMENT OF 14 JUNE 1985 BETWEEN THE GOVERNMENTS OF THE STATES OF THE BENELUX ECONOMIC UNION, THE FEDERAL REPUBLIC OF GERMANY AND THE FRENCH REPUBLIC ON THE GRADUAL ABOLITION OF CHECKS AT THEIR COMMON BORDERS SIGNED AT SCHENGEN ON 19 JUNE 1990, TO WHICH THE ITALIAN REPUBLIC ACCEDED BY THE AGREEMENT SIGNED AT PARIS ON 27 NOVEMBER 1990, AND TO WHICH THE KINGDOM OF SPAIN AND THE HELLENIC REPUBLIC ACCEDED BY THE AGREEMENTS SIGNED AT BONN ON 25 JUNE 1991

The Kingdom of Belgium, the Federal Republic of Germany, the French Republic, the Grand Duchy of Luxembourg and the Kingdom of the Netherlands, Parties to the convention implementing the Schengen Agreement of 14 June 1985 between the Governments of the States of the Benelux Economic Union, the Federal Republic of Germany and the French Republic on the gradual abolition of checks at their common borders signed at Schengen on 19 June 1990, hereinafter referred to as 'the 1990 Convention', as well as the Italian Republic, which acceded to the 1990 Convention by the agreement signed at Paris on 27 November 1990, and the Kingdom of Spain and the Portuguese Republic, which acceded to the 1990 Convention by the agreements signed at Bonn on 25 June 1991, of the one part,

and the Hellenic Republic, of the other part,

Having regard to the signature done at Madrid on 6 November 1992 of the protocol on the accession of the Government of the Hellenic Republic to the Schengen Agreement of 14 June 1985 between the Governments of the States of the Benelux Economic Union, the Federal Republic of Germany and the French Republic on the gradual abolition of checks at their common borders, as amended by the protocol on the accession of the Government of the Italian Republic signed at Paris on 27 November 1990 and the protocols on the accession of the Governments of the Kingdom of Spain and the Portuguese Republic signed at Bonn on 25 June 1991,

On the basis of Article 140 of the 1990 Convention,

HAVE AGREED AS FOLLOWS:

Article 1

The Hellenic Republic hereby accedes to the 1990 Convention.

Article 2

1. The officers referred to in Article 40(4) of the 1990 Convention as regards the Hellenic Republic shall be: police officers of the *Ελληνική Αστυνομία* (Greek police) and of the *Λιμενικό Σώμα* (port authority), each within the limits of their powers, as well as officials of the customs administration, under the conditions laid down in appropriate bilateral agreements referred to in Article 40(6) of the 1990 Convention, with respect to their powers regarding the illicit trafficking in narcotic drugs and psychotropic substances, trafficking in arms and explosives, and the illicit transportation of toxic and hazardous waste.

2. The authority referred to in Article 40(5) of the 1990 Convention as regards the Hellenic Republic shall be: the *Διεύθυνση Διεθνούς Αστυνομικής Συνεργασίας του Υπουργείου Δημοσίας Τάξεως* (Directorate of International Police Cooperation of the Ministry of Public Order).

Article 3

The competent ministry referred to in Article 65(2) of the 1990 Convention as regards the Hellenic Republic shall be the Ministry of Justice.

Article 4

For the purposes of extradition between the contracting parties to the 1990 Convention, the Hellenic Republic shall refrain from applying the reservations that it made in respect of Articles 7, 18 and 19 of the European Convention on Extradition of 13 December 1957.

Article 5

For the purposes of mutual assistance in criminal matters between the contracting parties to the 1990 Convention, the Hellenic Republic shall refrain from applying the reservation it made in respect of Articles 4 and 11 of the European Convention on Mutual Assistance in Criminal Matters of 20 April 1959.

Article 6

1. This agreement shall be subject to ratification, acceptance or approval. The instruments of ratification, acceptance or approval shall be deposited with the Government of the Grand Duchy of Luxembourg, which shall notify all the contracting parties thereof.

2. This agreement shall enter into force on the first day of the second month following the deposit of the instruments of ratification, acceptance or approval by the States for which the 1990 Convention has entered into force and by the Hellenic Republic.

With regard to the other States, this agreement shall enter into force on the first day of the second month following the deposit of their instruments of ratification, acceptance or approval, provided that this agreement has entered into force in accordance with the provisions of the preceding subparagraph.

3. The Government of the Grand Duchy of Luxembourg shall notify each of the contracting parties of the date of entry into force.

Article 7

1. The Government of the Grand Duchy of Luxembourg shall transmit to the Government of the Hellenic Republic a certified copy of the 1990 Convention in the Dutch, French, German, Italian, Portuguese and Spanish languages.

2. The text of the 1990 Convention drawn up in the Greek language is annexed to this agreement and shall be authentic under the same conditions as the texts of the 1990 Convention drawn up in the Dutch, French, German, Italian, Portuguese and Spanish languages.

In witness whereof, the undersigned, duly authorised to this effect, have signed this agreement.

Done at Madrid on 6 November 1992 in a single original in the Dutch, French, German, Greek, Italian, Portuguese and Spanish languages, all seven texts being equally authentic, such original remaining deposited in the archives of the Government of the Grand Duchy of Luxembourg, which shall transmit a certified copy to each of the contracting parties.

For the Government of the Kingdom of Belgium,

For the Government of the Federal Republic of Germany,

For the Government of the Hellenic Republic,

For the Government of the Kingdom of Spain,

For the Government of the French Republic,

For the Government of the Italian Republic,

For the Government of the Grand Duchy of Luxembourg,

For the Government of the Kingdom of the Netherlands,

For the Government of the Portuguese Republic.

FINAL ACT

I. At the time of signing the agreement on the accession of the Hellenic Republic to the convention implementing the Schengen Agreement of 14 June 1985 between the Governments of the States of the Benelux Economic Union, the Federal Republic of Germany and the French Republic on the gradual abolition of checks at their common borders signed at Schengen on 19 June 1990, to which the Italian Republic acceded by the agreement signed at Paris on 27 November 1990 and to which the Kingdom of Spain and the Portuguese Republic acceded by the accession agreements signed at Bonn on 25 June 1991, the Government of the Hellenic Republic has subscribed to the final act, the minutes and the joint declaration of the ministers and State secretaries which were signed at the same time as the 1990 Convention.

The Government of the Hellenic Republic has subscribed to the joint declarations and has taken note of the unilateral declarations contained therein.

The Government of the Grand Duchy of Luxembourg shall transmit to the Government of the Hellenic Republic a certified copy of the final act, the minutes and the joint declaration of the ministers and State secretaries, which were signed at the time of signing the 1990 Convention, in the Dutch, French, German, Italian, Portuguese and Spanish languages.

The texts of the final act, the minutes and the joint declaration of the ministers and State secretaries which were signed at the time of signing the 1990 Convention, drawn up in the Greek language, are annexed to this final act and shall be authentic under the same conditions as the texts drawn up in the Dutch, French, German, Italian, Portuguese and Spanish languages.

II. At the time of signing the agreement on the accession of the Hellenic Republic to the convention implementing the Schengen Agreement of 14 June 1985 between the Governments of the States of the Benelux Economic Union, the Federal Republic of Germany and the French Republic on the gradual abolition of checks at their common borders signed at Schengen on 19 June 1990, to which the Italian Republic acceded by the agreement signed at Paris on 27 November 1990 and to which the Kingdom of Spain and the Portuguese Republic acceded by the accession agreements signed at Bonn on 25 June 1991, the contracting parties adopted the following declarations.

1. Joint declaration on Article 6 of the accession agreement

The Signatory States shall, prior to the entry into force of the accession agreement, inform each other of all circumstances that could have a significant bearing on the areas covered by the 1990 Convention and on the bringing into force of the accession agreement.

This accession agreement shall not be brought into force between the States for which the 1990 Convention has been brought into force and the Hellenic Republic until the preconditions for implementation of the 1990 Convention have been fulfilled in these States and checks at the external borders are effective there.

With regard to the other States, this accession agreement shall only enter into force when all the preconditions for the implementation of the convention of 1990 have been fulfilled by the Signatory States to this accession agreement and controls at the external borders are effective there.

2. Joint declaration on Article 9(2) of the 1990 Convention

The contracting parties specify that at the time of signing the agreement on the accession of the Hellenic Republic to the 1990 Convention, the common visa arrangements referred to in Article 9(2) of the 1990 Convention shall be taken to mean the common arrangements applied by the Signatory Parties to the said convention since 19 June 1990.

3. Joint declaration on data protection

The contracting parties note that the Government of the Hellenic Republic undertakes to take all the necessary steps before the ratification of the agreement on the accession to the 1990 Convention to ensure that Greek legislation is supplemented in accordance with the Council of Europe Convention for the Protection of Individuals with regard to the Automatic Processing of Personal Data of 28 January 1981 and in accordance with Recommendation No R (87) 15 of 17 September 1987 of the Committee of the Ministers of the Council of Europe regulating the use of personal data in the police sector, so as to ensure the full application of the provisions of Articles 117 and 126 of the 1990 Convention relating to the protection of personal data, with the aim of achieving a level of protection compatible with the relevant provisions of the 1990 Convention.

4. Joint declaration on Article 41 of the 1990 Convention

The contracting parties note that, in view of the geographical situation of the Hellenic Republic, the provisions of Article 41(5)(b) preclude the application of Article 41 in relations between the Hellenic Republic and the other contracting parties. The Hellenic Republic has therefore not designated authorities within the meaning of Article 41(7) or made a declaration within the meaning of Article 41(9).

This procedure applied by the Greek Government does not conflict with the provisions of Article 137.

5. Joint declaration concerning Mount Athos

Recognising that the special status granted to Mount Athos, as guaranteed by Article 105 of the Hellenic Constitution and the Charter of Mount Athos, is justified exclusively on grounds of a spiritual and religious nature, the contracting parties will ensure that this status is taken into account in the application and subsequent preparation of the provisions of the 1985 Agreement and the 1990 Convention.

III. The contracting parties have taken note of the following declarations made by the Hellenic Republic.

1. Declaration by the Hellenic Republic on the agreements on the accession of the Italian Republic, the Kingdom of Spain and the Portuguese Republic

The Government of the Hellenic Republic takes note of the contents of the agreements on the accession of the Italian Republic, the Kingdom of Spain and the Portuguese Republic to the 1990 Convention, and of the contents of the final acts and declarations annexed to the said agreements.

The Government of the Grand Duchy of Luxembourg shall transmit a certified copy of the abovementioned instruments to the Government of the Hellenic Republic.

2. Declaration by the Hellenic Republic on mutual assistance in criminal matters

The Hellenic Republic undertakes to process requests for assistance from the other contracting parties with all due diligence, including when they are made directly to the Greek judicial authorities in accordance with the procedure laid down in Article 53(1) of the 1990 Convention.

3. Declaration on Article 121 of the 1990 Convention

The Government of the Hellenic Republic declares that, except in respect of fresh citrus fruit, cotton and lucerne seed, it shall apply the simplification of plant health checks and requirements referred to in Article 121 of the 1990 Convention from the date of signature of the agreement on the accession to the 1990 Convention.

Nevertheless, in respect of fresh citrus fruit, the Hellenic Republic shall transpose the provisions of Article 121 and related measures by 1 January 1993 at the latest.

Done at Madrid on 6 November 1992 in a single original in the Dutch, French, German, Greek, Italian, Portuguese and Spanish languages, all seven texts being equally authentic, such original remaining deposited in the archives of the Government of the Grand Duchy of Luxembourg, which shall transmit a certified copy to each of the contracting parties.

For the Government of the Kingdom of Belgium,

For the Government of the Federal Republic of Germany,

For the Government of the Hellenic Republic,

For the Government of the Kingdom of Spain,

For the Government of the French Republic,

For the Government of the Italian Republic,

For the Government of the Grand Duchy of Luxembourg,

For the Government of the Kingdom of the Netherlands,

For the Government of the Portuguese Republic.

DECLARATION OF THE MINISTERS AND STATE SECRETARIES

On 6 November 1992, the representatives of the Governments of the Kingdom of Belgium, the Federal Republic of Germany, the Kingdom of Spain, the French Republic, the Hellenic Republic, the Italian Republic, the Grand Duchy of Luxembourg, the Kingdom of the Netherlands and the Portuguese Republic signed at Madrid the agreement on the accession of the Hellenic Republic to the convention implementing the Schengen Agreement of 14 June 1985 between the Governments of the States of the Benelux Economic Union, the Federal Republic of Germany and the French Republic on the gradual abolition of checks at their common borders, signed at Schengen on 19 June 1990, to which the Italian Republic acceded by the agreement signed at Paris on 27 November 1990 and to which the Kingdom of Spain and the Portuguese Republic acceded by the agreements signed at Bonn on 25 June 1991.

They noted that the representative of the Government of the Hellenic Republic declared support for the declaration made at Schengen on 19 June 1990 by the ministers and State secretaries representing the Governments of the Kingdom of Belgium, the Federal Republic of Germany, the French Republic, the Grand Duchy of Luxembourg and the Kingdom of the Netherlands and for the decision confirmed on the same date upon signature of the convention implementing the Schengen Agreement, which declaration and decision the Governments of the Italian Republic, the Kingdom of Spain and the Portuguese Republic have also supported.

AGREEMENT ON THE ACCESSION OF THE REPUBLIC OF AUSTRIA

TO THE CONVENTION IMPLEMENTING THE SCHENGEN AGREEMENT OF 14 JUNE 1985 BETWEEN THE GOVERNMENTS OF THE STATES OF THE BENELUX ECONOMIC UNION, THE FEDERAL REPUBLIC OF GERMANY AND THE FRENCH REPUBLIC ON THE GRADUAL ABOLITION OF CHECKS AT THEIR COMMON BORDERS SIGNED AT SCHENGEN ON 19 JUNE 1990, TO WHICH THE ITALIAN REPUBLIC, THE KINGDOM OF SPAIN AND THE PORTUGUESE REPUBLIC, AND THE HELLENIC REPUBLIC ACCEDED BY THE AGREEMENTS SIGNED ON 27 NOVEMBER 1990, ON 25 JUNE 1991 AND ON 6 NOVEMBER 1992 RESPECTIVELY

The Kingdom of Belgium, the Federal Republic of Germany, the French Republic, the Grand Duchy of Luxembourg and the Kingdom of the Netherlands, Parties to the convention implementing the Schengen Agreement of 14 June 1985 between the Governments of the States of the Benelux Economic Union, the Federal Republic of Germany and the French Republic on the gradual abolition of checks at their common borders signed at Schengen on 19 June 1990, hereinafter referred to as 'the 1990 Convention', as well as the Italian Republic, the Kingdom of Spain and the Portuguese Republic, and the Hellenic Republic, which acceded to the 1990 Convention by the agreements signed on 27 November 1990, on 25 June 1991 and on 6 November 1992 respectively,

of the one part,

and the Republic of Austria, of the other part,

Having regard to the signature done at Brussels on 28 April 1995 of the protocol on the accession of the Government of the Republic of Austria to the Schengen Agreement of 14 June 1985 between the Governments of the States of the Benelux Economic Union, the Federal Republic of Germany and the French Republic on the gradual abolition of checks at their common borders, as amended by the protocols on the accession of the Government of the Italian Republic, the Kingdom of Spain and the Portuguese Republic, and the Hellenic Republic signed on 27 November 1990, on 25 June 1991 and on 6 November 1992 respectively,

On the basis of Article 140 of the 1990 Convention,

HAVE AGREED AS FOLLOWS:

Article 1

The Republic of Austria hereby accedes to the 1990 Convention.

Article 2

1. The officers referred to in Article 40(4) of the 1990 Convention as regards the Republic of Austria shall be:

(a) the officers of the *öffentlicher Sicherheitsdienst* (agencies responsible for maintaining public security), namely:

- the officers of the *Bundesgendarmerie* (federal gendarmerie);
- the officers of the *Bundessicherheitswachekorps* (federal police force under the command of the local chief of the federal police);
- the officers of the *Kriminalbeamtenkorps* (criminal police);
- the officials of the *rechtskundiger Dienst bei Sicherheitsbehörden* (legal department attached to the law enforcement authorities), authorised to issue direct orders and execute coercive measures.

(b) customs officers, under the conditions laid down in appropriate bilateral agreements referred to in Article 40(6) of the 1990 Convention, with respect to their powers regarding the illicit trafficking in narcotic drugs and psychotropic substances, trafficking in arms and explosives, and the illicit transportation of toxic and hazardous waste.

2. The authority referred to in Article 40(5) of the 1990 Convention as regards the Republic of Austria shall be: the *Generaldirektion für die öffentliche Sicherheit* (Directorate-General for Public Security) at the Federal Ministry of the Interior.

Article 3

The officers referred to in Article 41(7) of the 1990 Convention as regards the Republic of Austria shall be:

1. the officers of the *öffentlicher Sicherheitsdienst* (agencies responsible for maintaining public security), namely:

- the officers of the *Bundesgendarmerie* (federal gendarmerie);
- the officers of the *Bundessicherheitswachekorps* (federal police force under the command of the local chief of the federal police);
- the officers of the *Kriminalbeamtenkorps* (criminal police);
- the officials of the *rechtskundiger Dienst bei Sicherheitsbehörden* (legal department attached to the law enforcement authorities), authorised to issue direct orders and execute coercive measures.

2. customs officers, under the conditions laid down in appropriate bilateral agreements referred to in Article 41(10) of the 1990 Convention, with respect to their powers regarding the illicit trafficking in narcotic drugs and psychotropic substances, trafficking in arms and explosives, and the illicit transportation of toxic and hazardous waste.

Article 4

The competent ministry referred to in Article 65(2) of the 1990 Convention as regards the Republic of Austria shall be the Federal Ministry of Justice.

Article 5

1. This agreement shall be subject to ratification, acceptance or approval. The instruments of ratification, acceptance or approval shall be deposited with the Government of the Grand Duchy of Luxembourg, which shall notify all the contracting parties thereof.

2. This agreement shall enter into force on the first day of the second month following the deposit of the instruments of ratification, acceptance or approval by the States for which the 1990 Convention has entered into force and by the Republic of Austria.

With regard to other States, this agreement shall enter into force on the first day of the second month following the deposit of their instruments of ratification, acceptance or approval, provided that this agreement has entered into force in accordance with the provisions of the preceding subparagraph.

3. The Government of the Grand Duchy of Luxembourg shall notify each of the contracting parties of the date of entry into force.

Article 6

The Government of the Grand Duchy of Luxembourg shall transmit to the Government of the Republic of Austria a certified copy of the 1990 Convention in the Dutch, French, German, Greek, Italian, Portuguese and Spanish languages.

In witness whereof, the undersigned, duly authorised to this effect, have signed this agreement.

Done at Brussels on 28 April 1995 in a single original in the Dutch, French, German, Greek, Italian, Portuguese and Spanish languages, all seven texts being equally authentic, such original remaining deposited in the archives of the Government of the Grand Duchy of Luxembourg, which shall transmit a certified copy to each of the contracting parties.

For the Government of the Kingdom of Belgium,

For the Government of the Federal Republic of Germany,

For the Government of the Hellenic Republic,

For the Government of the Kingdom of Spain,

For the Government of the French Republic,

For the Government of the Italian Republic,

For the Government of the Grand Duchy of Luxembourg,

For the Government of the Kingdom of the Netherlands,

For the Government of the Republic of Austria,

For the Government of the Portuguese Republic.

FINAL ACT

I. At the time of signing the agreement on the accession of the Republic of Austria to the convention implementing the Schengen Agreement of 14 June 1985 between the Governments of the States of the Benelux Economic Union, the Federal Republic of Germany and the French Republic on the gradual abolition of checks at their common borders signed at Schengen on 19 June 1990, to which the Italian Republic, the Kingdom of Spain and the Portuguese Republic, and the Hellenic Republic acceded by the agreements signed on 27 November 1990, on 25 June 1991 and on 6 November 1992 respectively, the Government of the Republic of Austria has subscribed to the final act, the minutes and the joint declaration by the ministers and State secretaries which were signed at the time of signing the 1990 Convention.

The Government of the Republic of Austria has subscribed to the joint declarations and has taken note of the unilateral declarations contained therein.

The Government of the Grand Duchy of Luxembourg shall transmit to the Government of the Republic of Austria a certified copy of the final act, the minutes and the joint declaration by the ministers and State secretaries which were signed at the time of signing the 1990 Convention, in the Dutch, French, German, Greek, Italian, Portuguese and Spanish languages.

II. At the time of signing the agreement on the accession of the Republic of Austria to the convention implementing the Schengen Agreement of 14 June 1985 between the Governments of the States of the Benelux Economic Union, the Federal Republic of Germany and the French Republic on the gradual abolition of checks at their common borders signed at Schengen on 19 June 1990, to which the Italian Republic, the Kingdom of Spain and the Portuguese Republic, and the Hellenic Republic acceded by the agreements signed on 27 November 1990, on 25 June 1991 and on 6 November 1992 respectively, the contracting parties have adopted the following declarations:

1. Joint declaration on Article 5 of the accession agreement

The contracting parties shall, prior to the entry into force of the accession agreement, inform each other of all circumstances that could have a significant bearing on the areas covered by the 1990 Convention and on the bringing into force of the accession agreement.

The accession agreement shall not be brought into force between the States for which the 1990 Convention has been brought into force and the Republic of Austria until the preconditions for implementation of the 1990 Convention have been fulfilled in all these States and checks at the external borders are effective there.

With regard to each of the other States, this accession agreement shall not be brought into force until the preconditions for the implementation of the 1990 Convention have been fulfilled in that State and checks at the external borders are effective there.

2. Joint declaration on Article 9(2) of the 1990 Convention

The contracting parties specify that at the time of signing the agreement on the accession of the Republic of Austria to the 1990 Convention, the common visa arrangements referred to in Article 9(2) of the 1990 Convention shall be taken to mean the common arrangements applied by the Signatory Parties to the said convention since 19 June 1990.

III. The contracting parties have taken note of the declaration by the Republic of Austria on the agreements on the accession of the Italian Republic, the Kingdom of Spain, the Portuguese Republic, and the Hellenic Republic.

The Government of the Republic of Austria takes note of the contents of the agreements on the accession of the Italian Republic, the Kingdom of Spain and the Portuguese Republic, and the Hellenic Republic to the 1990 Convention, signed on 27 November 1990, on 25 June 1991 and on 6 November 1992 respectively and of the contents of the final acts and declarations annexed to the said agreements.

The Government of the Grand Duchy of Luxembourg shall transmit a certified copy of the abovementioned instruments to the Government of the Republic of Austria.

Done at Brussels 28 April 1995 in a single original in the Dutch, French, German, Greek, Italian, Portuguese and Spanish languages, all seven texts being equally authentic, such original remaining deposited in the archives of the Government of the Grand Duchy of Luxembourg, which shall transmit a certified copy to each of the contracting parties.

For the Government of the Kingdom of Belgium,

For the Government of the Federal Republic of Germany,

For the Government of the Hellenic Republic,

For the Government of the Kingdom of Spain,

For the Government of the French Republic,

For the Government of the Italian Republic,

For the Government of the Grand Duchy of Luxembourg,

For the Government of the Kingdom of the Netherlands,

For the Government of the Republic of Austria,

For the Government of the Portuguese Republic.

AGREEMENT ON THE ACCESSION OF THE KINDOM OF DENMARK

TO THE CONVENTION IMPLEMENTING THE SCHENGEN AGREEMENT OF 14 JUNE 1985 ON THE GRADUAL ABOLITION OF CHECKS AT THE COMMON BORDERS SIGNED AT SCHENGEN ON 19 JUNE 1990

The Kingdom of Belgium, the Federal Republic of Germany, the French Republic, the Grand Duchy of Luxembourg and the Kingdom of the Netherlands, Parties to the convention implementing the Schengen Agreement of 14 June 1985 between the Governments of the States of the Benelux Economic Union, the Federal Republic of Germany and the French Republic on the gradual abolition of checks at their common borders signed at Schengen on 19 June 1990, hereinafter referred to as 'the 1990 Convention', as well as the Italian Republic, the Kingdom of Spain and the Portuguese Republic, the Hellenic Republic, and the Republic of Austria, which acceded to the 1990 Convention by the agreements signed on 27 November 1990, on 25 June 1991, on 6 November 1992 and on 28 April 1995 respectively,

of the one part,

and the Kingdom of Denmark, of the other part,

Having regard to the signature done at Luxembourg on 19 December 1996 of the protocol on the accession of the Government of the Kingdom of Denmark to the Schengen Agreement of 14 June 1985 between the Governments of the States of the Benelux Economic Union, the Federal Republic of Germany and the French Republic on the gradual abolition of checks at their common borders, as amended by the protocols on the accession of the Governments of the Italian Republic, the Kingdom of Spain and the Portuguese Republic, the Hellenic Republic, and the Republic of Austria, signed on 27 November 1990, 25 June 1991, on 6 November 1992 and on 28 April 1995 respectively,

On the basis of Article 140 of the 1990 Convention,

HAVE AGREED AS FOLLOWS:

Article 1

The Kingdom of Denmark hereby accedes to the 1990 Convention.

Article 2

1. At the date of signing this agreement, the officers referred to in Article 40(4) of the 1990 Convention as regards the Kingdom of Denmark shall be:

(a) *Politijenestemaend hos lokale politimestre og hos Rigspolitichefen* (police officers working for local chief constables and for the Office of the Commissioner of Police;

(b) customs officers, under the conditions laid down in appropriate bilateral agreements referred to in Article 40(6) of the 1990 Convention, with respect to their powers regarding the illicit trafficking in narcotic drugs and psychotropic substances, trafficking in arms and explosives, and the illicit transportation of toxic and hazardous waste.

2. At the date of signing this agreement, the authority referred to in Article 40(5) of the 1990 Convention as regards the Kingdom of Denmark shall be the *Rigspolitichefen* (Office of the Commissioner of Police).

Article 3

As the date of signing this agreement, the officers referred to in Article 41(7) of the 1990 Convention as regards the Kingdom of Denmark shall be:

1. *Politijenestemaend hos lokale politimestre og hos Rigspolitichefen* (police officers working for local chief constables and for the Office of the Commissioner of Police;

2. customs officers, under the conditions laid down in appropriate bilateral agreements referred to in Article 41(10) of the 1990 Convention, with respect to their powers regarding the illicit trafficking in narcotic drugs and psychotropic substances, trafficking in arms and explosives, and the illicit transportation of toxic and hazardous waste.

Article 4

At the date of signing this agreement, the competent ministry referred to in Article 65(2) of the 1990 Convention as regards the Kingdom of Denmark shall be the *Justitsministeriet* (Ministry of Justice).

Article 5

1 The provisions of this agreement shall not apply to the Faeroe Islands or to Greenland.

2. Taking into account the fact that the Faeroe Islands and Greenland apply the provisions on the movement of persons laid down within the framework of the Nordic Passport Union, persons travelling between the Faeroe Islands or Greenland, of the one part, and the States parties to the 1990 Convention and the Cooperation Agreement with the Republic of Iceland and the Kingdom of Norway, of the other part, shall not be subject to border checks.

Article 6

The provisions of this agreement shall not prejudice cooperation within the framework of the Nordic Passport Union, insofar as such cooperation does not conflict with, or impede, the application of this agreement.

Article 7

1. This agreement shall be subject to ratification, acceptance or approval. The instruments of ratification, acceptance or approval shall be deposited with the Government of the Grand Duchy of Luxembourg, which shall notify all the contracting parties thereof.

2. This agreement shall enter into force on the first day of the second month following the deposit of the instruments of ratification, acceptance or approval by the States for which the 1990 Convention has entered into force and by the Kingdom of Denmark.

With regard to other States, this agreement shall enter into force on the first day of the second month following the deposit of their instruments of ratification, acceptance or approval, provided that this agreement has entered into force in accordance with the provisions of the preceding subparagraph.

3. The Government of the Grand Duchy of Luxembourg shall notify each of the contracting parties of the date of entry into force.

Article 8

1. The Government of the Grand Duchy of Luxembourg shall transmit to the Government of the Hellenic Republic a certified copy of the 1990 Convention in the Dutch, French, German, Greek, Italian, Portuguese and Spanish languages.

2. The text of the 1990 Convention drawn up in the Danish language is annexed to this agreement and shall be authentic under the same conditions as the texts of the 1990 Convention drawn up in the Dutch, French, German, Greek, Italian, Portuguese and Spanish languages.

In witness whereof, the undersigned, duly authorised to this effect, have signed this agreement.

Done at Luxembourg on 19 December 1996 in a single original in the Danish, Dutch, French, German, Greek, Italian, Portuguese and Spanish languages, all eight texts being equally authentic, such original remaining deposited in the archives of the Government of the Grand Duchy of Luxembourg, which shall transmit a certified copy to each of the contracting parties.

For the Government of the Kingdom of Belgium,

For the Government of the Kingdom of Denmark,

For the Government of the Federal Republic of Germany,

For the Government of the Hellenic Republic,

For the Government of the Kingdom of Spain,

For the Government of the French Republic,

For the Government of the Italian Republic,

For the Government of the Grand Duchy of Luxembourg,

For the Government of the Kingdom of the Netherlands,

For the Government of the Republic of Austria,

For the Government of the Portuguese Republic.

FINAL ACT

I. At the time of signing the agreement on the accession of the Kingdom of Denmark to the convention implementing the Schengen Agreement of 14 June 1985 between the Governments of the States of the Benelux Economic Union, the Federal Republic of Germany and the French Republic on the gradual abolition of checks at their common borders signed at Schengen on 19 June 1990, to which the Italian Republic, the Kingdom of Spain and the Portuguese Republic, the Hellenic Republic, and the Kingdom of Austria acceded by the agreements signed on 27 November 1990, on 25 June 1991, on 6 November 1992 and on 28 April 1995 respectively, the Government of the Kingdom of Denmark has subscribed to the final act, the minutes and the joint declaration by the ministers and State secretaries which were signed at the time of signing the 1990 Convention.

The Government of the Kingdom of Denmark has subscribed to the joint declarations and has taken note of the unilateral declarations contained therein.

The Government of the Grand Duchy of Luxembourg shall transmit to the Government of the Kingdom of Denmark a certified copy of the final act, the minutes and the joint declaration by the ministers and State secretaries which were signed at the time of signing the 1990 Convention, in the Danish, Dutch, French, German, Greek, Italian, Portuguese and Spanish languages.

II. At the time of signing the agreement on the accession of the Kingdom of Denmark to the convention implementing the Schengen Agreement of 14 June 1985 between the Governments of the States of the Benelux Economic Union, the Federal Republic of Germany and the French Republic on the gradual abolition of checks at their common borders signed at Schengen on 19 June 1990, to which the Italian Republic, the Kingdom of Spain and the Portuguese Republic, the Hellenic Republic, and the Kingdom of Austria acceded by the agreements signed on 27 November 1990, on 25 June 1991, on 6 November 1992 and on 28 April 1995 respectively, the contracting parties have adopted the following declarations.

1. Joint declaration on Article 7 of the accession agreement

The contracting parties shall, prior to the entry into force of the accession agreement, inform each other of all circumstances that could have a significant bearing on the areas covered by the 1990 Convention and on the bringing into force of the accession agreement.

This accession agreement shall be brought into force between the States for which the 1990 Convention has been brought into force and the Kingdom of Denmark when the preconditions for implementation of the 1990 Convention have been fulfilled in all these States and checks at the external borders are effective there, and once the Executive Committee has established that the rules which it deems necessary for the implementation of effective control and surveillance measures at the external borders of the Faroe Islands and Greenland and the necessary compensatory measures, including the implementation of the Schengen information system (SIS) have been applied and are effective.

With regard to each of the other States, this accession agreement shall be brought into force when the preconditions for the implementation of the 1990 Convention have been fulfilled in that State and when checks at the external borders are effective there.

2. Joint declaration on Article 9(2) of the 1990 Convention

The contracting parties specify that at the time of signing the agreement on the accession of the Kingdom of Denmark to the 1990 Convention, the common visa arrangements referred to in Article 9(2) of the 1990 Convention shall be taken to mean the common arrangements applied by the Signatory Parties to the said convention since 19 June 1990.

3. Joint declaration on the convention drawn up on the basis of Article K.3 of the Treaty on European Union relating to extradition

The States party to the 1990 Convention hereby confirm that Article 5(4) of the convention drawn up on the basis of Article K.3 of the Treaty on European Union relating to extradition between the Member States of the European Union, signed at Dublin on 27 September 1996, and their respective declarations annexed to the said convention, shall apply within the framework of the 1990 Convention.

III. The contracting parties have taken note of the declarations by the Kingdom of Denmark on the agreements on the accession of the Italian Republic, the Kingdom of Spain, the Portuguese Republic, the Hellenic Republic, and the Republic of Austria.

The Government of the Kingdom of Denmark takes note of the contents of the agreements on the accession of the Italian Republic, the Kingdom of Spain and the Portuguese Republic, the Hellenic Republic, and the Republic of Austria to the 1990 Convention, signed on 27 November 1990, on 25 June 1991, on 6 November 1992 and on 28 April 1995 respectively, and of the contents of the final acts and declarations annexed to the said agreements.

The Government of the Grand Duchy of Luxembourg shall transmit a certified copy of the abovementioned instruments to the Government of the Kingdom of Denmark.

Declaration by the Kingdom of Denmark on the agreements on the accession of the Republic of Finland and the Kingdom of Sweden to the 1990 Convention

At the time of signing this agreement, the Kingdom of Denmark takes note of the contents of the agreements on the accession of the Republic of Finland and the Kingdom of Sweden to the 1990 Conven-

tion and of the contents of the related final acts and declarations.

Done at Luxembourg on 19 December 1996 in a single original in the Danish, Dutch, French, German, Greek, Italian, Portuguese and Spanish languages, all eight texts being equally authentic, such original remaining deposited in the archives of the Government of the Grand Duchy of Luxembourg, which shall transmit a certified copy to each of the contracting parties.

For the Government of the Kingdom of Belgium,

For the Government of the Kingdom of Denmark,

For the Government of the Federal Republic of Germany,

For the Government of the Hellenic Republic,

For the Government of the Kingdom of Spain,

For the Government of the French Republic,

For the Government of the Italian Republic,

For the Government of the Grand Duchy of Luxembourg,

For the Government of the Kingdom of the Netherlands,

For the Government of the Republic of Austria,

For the Government of the Portuguese Republic.

DECLARATION BY THE MINISTERS AND STATE SECRETARIES

On 19 December 1996, the representatives of the Governments of the Kingdom of Belgium, the Kingdom of Denmark, the Federal Republic of Germany, the Hellenic Republic, the Kingdom of Spain, the French Republic, the Italian Republic, the Grand Duchy of Luxembourg, the Kingdom of the Netherlands, the Republic of Austria and the Portuguese Republic signed at Luxembourg the agreement on the accession of the Kingdom of Denmark to the convention implementing the Schengen Agreement of 14 June 1985 between the Governments of the States of the Benelux Economic Union, the Federal Republic of Germany and the French Republic on the gradual abolition of checks at their common borders, signed at Schengen on 19 June 1990, to which the Italian Republic, the Kingdom of Spain and the Portuguese Republic, the Hellenic Republic, and the Republic of Austria acceded by the agreements signed on 27 November 1990, on 25 June 1991, on 6 November 1992 and on 28 April 1995 respectively.

They noted that the representative of the Government of the Kingdom of Denmark declared support for the declaration made at Schengen on 19 June 1990 by the ministers and State secretaries representing the Governments of the Kingdom of Belgium, the Federal Republic of Germany, the French Republic, the Grand Duchy of Luxembourg and the Kingdom of the Netherlands and for the decision confirmed on the same date upon signature of the convention implementing the Schengen Agreement, which declaration and decision the Governments of the Italian Republic, the Kingdom of Spain, the Portuguese Republic, the Hellenic Republic and the Republic of Austria have also supported.

AGREEMENT ON THE ACCESSION OF THE REPUBLIC OF FINLAND

TO THE CONVENTION IMPLEMENTING THE SCHENGEN AGREEMENT OF 14 JUNE 1985 ON THE GRADUAL ABOLITION OF CHECKS AT THE COMMON BORDERS SIGNED AT SCHENGEN ON 19 JUNE 1990

The Kingdom of Belgium, the Federal Republic of Germany, the French Republic, the Grand Duchy of Luxembourg and the Kingdom of the Netherlands, Parties to the convention implementing the Schengen Agreement of 14 June 1985 between the Governments of the States of the Benelux Economic Union, the Federal Republic of Germany and the French Republic on the gradual abolition of checks at their common borders signed at Schengen on 19 June 1990, hereinafter referred to as 'the 1990 Convention', as well as the Italian Republic, the Kingdom of Spain and the Portuguese Republic, the Hellenic Republic, and the Republic of Austria, which acceded to the 1990 Convention by the agreements signed on 27 November 1990, on 25 June 1991, on 6 November 1992 and on 28 April 1995 respectively,

of the one part,

and the Republic of Finland, of the other part,

Having regard to the signature done at Luxembourg on 19 December 1996 of the protocol on the accession of the Government of the Republic of Finland to the Schengen Agreement of 14 June 1985 between the Governments of the States of the Benelux Economic Union, the Federal Republic of Germany and the French Republic on the gradual abolition of checks at their common borders, as amended by the protocols on the accession of the Governments of the Italian Republic, the Kingdom of Spain and the Portuguese Republic, the Hellenic Republic, and the Republic of Austria, signed on 27 November 1990, 25 June 1991, on 6 November 1992 and on 28 April 1995 respectively,

On the basis of Article 140 of the 1990 Convention,

HAVE AGREED AS FOLLOWS:

Article 1

The Republic of Finland hereby accedes to the 1990 Convention.

Article 2

1. At the date of signing this agreement, the officers referred to in Article 40(4) of the 1990 Convention as regards the Republic of Finland shall be:

(a) *Poliisin virkamiehistä poliisimiehet — av polisens tjänstemän polismän* (officers of the police);

(b) *Rajavartiolaitoksen virkamiehistä raja-vartiomiehet — av gränsbevakningsvä-*

sendets tjänstemän gränsbevakningsmän (frontier guard officials of the frontier guard), as regards trafficking in human beings referred to in Article 40(7) of the 1990 Convention;

(c) *Tullimiehet — tulltjänstemän* (customs officers), under the conditions laid down in appropriate bilateral agreements referred to in Article 40(6) of the 1990 Convention, with respect to their powers regarding the illicit trafficking in narcotic drugs and psychotropic substances, trafficking in arms and explosives, and the illicit transportation of toxic and hazardous waste.

2. At the date of signing this agreement, the authority referred to in Article 40(5) of the 1990 Convention as regards the Kingdom of Denmark shall be the *Keskusrikospoliisi — Centralkriminalpolisen* (the National Bureau of Investigation).

Article 3

As the date of signing this agreement, the officers referred to in Article 41(7) of the 1990 Convention as regards the Republic of Finland shall be:

1. *Poliisin virkamiehistä poliisimiehet — av polisens tjänstemän polismän* (officers of the police);

2. *Rajavartiolaitoksen virkamiehistä rajavartiomiehet — av gränsbevakningsväsendets tjänstemän gränsbevakningsmän* (frontier guard officials of the frontier guard), as regards trafficking in human beings referred to in Article 40(7) of the 1990 Convention;

3. *Tullimiehet — tulltjänstemän* (customs officers), under the conditions laid down in appropriate bilateral agreements referred to in Article 41(10) of the 1990 Convention, with respect to their powers regarding the illicit trafficking in narcotic drugs and psychotropic substances, trafficking in arms and explosives, and the illicit transportation of toxic and hazardous waste.

Article 4

At the date of signing this agreement, the competent ministry referred to in Article 65(2) of the 1990 Convention as regards the Republic of Finland shall be the *Oikeusministeriö — Justitieministeriet* (Ministry of Justice).

Article 5

The provisions of this agreement shall not prejudice cooperation within the framework of the Nordic Passport Union, insofar as such cooperation does not conflict with, or impede, the application of this agreement.

Article 6

1. This agreement shall be subject to ratification, acceptance or approval. The instruments of ratification, acceptance or approval shall be deposited with the Government of the Grand Duchy of Luxembourg, which shall notify all the contracting parties thereof.

2. This agreement shall enter into force on the first day of the second month following the deposit of the instruments of ratification, acceptance or approval by the States for which the 1990 Convention has entered into force and by the Republic of Finland.

With regard to other States, this agreement shall enter into force on the first day of the second month following the deposit of their instruments of ratification, acceptance or approval, provided that this agreement has entered into force in accordance with the provisions of the preceding subparagraph.

3. The Government of the Grand Duchy of Luxembourg shall notify each of the contracting parties of the date of entry into force.

Article 7

1. The Government of the Grand Duchy of Luxembourg shall transmit to the Government of the Republic of Finland a certified copy of the 1990 Convention in the Dutch, French, German, Greek, Italian, Portuguese and Spanish languages.

2. The text of the 1990 Convention drawn up in the Finnish language is annexed to this agreement and shall be authentic under the same conditions as the texts of the 1990 Convention drawn up in the Dutch, French, German, Greek, Italian, Portuguese and Spanish languages.

In witness whereof, the undersigned, duly authorised to this effect, have signed this agreement.

Done at Luxembourg on 19 December 1996 in a single original in the Dutch, Finnish, French, German, Greek, Italian, Portuguese and Spanish languages, all eight texts being equally authentic, such original remaining deposited in the archives of the Government of the Grand Duchy of Luxembourg, which shall transmit a certified copy to each of the contracting parties.

For the Government of the Kingdom of Belgium,

For the Government of the Federal Republic of Germany,

For the Government of the Hellenic Republic,

For the Government of the Kingdom of Spain,

For the Government of the French Republic,

For the Government of the Italian Republic,

For the Government of the Grand Duchy of Luxembourg,

For the Government of the Kingdom of the Netherlands,

For the Government of the Republic of Austria,

For the Government of the Portuguese Republic,

For the Government of the Republic of Finland.

FINAL ACT

I. At the time of signing the agreement on the accession of the Republic of Finland to the convention implementing the Schengen Agreement of 14 June 1985 between the Governments of the States of the Benelux Economic Union, the Federal Republic of Germany and the French Republic on the gradual abolition of checks at their common borders signed at Schengen on 19 June 1990, to which the Italian Republic, the Kingdom of Spain and the Portuguese Republic, the Hellenic Republic, and the Kingdom of Austria acceded by the agreements signed on 27 November 1990, on 25 June 1991, on 6 November 1992 and on 28 April 1995 respectively, the Government of the Republic of Finland has subscribed to the final act, the minutes and the joint declaration by the ministers and State secretaries which were signed at the time of signing the 1990 Convention.

The Government of the Republic of Finland has subscribed to the joint declarations and has taken note of the unilateral declarations contained therein.

The Government of the Grand Duchy of Luxembourg shall transmit to the Government of the Republic of Finland a certified copy of the final act, the minutes and the joint declaration by the ministers and State secretaries which were signed at the time of signing the 1990 Convention, in the Dutch, Finnish, French, German, Greek, Italian, Portuguese and Spanish languages.

II. At the time of signing the agreement on the accession of the Republic of Finland to the convention implementing the Schengen Agreement of 14 June 1985 between the Governments of the States of the Benelux Economic Union, the Federal Republic of Germany and the French Republic on the gradual abolition of checks at their common borders signed at Schengen on 19 June 1990, to which the Italian Republic, the Kingdom of Spain and the Portuguese Republic, the Hellenic Republic, and the Kingdom of Austria acceded by the agreements signed on 27 November 1990, on 25 June 1991, on 6 November 1992 and on 28 April 1995 respectively, the contracting parties have adopted the following declarations.

1. Joint declaration on Article 6 of the accession agreement

The contracting parties shall, prior to the entry into force of the accession agreement, inform each other of all circumstances that could have a significant bearing on the areas covered by the 1990 Convention and on the bringing into force of the accession agreement.

This accession agreement shall be brought into force between the States for which the 1990 Convention has been brought into force and the Republic of Finland when the preconditions for implementation of the 1990 Convention have been fulfilled in all these States and checks at the external borders are effective there.

With regard to each of the other States, this accession agreement shall be brought into force when the preconditions for the implementation of the 1990 Convention have been fulfilled in that State and when checks at the external borders are effective there.

2. Joint declaration on Article 9(2) of the 1990 Convention

The contracting parties specify that at the time of signing the agreement on the accession of the Republic of Finland to the 1990 Convention, the common visa arrangements referred to in Article 9(2) of the 1990 Convention shall be taken to mean the common arrangements applied by the Signatory Parties to the said convention since 19 June 1990.

3. Joint declaration on the convention drawn up on the basis of Article K.3 of the Treaty on European Union relating to extradition

The States party to the 1990 Convention hereby confirm that Article 5(4) of the convention drawn up on the basis of Article K.3 of the Treaty on European Union relating to extradition between the Member States of the European Union, signed at Dublin on 27 September 1996, and their respective declarations annexed to the said convention, shall apply within the framework of the 1990 Convention.

III. The contracting parties have taken note of the declarations by the Republic of Finland on the agreements on the accession of the Italian Republic, the Kingdom of Spain, the Portuguese Republic, the Hellenic Republic, and the Republic of Austria.

The Government of the Republic of Finland takes note of the contents of the agreements on the accession of the Italian Republic, the Kingdom of Spain and the Portuguese Republic, the Hellenic Republic, and the Republic of Austria to the 1990 Convention, signed on 27 November 1990, on 25 June 1991, on 6 November 1992 and on 28 April 1995 respectively, and of the contents of the final acts and declarations annexed to the said agreements.

The Government of the Grand Duchy of Luxembourg shall transmit a certified copy of the abovementioned instruments to the Government of the Republic of Finland.

Declaration by the Republic of Finland on the agreements on the accession of the Kingdom of Denmark and the Kingdom of Sweden to the 1990 Convention

At the time of signing this agreement, the Republic of Finland takes note of the contents of the agreements on the accession of the Kingdom of Denmark and the Kingdom of Sweden to the 1990 Convention and of the contents of the related final acts and declarations.

Declaration by the Government of the Republic of Finland on the Åland Islands

The Republic of Finland hereby declares that the obligations arising from Article 2 of Protocol No 2 to the Act concerning the conditions of accession of the Republic of

Austria, the Republic of Finland and the Kingdom of Sweden and the adjustments to the Treaties on which the European Union is found relating to the Åland Islands shall be complied with when implementing the 1990 Convention.

Done at Luxembourg on 19 December 1996 in a single original in the Dutch, Finnish, French, German, Greek, Italian, Portuguese and Spanish languages, all eight texts being equally authentic, such original remaining deposited in the archives of the Government of the Grand Duchy of Luxembourg, which shall transmit a certified copy to each of the contracting parties.

For the Government of the Kingdom of Belgium,

For the Government of the Federal Republic of Germany,

For the Government of the Hellenic Republic,

For the Government of the Kingdom of Spain,

For the Government of the French Republic,

For the Government of the Italian Republic,

For the Government of the Grand Duchy of Luxembourg,

For the Government of the Kingdom of the Netherlands,

For the Government of the Republic of Austria,

For the Government of the Portuguese Republic,

For the Government of the Republic of Finland.

DECLARATION BY THE MINISTERS AND STATE SECRETARIES

On 19 December 1996, the representatives of the Governments of the Kingdom of Belgium, the Federal Republic of Germany, the Hellenic Republic, the Kingdom of Spain, the Republic of Finland, the French Republic, the Italian Republic, the Grand Duchy of Luxembourg, the Kingdom of the Netherlands, the Republic of Austria and the Portuguese Republic signed at Luxembourg the agreement on the accession of the Republic of Finland to the convention implementing the Schengen Agreement of 14 June 1985 between the Governments of the States of the Benelux Economic Union, the Federal Republic of Germany and the French Republic on the gradual abolition of checks at their common borders, signed at Schengen on 19 June 1990, to which the Italian Republic, the Kingdom of Spain and the Portuguese Republic, the Hellenic Republic, and the Republic of Austria acceded by the agreements signed on 27 November 1990, on 25 June 1991, on 6 November 1992 and on 28 April 1995 respectively.

They noted that the representative of the Government of the Republic of Finland declared support for the declaration made at Schengen on 19 June 1990 by the ministers and State secretaries representing the Governments of the Kingdom of Belgium, the Federal Republic of Germany, the French Republic, the Grand Duchy of Luxembourg and the Kingdom of the Netherlands and for the decision confirmed on the same date upon signature of the convention implementing the Schengen Agreement, which declaration and decision the Governments of the Italian Republic, the Kingdom of Spain, the Portuguese Republic, the Hellenic Republic and the Republic of Austria have also supported.

AGREEMENT ON THE ACCESSION OF THE KINGDOM OF SWEDEN

TO THE CONVENTION IMPLEMENTING THE SCHENGEN AGREEMENT OF 14 JUNE 1985 ON THE GRADUAL ABOLITION OF CHECKS AT THE COMMON BORDERS SIGNED AT SCHENGEN ON 19 JUNE 1990

The Kingdom of Belgium, the Federal Republic of Germany, the French Republic, the Grand Duchy of Luxembourg and the Kingdom of the Netherlands, Parties to the convention implementing the Schengen Agreement of 14 June 1985 between the Governments of the States of the Benelux Economic Union, the Federal Republic of Germany and the French Republic on the gradual abolition of checks at their common borders signed at Schengen on 19 June 1990, hereinafter referred to as 'the 1990 Convention', as well as the Italian Republic, the Kingdom of Spain and the Portuguese Republic, the Hellenic Republic, and the Republic of Austria, which acceded to the 1990 Convention by the agreements signed on 27 November 1990, on 25 June 1991, on 6 November 1992 and on 28 April 1995 respectively,

of the one part,

and the Kingdom of Sweden, of the other part,

Having regard to the signature done at Luxembourg on 19 December 1996 of the protocol on the accession of the Government of the Kingdom of Sweden to the Schengen Agreement of 14 June 1985 between the Governments of the States of the Benelux Economic Union, the Federal Republic of Germany and the French Republic on the gradual abolition of checks at their common borders, as amended by the protocols on the accession of the Governments of the Italian Republic, the Kingdom of Spain and the Portuguese Republic, the Hellenic Republic, and the Republic of Austria, signed on 27 November 1990, 25 June 1991, on 6 November 1992 and on 28 April 1995 respectively,

On the basis of Article 140 of the 1990 Convention,

HAVE AGREED AS FOLLOWS:

Article 1

The Kingdom of Sweden hereby accedes to the 1990 Convention.

Article 2

1. At the date of signing this agreement, the officers referred to in Article 40(4) of the 1990 Convention as regards the Kingdom of Sweden shall be:

(a) *Polismän som är anställda av svenska polismyndigheter* (police officers of the Swedish police authorities);

(b) *Tulltjänstemän, som är anställda av svensk tullmyndighet i de fall de har polisiara befogenheter, dvs framst i samband med smugglingsbrott och andra brott i samband med inresa och utresa till och fran riket* (customs officers of the Swedish customs authorities, when working in a police capacity, mainly to deal with smuggling-related offences and other offences linked to entry to and exit from the country);

(c) Tjänstemän anställda vid den svenska Kustbevakningen i samband med övervakning till sjöss (officers of the Swedish Coast Guard responsible for sea surveillance).

2. At the date of signing this agreement, the authority referred to in Article 40(5) of the 1990 Convention as regards the Kingdom of Sweden shall be the *Rikspolisstyrelsen* (the Swedish National Police Board).

Article 3

As the date of signing this agreement, the officers referred to in Article 41(7) of the 1990 Convention as regards the Kingdom of Sweden shall be:

1. *Polismän som är anställda av svenska polismyndigheter* (police officers of the Swedish police authorities);

2. *Tulltjänstemän, som är anställda av svensk tullmyndighet i de fall de har polisiara befogenheter, dvs framst i samband med smugglingsbrott och andra brott i samband med inresa och utresa till och fran riket* (customs officers of the Swedish customs authorities, when working in a police capacity, mainly to deal with smuggling-related offences and other offences linked to entry to and exit from the country).

Article 4

At the date of signing this agreement, the competent ministry referred to in Article 65(2) of the 1990 Convention as regards the Kingdom of Sweden shall be the Utrikesdepartementet (Ministry of Foreign Affairs).

Article 5

The provisions of this agreement shall not prejudice cooperation within the framework of the Nordic Passport Union, insofar as such cooperation does not conflict with, or impede, the application of this agreement.

Article 6

1. This agreement shall be subject to ratification, acceptance or approval. The instruments of ratification, acceptance or approval shall be deposited with the Government of the Grand Duchy of Luxembourg, which shall notify all the contracting parties thereof.

2. This agreement shall enter into force on the first day of the second month following the deposit of the instruments of ratification, acceptance or approval by the States for which the 1990 Convention has entered into force and by the Kingdom of Sweden.

With regard to other States, this agreement shall enter into force on the first day of the second month following the deposit of their instruments of ratification, acceptance or approval, provided that this agreement has entered into force in accordance with the provisions of the preceding subparagraph.

3. The Government of the Grand Duchy of Luxembourg shall notify each of the contracting parties of the date of entry into force.

Article 7

1. The Government of the Grand Duchy of Luxembourg shall transmit to the Government of the Kingdom of Sweden a certified copy of the 1990 Convention in the Dutch, French, German, Greek, Italian, Portuguese and Spanish languages.

2. The text of the 1990 Convention drawn up in the Swedish language is annexed to this agreement and shall be authentic under the same conditions as the texts of the 1990 Convention drawn up in the Dutch, French, German, Greek, Italian, Portuguese and Spanish languages.

In witness whereof, the undersigned, duly authorised to this effect, have signed this agreement.

Done at Luxembourg on 19 December 1996 in a single original in the Dutch, French, German, Greek, Italian, Portuguese, Spanish and Swedish languages, all eight texts being equally authentic, such original remaining deposited in the archives of the Government of the Grand Duchy of Luxembourg, which shall transmit a certified copy to each of the contracting parties.

For the Government of the Kingdom of Belgium,

For the Government of the Federal Republic of Germany,

For the Government of the Hellenic Republic,

For the Government of the Kingdom of Spain,

For the Government of the French Republic,

For the Government of the Italian Republic,

For the Government of the Grand Duchy of Luxembourg,

For the Government of the Kingdom of the Netherlands,

For the Government of the Republic of Austria,

For the Government of the Portuguese Republic,

For the Government of the Kingdom of Sweden.

FINAL ACT

I. At the time of signing the agreement on the accession of the Kingdom of Sweden to the convention implementing the Schengen Agreement of 14 June 1985 between the Governments of the States of the Benelux Economic Union, the Federal Republic of Germany and the French Republic on the gradual abolition of checks at their common borders signed at Schengen on 19 June 1990, to which the Italian Republic, the Kingdom of Spain and the Portuguese Republic, the Hellenic Republic, and the Kingdom of Austria acceded by the agreements signed on 27 November 1990, on 25 June 1991, on 6 November 1992 and on 28 April 1995 respectively, the Government of the Kingdom of Sweden has subscribed to the final act, the minutes and the joint declaration by the ministers and State secretaries which were signed at the time of signing the 1990 Convention.

The Government of the Kingdom of Sweden has subscribed to the joint declarations and has taken note of the unilateral declarations contained therein.

The Government of the Grand Duchy of Luxembourg shall transmit to the Government of the Kingdom of Sweden a certified copy of the final act, the minutes and the joint declaration by the ministers and State secretaries which were signed at the time of signing the 1990 Convention, in the Dutch, French, German, Greek, Italian, Portuguese, Spanish and Swedish languages.

II. At the time of signing the agreement on the accession of the Kingdom of Sweden to the convention implementing the Schengen Agreement of 14 June 1985 between the Governments of the States of the Benelux Economic Union, the Federal Republic of Germany and the French Republic on the gradual abolition of checks at their common borders signed at Schengen on 19 June 1990, to which the Italian Republic, the Kingdom of Spain and the Portuguese Republic, the Hellenic Republic, and the Kingdom of Austria acceded by the agreements signed on 27 November 1990, on 25 June 1991, on 6 November 1992 and on 28 April 1995 respectively, the contracting parties have adopted the following declarations:

1. Joint declaration on Article 6 of the accession agreement

The contracting parties shall, prior to the entry into force of the accession agreement, inform each other of all circumstances that could have a significant bearing on the areas covered by the 1990 Convention and on the bringing into force of the accession agreement.

This accession agreement shall be brought into force between the States for which the 1990 Convention has been brought into force and the Kingdom of Sweden when the preconditions for implementation of the

1990 Convention have been fulfilled in all these States and checks at the external borders are effective there.

With regard to each of the other States, this accession agreement shall be brought into force when the preconditions for the implementation of the 1990 Convention have been fulfilled in that State and when checks at the external borders are effective there.

2. Joint declaration on Article 9(2) of the 1990 Convention

The contracting parties specify that at the time of signing the agreement on the accession of the Kingdom of Sweden to the 1990 Convention, the common visa arrangements referred to in Article 9(2) of the 1990 Convention shall be taken to mean the common arrangements applied by the Signatory Parties to the said convention since 19 June 1990.

3. Joint declaration on the convention drawn up on the basis of Article K.3 of the Treaty on European Union relating to extradition

The States party to the 1990 Convention hereby confirm that Article 5(4) of the convention drawn up on the basis of Article K.3 of the Treaty on European Union relating to extradition between the Member States of the European Union, signed at Dublin on 27 September 1996, and their respective declarations annexed to the said convention, shall apply within the framework of the 1990 Convention.

III. The contracting parties have taken note of the declarations by the Kingdom of Sweden on the agreements on the accession of the Italian Republic, the Kingdom of Spain, the Portuguese Republic, the Hellenic Republic, and the Republic of Austria.

The Government of the Kingdom of Sweden takes note of the contents of the agreements on the accession of the Italian Republic, the Kingdom of Spain and the Portuguese Republic, the Hellenic Republic, and the Republic of Austria to the 1990 Convention, signed on 27 November 1990, on 25 June 1991, on 6 November 1992 and on 28 April 1995 respectively, and of the contents of the final acts and declarations annexed to the said agreements.

The Government of the Grand Duchy of Luxembourg shall transmit a certified copy of the abovementioned instruments to the Government of the Kingdom of Sweden.

Declaration by the Kingdom of Sweden on the agreements on the accession of the Kingdom of Denmark and the Republic of Finland to the 1990 Convention

At the time of signing this agreement, the Kingdom of Sweden takes note of the contents of the agreements on the accession of the Kingdom of Denmark and the Republic of Finland to the 1990 Convention and of the contents of the related final acts and declarations.

Done at Luxembourg on 19 December 1996 in a single original in the Dutch, French, German, Greek, Italian, Portuguese, Spanish and Swedish languages, all eight texts being equally authentic, such original remaining deposited in the archives of the Government of the Grand Duchy of Luxembourg, which shall transmit a certified copy to each of the contracting parties.

For the Government of the Kingdom of Belgium,

For the Government of the Federal Republic of Germany,

For the Government of the Hellenic Republic,

For the Government of the Kingdom of Spain,

For the Government of the French Republic,

For the Government of the Italian Republic,

For the Government of the Grand Duchy of Luxembourg,

For the Government of the Kingdom of the Netherlands,

For the Government of the Republic of Austria,

For the Government of the Portuguese Republic,

For the Government of the Kingdom of Sweden.

DECLARATION BY THE MINISTERS AND STATE SECRETARIES

On 19 December 1996, the representatives of the Governments of the Kingdom of Belgium, the Federal Republic of Germany, the Hellenic Republic, the Kingdom of Spain, the Kingdom of Sweden, the French Republic, the Italian Republic, the Grand Duchy of Luxembourg, the Kingdom of the Netherlands, the Republic of Austria and the Portuguese Republic signed at Luxembourg the agreement on the accession of the Kingdom of Sweden to the convention implementing the Schengen Agreement of 14 June 1985 between the Governments of the States of the Benelux Economic Union, the Federal Republic of Germany and the French Republic on the gradual abolition of checks at their common borders, signed at Schengen on 19 June 1990, to which the Italian Republic, the Kingdom of Spain and the Portuguese Republic, the Hellenic Republic, and the Republic of Austria acceded by the agreements signed on 27 November 1990, on 25 June 1991, on 6 November 1992 and on 28 April 1995 respectively.

They noted that the representative of the Government of the Kingdom of Sweden declared support for the declaration made at Schengen on 19 June 1990 by the ministers and State secretaries representing the Governments of the Kingdom of Belgium, the Federal Republic of Germany, the French Republic, the Grand Duchy of Luxembourg and the Kingdom of the Netherlands and for the decision confirmed on the same date upon signature of the convention implementing the Schengen Agreement, which declaration and decision the Governments of the Italian Republic, the Kingdom of Spain, the Portuguese Republic, the Hellenic Republic and the Republic of Austria have also supported.

2. – DECISIONS OF THE EXECUTIVE COMMITTEE AND THE CENTRAL GROUP – DECLARATIONS OF THE CENTRAL GROUP

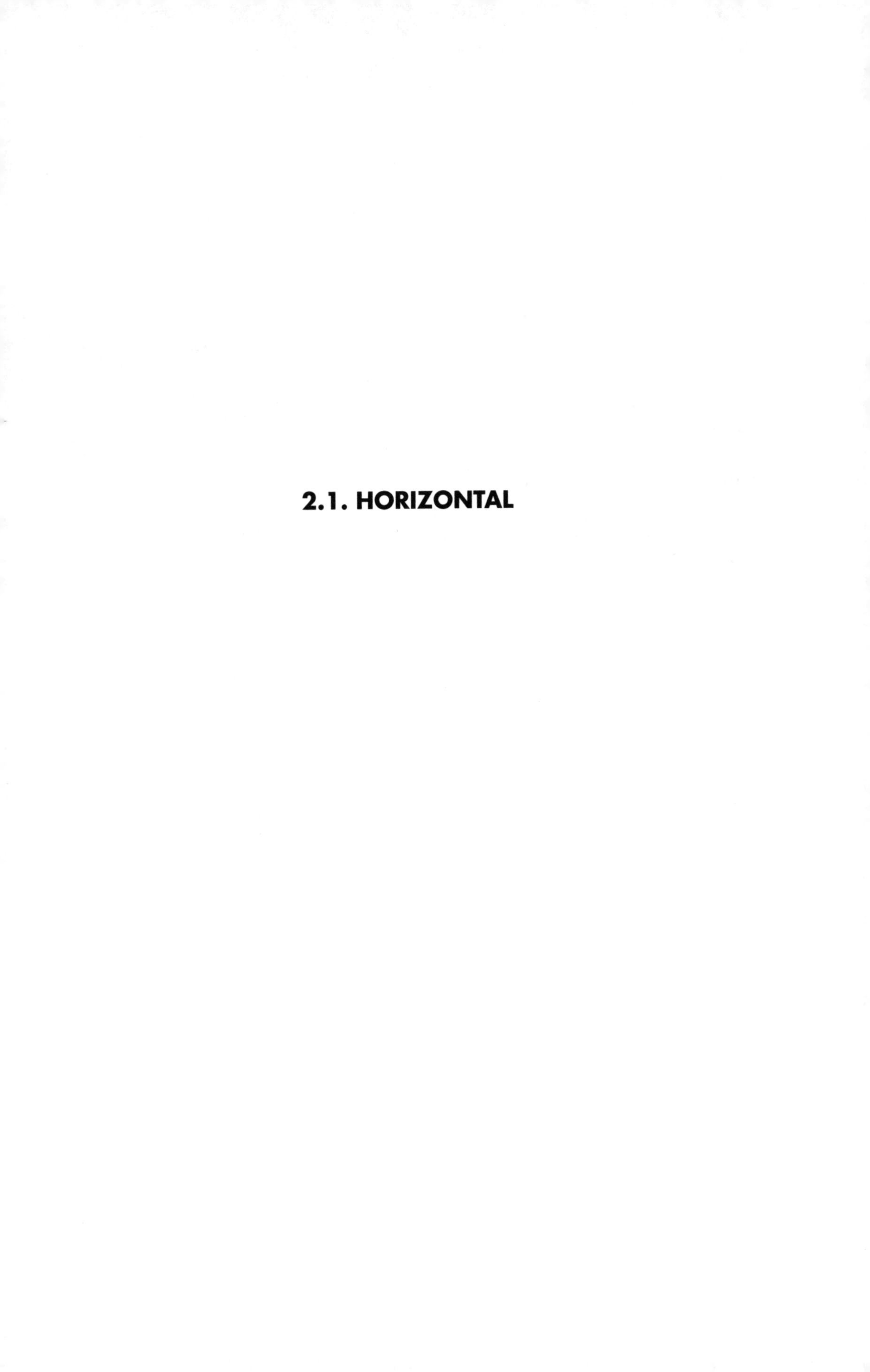

2.1. HORIZONTAL

DECISION OF THE EXECUTIVE COMMITTEE of 14 December 1993 concerning the declarations by the ministers and State secretaries

(SCH/Com-ex (93) 10)

The Executive Committee,

Having regard to Article 132 of the convention implementing the Schengen Agreement,

HAS DECIDED AS FOLLOWS:

the declarations by the ministers and State secretaries of 19 June 1992 (1) and 30 June 1993 regarding the bringing into force of the implementing convention and the fulfilment of the prerequisites are hereby confirmed.

Paris, 14 December 1993

The Chairman

A. LAMASSOURE

(1) The declarations of 19 June 1992 have not been taken over in the *acquis*.

Annex

Madrid, 30 June 1993
SCH/M (93) 14

DECLARATION OF THE MINISTERS AND STATE SECRETARIES

1. The ministers and State secretaries hereby agree to set the political goal of applying the 1990 Schengen Convention as of 1 December 1993.

2. The ministers and State secretaries note that the following preconditions have been fulfilled:

— the common manual;

— the arrangements for issuing the uniform visa and the common consular instructions on visas;

— the examination of applications for asylum;

— the airports, as agreed in the declaration of the ministers and State secretaries of 19 June 1992.

Great progress has been made in respect of the other preconditions, which have already been fulfilled to such an extent that the said application ought to be possible as of 1 December 1993. To this end, and in compliance with the 1990 Schengen Convention, additional efforts are necessary to give effect to the agreements already reached on external border controls and drugs.

The ministers and State secretaries confirm that an operational SIS is an essential condition for the abolition of controls at the internal borders. Significant progress has been accomplished in this area. They agree to step up work to enable the SIS to be brought into operation by degrees as the States successfully complete the tests and bring their N.SISs into operation.

3. At its meeting in October the Executive Committee will take final stock of progress made in realising the additional efforts mentioned above.

4. The 1990 Schengen Convention will apply in all the Member States which have fulfilled the preconditions and have an operational N.SIS.

To this end, all the Member States undertake to make all the necessary arrangements to complete the national procedures required for ratification of the convention and the accession agreements.

5. The ministers and State secretaries agree that the original Signatory States to the 1990 Schengen Convention which have not already done so must deposit their instruments of ratification as soon as possible and at the latest on a date which will allow the deadline set in paragraph 1 to be respected. Those Member States which have not already done so also agree to deposit, as soon as possible and at the latest on a date which will allow the deadline set in paragraph 1 to be respected, their instruments ratifying the accession agreements of those States whose N.SISs are being integrated into the system. This undertaking will also apply as the other acceding States reach the same stage with regard to their respective N.SISs.

The ministers and State secretaries agree that the declaration on Article 139 in the final act of the convention implies that the bringing into force of the convention is subject to an Executive Committee decision which must be adopted as soon as the preconditions have been fulfilled.

DECISION OF THE EXECUTIVE COMMITTEE of 14 December 1993 concerning the confidential nature of certain documents

(SCH/Com-ex (93) 22 rev)

The Executive Committee,

Having regard to Article 132 of the convention implementing the Schengen Agreement,

HAS DECIDED AS FOLLOWS:

1. Irrespective of the different national legal rules, certain documents must be kept confidential for the following three reasons:

— making some documents public would be directly contrary to the objectives set;

— moreover, some documents may contain personal data or a description of administrative procedures that should not be disclosed;

— Certain documents may also contain information relating to the production techniques or even the security of external relations.

2. The following documents shall remain confidential: Annexes 1, 5, 8, 9 and 10 to the common consular instructions, the list of countries subject to the visa requirement, the common manual, the Sirene manual, the three documents covered by the decision on narcotic drugs (tightening controls at external borders (SCH/Stup (92) 45), controlled deliveries (SCH/Stup (92) 46 rev 4) and measures on combating the illicit export of drugs (SCH/Stup (92) 72 rev 3)) ([1]).

3. The States may incorporate the content of the common manual, the Sirene manual and Annex 1 to the common consular instructions on visas (the list of countries subject to the visa requirement) into their own national instructions and manuals.

Paris, 14 December 1993

The Chairman

A. LAMASSOURE

([1]) See SCH/Com-ex (98) 17.

DECISION OF THE EXECUTIVE COMMITTEE of 22 December 1994 on bringing into force the convention implementing the Schengen Agreement of 19 June 1990

(SCH/Com-ex (94) 29 rev 2)

The Executive Committee,

Having regard to Article 2 of the convention implementing the Schengen Agreement,

Having regard to Article 131 of the abovementioned convention,

Having regard to Article 132 of the abovementioned convention,

Having regard to Article 139(2) in conjunction with paragraphs (1) and (2) of Joint Declaration I on Article 139 contained in the final act of the abovementioned convention,

HAS DECIDED AS FOLLOWS:

The convention implementing the Schengen Agreement (hereinafter the 'convention') shall be applied irreversibly:

(1) Bringing into force the rules and regulations

The convention shall be brought into force in its entirety on 26 March 1995 for the initial Signatory States namely Belgium, Germany, France, Luxembourg and the Netherlands and the acceding States Spain and Portugal.

From that date onwards all provisions of the convention shall apply to relations between the Schengen Contracting Parties in accordance with the decisions of the Executive Committee, in particular those relating to,

- the abolition of checks on persons at the internal borders, in particular the removal of obstacles to and restrictions on traffic at the road crossings on the internal borders (SCH/Com-ex (94) 1 rev 2),
- the introduction and application of Schengen arrangements at airports and aerodromes (SCH/Com-ex (94) 17 rev 4),

— the performance of checks at the external borders and measures to further enhance security at the external borders (SCH/Com-ex (93) 4 rev 2 corr [1]; SCH/Com-ex (94) decl. 8 corr [2]; SCH/Com-ex (94) 12*; SCH/Com-ex (94) 16 rev; SCH/Com-ex (94) 23 rev*),

— the common policy on visas (SCH/Com-ex (93) 6**; SCH/Com-ex (93) 7*; SCH/Com-ex (93) 19**; SCH/Com-ex (93) 24; SCH/Com-ex (93) 21; SCH/Com-ex (94) 15 rev; SCH/Com-ex (94) 2; SCH/Com-ex (94) 5*; SCH/Com-ex (94) 6*; SCH/Com-ex (94) 7*; SCH/Com-ex (94) 20 rev*; SCH/Com-ex (94) 24*),

— the fight against the illegal trafficking in narcotic drugs and psychotropic substances (SCH/Com-ex (93) 9; SCH/Com-ex (94) 28 rev),

— responsibility for examining asylum applications (SCH/Com-ex (93) 15 corr [3]; SCH/Com-ex (94) 3***; SCH/Com-ex (94) 11***) and

— international mutual judicial assistance (SCH/Com-ex (93) 14).

A decision shall be adopted at a later date for the other States which have acceded to the convention, namely Italy and Greece, as soon as they have satisfied the preconditions for the convention to be brought into force.

(2) Declaring Schengen information system (SIS) operational

The SIS shall be declared operational and accessible to the authorities entitled to consult directly the data contained therein on 26 March 1995.

The Sirene manual (SCH/Com-ex (93) 8 [4]) supplementing the SIS shall apply in its entirety with effect as of that date.

By reason of the conclusions of the report by the SIS Steering Committee, the Executive Committee considers that the SIS will be operational on that date and that the existing national data deemed essential within the meaning of its declaration of 18 October 1993 (SCH/Com-ex (93) decl. 1 [5]) shall then have been loaded in accordance with its declaration of 27 June 1994 (SCH/Com-ex (94) decl. 4 rev 2).

(1) See SCH/Com-ex (99) 13.
(2) This document is not taken over in the *acquis*.
(3) 'Asylum' provisions taken over in the Bonn Protocol (SCH/Com-ex (94) 3).
(4) Replaced by SCH/Com-ex (99) 5.
(5) This document is not taken over in the *acquis*.

As of that date the Joint Supervisory Authority provided for under Article 115 of the convention shall assume its functions.

The provisions of the convention on data protection shall apply in their entirety. The Executive Committee refers to the notification by the Provisional Joint Supervisory Authority for data protection that the Contracting Parties which have successfully completed the tests satisfy the data protection conditions required for the putting into operation of the SIS.

(3) Arrangements for the preparatory period (22 December 1994 to 26 March 1995)

The Executive Committee requests the Contracting Parties which have successfully completed the tests to adopt the following measures before 26 March 1995:

— to consolidate in terms of organisational and human resources the measures necessary for the full application of the Schengen rules and regulations, particularly in the fields of consular, judicial and police cooperation as well as in the fight against narcotic drugs; to continue to ensure that the competent staff are trained in the application of the Schengen rules and regulations;

— to complete the preparations in terms of technical, organisational and human resources with a view to bringing the N.SIS into operation in relation to the C.SIS and to complete preparations for end-user access to this system.

The Executive Committee instructs the SIS Steering Committee to confirm in good time before the abovementioned date that the SIS is ready for operation in terms of technical, organisational and human resources.

The Executive Committee requests the Contracting States to confirm that the system is accessible to the authorities entitled to direct consultation already notified to the Executive Committee (SCH/OR.SIS (94) 18 rev 3).

The Executive Committee requests the Contracting Parties to load retroactively during this period other data on persons or objects which go beyond the data deemed essential (SCH/Com-ex (94) decl. 4 rev 2 [1]). The SIS databases must be constantly updated.

The Executive Committee calls on the Contracting Parties to ensure that the airlines make the changes necessary for the free movement of persons at the latest by the change in flight schedules on 26 March 1995 and that airport operators complete the measures provided for, to this end, in the decision on the introduction and application of the Schengen arrangements at airports and aerodromes (SCH/Com-ex (94) 17 rev 4) and create the necessary organisational and technical preconditions for the free movement of persons by that date.

[1] This document is not taken over in the *acquis*.

The Contracting Parties are requested to inform the airlines and airport operators accordingly as soon as possible.

(4) Organisation of the application of the convention after its entry into force, particularly in the initial phase of application

The purpose of implementing the convention is to enhance the security of citizens in Europe whilst creating the preconditions necessary to achieve the free movement of persons within the meaning of Article 7a of the Treaty establishing the European Community.

The Executive Committee therefore attaches particular importance to the initial phase of the application of the convention in its entirety during the first three months after 26 March 1995.

Each Contracting Party shall be responsible for the application of the convention, particularly the abolition of checks at the internal borders during the initial phase of application. The Contracting Parties shall keep each other mutually informed, shall consult whenever necessary and shall work in close cooperation.

With a view to creating the instrument necessary for the administration of the convention, the Executive Committee hereby decides to set up a permanent follow-up structure composed of the existing central group and its working groups and subgroups.

The Executive Committee instructs the permanent follow-up structure during the initial phase of application to monitor particularly closely the application of the Schengen rules and regulations, to identify, analyse and resolve rapidly any technical problems and, if necessary, to take measures with a view to the more effective application of the convention.

The Executive Committee instructs the Presidency as of 1 January 1995 to prepare the work of this follow-up structure and to ensure particularly that the working groups identify any difficulties and rapidly devise solutions.

During the initial three-month application period, the working groups of the follow-up structure shall convene regularly and as often as necessary.

Should urgent decisions be required in particular cases, the Central Group may convene a select meeting at short notice as the follow-up committee. The follow-up committee shall be composed of either the heads of delegation of each Contracting Party or a high-ranking official designated by each of the Contracting Parties assisted by the representatives of the working groups which must be consulted to resolve any problems arising.

At the request of one Contracting Party, the Central Group shall also undertake a general analysis of the difficulties arising and shall propose solutions devised in collaboration with the working groups and subgroups.

In the absence of agreement within the Central Group, the matter shall be referred to the Executive Committee. In this respect, the Contracting Parties concerned must be granted the opportunity to give an opinion on its conclusions.

Each Contracting Party may also request the Central Group to assess situations which have only arisen on its own national territory.

Three months after the convention has been brought into force, the Central Group shall submit a preliminary report to the Executive Committee dealing with the functioning of the SIS, the efficacy of controls at the external borders, the efficiency of the fight against narcotic drugs and the results of police and judicial cooperation. The Central Group shall submit a general report to the Executive Committee by 31 March 1996.

Bonn, 22 December 1994

The Chairman

B. SCHMIDBAUER

DECISION OF THE EXECUTIVE COMMITTEE of 20 December 1995 on the procedure for applying Article 2(2) of the convention implementing the Schengen Agreement

(SCH/Com-ex (95) 20 rev 2)

The Executive Committee,

Having regard to Article 132 of the convention implementing the Schengen Agreement,

Having regard to Article 2 of the abovementioned convention,

HAS DECIDED AS FOLLOWS:

Document SCH/I (95) 40 rev 6 on the procedure for applying Article 2(2) of the convention is hereby approved. The principles and procedures set out therein shall be respected by any Contracting Party which wishes to invoke the derogation clause provided for in Article 2(2) of the convention and temporarily reinstate checks at its internal borders.

Ostend, 20 December 1995

The Chairman

J. VANDE LANOTTE

SCH/I (95) 40 rev. 6

PROCEDURE FOR THE APPLICATION OF ARTICLE 2(2) OF THE CONVENTION

'Article 2:

1. Internal borders may be crossed at any point without any checks on persons being carried out.

2. However, where public policy or national security so require, a Contracting Party may, after consulting the other Contracting Parties, decide that for a limited period national border checks appropriate to the situation will be carried out at internal borders. If public policy or national security require immediate action, the Contracting Party concerned shall take the necessary measures and at the earliest opportunity shall inform the other Contracting Parties thereof.'

The overall objective of the measures provided for in the Schengen Convention is to avoid invoking Article 2(2). The reinstatement of checks must remain a measure of exception.

1. Procedure for prior consultation (Article 2(2) first sentence).

A State which contemplates reinstating checks at its internal borders in the short term must send notification to the other States, together with the following information:

(a) Grounds for the planned measure: the State in question must specify which events constitute a threat to its public order or national security.

(b) Extent of the planned measure: the State in question must specify whether checks will be reinstated along all borders or only in certain areas.

(c) Duration of the planned measure: the State must specify the date as of which the measure will apply (after consultation) and what its probable duration will be.

(d) Request for consultation: the State must specify what measures it expects other States, individually or collectively, to adopt so as to avoid reinstating checks or, once checks have been reinstated, to supplement the measures taken by the requesting State.

Notification of the decision must be sent to: the members of the Executive Committee and the Central Group, and the General Secretariat.

In accordance with Article 131(2), the Presidency shall swiftly convene a meeting of the Executive Committee, possibly preceded by a Central Group meeting, in a plenary or restricted session, to conduct the consultations between the States. No extraordinary meeting need be held if an Executive Committee meeting is already planned to take place in the near future. In this case, an item should be added to the agenda accordingly.

Should the decision to reinstate border checks continue to apply after the consultation phase, the requesting State must inform the abovementioned recipients of the date and conditions for the application of the measures in connection with Article 2(2).

Under agreements on cross-border police cooperation, the border authorities of the requesting State must also inform the border authorities of the States concerned so as to expedite any reactions in the field.

2. Procedure for an immediate decision (Article 2(2) second sentence):

A State which deems it necessary to reinstate checks immediately so as to maintain public order or national security must send notification to the other States containing the elements listed under point 1, i.e. grounds, extent and probable duration of the measure.

The other criteria referred to in point 1 shall also apply (recipients of notification, bilateral talks, etc.).

The State must specify whether it requests assistance and cooperation from other States.

Taking circumstances into account, an Executive Committee meeting shall be convened as soon as possible after notification of the decision.

3. Procedure for extension or return to normal

The State which has applied the procedure under Article 2(2) shall confirm the date on which the checks are to be lifted and, either at the same time or shortly thereafter, shall submit a report on the implementation of the decision.

However, if the State deems that the duration of validity of the initial decision has to be extended, it shall notify its decision to this effect in accordance with the procedures under points 1 or 2.

DECISION OF THE EXECUTIVE COMMITTEE of 7 October 1997 on bringing into force the convention implementing the Schengen Agreement in Greece

(SCH/Com-ex (97) 29 rev 2)

The Executive Committee,

— Having regard to Articles 131 and 132 of the convention implementing the Schengen Agreement;

— Having regard to Article 6 of the accession agreement of Greece of 6 November 1992 in conjunction with the joint declaration on Article 6 in the final act of that accession agreement;

— Having regard to the declaration by the ministers and State secretaries of 19 June 1992 on bringing into force the implementing convention;

— Whereas the joint declaration on Article 139 in the final act of the convention implementing the Schengen Agreement and the joint declaration in the final act of the accession agreement with Greece provide that 'the convention shall not be brought into force until the preconditions for its implementation have been fulfilled in the Signatory States and checks at the external borders are effective';

— Whereas on 25 April 1997 the Executive Committee reaffirmed its political resolve to enable the Schengen Convention to be brought into force in Italy, Greece and Austria on 26 October 1997 on the basis of an Executive Committee decision;

— Whereas the progress made by Greece with a view to meeting the preconditions for the convention to be brought into force, laid down in the declaration of 19 June 1992, must enable the convention to be implemented in Greece;

— Pursuant to the Executive Committee declaration of 24 June 1997 on bringing into force the Schengen Convention in Italy, Greece and Austria, confirming the firm resolve to implement the Schengen Convention for Italy on 26 October 1997 and for Austria and Greece before the end of 1997;

— Whereas, however, the strengthening of external border checks and the conversion of the airports have not yet been fully completed;

— Confirming its political resolve to achieve the bringing into force of the convention in Greece as soon as possible;

HAS DECIDED AS FOLLOWS:

I. Bringing into force the convention implementing the Schengen Agreement

1. Without prejudice to the provisions of point 4, the initial phase for bringing into force the convention implementing the Schengen Agreement shall begin for Greece on 1 December 1997.

2. This decision shall apply to Greece subject to the completion of the procedures for the ratification, approval or acceptance of the instruments of accession by France and the Netherlands.

3. The fulfilment of the condition referred to in No 2 shall be established by notification from the depositary of the completion of the procedures for the ratification, approval or acceptance.

4. The dates and arrangements for the abolition of checks at the internal borders shall remain subject to a further Executive Committee decision — adopted on the basis of the fulfilment of all the necessary preconditions. In preparation for this decision, the subgroup on frontiers and the Central Group shall submit a report to the Executive Committee in 1998. The Executive Committee shall discuss this report at the latest during its last meeting in 1998 and adopt a decision.

5. The Executive Committee hereby acknowledges that Greece has made considerable efforts to carry out all border checks at the airports and external borders to the Schengen standard.

II. Operational status of the Schengen information system

The Executive Committee hereby declares Greece operational as of 1 December 1997. From that date onwards, the system shall be open to the Greek authorities authorised access.

1. The Greek N.SIS has successfully completed all test campaigns. Within the meaning of its declarations of 27 June 1994, the Executive Committee hereby finds the Greek N.SIS technically operational and the SIS technically operational with the Greek N.SIS.

2. Pursuant to Article 101(4) of the convention implementing the Schengen Agreement, each Contracting Party shall send the Executive Committee the list of the competent authorities authorised to search the data contained in the Schengen information system directly.

The Executive Committee hereby acknowledges the lists sent by Greece.

Pursuant to Article 108(1) of the convention implementing the Schengen Agreement, each Contracting Party shall designate an authority which shall have central responsibility for its national section of the Schengen information system.

The Executive Committee hereby acknowledges the notifications sent by Greece.

Pursuant to the declarations of the Executive Committee of 18 October 1993 and of 27 June 1994, a precondition for declaring the SIS operational is notification of accessibility for the authorities authorised to search SIS directly in the State in which the Schengen Convention is to be implemented.

In acknowledging the lists forwarded by Greece, the Executive Committee hereby confirms receipt of the notification of accessibility for the authorities authorised access within the meaning of the Executive Committee declarations of 18 October 1993, 26 April 1994 and of 27 June 1994.

3. The Executive Committee assumes that the loading of the existing national data deemed essential within the meaning of the Executive Committee declarations of 18 October 1993 and 27 June 1994, which is a precondition for the declaration that Greece is operational to take effect, will be completed for Greece by 1 December 1997.

The start of loading of the national data of Greece is tied to the entry into force of the instruments of accession. From that date onwards, the States already applying the Schengen Convention shall be empowered to use the alerts of Greece under the terms of that convention.

The SIS Steering Committee is hereby instructed to keep the Central Group and the Executive Committee constantly informed of the progress in real data loading.

4. The provisions on the protection of personal data laid down in the convention implementing the Schengen Agreement shall apply in their entirety in Greece.

Brussels, 7 October 1997

The Chairman

DECISION OF THE EXECUTIVE COMMITTEE of 23 June 1998 concerning the confidential nature of certain documents

(SCH/Com-ex (98) 17)

The Executive Committee,

Having regard to Article 132 of the convention implementing the Schengen Agreement,

HAS DECIDED AS FOLLOWS:

Paragraph 2 of the decision of 14 December 1993 (SCH/Com-ex (93) 22 rev) shall be replaced by the following paragraph:

'The following documents shall remain confidential: Annexes 5, 9 and 10 to the common consular instructions on visas, the common manual, the Sirene manual, and the three documents covered by the decision on narcotic drugs (tightening controls at external borders (SCH/Stup (92) 45 latest version), controlled deliveries (SCH/Stup (92) 46 latest version) and measures on combating the illicit exportation of drugs (SCH/Stup (92) 72 latest version)).'

Ostend, 23 June 1998

The Chairman

L. Tobback

DECISION OF THE EXECUTIVE COMMITTEE of 16 September 1998 setting up a Standing Committee on the evaluation and implementation of Schengen

(SCH/ Com-ex (98) 26 def)

The Executive Committee,

Having regard to Article 132 of the convention implementing the Schengen Agreement,

Having regard to Article 7 of the convention implementing the Schengen Agreement,

Having regard to the joint declaration concerning Article 139 in the final act annexed to the convention,

Whereas the initiative to set up the Standing Committee stems from a concern for complementarity with existing instruments within the European Union;

Mindful of the need to observe the principle of national sovereignty,

Whereas this Committee may in due course have to be adapted to take account of the operational framework of the European Union

HAS DECIDED AS FOLLOWS:

A Standing Committee on the evaluation and implementation of Schengen (hereinafter 'the Standing Committee') shall be set up under the aegis of the Executive Committee, firstly to establish whether all the preconditions for bringing the convention into force in a candidate State there to have been fulfilled and secondly to ensure that Schengen *acquis* is properly applied by the States already implementing the convention, notably by pinpointing problems and proposing solutions.

The Standing Committee shall have sole responsibility for drafting the reports with a view to evaluating the preparations by the candidate States to bring the Schengen Convention into force and verifying that all of the preconditions for the practical application of the Schengen Convention and the abolition of checks at the internal borders have been fulfilled.

The second task of the Standing Committee shall be to lay the foundations so that the Executive Committee can ensure the proper application of the Schengen Convention by the States which have already brought it into force, in particular by following up the recommendations made by the visiting committees to the external borders, by ensuring that follow-up action is taken to remedy the shortcomings mentioned in the Annual Report on the External Borders, by focusing greater attention on the joint efforts needed to improve the quality of controls at the external borders and by optimising the application of the convention in the fields of police cooperation, judicial cooperation and the SIS. The Standing Committee shall seek solutions to the problems detected and shall make proposals for the satisfactory and optimal implementation of the convention. Sole responsibility for checking to ensure that the convention is properly applied shall continue to remain with the Schengen States. The Standing Committee shall therefore confine itself to carrying out the verification procedures as defined in the following mandate.

These two tasks warrant the Standing Committee being awarded two separate mandates:

1. to prepare the reports to serve as a basis for establishing that all the preconditions for bringing the Schengen Convention into force in a candidate State have been satisfied. In these cases it shall be called the 'Evaluation Committee', and shall be in charge of evaluating how well these States are prepared;

2. to lay the foundations so that the Executive Committee can ensure the proper application of the convention in the States already implementing the convention with a view to optimising its application and cooperation between the Schengen partners. First, it has to find solutions to problems encountered since the bringing into force of the convention and make proposals on improving controls in accordance with the objectives set and the spirit of the convention. Here, it shall be called the 'Implementation Committee'.

I Evaluation Committee for candidate States to bring the convention into force

1. Tasks of the Evaluation Committee

Each time a State is a candidate to bring the convention into force, the Standing Committee, acting in the context of its evaluation remit, shall draw up a report laying down a list of the criteria to be satisfied by the candidate States. This list shall indicate precisely the standard to be reached in all of the areas covered by the convention. Once these criteria have been approved by the Executive Committee, the Standing Committee shall verify in another report whether a candidate State to bring the convention into force satisfies the criteria and complies with the standard required.

In each of the Committee's spheres of competence, it may instruct a group of competent experts to draft a report in its specific field. These reports shall deal with the qualitative, quantitative, operational, administrative and organisational aspects and should pinpoint shortcomings or weaknesses, whilst proposing solutions.

2. Spheres of competence

The Committee shall draft a detailed and exhaustive report and shall assess how well prepared the candidate States to bring into force the Schengen Convention are in all of the fields referred to in Decision SCH/Com-ex (93) 10 of 14 December 1993 and shall ensure that all of the preconditions for implementing the Schengen *acquis* are respected. The assessment shall cover the following areas in particular:

- checks at the external borders, in particular the application of the common manual;
- surveillance of external land and sea borders;
- visas, in particular the application of the common consular instructions;
- conditions governing the movement of aliens, including measures taken with regard to illegal immigration and aliens illegally on Schengen territory;
- residence permits and alerts for the purpose of refusing entry;
- police cooperation;
- mutual assistance in criminal matters, including extradition;
- drugs;
- SIS, in particular the application of the Sirene manual;
- protection of personal data;
- policy on expulsion and readmission;
- arrangements for movement within airports.

On the one hand, the Standing Committee shall take as its basis the following tasks in the areas relating to external borders, police cooperation, the SIS and visas; on the other, it shall draw up a list of tasks to be carried out by the experts in the other areas.

(a) Controls at the external borders and migratory flows, including bilateral and multilateral cooperation with third States and the question of readmission

Taking into account the local geographical situation and depending on the kind of external borders in the visited State, the experts shall:

— visit all external maritime borders in order to gather information *in situ* regarding the efficiency of surveillance measures on sea and land, particularly at night; and observe how checks are carried out on persons and freight in major ports;

— observe control measures at the land borders with the aim of verifying their efficiency day and night. They must obtain information on the fight against the smuggling of illegal immigrants, *inter alia* by means of interviews with the control authorities;

— visit all airports for the purpose of checking how Schengen provisions have been applied;

— visit in addition the Central Authorities in charge of external border and immigration controls and examine administrative structures and coordination between national and local levels;

— enquire about practices for the issue of visas at the border when visiting the border crossing points and the Central Authority;

— verify, when visiting the border crossing points and the Central Authority, that the SIS can be put into operation;

— assess the arrangements for carrying out checks at the external borders, at the official border crossing points and in the intervening areas;

— assess the technical means available at the external borders, *inter alia* to deal with false documents;

— assess the surveillance of land and sea borders;

— check whether there are sufficient staffing levels at the different borders visited, together with their training, *inter alia* on detecting false documents;

— check the measures taken at the external borders visited to tackle illegal immigration and more generally crime;

— check the measures taken vis-à-vis persons not admitted at the border or present illegally;

— check the means deployed to combat illegal immigration networks;

— assess cooperation with the bordering State(s).

The objective of the visit shall be to assess *in situ* the efficiency of surveillance measures and their compliance with the Schengen control standards laid down in the Schengen Convention, the common manual and the relevant Executive Committee decisions.

(b) Cooperation at the joint borders with States already applying the convention, mainly with regard to police and judicial cooperation, in particular the conclusion of bilateral agreements and the secondment of liaison officers

In this context, the Standing Committee shall have the task of verifying:

— the efficiency of day-to-day cooperation in the common border regions in implementation of the convention and bilateral agreements;

— the capacity and the willingness to implement and develop joint cross-border operations in compliance with the convention and bilateral agreements;

— the capacity and the willingness to implement and develop cooperation with liaison officers;

— the efficiency of cooperation with States adjacent to Schengen's external borders in the fight against crime and, in particular, the fight against illegal immigration networks;

— police access to databases and general training;

— the efficiency of cross-border cooperation structures;

— direct cooperation and relations between the authorities of the candidate State and the Schengen States;

— security means and staff level in the border region.

(c) The SIS, the Sirene bureaux, the protection of facilities and personal data

In this context, the Standing Committee shall have the task of verifying:

• *Technical aspects*

— the qualitative, quantitative, operational, organisational and technical aspects of the future N.SIS;

— the technical means and the procedures used to transfer information from the national information systems to the N.SIS (downloading to the SIS from national systems);

— the technical means for making SIS data available to users on the ground and ensuring synchronisation of N.SIS and C.SIS data;

— the technical availability of the N.SISs;

• *Aspects concerning data and their use*

— the quantity of data the State is prepared to integrate into the SIS;

— the quality of the data to be incorporated (completion of headings);

— the geographical location of terminals, the number of terminals and their operational state (accessibility of SIS data to end-users);

— training of employees authorised to use data contained in the SIS;

— the internal procedures and the instructions for issuing alerts and to be applied in the event of a hit;

— the use of different options for alerts;

— the operational capacity of the Sirene bureaux (coordination between services, reply times);

• *Protection of the facilities and data*

— the organisational and technical aspects of the protection of the facilities and personal data;

— measures to prevent access to the systems and to data;

— measures geared towards different levels of processing according to the user's responsibilities;

— the conditions governing the removal of alerts which have expired;

(d) The issue of visas

— general conditions governing the issue of visas compared to those laid down in the common consular instructions;

— provisions for consultation prior to the issue of visas;

— provisions for consulting the SIS prior to the issue of visas;

— provisions for procuring stickers and storage conditions.

The Standing Committee shall oversee the coordination of these reports and shall submit a general report to the Executive Committee.

II Implementation Committee for the States already applying the convention

1. Tasks

The Standing Committee shall provide the scope for detecting any problems encountered at external borders and for identifying situations which do not comply with the standard set in accordance with the spirit and objectives of the convention. By means of the Standing Committee, the State visited and the Executive Committee shall be informed of the problems encountered, together with solutions proposed for applying the convention in a satisfactory and most effective manner. As for any problems encountered since the bringing into force of the convention, it shall be up to the Committee to make technical proposals to improve checks, security and judicial cooperation, including extradition.

The Committee shall also check whether the recommendations and observations put forward by the visiting committees to external borders have been acted upon and have enabled any shortcomings in security to be overcome. The Committee shall also have the task of following up the problems highlighted in the annual report on the situation at the external borders of the States applying the convention.

Finally, the Committee shall perform its duties flexibly and objectively, in cooperation with the competent authorities and in compliance with the legal and ethical rules applicable at national level, and in so doing strive to meet the common objective of improving security and taking account of the interests of the other States applying the convention.

2. Areas to be covered

For those States already applying the convention, the Committee shall be granted a wider remit than that of the visiting committees, but it shall continue to focus on the practical aspects. The following areas, extending across the whole of the Schengen acquis, may undergo evaluation and therefore have to be taken into account:

— external border checks and surveillance;

— police cooperation at the border areas of States already applying the convention;

— the Schengen information system;

— the conditions for the issuing of Schengen visas (in particular the arrangements governing prior consultation of the partner States on sensitive nationalities);

— measures aimed at terminating the stay of aliens discovered to be illegally on the territory;

— mutual assistance in criminal matters, including extradition.

The following should be given priority:

(a) External border checks and surveillance

— provisions for carrying out checks at the authorised crossing points along the external borders and in the border areas;

— technical means available at the external borders, in particular for detecting counterfeit documents;

— determining whether staff levels are adequate for the particular border visited;

— external border checks and surveillance, encompassing mobile patrols as well as systems and methods of stationary surveillance;

— training for officials, *inter alia* in the detection of counterfeit documents;

— measures taken at the external borders visited to combat illegal immigration and crime in general;

— measures taken against individuals not granted admission at the border or individuals who are illegally on Schengen territory;

— means deployed to combat illegal immigration networks;

— existing forms of cooperation with neighbouring State(s);

— administrative organisation of the service(s) responsible for combating illegal immigration and for coordination between these services at national and local level;

— SIS use at border posts.

(b) Police cooperation in the border areas of States already applying the convention

— existence of bilateral agreements;

— exercising the right to pursuit and surveillance;

— organisation of cross-border cooperation;

— direct cooperation between services;

— equipment and staff deployed in the border region for security purposes;

— cooperation involving liaison officers.

(c) The Schengen information system

— downloading to the SIS from the national systems;

— technical availability of the N.SISs and the Sirene bureaux;

— end users' access to SIS data;

— conditions for deleting expired alerts;

— exploiting the different possibilities with regard to alerts;

— operational capacity of the Sirene bureaux: response time, etc.

(d) Conditions for the issue of Schengen visas

— provisions for consultation prior to the issue of visas, as laid down in Annex 5B to the common consular instructions;

— provisions for consulting the SIS prior to the issue of Schengen visas;

— VLTVs issued: quantity, target groups, grounds;

— provisions for procuring Schengen stickers and storage conditions.

III Principles governing the Standing Committee

- *Composition of the Standing Committee*

The Committee shall be a standing body. It shall be composed of one high-ranking representative from each Signatory State to the convention or the cooperation agreement. (This high-ranking representative may be accompanied). The Standing Committee shall be assisted by the Secretariat in connection with its meetings and various tasks.

The Standing Committee shall visit all of the countries, in an order and at intervals to be laid down by the Executive Committee.

For the performance of their tasks, the permanent members shall be able to call on the Schengen States to second temporarily experts in the each of the Committee's areas of competence, in particular for the purpose of carrying out the assignments in the countries, in line with the arrangements defined by the permanent members. Certain assignments involving experts may be carried out jointly or may focus on one area. Each State shall be entitled to appoint an expert to perform assignments in the framework of the Standing Committee. The Standing Committee shall, however, endeavour to maintain membership of the delegations at a level that is compatible with the technical constraints of the assignments.

Where there are several visits taking place at the same time involving groups of experts specialising in each of the specific areas, a coordination meeting shall be organised with all the experts before the end of the visit.

The experts must have the requisite qualifications and, in general, it would be desirable for the same experts to be designated each time.

The European Commission shall participate as an observer in the Standing Committee's work and in the activities of the working groups which serve the Committee, the Central Group and the Executive Committee.

- *Joint Supervisory Authority*

The Standing Committee shall carry out its tasks without prejudice to the powers of the Joint Supervisory Authority. The Committee shall be authorised to consult the Authority in areas within its sphere of competence.

- *Locations to be visited*

The Standing Committee shall, in conjunction with the respective working groups, select the locations to be visited and the information to be gathered on a case-by-case basis.

- *Language arrangements*

Details of the language arrangements to be used during the visits shall be determined for each visit.

- *Facilitating the activities of the Committee*

The authorities of the visited State shall ensure that its authorities afford the Committee the cooperation and assistance it requires to enable it to perform its tasks properly. The visited State must provide the Committee with the relevant information on the locations to be visited and all useful statistical, factual, analytical or other information (in one of the official Schengen languages) at least one month before the start of the visit.

- *Reimbursement of travel and accommodation expenses incurred during the visits*

The costs of travel and accommodation are to be met by the Committee members or their experts. The host State shall bear the costs of the logistical support *in situ*.

- *Drafting of the report*

The report shall be drafted on the basis of a standard model to be laid down by the Standing Committee in consultation with the competent working groups. The model may be adjusted according to needs and circumstances.

A preliminary draft of the report shall be written by the Presidency and submitted to the group of experts, who shall seek a consensus on how the report should be drafted. The representatives of the host State shall have observer status within this group. Once the report has been drawn up by the experts, it shall be submitted to the host State, which may draft an opinion. The report and the opinion shall be submitted to the Standing Committee, which shall attempt to find a consensus between the two documents. With regard to points that remain contentious, the Committee shall put the position of each of the Parties.

The reports must clearly show in which areas the objectives have been reached and those in which this is not the case, together with concrete proposals for measures to take with a view to remedying or improving the situation. Responsibility for adopting the final decision shall in any case rest with the Executive Committee.

- *Confidentiality*

The Committee members and the experts shall regard as confidential the information they acquire in the course of performing their duties. The reports drawn up pursuant to this decision shall be regarded as confidential.

Königswinter, 16 September 1998

The Chairman

M. KANTHER

DECISION OF THE EXECUTIVE COMMITTEE of 23 June 1998 on a catch-all clause to cover the whole technical Schengen *acquis*

(SCH/Com-ex (98) 29 rev)

The Executive Committee,

Having regard to Article 132 of the convention implementing the Schengen Agreement,

Having regard to Articles 92 and 93 of the abovementioned convention,

Hereby confirms that arrangements, procedures and other rules have been adopted for the functioning of the SIS at the organisational, operational and technical levels and for the protection of personal data and recommends that these be retained following the entry into force of the Treaty of Amsterdam.

Ostend, 23 June 1998

The Chairman

L. TOBBACK

DECISION OF THE EXECUTIVE COMMITTEE of 16 September 1998 setting up an Ad Hoc Committee for Greece

(SCH/Com-ex (98) 43 rev.)

The Executive Committee,

Having regard to Article 132 of the convention implementing the Schengen Agreement,

Whereas the agreement on the accession of the Hellenic Republic to the convention implementing the Schengen Convention was partially brought into force by a decision of 7 October 1997,

HAS DECIDED AS FOLLOWS:

1. An Ad Hoc Committee shall be set up to examine whether Greece fulfils all the preconditions for the abolition of checks on persons at the internal borders. All the Contracting Parties may participate by sending experts to the Committee.

2. The said Committee shall have the task of gathering information in the following:

areas:

— checks at the external borders, in particular the application of the common manual;

— surveillance of external land and sea borders;

— visas, in particular the application of the common consular instructions;

— conditions governing the movement of aliens, including measures taken with regard to illegal immigration and aliens illegally on Schengen territory;

— residence permits and alerts for the purpose of refusing entry;

— police cooperation;

— mutual assistance in criminal matters, including extradition;

— drugs;

— SIS, in particular the application of the Sirene manual;

— protection of personal data;

— policy on expulsion and readmission;

— arrangements for the movement of persons within airports.

3. The Committee shall evaluate the results of its inquiries in the areas of external border checks and arrangements for the movement of persons within airports. In the other areas it shall make observations.

4. The Committee shall draft a report containing a summary of the information gathered, as well as its evaluations and observations, for submission to the subgroup on frontiers and the Central Group. On the basis of this report the Executive Committee will adopt a decision, not later than at its meeting of December 1998, in accordance with the decision of the Executive Committee of 7 October 1997, adopted in Vienna.

Königswinter, 16 September 1998

The Chairman

M. KANTHER

DECISION OF THE EXECUTIVE COMMITTEE of 16 December 1998 on bringing into force the implementing convention in Greece

(SCH/Com-ex (98) 49 rev 3)

The Executive Committee,

Having regard to Article 132 of the convention implementing the Schengen Agreement,

Having regard to Article 6 of the accession agreement signed with Greece on 6 November 1992 in conjunction with the joint declaration on Article 6 of the final act of the aforesaid agreement,

Having regard to its decision of 7 October 1997 on bringing into force the convention implementing the Schengen Agreement in Greece (SCH/Com-ex (97) 29 rev 2),

Having regard to the report of the Ad Hoc Committee for Greece (SCH/C (98) 123 rev 2),

Having regard to the Ad Hoc Committee for Greece's various reports,

Confirming the political resolve of the Executive Committee of 7 October 1997 to bring the Schengen Convention fully into force for Greece, as expressed in Decision SCH/Com-ex (97) 29 rev 2,

Recognising and acknowledging that Greece has already satisfied the requirements for the full application of the Schengen Convention in the fields of visas, police and judicial cooperation, the fight against drug trafficking, the Schengen information system and data protection;

Whereas Greece has already made considerable progress, particularly at the airports, in adapting security at its external borders to take account of Schengen requirements,

HAS DECIDED AS FOLLOWS:

1. Greece shall notify the other Contracting Parties when it considers that it has satisfied Schengen requirements regarding security at the external maritime and land borders.

2. The checks on persons at Greece's internal borders shall be lifted when the Executive Committee finds on the basis of appropriate reviews and visits by the Ad Hoc Committee that the requirements to ensure Schengen standards of security at the external maritime and land borders of Greece have been satisfied.

3. Fulfilment of the requirements relating to manpower levels and material resources, the training of border check and surveillance services and coordination between the departments concerned shall be examined on the basis of visits. The necessary improvements in the areas of:

— maritime surveillance strategy

— flexible deployment of mobile units and

— application of Article 26 of the convention

may be demonstrated by the presentation of documentary evidence.

4. The Executive Committee shall take a decision before the end of 1999 if possible.

Berlin, 16 December 1998

The Chairman,

C. H. SCHAPPER

2.2. ABOLITION OF CHECKS AT INTERNAL BORDERS AND MOVEMENT OF PERSONS

DECISION OF THE EXECUTIVE COMMITTEE of 14 December 1993 extending the uniform visa

(SCH/Com-ex (93) 21)

The Executive Committee,

Having regard to Article 132 of the convention implementing the Schengen Agreement,

Having regard to Article 17(3)(e) of the abovementioned convention,

HAS DECIDED AS FOLLOWS:

Uniform visas shall be extended in accordance with the common principles laid down in the document annexed hereto.

Paris, 14 December 1993

The Chairman

A. LAMASSOURE

ANNEX ON EXTENDING UNIFORM VISAS

COMMON PRINCIPLES

(1) Article 17(3)(e) of the implementing convention lays down that the Executive Committee shall take the necessary decisions on the conditions for extending visas in accordance with the interests of all the Contracting Parties. This provision shall be the legal basis for the common principles defined below.

(2) A visa may be extended if new facts have arisen since the visa was issued. Applications to extend visas on the following grounds must be duly substantiated: *force majeure*; humanitarian, serious occupational or personal reasons. Applications may not, under any circumstances, result in the purpose of the visa being changed. It shall be for the competent administrative authority to assess whether or not the reason actually given constitutes grounds for an extension.

(3) A visa extension shall not result in the duration of the stay exceeding 90 days.

(4) A visa shall be extended in accordance with national procedures.

(5) The competent authority shall be that of the Contracting Party on whose territory the alien happens to be when the application is submitted even if extension of the visa means the applicant will travel to the territory of another Contracting Party.

In each of the Contracting Parties, the following administrative authorities shall be responsible for extending visas:

France: Prefectures (in Paris, the police headquarters);

Spain: For ordinary passports: 'gobiernos civiles y por su delegacion las comisarias de policia' (prefectures and, where authorised by delegation, police stations);

Italy: 'Ufficio degli Stranieri (Questure Republica)' (Aliens Dept. (Prefectures of the police of the Italian Republic);

Greece: 'Υπουργείο Δημόσιας Τάξης (Γραφεία Αλλοδαπών)' (Ministry of Public Order — Aliens Dept.);

Portugal: 'Serviço de Estrangeiros e Fronteiras' 'Ministério da Administracão Interna' (Aliens and Borders Department at the Ministry of the Interior).

Germany: 'Ausländeramt der jeweiligen Stadt oder des Landkreises' (Aliens Department of the town or the administrative district);

Belgium: For ordinary visas: Provincial governments; for diplomatic and service visas: Ministry of Foreign Affairs;

The Netherlands: For ordinary visas: 'Hoofden van de plaatselijke politie' (Local Police Chiefs); for diplomatic and service visas: 'Ministerie van Buitenlandse Zaken' (Ministry of Foreign Affairs);

Luxembourg: For all visas: Passport and visa office at the Ministry of Foreign Affairs.

(6) Depending on the national procedures, extension of uniform visas shall take the form of a new visa sticker or a stamp.

(7) A fee may be charged for extending visas.

(8) Where applicants are nationals of countries, or belong to one of the categories subject by one or more Contracting Parties to the consultation procedure involving the central authorities, visa extensions shall continue to be granted only in exceptional cases. If the visa is extended, the central authority of the country whose consular representation issued the visa shall be informed thereof.

(9) Unless otherwise decided by the administrative authority which extends the visa, the extended visa shall remain a uniform visa, entitling entry to the territory of all the Contracting Parties for which this visa was valid at the time of issue.

DECISION OF THE EXECUTIVE COMMITTEE of 14 December 1993 on the common principles for cancelling, rescinding or shortening the length of validity of the uniform visa

(SCH/Com-ex (93) 24)

The Executive Committee,

Having regard to Article 132 of the convention implementing the Schengen Agreement,

Having regard to Article 131 of the abovementioned convention,

HAS DECIDED AS FOLLOWS:

The procedures for cancelling, rescinding or shortening the length of validity of the uniform visa shall comply with the principles defined in the document attached hereto.

Paris, 14 December 1993

The Chairman

A. LAMASSOURE

The procedures for cancelling, rescinding or shortening the length of validity of a uniform visa, as laid down by the Executive Committee pursuant to Article 131, shall be either to prevent access to the territory of the signatory States to the Schengen Convention as granted by the issue of a uniform visa, or to shorten the length of validity of the visa or the length of the initially intended duration of the stay.

A distinction can be made between:

— cancellation,

— rescission,

— and shortening of the length of validity.

1. Cancellation

The visa shall be cancelled at the border (1) and the procedure carried out by the officers responsible for border controls (see Common Manual II — 1.4.4) (2). The purpose is to prevent access to the territory of the signatory States to the Schengen Convention, notably where a visa has been issued in error to an alien who is the subject of an alert refusing entry as an undesirable person. If a visa is cancelled it is considered as never having existed.

Cancellation is not the same as refusal of admission, a procedure whereby the border control officers do not cancel the visa but refuse the holder entry to their territory, for example because the latter lacks the documents to justify the purpose of the stay.

The decision to cancel the visa is taken by the national administrative authorities responsible for border checks.

For practical purposes, an interlineation or some kind of indication may be attached to the visa sticker that clearly shows that the visa has been cancelled. It is recommended that the sticker kinegramme be scored through with a pointed metal object.

The central authority of the State that issued the visa shall be notified that the visa has been cancelled, and the following information shall be communicated:

— the date and grounds for cancellation,

— the name of the visa holder,

— nationality,

— travel document type and issue number,

— visa sticker number,

(1) A visa may also be cancelled by the consular authorities if the visa appears to have been issued in error.

(2) Confidential document. See SCH/Com-ex (98) 17.

— type of visa,
— date and place of issue of the visa.

2. Rescission

Some States draw a distinction between rescinding a uniform visa and cancelling it.

By rescinding a visa, a measure which does not have retroactive effect, it is possible to cancel the remaining period of validity of a uniform visa after the holder has entered the territory.

Pursuant to Article 23 of the Schengen Convention, the visa shall be rescinded if checks reveal that the alien holding a visa issued correctly does not fulfil, or no longer fulfils, one or several of the conditions set out in Article 5(1), (c), (d), (e) of the Schengen Convention. The visa shall be rescinded according to the national procedures of the Contracting Party on whose territory the visa holder is located. The Contracting Party that rescinds the visa shall inform the Contracting Party which issued the visa. It shall give the reasons for its decision.

3. Shortening of the length of validity of the uniform visa

Pursuant to Article 23 of the Schengen Convention, some States use this procedure prior to the expulsion of an alien. It entails shortening the length of the stay to the number of days between the date on which the border was crossed and the date set for the alien's expulsion.

The border control officer may also decide to shorten the length of validity of a uniform visa if it is established that the alien does not have adequate means of support for the initially intended duration of the stay.

DECISION OF THE EXECUTIVE COMMITTEE of 26 April 1994 on adjustment measures aiming to remove the obstacles to, and restrictions on, traffic at road crossing points at internal borders

(SCH/Com-ex (94) 1 rev 2)

The Executive Committee,

Having regard to Article 132 of the convention implementing the Schengen Agreement,

Having regard to Article 2 of the abovementioned convention,

Hereby acknowledges and approves the document on the abolition of checks on persons at the internal borders (SCH/I-Front (94) 1 rev 3) referred to it and

HAS DECIDED AS FOLLOWS:

The adjustment measures aiming to remove obstacles to, and restrictions on, traffic at road crossing points at internal borders shall be implemented in accordance with the document attached hereto. The implementation of these adjustment measures falls within the national competence of the Contracting Parties.

Bonn, 26 April 1994

The Chairman

BERND SCHMIDBAUER

Adjustment measures aiming to removing obstacles to, and restrictions on, traffic at road crossing points of internal borders

Completing the abolition of checks at the internal borders between the Schengen States also involves the removal of the obstacles restricting travel, in particular those constituted by the installations formerly required for checks.

The Contracting Parties therefore intend to begin immediately dismantling these obstacles progressively as soon as positive indications as to the prospects of bringing the Schengen information system into operation have been received.

Phase 1 will consist of measures which are particularly necessary to guarantee that the internal borders may be crossed swiftly and which may be implemented relatively quickly without incurring unreasonable expense.

To this end the following measures, in particular, must be taken:

— opening carriageways and lanes previously blocked for border checks, particularly at motorway border crossing points;

— removing customs sheds from central lanes so as not to hinder vehicles passing at high speed;

— dismantling roofs jutting out over the road at border crossing points to improve visibility and reduce nuisance caused by air pressure changes;

— removing speed limits; the sole criteria for introducing any new speed limits is road safety;

— technical adjustments in order to enable vehicles to turn round on motorways and comparable roads in case checks at the internal borders are temporarily reinstated on grounds of public policy or national security and vehicles are refused entry.

The implementation of these programmes shall be the national responsibility of each Contracting Party and — if necessary or expedient from a legal or a practical point of view — by mutual consultation or agreement.

As many as possible of the measures referred to in Phase 1 should be completed by the time the convention implementing the Schengen Agreement is brought into force, or at least those which can be implemented quickly without any lengthy preparations (e.g. the removal of road barriers).

Preparations for the remaining adjustment measures in Phase 1 shall be made in accordance with the following timetable:

1. During the period from 1 July to 15 September 1994, a review of the situation is to be made and a list drawn up of the steps to be taken at each internal border crossing point with a view to implementing the adjustment measures.

It should be borne in mind that installations for police cooperation are to be kept provisionally at certain border crossing points which means, for instance, that the speed limits should be retained for access roads to the services concerned.

2. The period from 15 September to 31 October 1994 is the phase for consultation between neighbouring States. During this period, they are to inform each other of the activities required to put into practice the adjustment measures at each border crossing point.

3. The Contracting Parties shall ensure that the necessary arrangements for bringing into force the convention implementing the Schengen Agreement are completed by 31 December 1994.

At the end of each of the three preparatory phases, the Contracting Parties shall report to the Central Group on progress made towards completing the timetable, whilst providing detailed overviews.

SCH/I-Front (94) 1 rev 3

Abolition of checks on persons at the internal borders

After years of intensive preparation, almost all the various compensatory measures provided for by the Schengen Convention of 19 June 1990 have been fully implemented, and the work that remains to be done in this area, e.g. on the Schengen information system, is currently proceeding at a steady pace.

However, certain arrangements that were designed to achieve the objective which these compensatory measures were supposed to permit, i.e. the abolition of checks on persons at the internal borders, are still not in place. The avoidance of any further delay in abolishing such checks at the common borders even after all the compensatory measures have been implemented is contingent on the necessary preconditions being fulfilled. In this connection it is important not only to dispense with the formalities that accompany such checks but to remove the obstacles to freedom of movement at the internal borders that were previously necessary for the purpose of carrying out controls.

In order to ensure that this operation proceeds in an orderly fashion, there must be a concrete action programme for implementing the various stages.

1. Abolition of checks on persons and of the requirement to present cross-border travel documents at land borders, ports and airports

1.1. Abolition of checks on persons

Under Article 2(1) of the Schengen Convention, the internal borders may be crossed at any point without checks on persons being carried out.

Consequently, the competent authorities should dispense with internal border checks except in the cases provided for in Article 2(2) of the convention.

On the other hand, this would have the effect of exempting all travellers, whatever their nationality, from police checks when crossing the border. Furthermore, they would no longer be obliged to use authorised border crossing points.

The abolition of checks on persons at the internal borders is without prejudice to the provisions of Article 22 of the Schengen Convention. Nor does it affect the exercise by the competent authorities of a Contracting Party, on its national territory, including the border areas, of their powers under national law for the purpose of monitoring compliance with the obligation to possess, carry and present papers and travel documents.

Alternative border checks are incompatible with the provisions of the Schengen Convention on the abolition of controls. Here, however, they are taken to mean systematic checks on persons carried out for the purpose of crossing the border, in a hinterland area adjacent to the border or in defined border areas. This does not contravene the provisions of Article 2(2).

Persons entering via airports and seaports are exempt from checks only if they cross a common border, e.g. in the case of air and sea travel inside the Schengen area. Since passengers are channelled into Schengen and non-Schengen flows, checks cannot in practice be abolished for air and sea travel unless airports and seaports have the requisite separate handling areas.

The Contracting Parties should take appropriate steps to inform

the public,

the authorities responsible for border protection,

the police, and

the airport and seaport operators and the carriers

of the various features of the new situation at the internal borders with regard to the abolition of checks.

1.2. Abolition of the requirement to present cross-border travel documents when crossing internal borders

The abolition of border controls goes hand in hand with abolition of the requirement to produce or present a valid document that permits the holder to cross borders.

This does not conflict with national provisions on holding, carrying and presenting identity and residence papers that are applicable on the national territory.

Delegations were to communicate the relevant national provisions before the end of April 1994 and provide details of the identity documents used in their countries and of the checks provided for under their national law.

2. Adjustment measures aimed at eliminating obstacles to and restrictions on movement at road crossing points

The abolition of checks on persons is the main instrument for achieving freedom of movement at the borders. To attain this objective, however, it is necessary to remove infrastructures the existence of which was hitherto justified by the need to conduct checks and which restrict freedom of movement.

2.1. General observations

(a) Crossing points at internal borders — the largest and most important at any rate — consist of numerous buildings and facilities that form a complex.

In the initial phase, the activities undertaken by the Contracting Parties for the purpose of complementing the abolition of checks by accompanying measures will consist solely of steps aimed at guaranteeing that there are no obstacles to crossing the borders.

The question of dismantling other buildings or putting them to a different use, collection of the barriers used previously and important tasks such as rectifying the layout will be tackled during the second stage.

(b) Most of the Schengen States have concluded bilateral agreements with neighbouring States determining that checks on cross-border traffic may take the form of joint checks carried out on the territory of either State. Accordingly, the implementing agreements provided for checks to be combined at virtually all crossing points. Consequently, adaptations for the purpose of implementing the Schengen system presuppose the agreement of the two neighbouring States in question. The Contracting Parties should reach such agreement quickly and inform the Executive Committee accordingly.

2.2. Infrastructural modifications of a technical nature

In the first instance, the following measures in particular should be prepared at a number of crossing points, especially on motorways, provision has been made for traffic lanes for vehicles but these are blocked by security ramps or crash barriers. These lanes can be opened to traffic and measures to this end should be taken as soon as possible.

The control booths erected in the middle lanes, particularly on motorways, are too close to the traffic lane and constitute a safety hazard for vehicles travelling at high speed. They should therefore be demolished.

If vehicles are allowed to travel at higher speeds, the roofs which overhang the road at border crossing points should be demolished in order to improve visibility and reduce the nuisance caused by air currents.

2.3. Abolition of traffic restrictions

Once the necessary tasks have been completed, it will be possible to abolish the speed limits currently in force. The introduction of new speed limits will be dictated solely by road safety requirements.

2.4. Arrangements for the temporary reintroduction of checks at internal borders

Should it prove necessary to reintroduce internal border checks temporarily in accordance with the provisions of Article 2(2) of the convention, mobile units of the border police can impose the speed restrictions necessary for conducting checks by means of ad hoc signalling. This obviates the need to install permanent signs for this purpose.

However, in order to enforce a decision to refuse entry, provision needs to be made for installing a device that enables traffic to reverse. Steps therefore need to be taken to ensure that movable components capable of being opened immediately if necessary are installed in the security barriers located in the middle of motorways and similar roads.

2.5. Action programmes

With a view to the practical implementation of the Schengen Convention, the Contracting Parties should draft detailed programmes for the first phase of infrastructural adaptation at the border crossing points and submit them to the Executive Committee.

The following measures in particular must be taken in due course for the purpose of bringing the convention into force.

— Road lanes, especially those at motorway crossing points that have up to now been closed for the purpose of conducting border checks, should be opened to traffic;

— The control booths situated on the middle lanes should be demolished so as not to hamper vehicles travelling past at high speed;

— The roofs overhanging the road at the border crossing points should be removed to improve visibility and reduce the nuisance caused by air currents;

— Speed limits should be abolished, and the introduction of new restrictions should be determined solely by road safety considerations;

— Technical modifications should be carried out to enable vehicles to make a U-turn on motorways and similar roads in the event that internal border checks are temporarily reintroduced on public order or national security grounds.

These programmes are the responsibility of each Contracting Party and should be implemented jointly or by mutual agreement, in so far as circumstances or legal considerations make this necessary or advisable. The Contracting Parties should report to the General Secretariat on the measures they have taken.

3. Information on the abolition of checks prior to the implementation of the Schengen Convention

The strategy underlying the Schengen Convention is that the abolition of internal border checks should be preceded by the introduction of compensatory measures.

One of the principal compensatory measures, the Schengen information system, has yet to be completed, which means that checks on persons must in principle be maintained at the internal borders.

In the opinion of the Contracting Parties, internal border checks may, where appropriate, be discontinued by bilateral agreement in some cases, as a symbolic gesture and for a trial period, provided that security is not (seriously) undermined (pilot projects).

If the Contracting Parties envisage abolishing checks before the compensatory measures are in place, they should notify the Executive Committee accordingly.

4. Consultation in the event that alternative border checks are carried out

Article 2(2) of the convention lays down that a Contracting Party which decides to carry out national border checks for a limited period on public order or national security grounds should consult the other Contracting Parties in advance.

Given the substance and purpose of the above provision, this requirement also applies in the case of alternative border checks carried out in a hinterland area adjacent to the border or in defined border areas (see Section 1.1).

If a Contracting Party is planning to take such a measure, it should proceed as in the case of checks carried out for a temporary period directly at the internal borders and inform the other partners accordingly.

DECISION OF THE EXECUTIVE COMMITTEE of 26 April 1994 on the issue of uniform visas at borders

(SCH/Com-ex (94) 2)

The Executive Committee,

Having regard to Article 132 of the convention implementing the Schengen Agreement,

Having regard to Article 17(3)(c) and (d) of the abovementioned convention,

HAS DECIDED AS FOLLOWS:

Uniform visas shall be issued at borders in accordance with the common principles laid down in the document annexed hereto.

Berlin, 26 April 1994

The Chairman

B SCHMIDBAUER

ANNEX
Annex on the issue of uniform visas at borders

1. Article 12(1) of the implementing convention provides for uniform visas to be issued by the diplomatic and consular missions of the Contracting Parties and, where appropriate, by the authorities designated under Article 17. Article 17(3)(c) provides in particular for the Executive Committee to take decisions relating to the issue of visas at borders.

Furthermore, the common manual (Part II, point 5) stipulates that if 'due to lack of time and for pressing reasons an alien has been unable to apply for a visa, in exceptional circumstances the authorities responsible may issue him with a short-stay visa at the border'. The issue of visas in such cases is subject to a series of conditions in the common manual:

— the alien must hold a valid document authorising him to cross the border;

— he must fulfil the conditions laid down in Article 5(1)(a), (c), (d) and (e) of the convention;

— he must submit supporting documents substantiating 'unforeseeable and imperative' reasons for entry;

— return to his country of origin or transit to a third State is assured.

2. It clearly ensues from the above that visas are usually issued by the diplomatic posts and consular missions and that the issue of visas at borders therefore constitutes an exception for specific and duly justified cases.

3. Visas issued at borders may, on a case by case basis, depending on national rules and provided the abovementioned conditions are respected, be:

— a uniform visa without restrictions on territorial validity;

— a visa with limited territorial validity within the meaning of Article 10(3) of the implementing convention.

In both of the above cases, the visa issued must not be valid for more than one entry. The validity of short-stay visas must not exceed 15 days.

4. An alien in a category of persons on whom the central authorities are obliged to consult one or more of the other Contracting Parties shall not, in principle, be issued with a visa at the border, particularly given the required minimum seven-day reply period.

Nevertheless, a visa may be issued at the border for these categories of persons in exceptional cases. In such cases a visa may only be issued with territorial validity restricted to the State of issue. This visa may only be issued in the cases provided for under Article 5(2) of the implementing convention, namely on humanitarian grounds, in the national interest or on account of international obligations. The central authorities of the other Contracting Parties must be notified immediately of the issue thereof.

5. The border control authorities shall issue visas in accordance with national provisions. In practice, the visa may take the form of a Schengen visa sticker or a special stamp which is affixed.

6. Statistics must be kept on visas issued at borders. The Contracting Parties shall exchange these statistics once a month via the Schengen General Secretariat.

DECISION OF THE EXECUTIVE COMMITTEE of 21 November 1994 introducing a computerised procedure for consulting the central authorities referred to in Article 17(2) of the convention

(SCH/Com-ex (94) 15 rev)

The Executive Committee,

Having regard to Article 132 of the convention implementing the Schengen Agreement,

Having regard to Article 17(2) of the abovementioned convention,

HAS DECIDED AS FOLLOWS:

1. In implementation of the provisions relating to the issue of visas, the computerised procedure for consulting the central authorities of the other Contracting Parties when issuing visas shall be applied in pursuant to the principles laid down in the data dictionary attached hereto (SCH/II-VISION (93) 20 rev 3 ([1])) with effect as of the bringing into force of the convention implementing the Schengen Agreement. Should certain Contracting Parties not satisfy the technical requirements for applying the computerised procedure after the implementing convention has been brought into force, the consultation data for these Contracting Parties shall be transmitted by conventional methods in accordance with the provisions of the common consular instruction.

2. The Executive Committee calls on all Contracting Parties to create the technical conditions necessary for application of the computerised procedure as soon as possible.

3. As long as the Sirene network (Phase II) planned for the transmission of data for consultation is not available when the abovementioned procedural principles begin to apply, the Contracting Parties concerned shall take the necessary steps to ensure that the data can be transmitted via public lines. The Contracting Parties shall guarantee an appropriate level of security when transmitting data.

4. Each Contracting Party shall bear the costs incurred for the installations required for the computerised consultation procedure in its country. Twelve months after the system has been brought into operation, the Contracting Parties shall consult regarding any compensatory payments for the transmission of data, taking into account the principle that the generator of the costs is liable. In this connection the Contracting States shall take

([1]) Confidential document.

into account that in the consultation procedure, the consulted State also safeguards the legitimate security interests of the consulting State.

The Contracting Parties shall record the costs occasioned by the running of the consultation procedure from the date on which the system is brought into operation and shall submit an overview of these costs after not more than 12 months.

Heidelberg, 21 November 1994

The Chairman

B. SCHMIDBAUER

DECISION OF THE EXECUTIVE COMMITTEE of 21 November 1994 on the acquisition of common entry and exit stamps

(SCH/Com-ex (94) 16 rev)

The Executive Committee,

Having regard to Article 132 of the convention implementing the Schengen Agreement,

Having regard to Article 6 of the abovementioned convention,

Takes note of and approves document SCH/I-Front (94) 43 and

HAS DECIDED AS FOLLOWS:

The acquisition of common entry and exit stamps by the Contracting Parties shall take place in accordance with the principles laid down in document SCH/Gem-Handb (93) 15 ([1]).

Heidelberg, 21 November 1994

The Chairman

BERND SCHMIDBAUER

([1]) Confidential document. See SCH/Com-ex (98) 17.

(SCH/I-Front (94) 43)

Acquisition of common entry and exit stamps

The Contracting Parties shall take the specifications for manufacturing common entry and exit stamps, dated 17 September 1993 (SCH/Gem-Handb (93) 15), as the basis for the acquisition of stamps certifying entry and exit through the external borders to Schengen territory. These specifications specifically provide that two-colour ink stamps be used.

By way of exception, common entry and exit stamps employing a single colour which have already been manufactured and distributed to the border authorities may be used until they are due to be replaced. The replacement stamps must in any event be two-coloured.

DECISION OF THE EXECUTIVE COMMITTEE of 22 December 1994 introducing and applying the Schengen arrangements in airports and aerodromes

(SCH/Com-ex (94) 17 rev 4)

The Executive Committee,

Having regard to Article 132 of the convention implementing the Schengen Agreement,

Having regard to Articles 4 and 6 of the Schengen Convention,

Takes note of and approves the document introducing and applying the Schengen arrangements in airports and aerodromes (SCH/I-Front (94) 39 rev 9) and

HAS DECIDED AS FOLLOWS:

The measures set out in the annex hereto shall be implemented with a view to introducing and applying the Schengen arrangements in airports and aerodromes.

Bonn, 22 December 1994

The Chairman

BERND SCHMIDBAUER

SCH/I-Front (94) 39 rev 9

Decision on introducing and applying the Schengen arrangements in airports and aerodromes (secondary airports)

When introducing the Schengen arrangements in airports and aerodromes, the importance of the airways for illegal immigration and the function of airports as internal and external borders should be taken into account. The Contracting Parties consider it necessary to introduce the following new measures.

1. Given the need to prevent the intermingling of passenger flows from domestic and international flights — at entry points, before border police checks, and at exit points, after such checks — and whereas before the Schengen Convention is brought into force the infrastructure necessary to ensure the physical separation of such passenger flows should be in place at all airports (apart from Schiphol Airport in Amsterdam which has been granted an exemption until the end of 1995 on condition that during this period it takes procedural measures to ensure that passenger flows are clearly separated), the Schengen Convention will also be brought into force for air traffic on the date set by the Executive Committee [1].

During the preparatory stage — between 22 December 1994 and 26 March 1995 — the Contracting Parties will inform each other of the measures that are adopted.

2. In the case of controls on international flights, to reduce delays for persons covered by Community law, who are generally subject only to an identity check, provision will be made for separate checkpoints bearing uniform minimal markings in all the Schengen States — the European Union emblem with the letters 'EU' in a circle of stars. The checkpoints intended for third-country nationals will indicate 'non-EU nationals'. Checkpoints in Romance-language countries will use the abbreviations 'UE' and 'non-UE'.

3. In aerodromes — airports which do not hold the status of international airport under the relevant national law but which are authorised to serve international flights — conditions governing controls will be aligned on the conditions that apply in airports, with the following exceptions.

[1] This provision is based on the assumption that the decision bringing the Schengen Convention into force will be adopted on 22 September 1994 and that there will be a three-month period between this decision and the date of entry into force.

— To obviate risks, checks must be carried out on passengers from flights where uncertainty exists as to whether they are exclusively coming from, or solely bound for, the territories of the Contracting Parties without landing on the territory of a third country.

— Where the volume of traffic allows, border control staff need not be present in aerodromes at all times, provided that there is a guarantee that the requisite personnel can be deployed in good time should the need arise. The manager of the aerodrome is required to give the border control authorities adequate notice of the arrivals and departures of international flights. Use of extra police officers is authorised provided that this is permissible under national law.

In general it will not be necessary to make arrangements in aerodromes to ensure that passenger flows from domestic and international flights are physically separated.

Provisions on aerodromes will be added to the common manual.

Introducing and applying the Schengen arrangements in airports and aerodromes (secondary airports)

Airports play a key role in the Schengen system: firstly, they are of considerable importance as an access point for an ever-increasing number of travellers and consequently also for illegal immigrants; secondly, they serve as both internal and external borders and therefore constitute a specific sector facing a series of specific problems.

In concrete terms, the following aspects need to be take into account:

— bringing into force of the Schengen Convention;

— channelling of passenger flows in airports;

— adaptation of the level of checks on civil air traffic to the Schengen provisions;

— specific features of aerodromes.

1. Bringing into force of the Schengen Convention

The Schengen arrangements introduce an important new feature: irrespective of their nationality, domestic flight passengers will no longer be subject to any checks whereas international flight passengers will undergo checks on entry and departure, the thoroughness of which will vary depending on their nationality. To fulfil both objectives simultaneously, these two categories of passenger have to be separated. Steps must be taken to prevent checks from being carried out on domestic flight passengers, on the one hand, and international flight passengers from entering the territory of the Schengen States without undergoing checks, on the other.

Total separation can only be achieved by physical measures, mainly by putting in place the necessary infrastructure. Means of separation include building partitions in existing control areas, the use of different levels in existing buildings or dealing with traffic in different terminals.

Given that, when the Schengen Convention is brought into force, the necessary infrastructure should be in place at all airports apart from Schiphol Airport, which has been granted an exemption until the end of 1995 on condition that during this period it takes procedural measures to ensure that passenger flows are separated, the Schengen Convention will also be brought into force for air traffic on the date set by the Executive Committee [1].

(1) This provision is based on the assumption that the decision bringing into force the Schengen Convention will be adopted on 22 September 1994 and that there will be a three-month period between this decision and the date of entry into force.

During the preparatory stage — between 22 December 1994 and 26 March 1995 — the Contracting Parties will inform each other of the measures that are adopted.

2. Channelling of passenger flows in airports

Tests have shown that implementation of the Schengen provisions on controls, in particular controls on third-country nationals, considerably increases the duration of controls and gives rise to long delays. To ensure that the amount of time spent at checkpoints remains acceptable, at least for persons covered by Community law, greater emphasis must be placed on speeding up controls for those travellers.

In this context, one solution would be to provide checkpoints specifically for persons covered by Community law, so that these travellers, who are generally subject only to minimal checks, are not delayed on account of having to go to the same counter as third-country nationals who must undergo thorough and lengthy checks. Nevertheless, experience has shown that passengers only queue at the right checkpoints when the signs are comprehensible to all. Greater uniformity would probably lead to better compliance with signs. The objective should be to achieve concerted practice in all the Schengen States.

For persons covered by Community law, provision will be made for separate checkpoints bearing uniform minimal markings in all the Schengen States — the European Union emblem with the letters 'EU' in a circle of stars. The checkpoints intended for third-country nationals will indicate 'non-EU nationals'. Checkpoints in Romance-language countries will use the abbreviations 'UE' and 'non-UE'.

3. Adaptation of the level of checks on civil air traffic to the Schengen provisions

The principles governing checks at airports, being external borders, are the same as those governing checks on travellers elsewhere, for instance at road checkpoints. However, in contrast to the latter, time is a key factor in air traffic, largely on account of flight connections.

Hence the need to reconcile security requirements and time constraints. In cases of doubt, however, priority should always be given to security requirements.

The duration of the entire control procedure depends on the workload of the border control staff but also on a range of other factors such as the number of passengers, their make-up, the structure of the buildings, etc. Circumstances vary from one airport to another. According to studies undertaken by IATA, if the average duration of checks on passengers exceeds 40 seconds, the airport's functioning is considerably disrupted. These results are borne out by tests carried out on the basis of the Schengen provisions on controls. Given that space and reception facilities are limited, this situation cannot be changed overnight, even if staff levels are increased.

This is why, in addition to deploying extra staff, special arrangements must be made at airports to enable compliance with the level of Schengen controls and to ensure that time spent on checks is not incompatible with the time constraints imposed by the other systems that must be taken into account, such as international air traffic.

A distinction should be made between organisational measures which are feasible in the short term and measures based on complex technology which, by their very nature, take longer to implement.

The Contracting Parties propose examining the expediency of the following measures.

3.1. Organisational measures

The measures falling under this category should make it possible to rationalise and speed up the control procedure without causing any security deficits.

— Instituting a second set of controls allowing staff at a first checkpoint to pass on difficult cases to staff at a second checkpoint should make it possible to maintain a brisk pace during checks on passenger flows.

— Pursuant to the decision by the ministers and State secretaries of 6 November 1992, external border controls are effective in terms of Schengen requirements if their level of intensity matches the risks and threats posed by the different third countries. The Schengen Contracting Parties will inform each other of the implementing provisions.

  To this end, the Contracting Parties intend to ask their security forces to establish what risks and threats are posed by third countries.

— Automated border controls are another way of speeding up passenger checks while at the same time economising on staff. This automated method involves an electronic reading of a travel document or a card containing a special microchip. Faster controls mainly result from the installation of a large number of automatic readers which do not take up much room and which are significantly cheaper than a checkpoint manned by an officer.

  This procedure provides the means to carry out immediate comprehensive checks to establish whether all the entry conditions are met by means of access to automated search data, checks carried out before authorisation to use the automated system was granted, and repeat controls. Moreover, the border control authorities may at any time carry out additional controls considered necessary.

3.2. Advanced passenger information system

To adapt the level of air traffic controls to Schengen requirements, new avenues must be explored. Since the scope for increasing the duration of controls once a plane has landed cannot be widened at will, this situation has to be remedied by carrying out advance checks on passengers before the aeroplane lands. This procedure is already used to a certain extent in international air transport and is organised in such a way that passenger data are electronically transmitted to the airport of arrival once the aeroplane has taken off. The border control authorities at the airport of destination can then start to compare these details with their data and search files and generally have enough time to do so.

3.3. Pre-flight inspections

Pre-flight inspections are another means of carrying out advance checks on passengers. Under this system, border control officials of the country of destination may, on the basis of international agreements, carry out checks in the airport of departure to determine whether passengers fulfil certain conditions for entering the territory of the Schengen State of destination and whether they can board the flight. Pre-flight inspections constitute an extra entry control, but do not replace the entry controls carried out at the airport of arrival.

4. Specific features of aerodromes

In aerodromes — airports which do not hold the status of international airport under the relevant national law but which are authorised to serve international flights — passengers from international flights are subject to checks on persons (Section II, point 3.3.3 of the common manual ([1])).

To obviate risks, checks must be carried out on passengers from flights where uncertainty exists as to whether they are exclusively coming from, or solely bound for, the territories of the Contracting Parties without landing on the territory of a third country.

Where the volume of traffic allows, border control staff need not be present in aerodromes at all times, provided that there is a guarantee that the requisite personnel can be deployed in good time should the need arise. The manager of the aerodrome is required to give the border control authorities adequate notice of the arrivals and departures of international flights. Use of extra police officers is authorised provided that this is permissible under national law.

Since traffic at aerodromes is usually sporadic, in general it will not be necessary to put in place the infrastructure to physically separate passengers from domestic and international flights.

Provisions on aerodromes will be added to the common manual.

([1]) Confidential document: see SCH/Com-ex (98) 17.

DECISION OF THE EXECUTIVE COMMITTEE of 22 December 1994 on the exchange of statistical information on the issuing of uniform visas

(SCH/Com-ex (94) 25)

The Executive Committee,

Having regard to Article 132 of the convention implementing the Schengen Agreement,

Having regard to Article 12(3) of the abovementioned convention,

HAS DECIDED AS FOLLOWS:

1. The Contracting Parties shall exchange statistical information with each other on the issuing of uniform visas. The table attached hereto indicates what information is to be gathered and the intervals at which these exchanges are to take place.

2. The Contracting Parties shall transmit the statistical information to the Schengen General Secretariat. The Secretariat shall collate this information and compile global tables giving an overview of each period, which it shall make available to the Contracting Parties.

3. Notwithstanding the above exchanges, statistical information may also be exchanged locally within the framework of consular cooperation in accordance with a procedure agreed upon by the representations concerned.

Bonn, 22 December 1994

The Chairman

B. SCHMIDBAUER

Exchange of statistics on the issuing of visas

Type of visa	Frequency	Information to be exchanged
Uniform visa issued by the diplomatic and consular representations	six-monthly	— issuing representation — type of visa (short-stay, transit visa, airport transit visa) — type of travel document — nationality
Uniform visa (issued at the border)	quarterly	— issuing border post — type of visa — type of travel document — nationality
Visa with limited territorial validity	quarterly	— Issuing representation/border post — nationality (statistics shall be collated without prejudice to the obligation to inform the other Contracting Parties)
Visa issued after consultation with central authorities of other Contracting Parties	annually	— cf. document SCH/II-Vision (93) 20 rev 3 [1]

[1] Confidential document. See SCH/Com-ex (94) 15.

DECISION OF THE EXECUTIVE COMMITTEE of 28 April 1995 on common visa policy

Decision contained in the minutes of the meeting of the Executive Committee held in Brussels on 28 April 1995 (SCH/Com-ex (95) PV 1 rev)

8. Other business

— Visa policy with regard to Indonesia

The Executive Committee re-examined the item on visa policy with regard to Indonesia, which appeared on the agenda of the follow-up committee, and agreed on the following solution, which would apply temporarily and by way of exception:

(1) Visa applications lodged by Indonesians who have stated that they intend to enter or transit through the national territory of Portugal:

— shall be subject to prior consultation; Indonesians may only enter Portuguese territory if they have received official authorisation from the Portuguese State;

(2) Visa applications lodged by Indonesians who have stated that they have no intention of entering or transiting through the national territory of Portugal:

— do not require prior consultation. In such cases, to ensure Indonesian nationals cannot travel freely to Portugal, the other Schengen States shall issue such nationals a visa with limited territorial validity authorising the holder to enter the territory of one or several Contracting Parties with the exception of Portuguese territory.

The Executive Committee would examine this question again at the end of the year.

DECISION OF THE EXECUTIVE COMMITTEE of 20 December 1995 on the swift exchange between the Schengen States of statistical and specific data on possible malfunctions at the external borders

(SCH/Com-ex (95) 21)

The Executive Committee,

Having regard to Article 132 of the convention implementing the Schengen Agreement,

Having regard to Articles 7 and 131 of the abovementioned convention,

HAS DECIDED AS FOLLOWS:

The Schengen States shall exchange as quickly as possible statistical and specific data which reveal any possible malfunctions at the external borders.

The Schengen States shall communicate any specific data they might have to the Presidency via the General Secretariat.

The subgroup on 'borders' shall examine this data at every meeting and put forward practical solutions.

Ostend, 20 December 1995

The Chairman

J. VANDE LANOTTE

SCH/I-Front (95) 45 rev 2 corr

NOTE TO THE CENTRAL GROUP

Following the mandate given to the Central Group by the Executive Committee on 24 October 1995, the subgroup on frontiers was instructed to look into the problems encountered with regard to checks at external frontiers.

For this purpose, in implementation of Article 7 of the Schengen Convention and in order to give a factual content to the provisions of point 4.1 of the joint handbook, a statistical tool has been devised, based on the work of Cirefi.

Each State undertakes to forward to the Schengen Secretariat, within 30 days of its being gathered, statistical information permitting better monitoring and knowledge of migration phenomena, in the form of the attached tables.

The Schengen Secretariat is instructed to forward that information to all the Schengen States immediately.

The Schengen Secretariat, in liaison with the FMAD (seconded officials), will collate the information. The FMAD may undertake on the Presidency's behalf an initial analysis of problems which might appear on examination of such information. Each Member State also retains the right to raise questions which it thinks should be looked into.

Parallel to the forwarding of statistical information each Member State must communicate information on current difficulties in carrying out controls at external frontiers; that information may also be analysed in accordance with the arrangements referred to in the preceding paragraph.

For this purpose the national authorities of the Schengen States, acting through their departments responsible for external frontiers controls and through liaison officers — insofar as bilateral agreements on the secondment of officials make provision for such duties — are to collect all information on specific problems arising at external frontiers which suggest a dysfunctioning at frontier control level. National authorities are to compile and analyse this information and inform the Presidency through the Secretariat.

Each meeting of the subgroup on frontiers must devote an item on its agenda to any observations made on those statistics and on these problems.

SCHENGEN

I — EVALUATION REGARDING LAND FRONTIERS

Period		**F/United Kingdom**	**F/Belgium**	**F/Luxembourg**	**F/Germany**	**F/Swiss Confederation**	**F/Italy**	**F/Spain**	**F/Andorra**	**TOTAL**
Aliens refused entry ([1])	During the period									
	During the corresponding period of the previous year									
	Trend (%)									
Illegal aliens apprehended near the frontier ([2])	During the period									
	During the corresponding period of the previous year									
	Trend (%)									
Aliens readmitted ([3])	During the period									
	During the corresponding period of the previous year									
	Trend (%)									
Couriers apprehended	During the period									
	During the corresponding period of the previous year									
	Trend (%)									
Aliens apprehended carrying false or falsified documents	During the period									
	During the corresponding period of the previous year									
	Trend (%)									

NB: Each Contracting Party is to modify Table I according to its neighbouring countries.

II — EVALUATION REGARDING MARITIME AND AIR FRONTIERS					
Period:		**MARITIME FRONTIERS**		**AIR FRONTIERS**	
		Internal	**External**	**Internal**	**External**
Aliens refused entry ([1])	During the period				
	During the corresponding period of the previous year				
	Trend (%)				
Aliens readmitted ([3])	During the period				
	During the corresponding period of the previous year				
	Trend (%)				
Aliens apprehended carrying false or falsified documents	During the period				
	During the corresponding period of the previous year				
	Trend (%)				

([1]) Aliens refused entry: This term means the number of aliens who have been the subject of a readmission procedure in accordance with point 1.4 of the joint handbook.
([2]) Illegal aliens apprehended near the frontier: This term means the number of aliens who could be the subject of a readmission procedure without formalities in a non-Schengen State.
([3]) Aliens readmitted: This term means the number of aliens who could be the subject of a readmission procedure in a non-Schengen State.

NB: For countries for which no readmission agreement applies, these are illegal aliens apprehended in an irregular situation in a geographical area defined by those States.

DECISION OF THE EXECUTIVE COMMITTEE of 27 June 1996 on the principles for issuing Schengen visas in accordance with Article 30(1)(a) of the convention implementing the Schengen Agreement

(SCH/Com-ex (96) 13 rev 1)

The Executive Committee,

Having regard to Article 132 of the convention implementing the Schengen Agreement,

Having regard to Articles 9, 17 and 30 of the abovementioned convention,

Whereas it is in the interest of all Schengen States to define the rights and obligations of representing and represented States, since all Schengen States have representations in which they represent other States and places where they themselves are represented,

Whereas the main principle underlying cooperation between the Schengen States is absolute confidence in the way in which the Schengen representation system is applied,

HAS DECIDED AS FOLLOWS:

The issue of Schengen visas in third States where not all Schengen States are represented pursuant to Article 30(1)(a) of the agreement implementing the Schengen Convention shall take place in accordance with the following principles:

(a) Representation with respect to the issue of visas shall apply to airport transit visas, uniform transit visas and short-stay visas issued within the framework of the Schengen Convention and in accordance with the common consular instructions.

    The representing State shall be obliged to apply the provisions of the common consular instructions with the same urgency as is accorded to the issue of national visas of this kind and validity.

(b) Except where otherwise provided for in specific bilateral agreements, the representation arrangement shall not apply to visas issued to persons intending to take up paid employment or an activity which is subject to the prior approval of the State where it will take place. Persons applying for such visas must refer to the accredited consular representation of the State where the said activity is to be carried out.

(c) It shall not be obligatory for Schengen States to be represented in every third country for the purpose of issuing visas. Schengen States may decide that visa applications in certain third countries or applications for a certain category of visa have to be submitted to a representation of the State which is the applicant's main travel destination.

(d) Assessment of the risk of illegal immigration when the visa application is lodged shall be entirely at the discretion of the diplomatic or consular representation processing the visa application.

(e) The represented States shall accept responsibility for asylum applications lodged by holders of a visa issued by the representing States on their behalf, whereby such visas shall explicitly state that they were issued in the framework of representation (in accordance with Annex 13 of the common consular instructions) ([1]).

(f) In exceptional cases, bilateral agreements may stipulate that the representing State shall either send the visa applications lodged by certain categories of aliens to the authorities of the represented State which is also the main travel destination, or to a diplomatic mission of this State. These categories should be established in writing (if necessary for each diplomatic or consular representation). The visa shall thus be deemed to have been issued with the authorisation of the represented State, as provided for under Article 30(1)(a) of the Schengen Convention.

(g) Bilateral agreements may be adapted in due course in the light of national assessments of applications for asylum lodged within a fixed period by holders of visas issued in the framework of representation, and other relevant data pertaining to the issue of visas. On the basis of the results, it may be agreed to withdraw representation in the case of certain representations (and possibly, for certain nationalities).

(h) Representation shall apply only to the issue of visas. If the visa cannot be issued because the alien has not been able to provide sufficient documentary evidence that he or she has satisfied the conditions, the alien should be informed of the possibility of submitting his application to a diplomatic representation of the State which is his or her main travel destination.

([1]) Annex 13 of the common consular instructions will be adapted accordingly. See SCH/Com-ex (99) 13.

(i) The representation arrangement can be further improved by extending the consultation network, and by developing software which would enable the representations of the representing State to consult the central authorities of the represented State without difficulty.

(j) Attached to this document is a table on representation for the issue of Schengen visas in third States where not all Schengen States are represented. The Central Group takes note of the amendments made to this table after consultation between the Schengen States concerned ([1]).

The Hague, 27 June 1996

The Chairman

M. PATIJN

([1]) See document SCH/Com-ex (99) 13, Annex 4.

DECISION OF THE EXECUTIVE COMMITTEE of 19 December 1996 on issuing visas at borders to seamen in transit

(SCH/Com-ex (96) 27)

The Executive Committee,

Having regard to Article 132 of the convention implementing the Schengen Agreement,

Having regard to Article 134 of the abovementioned convention,

Having regard to sub-paragraphs (c) and (d) of Article 17(3) of the abovementioned convention,

HAS DECIDED AS FOLLOWS:

The procedure for issuing visas at borders to seamen in transit shall comply with the common principles defined in the documents set out in annex (SCH/II-Visa (96)11 rev 4, SCH/I-Front (96) 58 rev 3, SCH/I-Front (96) 78 rev 2 and SCH/SG (96) 62 rev). These instructions shall apply from 1 February 1997.

Luxembourg, 19 December 1996

The Chairman,

M. FISHBACH

SCH/II-Visa (96) 11 rev 4

Subject: Issuing visas to seamen in transit

Issuing visas to seamen is causing a number of specific problems as it is often the case that the vessel's port of call is not known in advance and the seamen rarely know exactly where they will end their service. Sometimes seamen also have to sign on at a port at very short notice. Given the unpredictable itineraries and the very short periods of notice, seamen subject to visa requirements frequently present themselves at both maritime ports and airports at the external borders of Schengen without actually holding a visa.

Before the Schengen Convention was applied, under such circumstances a transit visa could be issued at the internal borders. These borders may now be crossed without any checks being carried out.

In order, firstly, to guarantee that the Schengen provisions on visas are respected and, secondly, to avoid damaging the interests of the merchant navy, implementing procedures ought to be defined so that seamen who present themselves at borders at the start or the end of their service can enter and/or pass through Schengen territory.

(a) Seamen requiring a visa who are passing through Schengen territory in order to sign on a vessel, leave their service or join another vessel should, in principle, be in possession of a standard Schengen visa.

(b) According to decision SCH/Com-ex (94) 2 rev., a visa may be issued to seamen who present themselves at an external border without an entry visa owing to insufficient time and for compelling grounds, subject to the condition that they do not belong to the category of aliens who cannot be granted a visa without prior consultation pursuant to Annex 5B of the common consular instructions ([1]). The visa issued should be a transit visa valid for a maximum of five days and should mention that the holder is a seaman.

(c) Seamen who belong to the category of aliens who cannot be granted a visa without prior consultation pursuant to Annex 5B of the common consular instructions may (according to Decision SCH/Com-ex (94) 2 rev.) be issued a limited visa for the territory of the visa issuing State.

(d) A check should be carried out at the border to verify that seamen without a Schengen visa meet the conditions for entering Schengen territory.

([1]) Confidential document. See SCH/Com-ex (98) 17.

(e) A system should be set up for exchanging information between the external border authorities in order to be able to assess the factual situation, and in particular to be able to check the information on vessels' journeys, the muster rolls and seamen arriving and leaving.

(f) Checks to verify that the entry conditions are respected are based in particular on the necessary information obtained from this exchange system. If seamen meet these entry conditions, they may be issued a visa at the border.

(g) Before the authorities can issue a visa at the border, an information form on the seaman concerned, the vessel, the ship owner, departure dates, etc. must be produced.

(h) There must be good grounds for integrating the provisions on issuing visas to seamen in transit at the border into the common manual (Annex 14) and into the common consular instructions.

(i) The problem of seamen who are subject to prior consultation under the above stated conditions and who wish to transit through two or more Schengen States will be studied later in the light of experience acquired.

SCH/I-Front (96) 58 rev 3

Subject ([1]): Draft operational instructions for issuing visas at the border to seamen in transit

Operational instructions for issuing visas at the border to seamen in transit who are subject to visa requirements

The sole objective of these operational instructions (which are based on document SCH/II-Visa 11, 3rd rev.) is to provide regulations for the exchange of information between the border control authorities of the various Schengen States with respect to seamen in transit subject to visa requirements. Insofar as a visa is issued at the border on the basis of the information that has been exchanged, the responsibility lies with the Schengen State issuing the visa.

I. Signing on at a ship situated in or expected at a Schengen port:

a) Entry into Schengen territory via an airport situated in another Schengen State

- The shipping company or agency informs the border control authorities in the Schengen port where the ship is berthed or expected that seamen subject to visa requirements are due to enter via a Schengen airport. The shipping company or agency signs a guarantee in respect of these seamen.

- The said border control authorities verify as soon as possible whether the information provided by the shipping company or agency is correct and examine whether the other conditions, referred to in the common manual and which they are able to check, for entry into Schengen territory have been satisfied. Within the framework of this investigation the travel route within Schengen territory is also verified by, for example, checking airline tickets.

- The border control authorities of the Schengen port inform the border control authorities of the Schengen airport of entry by means of a duly completed Schengen form (see Annex I), preferably by fax (see Annex II for faxes and phone numbers of contacts at the most important external border posts) of the results of the

([1]) These instructions do not apply to seamen who may only be issued a visa subject to prior consultation, in accordance with Annex 5 of the common consular instructions.

verification and indicate whether a visa can in principle be issued at the border on the basis of these results.

– Where the verification of the available data is positive and the outcome concurs with the seaman's declaration or documents, the border control authorities of the Schengen airport of entry or exit may issue a Schengen transit visa at the border with a maximum validity of five days. Furthermore, in such cases the seaman's travel document referred to above has to be stamped with a Schengen entry or exit stamp and given to the seaman concerned.

(b) Entry into Schengen via a land or sea border situated in another Schengen State

In this case the same procedure applies with respect to entry via a Schengen airport except that the border control authorities of the border crossing point through which the seamen concerned enter Schengen territory, are informed.

II. Signing-off from a ship that has entered a Schengen port:

(a) Exit from Schengen territory via an airport situated in another Schengen Member State

– The shipping company or agency informs the border control authorities in the said Schengen port of the entry of seamen subject to visa requirements who are signing off and will leave Schengen territory via a Schengen airport. The shipping company or agency signs a guarantee in respect of these seamen.

– The said border control authorities verify as soon as possible the accuracy of the elements communicated by the shipping company or its agent and ascertain whether the other conditions, referred to in the common manual and which they are able to check, for entering Schengen territory have been satisfied. Within the framework of this investigation the travel route within Schengen territory is also verified by, for example, checking airline tickets.

– Where the verification of the data available is positive, the border control authorities may issue a Schengen transit visa with a maximum validity of five days.

(b) Exit Schengen territory via a land or sea border situated in another Schengen State

– In this case the same procedure applies with respect to exit via a Schengen airport.

III. Transferring from a ship that entered a Schengen port to a ship that will sail from a port situated in another Schengen State

— The shipping company or agency informs the border control authorities in the abovementioned Schengen port, of the entry of seamen subject to visa requirements who are due to sign-off and who will leave Schengen territory via another Schengen port. The shipping company or shipping agency signs a guarantee in respect of these seamen.

— The said border control authorities verify as soon as possible the bona fide nature of the shipping company's or agency's report and examine whether the other conditions, referred to in the common manual and which they are able to check, for entry into Schengen territory have been satisfied. The border control authorities of the Schengen port from which the seamen will leave Schengen territory by ship will be contacted for the verification. A check will be carried out to establish whether the ship they have signed on is berthed there or expected. Within the framework of this investigation the travel route within Schengen territory is also verified, for example by checking airline tickets.

— Where the verification of the available information is positive, the border control authorities may issue a Schengen visa with a maximum validity of five days.

Annexes ([1]): 1: Schengen form for seamen in transit

2: List of addresses and phone numbers of contact points at border posts

([1]) Not published.

DECISION OF THE EXECUTIVE COMMITTEE of 15 December 1997 on the harmonisation of visa policy

(SCH/Com-ex (97) 32)

The Executive Committee,

Having regard to Article 132 of the convention implementing the Schengen Agreement, hereinafter 'the Schengen Convention',

Having regard to Article 9 of the abovementioned convention,

Whereas it is in the interest of all Schengen partners to harmonise by mutual agreement their visa policies in the framework of their common policy on the movement of persons in order to avoid any adverse consequences that the absence of harmonisation could cause in the area of entry and internal security;

Wishing to eliminate as quickly as possible the existing differences between the various visa regulations in the States listed in Title III of Annex I to the common consular instructions;

Taking as a base the document entitled 'Essential criteria for including countries on the joint list of countries whose nationals require visas' (SCH/M (92) 32 rev), adopted by the ministers and State secretaries in Madrid on 15 December,

Guided by the principle of solidarity among the Schengen partners;

HAS DECIDED AS FOLLOWS:

1. The Schengen States shall initiate the measures necessary to abolish the visa requirement for nationals of Australia, Brunei, Costa Rica, Croatia, El Salvador, Guatemala, Honduras, Malaysia, Nicaragua, Panama, Paraguay, Singapore and Venezuela in good time for this abolition to take effect on 1 January 1999 at the latest.

2. The States Bosnia-Herzegovina, Jamaica, Malawi and Kenya shall be added to Section I of Annex I to the common consular instructions (joint list of States whose nationals are subject to the visa requirement by all the Schengen States) [1].

3. The visa requirement for nationals of the States mentioned under point 2 above shall take effect on 1 January 1999 at the latest.

[1] See SCH/Com-ex (99) 13.

4. With regard to Bolivia, Colombia and Ecuador, the Schengen States undertake to bring about the solution to be achieved pursuant to Article 100c of the EC Treaty by 1 January 1999 at the latest.

Vienna, 15 December 1997

The Chairman

K. SCHLÖGL

DECISION OF THE EXECUTIVE COMMITTEE of 15 December 1997 on the implementation of the joint action concerning a uniform format for residence permits

(SCH/Com-ex (97) 34 rev)

The Executive Committee,

Having regard to Article 132(2) of the convention implementing the Schengen Agreement, signed in Schengen on 19 June 1990 (hereinafter 'the Schengen Convention'),

Having regard to Article 134 of the abovementioned convention,

Having regard to the decision of the Central Group of 14 May 1997,

Recalling the outcome of the Central Group meeting of 28 October 1997,

HAS DECIDED AS FOLLOWS:

The Schengen States shall endeavour to implement the joint action of 16 December 1996 concerning a uniform format for residence permits (Joint Action 97/11/JAI, published in OJ L 7, 10 January 1997, p. 1) as soon as possible, if necessary by phasing it in, before the end of the transitional periods stipulated in the joint action.

Vienna, 15 December 1997

The Chairman

K. SCHLÖGL

DECISION OF THE EXECUTIVE COMMITTEE of 15 December 1997 on the guiding principles for means of proof and indicative evidence within the framework of readmission agreements between Schengen States

(SCH/Com-ex (97) 39 rev)

The Executive Committee,

Having regard to Article 132 of the convention implementing the Schengen Agreement,

Having regard to Article 23(4) of the abovementioned convention,

HAS DECIDED AS FOLLOWS:

Document SCH/II-Read (97) 3 rev 6 on the guiding principles for means of proof and indicative evidence under readmission agreements between Schengen States, attached hereto, is hereby approved. The application of these principles is recommended as of the date of adoption of this decision.

Vienna, 15 December 1997

The Chairman

K. SCHLÖGL

SCH/II-Read (97) 3 rev 7

SUBJECT:
Guiding principles for means of proof and indicative evidence under readmission agreements between Schengen States

Whereas problems have arisen in practice when applying readmission agreements, notably with the means of proof establishing the illegal residence in or transit through the territory of the requested Contracting Party by foreign nationals:

— the Contracting Parties have adopted the following guiding principles which may be of use to the Contracting Parties when applying future readmission agreements.

1. The following documents *inter alia* may be deemed to provide proof of residence or transit:

— an entry stamp affixed to the travel document by the requested Contracting Party;

— an exit stamp of a State adjacent to a Contracting Party, taking into account the travel route and date of the frontier crossing;

— an entry stamp affixed to a false or falsified travel document by the requested Contracting Party;

— travel tickets issued by name which can formally establish entry;

— fingerprints;

— a valid residence permit;

— a valid visa issued by the requested Contracting Party;

— an embarkation/disembarkation card showing the date of entry into the territory of the requested Contracting Party.

2. A presumption of residence or transit may be established *inter alia* by the following indicative evidence:

— statements by officials;

— statements by third parties;

— statements by the person to be transferred;

— an expired residence permit issued by the requested Contracting Party, whatever the type;

— an expired visa issued by the requested Contracting Party;

— documents issued by name in the territory of the requested Contracting Party;

— travel tickets;

— hotel bills;

— cards for access to public or private amenities in the Contracting Parties;

— appointment cards for doctors, dentists, etc.;

— data showing that the person to be transferred has used the services of a facilitator or travel agency.

3. Insofar as the Schengen partners take into account the means of proof listed under point 1 when concluding future readmission agreements, these shall provide conclusive proof of residence or transit. In principle, no further investigation shall be carried out. Evidence to the contrary shall, however, be admissible (e.g. showing a document to be falsified or forged).

4. Insofar as the Schengen partners take into account the evidence listed under point 2 when concluding future readmission agreements, such evidence shall establish a presumption of residence or transit. It is by nature rebuttable by evidence to the contrary.

DECISION OF THE EXECUTIVE COMMITTEE of 21 April 1998 on the activities of the task force

(SCH/Com-ex (98) 1 rev 2)

The Executive Committee,

Having regard to Article 132 of the convention implementing the Schengen Agreement,

Having regard to Article 6 of the abovementioned convention,

HAS DECIDED AS FOLLOWS:

Given the increase in the number of foreign nationals immigrating into the Schengen States, in particular nationals of Iraq and other States, it is necessary — in the context of recommendations either already made or still under discussion in the European Union — to step up external border checks and take practical steps to underpin the effectiveness of such checks in accordance with a joint plan.

In accordance with the rule of specific powers, it is possible within the bounds of the Schengen remit to focus particular attention on the pull factors underlying this irregular immigration flow without losing sight of the fact that other bodies are to deal with the causes of this phenomenon in the regions of origin and transit.

The Executive Committee proposes that the Schengen States immediately begin to implement the following measures for checks at the external borders, whilst taking into account the recommendations contemplated within the European Union in other areas and whilst stressing the need for appropriate steps also to be taken in implementation of the Dublin Convention:

- the reinforcement of entry checks at the external borders by deploying extra personnel and modern technology;

- securing the areas at airports not accessible to the public with regard to flights from outside the Schengen area and transfer passengers; parallel measures at ports serving international traffic;

- the provision of mutual assistance in the initial and further training both of staff responsible for carrying out checks at airports and ports and of airline personnel, for instance by means of bilateral exchange programmes; greater use and the reciprocal provision of modern technology and an increase in the number of staff deployed;

— the inspection of ferries both during loading and when putting out to sea;

— implementing and fostering the harmonisation of sanctions on and arrangements with carriers transporting illegal immigrants to the Schengen area;

— the performance of pre-boarding checks at high-risk points of departure still to be specified;

— the exchange of information on routes and modus operandi used for smuggling illegal immigrants, stepping up practical cooperation between police authorities and border protection authorities, stepping up cooperation between these authorities and liaison officers from Schengen States working in third countries; the exchange of officials from the Contracting Parties by mutual agreement in order to monitor the effectiveness of measures to prevent illegal immigration;

— in compliance with the relevant national law, the fingerprinting of every foreign national entering the Schengen area illegally whose identity cannot be established with certainty on the basis of valid documents; retention of fingerprints for the purpose of informing the authorities in other Schengen States; the principles of personal data protection law applicable in the European Union are to be observed;

— in compliance with the relevant national law, preventing foreign nationals who have entered the Schengen area illegally and whose identity cannot be established with certainty from absconding, either until such time as their identity has been clearly established or until the measures required by the aliens police have been ordered and implemented;

— the immediate expulsion of foreign nationals who have entered the territory of the Contracting States illegally insofar as they have no right to remain;

— supporting negotiations on a readmission agreement between the Schengen States on the one hand and Turkey, the Czech Republic, the Slovak Republic, Hungary and Slovenia on the other;

— improving practical cooperation between Schengen States in the application of the Dublin Convention.

These measures shall be implemented:

— whilst respecting the national sovereignty of each of the States;

— in accordance with the law of the Contracting States, in other words, if national law so permits;

— without prejudice to the provisions of existing bilateral agreements;

— in accordance with the Schengen implementing convention, and in particular Articles 134 and 142 thereof, in particular regarding the Dublin Convention.

In view of the need to steer the implementation of these measures and build on them, the Presidency is requested to set up a task force composed at least of representatives of the six most affected States. This task force should meet at short intervals and report to the next Executive Committee.

This decision is to be implemented as a complement to the EU action plan. The necessary coordination is to take place at the level of the K4 Committee and the Central Group.

Brussels, 21 April 1998

The Chairman

J. VANDE LANOTTE

DECISION OF THE EXECUTIVE COMMITTEE of 21 April 1998 on cooperation between the Contracting Parties in returning foreign nationals by air

(SCH/Com-ex (98) 10)

The Executive Committee,

Having regard to Article 132 of the convention implementing the Schengen Agreement,

Having regard to Article 23 of the abovementioned convention,

HAS DECIDED AS FOLLOWS:

Document SCH/II-read (97) 5 rev 5 on cooperation between the Contracting Parties in connection with the expulsion of foreign nationals by air, attached hereto, is hereby approved. These principles shall be applied from the date of this decision's adoption.

Brussels, 21 April 1998

The Chairman

J. VANDE LANOTTE

SCH/II-Read (97) 5 rev 5

SUBJECT:
Cooperation between the Contracting Parties in connection with the expulsion of foreign nationals by air

Having regard to the need to give effective shape to the willingness to cooperate that exists between all the Contracting Parties to facilitate the implementation of measures leading to the expulsion of foreign nationals from the Schengen area;

Conscious that the existence of a common area for the free movement of persons must serve as an incentive for cooperation between the bodies responsible for border checks and for applying the legislation on foreign nationals, whenever this proves necessary;

Having regard to the difficulties experienced by the Contracting Parties in the expulsion of foreign nationals transiting the territory of the other Contracting Parties;

Taking into account the recommendation of the Council of the European Union of 30 November 1992 on the adoption of a document on transit for expulsion purposes, the Portuguese Presidency proposes that all the Contracting Parties use a uniform document to request transit (set out in the annex) for the expulsion of foreign nationals.

Request to facilitate transit of foreign nationals for the purposes of their expulsion

The proposed form is to be used on the basis of the following general criteria and aims

- The request to facilitate transit for the purposes of expulsion must be sent to the authority of the State through which the foreign national will transit as quickly as possible but in principle at least two days in advance, except in emergencies, when appropriate justification should be provided.

- The request must contain all the essential information on the persons(s) to be expelled from the Schengen area, i.e. their identity, final destination, travel document used, flight details, as well as the identity of members of the escort and details of the date/time of the flight's arrival at the airport of the requested Contracting Party.

- Under these conditions, all the requested Parties undertake to forward the information relating to the approved transit to the border control officials where the transit is to take place, so that it may be facilitated effectively.

- To this end the procedure to facilitate transit must include, alongside enforcement, other precautionary measures and on each occasion that this proves essential for the satisfactory enforcement part of the expulsion procedure: an escort by a representative of the border authorities from the requested State from the time of arrival, use of the premises of the requested State, and if necessary, contacts with other airport representatives.

— The request may be refused, especially when the declared period of transit exceeds that permitted by the national law of the requested State.

— The Contracting Parties undertake to provide each other with information on the competent authorities and the respective contact persons to whom the requests in question should be sent.

REQUEST TO FACILITATE TRANSIT FOR THE PURPOSES OF EXPULSION BY AIR

____________________ Fax: ____________________

____________________ Tel.: ____________________

Requesting authority

.... Date:

Official

Signature: ....

____________________ Fax: ____________________

____________________ Tel.: ____________________

Requested authority: ____________________

EXPULSION INVOLVING TRANSIT

I.

Name	Forename	Nationality/Date and place of birth	Travel document No/-Type/Expiry date
....	....	....	....
....	....	....	....
....	....	....	....

II.

Escort yes/no Name/s: ....

III.

Route/Date/Transit via/Destination

.... at .... on flight .... Date: ....

.... at .... on flight .... Date: ....

.... at .... on flight .... Date: ....

.... at .... on flight .... Date: ....

Decision of the requested authority ....

Yes/no (Name/Signature/Date)

IV.

Remarks/Observations: ....

DECISION OF THE EXECUTIVE COMMITTEE of 21 April 1998 on the exchange of statistics on issued visas

(SCH/Com-ex (98) 12)

The Executive Committee,

Having regard to Article 9 of the convention implementing the Schengen Agreement,

Having regard to Article 16 of the abovementioned convention,

Whereas the exchange of statistics at local level on visas which have been issued and officially refused will enable the various representations to gain an insight into the overall trends in visa applications from countries within their jurisdiction and any possible shifts in applications from one Schengen partner mission on post to another,

Whereas the above overview will enable local consular cooperation to examine the reasons for any trends observed, in particular relating to visa shopping, to draw practical conclusions and, where appropriate, to make the necessary recommendations to their respective national authorities,

Having regard to the heavy administrative burden on the diplomatic missions and consular posts as a result of having to exchange monthly statistics on short-stay visas which have been issued and officially refused requested in note SCH/II (95) 50 rev 2 from Working Group II to the Central Group,

Whereas on the other hand, given that LTVs should only be issued in exceptional cases, the monthly exchange at local level of statistics on the issue of such visas should continue on a monthly basis,

HAS DECIDED AS FOLLOWS:

1. Statistics on short-stay visas which have been issued and officially refused, transit visas and airport transit visas shall be exchanged every quarter.

2. Without prejudice to the obligations arising from Article 16 of the Schengen Convention and explained in Annex 14 to the common consular instructions, according to which the Schengen States shall communicate any data relating to the issuing of LTVs

within a period of 72 hours, the Schengen diplomatic missions and consular posts are hereby earnestly reminded of their obligation (SCH/Com-ex decl. 4) to exchange on a monthly basis statistics on LTVs issued the previous month and to pass on these statistics to their respective central authorities.

3. Chapter VIII of the common consular instructions shall be completed accordingly [1].

Brussels, 21 April 1998

The Chairman

J. VANDE LANOTTE

(1) See SCH/Com-ex (99) 13.

DECISION OF THE EXECUTIVE COMMITTEE of 23 June 1998 on measures to be taken in respect of countries posing problems with regard to the issue of documents required for expulsion from the Schengen territory

(SCH/Com-ex (98) 18 rev)

The Executive Committee,

Having regard to Article 132 of the convention implementing the Schengen Agreement,

Having regard to Article 23 of the abovementioned convention,

HAS DECIDED AS FOLLOWS:

The measures to be taken vis-à-vis countries posing problems with regard to the issue of documents required for expulsion from the Schengen territory shall be adopted in accordance with the procedure laid down in the document annexed hereto.

Ostend, 23 June 1998

The Chairman

L. TOBBACK

SCH/II-Read (98) 2 rev 2

Subject:
Measures to be taken in respect of countries posing problems with regard to the issue of documents required for expulsion from the Schengen territory

The Belgian Presidency has, on several occasions (the Executive Committee meeting on 15 December 1997 in Vienna, the Central Group meetings on 14 January 1998 in Brugge and on 23 February in Luxembourg), expressed its willingness to find solutions to the problems related to the readmission of illegal foreign nationals.

This specifically concerns difficulties encountered in the area of repatriation, due to a lack of cooperation from foreign consulates in the Schengen capitals in issuing *laissez-passers*. Although initial steps to find solutions are currently being contemplated at national level, a joint Schengen approach to this problem might result in more effective solutions.

One of the approaches favoured by Belgium is as follows: a Schengen State finds that it is experiencing serious difficulties in obtaining a *laissez-passer* to repatriate illegal foreign nationals. The Schengen State informs its ambassador in the country concerned and instructs him/her to draw up the measures to be taken locally together with Schengen colleagues.

The Schengen ambassadors might, in the first instance, make contact with the local authorities to alert them to the problem of readmitting their nationals and to make arrangements for ad hoc solutions. The advantage of taking action at local level is that a country's national authorities are sometimes better placed to negotiate the readmission of their nationals than its consular staff in the Schengen capitals.

The readmission subgroup will be informed of any 'local action' taken. The Central Group will inform the Executive Committee of any action taken and the outcome of this action.

Should such contact not produce results, it would be necessary to use other means — undoubtedly of a more binding nature — to raise awareness of the problem, for instance, policy on issuing visas. These measures will be examined within the Group on Visas.

Each Schengen State shall retain the right to decide whether or not it wants to use any retaliatory measures proposed.

DECISION OF THE EXECUTIVE COMMITTEE of 23 June 1998 on Monegasque residence permits

(SCH/Com-ex (98) 19)

The Executive Committee:

Whereas freedom of movement between France and Monaco was instituted prior to the entry into force of the convention implementing the Schengen Agreement;

Whereas the Contracting Parties to the convention implementing the Schengen Agreement have not called into question these rules on freedom of movement,

Whereas on the basis of the agreement on good neighbourly relations between France and Monaco of 18 May 1963, as revised and supplemented by an exchange of letters between France and Monaco of 15 December 1997, the French authorities apply the rules and checks laid down in the convention implementing the Schengen Agreement when carrying out checks on the entry, stay and establishment of foreign nationals in the Principality of Monaco,

HAS DECIDED AS FOLLOWS:

— Monegasque residence permits shall be included in the French section of Annex IV to the common consular instructions ([1]) set aside for the French authorities;

— Monaco-Héliport and Monaco-Port de la Condamine shall be added to the authorised external border crossing points in Annex 1 to the common manual ([2]);

— Monegasque residence permits shall be included in the section of Annex XI to the common manual set aside for the French authorities;

— that the issue or renewal of a Monegasque residence permit shall not oblige a Contracting Party to withdraw an alert for the purposes of refusal of entry from the SIS.

Ostend, 23 June 1998

The Chairman

L. Tobback

([1]) See SCH/Com-ex (99) 13.

([2]) Confidential document. See SCH/Com-ex (98) 17.

DECISION OF THE EXECUTIVE COMMITTEE of 23 June 1998 on the stamping of passports of visa applicants

(SCH/Com-ex (98) 21)

The Executive Committee,

Having regard to Article 9 of the convention implementing the Schengen Agreement,

Having regard to Article 17 of the abovementioned convention,

Whereas it is in the interest of all the Schengen partners to harmonise, by mutual consent, their procedures for issuing visas as part of their common policy on the free movement of persons in order to prevent the same person from lodging multiple visa applications,

Desiring to strengthen consular cooperation for the purpose of combating illegal immigration and illegal networks,

Based on Chapter VIII of the common consular instructions (CCI) ([1]) on consular cooperation at local level,

Whereas the mutual exchange of information between the Schengen partners on the fact that a visa application has been lodged in one of their States is a means of preventing multiple or consecutive applications,

Whereas the affixing of a stamp to identify visa applications is a means of preventing the same person from lodging multiple or successive visa applications,

Whereas standardisation of the practice whereby a stamp is affixed to all visa applications irrespective of the country in which these are lodged would help to allay any reluctance that differing practices might create,

HAS DECIDED AS FOLLOWS:

1. The stamp shall be affixed to the passports of all visa applicants. The competent mission or post which receives the application shall decide whether or not to affix a stamp to diplomatic and service passports.

2. The stamp shall contain a third space reserved for the code of the type of visa requested.

([1]) See SCH/Com-ex (99) 13.

3. The stamp may also be affixed in the case of applications for long-stay visas.

4. The stamp shall be affixed when a Schengen State is representing another Schengen State. In this case, the third space reserved for designating the code of the type of visa requested shall also contain a note indicating that the State is representing another.

5. In exceptional circumstances when it is impracticable to affix a stamp, the mission or post of the Presidency-in-office shall inform the relevant Schengen group, after carrying out local consular consultation, and shall submit for the group's approval an alternative proposal, for instance involving the exchange of photocopies of passports or lists of rejected visa applications giving grounds for the refusal.

6. As a consequence of point 2, Chapter VIII of the CCI [1] shall be amended as follows:

'The exchange of information between missions and posts and the identification of applications by means of a stamp or by other means are aimed at preventing the same person from lodging multiple or successive visa applications, either whilst an application is being examined, or after an application has been refused, with the same mission or post or by a different mission or post.

Without prejudice to the consultation which may take place between the missions and posts and the exchange of information which they may carry out, the mission or post with which an application is lodged shall affix to the passports of all visa applicants a stamp stipulating 'Visa applied for on ... at ...'. The space following 'on' shall be filled in with six figures (two for the day, two for the month and two for the year); the second space shall be reserved for the diplomatic mission or consular post concerned; the third space shall be filled in with the code of the type of visa requested.

The competent mission or post which receives the application shall decide whether or not to affix a stamp to diplomatic and service passports.

The stamp may also be affixed in the case of applications for long-stay visas.

When a Schengen State is representing another Schengen State, the third space on the stamp shall show, after the code of the type of visa requested, the indication 'R' followed by the code of the represented State.

Where the visa is issued, the sticker shall, as far as possible, be affixed on top of the identification stamp.

[1] See SCH/Com-ex (99) 13.

In exceptional circumstances when it is impracticable to affix a stamp, the mission or post of the Presidency in office shall inform the relevant Schengen group and submit for the group's approval an alternative proposal, for instance involving the exchange of photocopies of passports or lists of rejected visa applications giving grounds for the refusal.

The heads of the diplomatic missions or consular posts may, on the initiative of the Presidency, adopt at local level additional preventative measures, if such measures prove necessary.'

Ostend, 23 June 1998

The Chairman

L. Tobback

DECISION OF THE EXECUTIVE COMMITTEE of 27 October 1998 on the adoption of measures to fight illegal immigration

(SCH/Com-ex (98) 37 def 2)

The Executive Committee,

Having regard to Article 132 of the convention implementing the Schengen Agreement,

Having regard to Article 6 of the abovementioned convention,

— emphasising the necessity to respect human rights and underlining each Contracting State's obligations arising from the European Convention for the Protection of Human Rights and Fundamental Freedoms and its protocols, the Geneva Convention on the Legal Status of Refugees and the New York Protocol, the Convention against Torture and other Cruel, Inhuman or Degrading Treatment or Punishment, the Convention on the Elimination of all forms of Discrimination against Women and the Convention on the Rights of the Child;

— taking into account the measures taken by and within the EU to fight illegal immigration and recognising the need for an integrated approach;

— recognising that a policy to combat illegal immigration must lay down appropriate provisions for the examination of asylum applications in compliance with public international law;

HAS DECIDED AS FOLLOWS:

The Schengen States are at present particularly affected by substantial waves of immigration.

The Schengen States find it necessary to take the following measures to fight against this immigration:

— drafting and constant updating of a situation report and formulation of proposals for the adaptation of measures by the task force;

— close cooperation with the competent agencies of the countries of origin and transit countries in accordance with national law in the Schengen States, especially with regard to the provision of advice and support by liaison officers of the Schengen States;

— provision of assistance by liaison officers from the Schengen States to the countries of origin and the transit countries, subject to the conditions laid down in No 2, in the form of advice on preventing illegal migration, in accordance with the applicable domestic law, so as to fight against illegal immigration into a Schengen State;

— regular reciprocal briefing of all the Schengen States on the results of expert missions to the countries of origin and transit, especially those applying for EU membership, a factor to be taken into account in connection with support measures;

— implementation of intensive controls at authorised border crossing points at the external borders in accordance with Schengen standards, with special emphasis placed on border sectors affected by immigration;

— fullest possible surveillance of land and sea borders outside authorised border crossing points and in the area behind the border, particularly the border sectors affected by illegal immigration, via the deployment of mobile units;

— checking of non-public areas in ports serving international maritime traffic;

— controls on ferries during loading and embarkation;

— intensification of police measures at national level in accordance with domestic law, particularly on the main transport routes, if possible in concert and in close cooperation with the Schengen partners;

— in compliance with the relevant national law, the fingerprinting of every alien illegal immigrant whose identity cannot be established with certainty; retention of fingerprints for the purpose of informing the authorities in other Schengen States; the principles of data protection law applicable in the framework of Schengen cooperation and in the European Union are to be observed;

— in compliance with the relevant national law, preventing foreign nationals who have entered the Schengen territory illegally and whose identity cannot be established with certainty from absconding, either until such time as their identity has been clearly established or until the measures required by the aliens police have been ordered and implemented;

— immediate and systematic return of third-country nationals who have entered the Schengen States without authorisation provided no right to stay exists and there are no obstacles based on compelling humanitarian grounds or international law;

— imposition of sanctions against carriers which transport passengers without the required entry and transit documents to Schengen States;

— exchange of information — in cooperation with Europol, to the extent that this is permissible in the case of personal data and subject to the agreement of the bodies laid down in the Europol Convention — between the Schengen States' designated central contact points about the situation as it develops, the measures taken and persons apprehended, focusing particularly on organisations involved in smuggling persons and the routes used, and faster transmission of this information to the relevant services;

— coordination of the fight against criminal networks involved in smuggling via information exchange — in cooperation with Europol, to the extent that this is permissible in the case of personal data and subject to the agreement of the bodies laid down in the Europol Convention — between the services responsible for conducting investigations, in accordance with the provisions of the Schengen Convention and subject to national law, together with the coordination of operational measures;

— application *mutatis mutandis* of the relevant measures contained in the EU action plan for preventing the influx of migrants from Iraq and the neighbouring region of 26 January 1998 (EU doc. 5573/98).

DECISION OF THE CENTRAL GROUP of 27 October 1998 on the adoption of measures to fight illegal immigration

(SCH/C (98) 117)

The Central Group,

Having regard to Article 132 of the convention implementing the Schengen Agreement in conjunction with the Executive Committee decision of 16 September 1998,

HAS DECIDED AS FOLLOWS:

The revised and finalised version of the action plan annexed hereto concerning measures to combat illegal immigration (SCH/Com-ex (98) 37 def) shall be brought into force pursuant to the mandate from the Executive Committee of 16 September 1998.

Brussels, 27 October 1998

The Chairman

B. Schattenberg

DECISION OF THE EXECUTIVE COMMITTEE of 16 December 1998 on the abolition of the grey list of States whose nationals are subject to the visa requirement by certain Schengen States

(SCH/Com-ex (98) 53 rev 2)

The Executive Committee,

Having regard to Article 132 of the convention implementing the Schengen Agreement,

Having regard to Article 9 of the abovementioned convention;

Whereas it is in the interest of all the Schengen States to continue harmonising their visa-issue policy in the context of their common policy on the movement of persons, with a view to preventing possible negative consequences as regards immigration and internal security,

Wishing to abolish, as quickly as possible, the differences which currently exist between the visa rules applied by the Schengen States as regards States mentioned in Section III of the Annex I to the common consular instructions ([1]), namely Bolivia and Ecuador,

Having regard to the document entitled 'Basic criteria for inclusion in the Schengen joint list of States subject to the visa requirement' (SCH/M (92) 32 rev) adopted by the ministers and State secretaries in Madrid on 15 December 1992 and the decision of the Executive Committee adopted in Vienna on 15 December 1997 (SCH/Com-ex (98) 32),

Acknowledging that the measures laid down under points 1 and 2 of the decision of the Executive Committee of 15 December 1997 (SCH/Com-ex (97) 32) have been introduced,

HAS DECIDED AS FOLLOWS:

1. Bolivia and Ecuador shall be included in the schedule of States whose nationals are exempted from the visa requirement by all Schengen States.

2. The Schengen States shall introduce the measures necessary for abolishing the visa requirement for Estonia, Latvia and Lithuania by 1 March 1999 at the latest.

3. The Schengen States shall request the Baltic States to accede to the UN convention of 28 September 1954 relating to the status of stateless persons so that all residents of the Baltic States are able to enjoy visa-free travel in the future to the Schengen States.

([1]) See SCH/Com-ex (99) 13.

This decision shall enter into force when the Schengen States have given notification that the measures have been implemented.

Berlin, 16 December 1998

The Chairman,

C. H. SCHAPPER

DECISION OF THE EXECUTIVE COMMITTEE of 16 December 1998 concerning the compilation of a manual of documents to which a visa may be affixed

(SCH/Com-ex (98) 56)

In accordance with Article 17(3)(a) of the convention implementing the Schengen Agreement, the Executive Committee has drawn up in Annex 11 of the common consular instructions ([1]) criteria for documents to which a visa may be affixed.

Pursuant thereto, the subgroup on visas has completed the task of collecting and examining all travel documents in use throughout the world, an activity that has spanned several presidencies. The edited collection of travel documents to which a visa may be affixed makes it possible to give effect to the procedure required under the Schengen Convention whereby a visa valid for all user States may only be issued if the travel document that is to bear the visa is recognised as a valid entry document by all user States.

Starting with Part I, which is now complete, a manual of documents to which a visa may be affixed will be drawn up containing the following sections:

Part I Travel documents to which a visa may be affixed

Part II Aliens' passports issued by the Schengen States to which a visa may be affixed

Part III A list of the travel documents issued by international organisations

Part IV Gradual compilation of a documentary record containing copies of originals

Part V Information on known fictitious passports

Individual sections of the manual will be issued to diplomatic missions and consular posts when they are complete. Completed sections may therefore be issued, without the need for subsequent sections to be finished.

The Executive Committee takes note of the fact that Part I, entitled 'Travel documents to which a visa may be affixed', has been forwarded to the diplomatic missions and consular posts for use (see annex — Doc. SCH/II-Visa (96) 59 rev 6) and requests that a report be

([1]) See SCH/Com-ex (99) 13.

sent to it on the effectiveness of this measure before June 1999. The diplomatic missions and consular posts are requested to assess the usefulness of this document and report their findings in March 1999.

The manual can be prepared by the General Secretariat on the basis of relevant notes submitted by the delegations.

Berlin, 16 December 1998

The Chairman,

C. H. SCHAPPER

TABLE OF TRAVEL DOCUMENTS ENTITLING THE HOLDER TO CROSS THE EXTERNAL BORDERS AND TO WHICH A VISA MAY BE AFFIXED

GENERAL COMMENTS

Collective passports

Portugal and Spain only recognise collective passports issued in accordance with the European agreement on travel by young persons on collective passports between the member countries of the Council of Europe of 16 December 1961 (up to a maximum of 25 persons as far as Portugal is concerned). However, Portugal does consent to its partners affixing the uniform visa. Spain also accepts other collective passports on a case-by-case basis according to the rule of reciprocity. The visa is affixed on a loose-leaf.

Travel documents for Stateless persons

Austria, Portugal and Iceland are not parties to the Convention on the Status of Stateless Persons, done at New York on 28 September 1954. Austria and Portugal nevertheless consent to their partners affixing the uniform visa to documents issued by the States signatory to the convention. Iceland will make its position known later.

Laissez-passer

A laissez-passer is, in general, only recognised for transit for the purpose of returning to the State of issue.

The following provisions apply as far as Germany is concerned

The official identity documents listed in points 1 to 9 and issued by one of the States which Germany recognises internationally but which have not yet been officially recognised, are accepted as passports or passport replacement documents even if they are not known, subject to certain conditions and in accordance with the law. They may therefore be endorsed with a visa as long as their non-recognition has not been officially pronounced. For the other Schengen States, documents may not be endorsed with a visa if they do not contain the following indications and features: name and surname, date of birth, nationality (apart from refugees' and Stateless persons' passports), photograph, holder's signature and authorisation of return if the document is issued to people other than nationals: these documents are marked with a cross and an asterisk (X*).

The following provisions apply as far as Austria is concerned

If a travel document is not expressly marked 'not recognised' in the following list, it may be endorsed with a visa for Austria — even if it is marked with a 'X' — if:

— it was issued by a duly empowered subject under international law;

— it clearly indicates the identity of the holder;

— it is valid in terms of time;

— it is applicable to the Republic of Austria;

— the right of return to the State which issued the document is guaranteed.

Codes

1 Ordinary passport

2 Diplomatic passport

3 Service passport

4 Special passport

5 Collective passport

6 Children's identity document

7 Seaman's book

8 Refugee's travel document (Geneva Convention of 28 July 1951)

9 Stateless person's travel document (New York Convention of 28 September 1954)

10 Alien's travel document

11 Other travel documents

[X] The document entitles the holder to cross the external borders and may be endorsed with a visa.

[O] The document is not recognised by this contracting party.

[ ] 'The document does not exist' or 'one or the Contracting State(s) has (have) not provided the relevant information'. The document is dealt with as non-recognised document **O**. If the travel document fulfils the conditions fixed by Austria, a visa for Austria may be affixed.

(X) It is not certain whether or not the document is issued.

Country codes

European Union:

Code	Country
A	Austria
B	Belgium
DK	Denmark
FIN	Finland
F	France
D	Germany
EL	Greece
IRL	Ireland
I	Italy
L	Luxembourg
NL	Netherlands
P	Portugal
E	Spain
S	Sweden
UK	United Kingdom

Non-EU countries:

Code	Country
AF	Afghanistan
AL	Albania
DZ	Algeria
AD	Andorra
AO	Angola
AG	Antigua and Barbuda
AR	Argentina
AM	Armenia
AU	Australia
AZ	Azerbaijan
BH	Bahrain
BD	Bangladesh
BB	Barbados
BY	Belarus
BZ	Belize
BJ	Benin
BT	Bhutan
BO	Bolivia
BA	Bosnia and Herzegovina
BW	Botswana
BR	Brazil
BN	Brunei
BG	Bulgaria
BF	Burkina Faso
BI	Burundi
KH	Cambodia
CM	Cameroon
CA	Canada
CV	Cape Verde
CF	Central African Republic
TD	Chad
CL	Chile

CN China
CO Colombia
CG Congo
CR Costa Rica
CI Côte d'Ivoire
HR Croatia
CU Cuba
CY Cyprus
CZ Czech Republic
CD Democratic Republic of the Congo
DJ Djibouti
DM Dominica
DO Dominican Republic
EC Ecuador
EG Egypt
SV El Salvador
GQ Equatorial Guinea
ER Eritrea
EE Estonia
ET Ethiopia
FJ Fiji
MK[1] Former Yugoslav Republic of Macedonia
GA Gabon
GE Georgia
GH Ghana
GD Grenada
GT Guatemala
GN Guinea
GW Guinea-Bissau
GY Guyana
HT Haiti
HN Honduras
HU Hungary
IS Iceland
IN India
ID Indonesia
IR Iran
IQ Iraq
IL Israel
JM Jamaica
JP Japan

(1) Provisional code which does not prejudge in any way the definitive nomenclature for this country, which will be agreed following the conclusion of negotiations currently taking place on this subject at the United Nations.

JO Jordan
KZ Kazakhstan
KE Kenya
KI Kiribati
KW Kuwait
KG Kyrgyzstan
LA Laos
LV Latvia
LB Lebanon
LS Lesotho
LR Liberia
LY Libya
LI Liechtenstein
LT Lithuania
MG Madagascar
MW Malawi
MY Malaysia
MV Maldives
ML Mali
MT Malta
MH Marshall Islands
MR Mauritania
MU Mauritius
MX Mexico
FM Micronesia
MD Moldova
MC Monaco
MN Mongolia
MA Morocco
MZ Mozambique
MM Myanmar
NA Namibia
NR Nauru
NP Nepal
NZ New Zealand
NI Nicaragua
NE Niger
NG Nigeria
KP North Korea
NO Norway
OM Oman
PK Pakistan
PW Palau
PS Palestinian Authority
PA Panama
PG Papua New Guinea

PY Paraguay
PE Peru
PH Philippines
PL Poland
QA Qatar
RO Romania
RU Russia
RW Rwanda
KN Saint Kitts and Nevis
LC Saint Lucia
VC Saint Vincent and the Grenadines
SM San Marino
ST São Tomé and Príncipe
SA Saudi Arabia
SN Senegal
SC Seychelles
SL Sierra Leone
SG Singapore
SK Slovakia
SI Slovenia
SB Solomon Islands
SO Somalia
ZA South Africa
KR South Korea
LK Sri Lanka
SD Sudan
SR Suriname
SZ Swaziland
CH Switzerland
SY Syria
TW Taiwan
TJ Tajikistan
TZ Tanzania
TH Thailand
BS The Bahamas
KM The Comoros
GM The Gambia
TG Togo
TO Tonga
TT Trinidad and Tobago
TN Tunisia
TR Turkey
TM Turkmenistan
TV Tuvalu
UG Uganda
UA Ukraine
AE United Arab Emirates
US United States
UY Uruguay
UZ Uzbekistan
VU Vanuatu
VA Vatican City
VE Venezuela
VN Vietnam
WS Western Samoa
YE Yemen
YU Yugoslavia
ZM Zambia
ZW Zimbabwe

AD — Andorra

	A	B/NL/L	D	DK	E	EL	F	FIN	I	IS	NO	P	S
1	X	X	X	X	X	X	X	X	X	X	X	X	X
2	X	X		X	X	X	X	X		X	X	X	
3													
4													
5													
6													
7													
8													
9													
10													
11 — *identity document for Andorrans*	X	X			X	X	X		X			X	

AE — United Arab Emirates

	A	B/NL/L	D	DK	E	EL	F	FIN	I	IS	NO	P	S
1	X	X	X	X	X	X	X	X	X	X	X	X	X
2	X	X	X	X	X	X	X	X	X	X	X	X	X
3	X	X	X	X	X	X	X	X	X	X	X	X	X
4			X				X						X
5													
6													
7		X				X	O	X					
8													
9													
10													
11 — *temporary passport* — *travel document (brown cover)*							O						

AF — Afghanistan

	A	B/NL/L	D	DK	E	EL	F	FIN	I	IS	NO	P	S
1	X	X	X	X	X	X	X	X	X	X	X	X	X
2	X		X	X	X	X	X	X	X	X	X	X	X
3	X		X		X	X	X	X	X	X	X	X	X
4													
5													
6													
7													
8													
9													
10													
11 — *business passport*	X		X				X ([1])		X				

([1]) Treated as an ordinary passport.

AG — Antigua and Barbuda

	A	B/NL/L	D	DK	E	EL	F	FIN	I	IS	NO	P	S
1	X	X	X	X	X	X	X	X	X	X	X	X	X
2	X	X	X	X	X	X	X	X	X	X	X	X	X
3	X	X			X			X	X	X	X	X	
4													
5													
6													
7		X			X	X	X	X	X			X	
8	X	X	X*	X	X	X	X	X	X	X	X	X	X
9	X	X		X	X	X	X	X	X		X		X
10													
11													

AL — Albania

	A	B/NL/L	D	DK	E	EL	F	FIN	I	IS	NO	P	S
1	X	X	X	X	X	X	X	X	X	X	X	X	X
2	X	X	X	X	X	X	X	X	X	X	X	X	X
3	X	X	X	X	X	X	X	X	X	X	X	X	X
4													
5													
6 (1)			O				O						
7			X										
8	X	X	X*	X	X	X	X	X	X	X	X	X	X
9													
10													
11 — *laissez-passer*		O			O	X	O						

(1) Laissez-passer (loose-leaf card).

AM — Armenia

	A	B/NL/L	D	DK	E	EL	F	FIN	I	IS	NO	P	S
1	X	X	X	X	X	X	X	X	X	X	X	X	X
2	X	X	X	X	X	X	X	X	X	X	X	X	X
3	X	X	X*	X	X	X	X	X	X	X	X	X	
4													
5													
6			O										
7													
8	X	X	X	X	X	X	X	X	X	X	X	X	X
9	X	X		X	X	X	X	X	X		X		X
10													
11 — *certificate of repatriation to the Republic of Armenia*							X (1)						

(1) Recognised for exit or transit for return to Armenia.

AO — Angola

	A	B/ NL/ L	D	DK	E	EL	F	FIN	I	IS	NO	P	S
1	X	X	X	X	X	X	X	X	X	X	X	X	X
2	X	X	X	X	X	X	X	X	X	X	X	X	X
3	X	X	X	X	X	X	X	X	X	X	X	X	X
4													
5													
6													
7		X			X	X	X	X	X			X	X
8	X	X	X*	X	X	X	X	X	X	X	X	X	X
9													
10													
11 — salvo conduto *issued by diplomatic missions* — salvo conduto *issued by the Emigration and Borders Department*			X (1)				X (2) **O**					X (2)	

(1) Only for the purpose of transit if the route crosses the territory of the Federal Republic of Germany and the FRG is not explicitly excluded from the territorial scope of the document.
(2) Recognised for exit or transit to return to Angola.

AR — Argentina

	A	B/ NL/ L	D	DK	E	EL	F	FIN	I	IS	NO	P	S
1	X	X	X	X	X	X	X	X	X	X	X	X	X
2	X	X	X*	X	X	X	X	X	X	X	X	X	X
3	X	X	X	X	X	X	X	X	X	X	X	X	X
4													
5													
6													
7		X				X	X	X					X
8	X	X	X*	X	X	X	X	X	X	X	X	X	X
9	X	X		X	X	X	X	X	X		X		X
10 (1)							O						
11 — certificado de viaje — *consular passport category C* — pasaporte provisorio *category A (valid 60 days)*							 O X (2) X (3)						

(1) *Pasaporte especial para extranjeros.*
(2) Treated like an ordinary passport.
(3) Recognised for exit or transit to return to Argentina.

AU — Australia

	A	B/ NL/ L	D	DK	E	EL	F	FIN	I	IS	NO	P	S
1	X	X	X	X	X	X	X	X	X	X	X	X	X
2	X	X	X	X	X	X	X	X	X	X	X	X	X
3	X	X	X	X	X	X	X	X	X	X	X	X	X
4													
5													
6													
7								X					
8 (1)	X	X	X*	X	X	X	X	X	X	X	X	X	X
9	X	X		X	X	X	X	X	X		X		X
10													
11 — *document of identity* — *certificate of identity* — *emergency travel document (separate sheet)*	 X (2) X (2)	 X (2)	 X (2) X (2)		 O O	 O O	 O O O		 O O			 X (2) X (2)	

(1) Document not issued on 7.5.1998.
(2) Only recognised if the document contains an authorisation of return.

AZ — Azerbaijan

	A	B/ NL/ L	D	DK	E	EL	F	FIN	I	IS	NO	P	S
1	X	X	X	X	X	X	X	X	X	X	X	X	X
2	X	X	X	X	X	X	X	X	X	X	X	X	X
3	X	X	X	X	X	X	X	X	X	X	X	X	X
4													
5													
6													
7					X			X				X	
8	X	X	X	X	X	X	X	X	X	X	X	X	X
9					X		X	X	X				
10													
11													

BA — Bosnia and Herzegovina

	A	B/ NL/ L	D	DK	E	EL	F	FIN	I	IS	NO	P	S
1	X	X	X	X	X	X	X	X	X	X	X	X	X
2	X	X	X	X	X	X	X	X	X	X	X	X	X
3	X	X	X	X	X	X	X	X	X	X	X	X	X
4													
5							O					O	
6													
7													
8	X	X	X*	X	X	X	X	X	X	X	X	X	X
9	X	X	X*	X	X	X	X	X	X		X		X
10													
11													

BB — Barbados

	A	B/NL/L	D	DK	E	EL	F	FIN	I	IS	NO	P	S
1	X	X	X	X	X	X	X	X	X	X	X	X	X
2	X	X	X*	X	X	X	X	X	X	X	X	X	X
3	X	X	X*	X	X	X	X	X	X	X	X	X	X
4													
5													
6													
7		X			X	X	X	X	X			X	
8													
9 (1)	X	X		X	X	X	X	X	X		X		X
10													
11													
— *certificate of identity*					O		O						
— *emergency passport (valid for a single journey only)*					O		O		O				

(1) Document not issued on 7.5.1998.

BD — Bangladesh

	A	B/NL/L	D	DK	E	EL	F	FIN	I	IS	NO	P	S
1	X	X	X	X	X	X	X	X	X	X	X	X	X
2	X	X	X	X	X	X	X	X	X	X	X	X	X
3	X	X	X*	X	X	X	X	X	X	X	X	X	X
4													
5													
6													
7		X				X	O	X					
8													
9													
10													
11													

BF — Burkina Faso

	A	B/NL/L	D	DK	E	EL	F	FIN	I	IS	NO	P	S
1	X	X	X	X	X	X	X	X	X	X	X	X	X
2	X	X	X	X	X	X	X	X	X	X	X	X	X
3	X	X	X	X	X	X	X	X	X	X	X	X	X
4													
5													
6													
7													
8	X	X	X*	X	X	X	X	X	X	X	X	X	X
9													
10			O										
11 — *pilgrim's passport* — *laissez-passer (loose-leaf)* — *safe conduct (for aliens)*					O		O O O					O	

BG — Bulgaria

	A	B/NL/L	D	DK	E	EL	F	FIN	I	IS	NO	P	S
1	X	X	X	X	X	X	X	X	X	X	X	X	X
2	X	X	X	X	X	X	X	X	X	X	X	X	X
3	X	X	X	X	X	X	X	X	X	X	X	X	X
4													
5	X		O				O						
6													
7	X	X	X		X	X	X	X	X			X	
8	X	X	X*	X	X	X	X	X	X	X	X	X	X
9													
10 (1)			X (2)										
11 — *Bulgarian boatman's card for the Danube* — *travel document for return to Bulgaria* (feuille de route)	X X		X				O X (3)					O X (3)	

(1) Travel document issued to individuals without persons in their charge (blue cover).
(2) If the requisite return visa is contained in English, French or German in the passport replacement document.
(3) Recognised for exit or transit for return to Bulgaria.

BH — Bahrain

	A	B/ NL/ L	D	DK	E	EL	F	FIN	I	IS	NO	P	S
1	X	X	X	X	X	X	X	X	X	X	X	X	X
2	X	X	X	X	X	X	X	X	X	X	X	X	
3													
4	X	X		X	X	X	X	X	X	X	X	X	
5													
6													
7													
8													
9													
10													
11 — *laissez-passer*			X ([1])										

([1]) If the passport replacement document is valid for the Federal Republic of Germany and contains the required authorisation of return.

BI — Burundi

	A	B/ NL/ L	D	DK	E	EL	F	FIN	I	IS	NO	P	S
1	X	X	X	X	X	X	X	X	X	X	X	X	X
2	X	X	X	X	X	X	X	X	X	X	X	X	X
3	X	X	X	X	X	X	X	X	X	X	X	X	X
4													
5													
6													
7													
8	X	X	X	X	X	X	X	X	X	X	X	X	X
9													
10													
11													

BJ — Benin

	A	B/ NL/ L	D	DK	E	EL	F	FIN	I	IS	NO	P	S
1	X	X	X	X	X	X	X	X	X	X	X	X	X
2	X	X	X	X	X	X	X	X	X	X	X	X	X
3	X	X	X	X	X	X	X	X	X	X	X	X	X
4													
5													
6													
7							X	X					
8	X	X	X*	X	X	X	X	X	X	X	X	X	X
9													
10													
11													

BN —Brunei

	A	B/ NL/ L	D	DK	E	EL	F	FIN	I	IS	NO	P	S
1	X	X	X	X	X	X	X	X	X	X	X	X	X
2	X	X	X	X	X	X	X	X	X	X	X	X	X
3	X	X		X		X		X	X	X	X	X	
4													
5													
6													
7													
8													
9													
10													
11 — *international certificate of identity (issued to Stateless persons)* — *emergency certificate*		 O	 X ([1]) O				 O						

([1]) Recognised for a stay of a maximum of three months if the requisite re-entry visa is already contained in the passport replacement document on exit.

BO — Bolivia

	A	B/NL/L	D	DK	E	EL	F	FIN	I	IS	NO	P	S
1	X	X	X	X	X	X	X	X	X	X	X	X	X
2	X	X	X	X	X	X	X	X	X	X	X	X	X
3	X	X	X	X	X	X	X	X	X	X	X	X	X
4						X							
5													
6													
7													
8	X	X	X*	X	X	X	X	X	X	X	X	X	X
9	X	X		X	X	X	X	X	X		X		X
10													
11													

BR — Brazil

	A	B/NL/L	D	DK	E	EL	F	FIN	I	IS	NO	P	S
1	X	X	X	X	X	X	X	X	X	X	X	X	X
2	X	X	X	X	X	X	X	X	X	X	X	X	X
3	X	X	X	X	X	X	X	X	X	X	X	X	X
4													
5													
6													
7		X			X	X	X	X	X			X	
8	X	X	X*	X	X	X	X	X	X	X	X	X	X
9	X	X	X*	X	X	X	X	X	X		X		X
10 (1)	X		X				O		O			X (2)	
11													
— *nationality certificate*									O			X (3)	
— *safe conduct*									O				
— autorização de retorno ao Brazil							X (3)					X (4)	
— *laissez-passer (double loose-leaf)*							O						

(1) *Pasaporte para estrangeiros* (yellow cover) and laissez-passer for aliens (brown cover).
(2) Recognised if the document contains a return permit.
(3) Recognised for exit or transit for return to Brazil.
(4) Recognised for exit from Portugal.

BS — The Bahamas

	A	B/ NL/ L	D	DK	E	EL	F	FIN	I	IS	NO	P	S
1	X	X	X	X	X	X	X	X	X	X	X	X	X
2	X	X	X	X	X	X	X	X	X	X	X	X	X
3	X	X	X*	X	X	X	X	X	X	X	X	X	X
4													
5													
6													
7							X	X					
8	X	X	X*	X	X	X	X	X	X	X	X	X	X
9													
10													
11 — *certificate of identity*			O		O		O						

BT — Bhutan

	A	B/ NL/ L	D	DK	E	EL	F	FIN	I	IS	NO	P	S
1	X	X	X*		X	X	X	X	X		X	X	
2	X	X	X*		X	X	X	X	X		X	X	
3	X	X			X		X	X	X		X	X	
4													
5													
6													
7													
8													
9													
10													
11													

BW — Botswana

	A	B/NL/L	D	DK	E	EL	F	FIN	I	IS	NO	P	S
1	X	X	X	X	X	X	X	X	X	X	X	X	X
2	X	X	X	X	X	X	X	X	X	X	X	X	X
3	X	X	X	X	X	X	X	X	X	X	X	X	X
4													
5													
6													
7													
8	X	X	X*	X	X	X	X	X	X	X	X	X	X
9	X	X		X	X	X	X	X	X		X		X
10													
11													

BY — Belarus

	A	B/NL/L	D	DK	E	EL	F	FIN	I	IS	NO	P	S
1	X	X	X	X	X	X	X	X	X	X	X	X	X
2	X	X	X	X	X	X	X	X	X	X	X	X	X
3	X	X	X	X	X	X	X	X	X	X	X	X	X
4													
5													
6													
7						X	O	X				X	X
8													
9													
10													
11 — *certificate of returning to the Republic of Belarus*							X (1)						

(1) Recognised for exit or transit for return to Belarus.

BZ — Belize

	A	B/ NL/ L	D	DK	E	EL	F	FIN	I	IS	NO	P	S
1	X	X	X	X	X	X	X	X	X	X	X	X	X
2	X	X	X	X	X	X	X	X	X	X	X	X	
3	X	X	X	X	X		X	X	X	X	X	X	
4													
5													
6													
7		X			X		X	X	X			X	
8	X	X	X*	X	X	X	X	X	X	X	X	X	X
9													
10													
11 — *passport office (on double loose-leaf)* — *temporary passport (on double loose-leaf)*							O O						

CA — Canada

	A	B/ NL/ L	D	DK	E	EL	F	FIN	I	IS	NO	P	S
1	X	X	X	X	X	X	X	X	X	X	X	X	X
2	X	X	X	X	X	X	X	X	X	X	X	X	X
3													X
4	X	X*	X	X	X	X	X	X	X	X	X	X	
5													
6													
7		X			X	X	X	X	X			X	
8	X	X	X*	X	X	X	X	X	X	X	X	X	X
9													
10													
11 — *certificate of identity* — *emergency passport for a single journey only*		O	O		O		O X ([1])		O				

([1]) Recognised for exit and transit for return to Canada.

CD — Democratic Republic of the Congo

	A	B/NL/L	D	DK	E	EL	F	FIN	I	IS	NO	P	S
1 (1)	X	X	X	X	X	X	X	X	X	X	X	X	
2 (2)	X	X	X	X	X	X	X	X	X	X	X	X	X
3 (3)	X	X	X	X	X	X	X	X	X	X	X	X	
4													
5													
6													
7						X		X	O			X	
8	X	X		X	X	X	X (3)	X	X	X	X	X	X
9													
10													
11													

(1) Only ordinary passports issued by the Ministry of Foreign Affairs may be endorsed.
(2) Bearing the indication 'République Démocratique du Congo'.
(3) This document was not issued on 7.5.1998.

CF — Central African Republic

	A	B/NL/L	D	DK	E	EL	F	FIN	I	IS	NO	P	S
1	X	X	X	X	X	X	X	X	X	X	X	X	X
2	X	X	X	X	X	X	X	X	X	X	X	X	X
3	X	X	X	X	X	X	X	X	X	X	X	X	X
4													
5													
6													
7													
8	X	X	X*	X	X	X	X	X	X	X	X	X	X
9													
10													
11													
— *six-month special passport*					O							O	
— *safe-conduct replacing the provisional passport*		O					O						
— *service passport (in loose-leaf form)*							O						
— *non-consular laissez-passer*							O						

CG — Congo

	A	B/NL/L	D	DK	E	EL	F	FIN	I	IS	NO	P	S
1 (1)	X	X	X	X	X	X	X	X	X	X	X	X	
2	X	X	X	X	X	X	X	X	X	X	X	X	
3	X	X	X	X	X	X	X	X	X	X	X	X	
4													
5													
6 (2)	X (3)	X (3)	X				O		X (3)				
7		X	O		X	X	X	X					
8	X	X	X*	X	X	X	X (4)	X	X	X	X	X	X
9													
10													
11 — *safe conduct* — *certificate of identity and travel valid as a provisional passport* — *laissez-passer replacing a diplomatic passport*							 O O O						

(1) Does not cover passports (red cover) issued between 5.6.1997 and 1.12.1998 not recognised by the Congolese authorities. The new passports introduced since 1.12.1998 have a brown cover.
(2) Certificate of identity for travel for children aged under three.
(3) Only valid if the holders are accompanied by their parents.
(4) This document was not issued on 7.5.1998.

CH — Switzerland

	A	B/ NL/ L	D	DK	E	EL	F	FIN	I	IS	NO	P	S
1	X	X	X	X	X	X	X	X	X	X	X	X	X
2	X	X	X	X	X	X	X	X	X	X	X	X	X
3	X	X	X	X	X	X	X	X	X	X	X	X	X
4	X	X	X		X	X	X		X			X	
5	X	X (1)			X		X (1)		X			X	
6	X	X					X		X				
7	X	X				X	X		X				
8	X	X	X	X	X	X	X	X	X	X	X	X	X
9	X	X		X	X	X	X	X	X		X		X
10 (2)			X				O						X
11 — *Swiss identity card*	X	X	X	X	X	X	X	X	X	X	X	X	

(1) Group passports issued in accordance with the European Convention of 16.12.1961 and group passport for young persons.
(2) Passport for aliens (burgundy cover) and certificate for aliens without papers (grey cover).

CI — Côte d'Ivoire

	A	B/ NL/ L	D	DK	E	EL	F	FIN	I	IS	NO	P	S
1	X	X	X	X	X	X	X	X	X	X	X	X	X
2	X	X	X	X	X	X	X	X	X	X	X	X	X
3	X	X	X	X	X	X	X	X	X	X	X	X	X
4													
5													
6													
7		X			X	X	X	X	X				
8	X	X	X*	X	X	X	X	X	X	X	X	X	X
9													
10													
11 — *safe conduct* — *laissez-passer*			X				O						

CL — Chile

	A	B/NL/L	D	DK	E	EL	F	FIN	I	IS	NO	P	S
1	X	X	X	X	X	X	X	X	X	X	X	X	X
2	X	X	X	X	X	X	X	X	X	X	X	X	X
3	X	X	X	X	X	X	X	X	X	X	X	X	X
4		X	X				X					X	
5													
6 (1)			X			O	O						
7		X					X	X					
8	X	X	X*	X	X	X	X	X	X	X	X	X	X
9													
10													
11 — *consular passport* — documento de viaje para extranjeros — titulo de viaje para extranjeros — salvo conducto *(laissez-passer)*			 X X O 				 X (2)						

(1) *Documento de viaje*/travel document for children of Chilean nationals aged under 21, born abroad.
(2) Recognised for exit and transit for return to Chile.

CM — Cameroon

	A	B/NL/L	D	DK	E	EL	F	FIN	I	IS	NO	P	S
1	X	X	X	X	X	X	X	X	X	X	X	X	X
2	X	X	X	X	X	X	X	X	X	X	X	X	X
3	X	X	X	X	X	X	X	X	X	X	X	X	X
4			O				O						
5													
6													
7		X			X		X	X	X			X	
8	X	X	X*	X	X	X	X	X	X	X	X	X	X
9													
10													
11 — *temporary diplomatic passport (loose-leaf)*							O					O	

CN — China

	A	B/NL/L	D	DK	E	EL	F	FIN	I	IS	NO	P	S
1	X	X	X	X	X	X	X	X	X	X	X	X	X
2	X	X	X	X	X	X	X	X	X	X	X	X	X
3	X	X	X	X	X	X	X	X	X	X	X	X	X
4													
5													
6													
7		X	X			X	X	X	X				
8 (1)	X	X	X*	X	X	X	X	X	X	X	X	X	X
9													
10 (2)							O						
11													
— *public affairs passport*	X	X	X				X (7)		X				
— *travel permit*		O					O						
— *HKSAR (Special Administrative Region of Hong Kong passport)*	X	X	X (5)	X	X	X	X	X	X	X	X	X	X
— *document of identity for visa purposes (HK)*	X (4)	O	X (6)	X	O	O	O	X	X (5)	X		X	
— *certificate of identity (HK)* (3)	X	X	X (6)	X	O	X	X	X	X (5)	X		X	
— *repatriation certificate*							X (8)						
— *laissez-passer*							O						

(1) Document not issued on 7.5.1998.
(2) Aliens' travel document/travel document for foreigners (booklet with a grey cover).
(3) The issue of identity certificates has been discontinued since 1 July 1997 and identity certificates can therefore not be renewed. These are valid for 10 years. This only concerns certificates issued before 1 July 1997.
(4) If page 4 of the document contains the entry 'the holder of this document may return to HK during its validity without a visa'.
(5) Holders and Chinese nationals are subject to the visa requirement.
(6) If the requisite return permit is contained in the passport replacement document the holder is subject to the visa requirement.
(7) Treated like an ordinary passport.
(8) Recognised for exit or transit for return to China.

CO — Colombia

	A	B/NL/L	D	DK	E	EL	F	FIN	I	IS	NO	P	S
1	X	X	X	X	X	X	X	X	X	X	X	X	X
2	X	X	X	X	X	X	X	X	X	X	X	X	X
3	X	X	X	X	X	X	X	X	X	X	X	X	X
4													
5													
6													
7		X				X	X	X					
8	X	X	X*	X	X	X	X	X	X	X	X	X	X
9													
10													
11 — Documento de viaje — Pasaporte provisional			 O				 O X (1)					 X (2)	

(1) Recognised for exit and transit for return to Colombia.
(2) Recognised by Portugal if the document contains an authorisation to return.

CR — Costa Rica

	A	B/NL/L	D	DK	E	EL	F	FIN	I	IS	NO	P	S
1	X	X	X	X	X	X	X	X	X	X	X	X	X
2	X	X	X	X	X	X	X	X	X	X	X	X	
3	X	X	X	X	X	X	X	X	X	X	X	X	
4													
5													
6													
7													
8	X	X	X*	X	X	X	X	X	X	X	X	X	X
9	X	X	X*	X	X	X	X	X	X		X		X
10 (1)			O		O		O		O				
11 — *safe conduct (in the form of a booklet)/provisional passport (dark green booklet)* — consular passport			 X (2) X				 O		 O				

(1) *Documento de identidad y viaje* (bright green card).
(2) Holders are subject to the visa requirement.

CU — Cuba

	A	B/ NL/ L	D	DK	E	EL	F	FIN	I	IS	NO	P	S
1	X	X	X (1)	X	X	X	X	X	X	X	X	X	X
2	X	X	X	X	X	X	X	X	X	X	X	X	X
3 (2)	X	X	X	X	X	X	X	X	X	X	X	X	X
4													
5													
6													
7					X	X	X	X	X			X	X
8													
9													
10													
11 — Certificado de identidad y viaje							O						

(1) Recognised by Germany subject to certain conditions (existence of an exit permit (*permiso de salida*) and an entry permit (*permiso de regresso*)).
(2) *Pasaporte oficial and pasaporte de servicio.*

CV — Cape Verde

	A	B/ NL/ L	D	DK	E	EL	F	FIN	I	IS	NO	P	S
1	X	X	X	X	X	X	X	X	X	X	X	X	X
2	X	X	X	X	X	X	X	X	X	X	X	X	X
3	X	X	X	X	X	X	X	X	X	X	X	X	X
4													
5													
6													
7		X					X	X				X	
8													
9													
10													
11 — *travel document*							O						

CY — Cyprus

	A	B/NL/L	D	DK	E	EL	F	FIN	I	IS	NO	P	S
1	X	X	X	X	X	X	X	X	X	X	X	X	X
2	X	X	X*	X	X	X	X	X	X	X	X	X	X
3	X	X	X*	X	X	X	X	X	X	X	X	X	X
4													
5							X						
6													
7						X	O	X					
8	X	X	X*	X	X	X	X	X	X	X	X	X	X
9													
10													
11 — *certificate of identity*	X	X	O			X	O		O			X (1)	

(1) Recognised by Portugal if the document contains an authorisation of return.

CZ — Czech Republic

	A	B/NL/L	D	DK	E	EL	F	FIN	I	IS	NO	P	S
1	X	X	X	X	X	X	X	X	X	X	X	X	X
2	X	X	X	X	X	X	X	X	X	X	X	X	X
3	X	X	X	X	X	X	X	X	X	X	X	X	X
4													
5													
6													
7					X		X	X					X
8	X	X	X	X	X	X	X	X	X	X	X	X	X
9													
10 (1)			X (2)		O		O						
11 — *emergency passport/* Cestovni Prukaz			X				X (3)						

(1) *Cestovni Prukas Totosnoti* (in booklet and loose-leaf form).
(2) *Cesterni Prakaz Tataznesti* in booklet form, if the requisite return visa sticker has been filled in and is contained in the document replacing the passport. The return permit printed on page 2 of the specimen passport is not sufficient; the document is not recognised if it is in loose-leaf format.
(3) Recognised for exit or transit to return to the Czech Republic.

DJ — Djibouti

	A	B/ NL/ L	D	DK	E	EL	F	FIN	I	IS	NO	P	S
1	X	X	X	X	X	X	X	X	X	X	X	X	
2	X	X	X	X	X	X	X	X	X	X	X	X	X
3	X	X	X*	X	X	X	X	X	X	X	X	X	X
4													
5													
6													
7		X	X*		X	X	X	X	X			X	
8	X	X	X*	X	X	X	X	X	X	X	X	X	X
9													
10													
11 — *laissez-passer replacing passport (loose-leaf)* — *special laissez-passer*							 O O						

DM — Dominica

	A	B/ NL/ L	D	DK	E	EL	F	FIN	I	IS	NO	P	S
1	X	X	X	X	X	X	X	X	X	X	X	X	X
2	X	X	X	X	X	X	X	X	X	X	X	X	X
3	X	X	X	X	X		X	X	X	X	X	X	X
4													
5							O						
6													
7		X	X (1)		X	X	X	X	X			X	
8	X	X	X*	X	X	X	X	X	X	X	X	X	X
9													
10													
11 — *intercommonwealth Caribbean travel document* — *certificate of identity* — *emergency passport*							 O O O						

(1) Seamen's certificate.

DO — Dominican Republic

	A	B/NL/L	D	DK	E	EL	F	FIN	I	IS	NO	P	S
1	X	X	X	X	X	X	X	X	X	X	X	X	
2	X	X	X	X	X	X	X	X	X	X	X	X	X
3	X	X	X	X	X	X	X	X	X	X	X	X	X
4													
5													
6													
7			X (1)				X	X	X				
8	X	X	X*	X	X	X	X	X	X	X	X	X	X
9													
10													
11													

(1) Seamen's certificate.

DZ — Algeria

	A	B/NL/L	D	DK	E	EL	F	FIN	I	IS	NO	P	S
1	X	X	X	X	X	X	X	X	X	X	X	X	X
2	X	X	X	X	X	X	X	X	X	X	X	X	X
3	X	X	X (1)	X	X	X	X	X	X	X	X	X	X
4													
5													
6													
7		X	X		X		X	X	X			X	X
8	X	X	X*	X	X	X	X	X	X	X	X	X	X
9	X	X		X	X	X	X	X	X		X		X
10													
11													
— *diplomatic laissez-passer*			X										
— *laissez-passer*							X (2)						

(1) Only if the place and date of birth are indicated.
(2) Recognised for exit or transit to return to Algeria.

EC — Ecuador

	A	B/ NL/ L	D	DK	E	EL	F	FIN	I	IS	NO	P	S
1	X	X	X	X	X	X	X	X	X	X	X	X	X
2	X	X	X	X	X	X	X	X	X	X	X	X	X
3	X	X	X	X	X	X	X	X	X	X	X	X	X
4		X	X			X	X	X	X			X	
5							X						
6													
7							X						
8	X	X	X*	X	X	X	X	X	X	X	X	X	X
9	X	X		X	X	X	X	X	X		X		X
10													
11													

EE — Estonia

	A	B/ NL/ L	D	DK	E	EL	F	FIN	I	IS	NO	P	S
1	X	X	X	X	X	X	X	X	X	X	X	X	X
2	X	X	X	X	X	X	X	X	X	X	X	X	X
3													
4													
5													
6													
7		X	X (1)				**O**	X	X (1)			**O**	
8 (2)	X	X	X*	X	X	X	X	X	X	X	X	X	X
9													
10 (3)	X	X	X (4)		X	X	**O**		X	X		X (5)	X
11 — *temporary travel document* — *certificate of return to Estonia*					**O**		**O** **X** (6)	X	**O**				X

(1) Not recognised when issued to a third-country national. The recognised seaman's book is only issued to Estonian nationals and is called a 'seaman's discharge book'.
(2) The document was not issued on 7.5.1998.
(3) Alien's passport.
(4) If the passport replacement document contains the requisite return permit (authorisation of stay for a limited or unlimited period for Estonia) with sufficient length of validity.
(5) Recognised by Portugal if it contains a residence permit.
(6) Recognised for exit or transit to return to Estonia.

EG — Egypt

	A	B/NL/L	D	DK	E	EL	F	FIN	I	IS	NO	P	S
1	X	X	X	X	X	X	X	X	X	X	X	X	X
2	X	X	X	X	X	X	X	X	X	X	X	X	X
3	X	X	X	X	X	X	X	X	X	X	X	X	X
4		X	X		X	X	X		X			X	
5		X					O						
6													
7		X	X			X	X	X	X				
8	X	X	X	X	X	X	X	X	X	X	X	X	X
9													
10													
11													
— *student's passport (blue cover)*		X					X [1]		O				
— *travel document for Palestinian refugees*			X				X [2]		O				
— *provisional travel document*					O		O						
— *laissez-passer (brown)*							O						

[1] Dealt with like an ordinary passport.
[2] Can be covered only if it contains a return permit.

ER — Eritrea

	A	B/NL/L	D	DK	E	EL	F	FIN	I	IS	NO	P	S
1	X	X	X	X	X	X	X	X	X	X	X	X	X
2	X	X	X	X	X	X	X	X	X	X	X	X	X
3													
4													
5													
6													
7													
8													
9													
10													
11													
— *laissez-passer*			X										

ET — Ethiopia

	A	B/ NL/ L	D	DK	E	EL	F	FIN	I	IS	NO	P	S
1	X	X	X	X	X	X	X	X	X	X	X	X	X
2	X	X	X	X	X	X	X	X	X	X	X	X	X
3			X										
4	X	X		X	X	X		X	X	X	X	X	X
5													
6													
7		X						X					
8	X	X	X*	X	X	X	X	X	X	X	X	X	X
9													
10													
11													
— *laissez-passer*	X		O				O						
— *emergency document of identity for non-Ethiopian nationals*	X					O	O						

FJ — Fiji

	A	B/ NL/ L	D	DK	E	EL	F	FIN	I	IS	NO	P	S
1	X	X	X	X	X	X	X	X	X	X	X	X	X
2	X	X	X	X	X	X	X	X	X	X	X	X	X
3													
4													
5													
6													
7					X		X	X					
8	X	X	X*	X	X	X	X	X	X	X	X	X	X
9	X	X		X	X	X	X	X	X		X		X
10													
11													
— *certificate of identity*					O		O		O				

FM — Micronesia

	A	B/NL/L	D	DK	E	EL	F	FIN	I	IS	NO	P	S
1	X	X	X	X	X	X	X	X	X	X	X	X	
2	X	X	X*	X	X	X	X	X	X	X	X	X	
3	X	X	X	X	X	X	X	X	X	X	X	X	
4													
5													
6													
7													
8													
9													
10													
11													

GA — Gabon

	A	B/NL/L	D	DK	E	EL	F	FIN	I	IS	NO	P	S
1	X	X	X	X	X	X	X	X	X	X	X	X	
2	X	X	X	X	X	X	X	X	X	X	X	X	
3	X	X	X	X	X	X	X	X	X	X	X	X	
4					O								
5													
6													
7						X	X	X					
8	X	X	X	X	X	X	X	X	X	X	X	X	X
9													
10													
11													

GD — Grenada

	A	B/NL/L	D	DK	E	EL	F	FIN	I	IS	NO	P	S
1	X	X	X	X	X	X	X	X	X	X	X	X	X
2	X	X	X	X	X	X	X	X	X	X	X	X	X
3	X	X	X	X	X	X	X	X	X	X	X	X	X
4													
5													
6													
7		X			X		X	X	X				
8													
9													
10													
11													
— *'British West India' travel permit*							O						
— *provisional passport / emergency passport*							O						

GE — Georgia

	A	B/NL/L	D	DK	E	EL	F	FIN	I	IS	NO	P	S
1	X	X	X	X	X	X	X	X	X	X	X	X	X
2	X	X	X	X	X	X	X	X	X	X	X	X	X
3	X	X	X	X	X	X	X	X	X	X	X	X	X
4													
5													
6													
7			X (1)				X		X				
8													
9													
10													
11													
— *laissez-passer*		X (2)											
— *identification document*			O				O						

(1) Only if the seaman's book shows that the person concerned is a Georgian national.
(2) Issued to Georgian nationals with re-entry visa.

GH — Ghana

	A	B/NL/L	D	DK	E	EL	F	FIN	I	IS	NO	P	S
1	X	X	X	X	X	X	X	X	X	X	X	X	X
2	X	X	X*	X	X	X	X	X	X	X	X	X	X
3	X	X	X*	X	X	X	X	X	X	X	X	X	X
4													
5													
6													
7		X			X	X	X	X	X			X	
8	X	X	X (1)	X	X	X	X	X	X	X	X	X	X
9													
10													
11													
— alien's identity certificate					O		O					O	
— travel booklet					O		O						

(1) If the passport replacement document contains a return permit with a sufficient period of validity.

GM — The Gambia

	A	B/NL/L	D	DK	E	EL	F	FIN	I	IS	NO	P	S
1	X	X	X	X	X	X	X	X	X	X	X	X	X
2	x	X	X*	X	X	X	X	X	X	X	X	X	X
3	X	X	X*	X	X	X	X	X	X	X	X	X	X
4													
5													
6													
7							X						
8	X	X	X*	X	X	X	X	X	X	X	X	X	X
9													
10													
11													

GN — Guinea

	A	B/ NL/ L	D	DK	E	EL	F	FIN	I	IS	NO	P	S
1	X	X	X	X	X	X	X	X	X	X	X	X	X
2	X	X	X	X	X	X	X	X	X	X	X	X	X
3	X	X	X	X	X	X	X	X	X	X	X	X	X
4													
5													
6													
7						X	X	X					X
8	X	X	X*	X	X	X	X	X	X	X	X	X	X
9	X	X		X	X	X	X	X	X		X		X
10													
11													
— *travel document replacing passport*							O						
— *diplomatic loose-leaf document*			X										

GQ — Equatorial Guinea

	A	B/ NL/ L	D	DK	E	EL	F	FIN	I	IS	NO	P	S
1	X	X	X	X	X	X	X	X	X	X	X	X	
2	X	X	X	X	X	X	X	X	X	X	X	X	
3 [1]	X	X	X	X	X	X	X	X	X	X	X	X	
4			X										
5													
6					X								
7													
8 [2]	X	X	X*	X	X	X	X	X	X	X	X	X	X
9													
10													
11													

[1] *Pasaporte de servicio* (blue cover) and official-duty passport (brown cover).
[2] Document not issued on 7.5.1998.

GT — Guatemala

	A	B/ NL/ L	D	DK	E	EL	F	FIN	I	IS	NO	P	S
1	X	X	X	X	X	X	X	X	X	X	X	X	X
2	X	X	X*	X	X	X	X	X	X	X	X	X	X
3	X	X	X	X	X	X	X	X	X	X	X	X	
4													
5							O					O	
6													
7					X		X	X					
8	X	X	X*	X	X	X	X	X	X	X	X	X	X
9													
10													
11 — *consular passport* — cedula de identidad refugiado	 X						 X O						

GW — Guinea-Bissau

	A	B/ NL/ L	D	DK	E	EL	F	FIN	I	IS	NO	P	S
1	X	X	X	X	X	X	X	X	X	X	X	X	X
2	X	X	X	X	X	X	X	X	X	X	X	X	X
3	X	X	X	X	X	X	X	X	X	X	X	X	X
4													
5													
6													
7		X			X	X	X	X	X			X	
8 (1)	X	X	X*	X	X	X	X	X	X	X	X	X	X
9													
10													
11 — *laissez-passer* — *travel document*							 O					 X (2)	

(1) Document not issued on 7.5.1998.
(2) Recognised for exit or transit for return to State of residence.

GY — Guyana

	A	B/ NL/ L	D	DK	E	EL	F	FIN	I	IS	NO	P	S
1	X	X	X	X	X	X	X	X	X	X	X	X	X
2	X	X	X*	X	X	X	X	X	X	X	X	X	X
3	X	X	X*	X	X	X	X	X	X	X	X	X	
4													
5													
6													
7		X			X	X	X	X	X			X	
8													
9													
10													
11 — *inter-Caribbean travel document*	O												

HN — Honduras

	A	B/ NL/ L	D	DK	E	EL	F	FIN	I	IS	NO	P	S
1	X	X	X	X	X	X	X	X	X	X	X	X	X
2	X	X	X	X	X	X	X	X	X	X	X	X	X
3	X	X	X*	X	X	X	X	X	X	X	X	X	X
4		X	X (2)				X						
5													
6													
7		X	X (3)		X	X	X	X	X			X	
8 (1)	X	X	X	X	X	X	X	X	X	X	X	X	X
9													
10													
11 — *emergency passport*							O		O				

(1) Document not issued on 7.5.1998.
(2) If the date of birth is indicated in the passport.
(3) Only if the seaman's book shows that the person concerned is a Honduran national.

HR — Croatia

	A	B/NL/L	D	DK	E	EL	F	FIN	I	IS	NO	P	S
1	X	X	X	X	X	X	X	X	X	X	X	X	X
2	X	X	X*	X	X	X	X	X	X	X	X	X	X
3	X	X	X*	X	X	X	X	X	X	X	X	X	X
4													
5	X (2)		X (3)				O						
6													
7	X		X (3)			X	X	X	X				
8	X	X	X*	X	X	X	X	X	X	X	X	X	X
9	X	X		X	X	X	X	X	X		X		X
10 (1)			O				O						
11													
— Brodarska Knjizica Schif-fausweis *(staff ID card for navigation within Croatia)*	X		X (3)				O						
— *laissez-passer* (Putni list)			X (4)				X (5)					X (5)	

(1) *Putni list za stranca* (travel document for foreign nationals).
(2) With photograph of each person entered on the group passport.
(3) Holders are subject to the visa requirement.
(4) Only for the purpose of transit if the logical route of return to Croatia crosses the Federal Republic of Germany.
(5) Recognised for exit and transit for return to Croatia.

HT — Haiti

	A	B/NL/L	D	DK	E	EL	F	FIN	I	IS	NO	P	S
1	X	X	X	X	X	X	X	X	X	X	X	X	X
2	X	X	X	X	X	X	X	X	X	X	X	X	X
3	X	X	X	X	X	X	X	X	X	X	X	X	X
4													
5													
6													
7													
8 (1)	X	X	X*	X	X	X	X	X	X	X	X	X	X
9													
10													
11 — *identity and travel certificate*							O						

(1) Document not issued on 7.5.1998.

HU — Hungary

	A	B/ NL/ L	D	DK	E	EL	F	FIN	I	IS	NO	P	S
1	X	X	X	X	X	X	X	X	X	X	X	X	X
2	X	X	X	X	X	X	X	X	X	X	X	X	X
3	X	X	X	X	X	X	X	X	X	X	X	X	X
4													
5			O										
6													
7		X	X			X	X	X				X	
8	X	X	X	X	X	X	X	X	X	X	X	X	X
9													
10 (1)	O	X	X (2)		O		O					X (3)	
11													
— *boatman's service passport*	X		O				O		X			O	
— *certificate of returning home for Hungarian nationals (in loose-leaf form)*		O	X (4)				X (3)					X (3)	
— *travel document issued for a single journey (in loose-leaf)*							O						

(1) Travel document for Stateless persons.
(2) Recognised provided the authorisation of stay is written in a Germanic or Romance language.
(3) Recognised for exit or transit for return to Hungary.
(4) Only for the purposes of transit if the logical route for return to Hungary crosses the territory of the Federal Republic of Germany; holders are subject to the visa requirement.

ID — Indonesia

	A	B/NL/L	D	DK	E	EL	F	FIN	I	IS	NO	P	S
1	X	X	X	X	X	X	X	X	X	X	X	X	X
2	X	X	X	X	X	X	X	X	X	X	X	X	X
3	X	X	X	X	X	X	X	X	X	X	X	X	X
4													
5													
6													
7		X	X			X	O	X					
8													
9													
10 ([1])		O					O		O			O	
11													
— *'passport-like travel document for Indonesian citizens'*							O		X				
— *'Haj passport' (pilgrim's passport)*							O		O			O	

([1]) Travel document in lieu of a passport for foreigners.

IL — Israel

	A	B/NL/L	D	DK	E	EL	F	FIN	I	IS	NO	P	S
1	X	X	X	X	X	X	X	X	X	X	X	X	X
2	X	X	X	X	X	X	X	X	X	X	X	X	X
3	X	X	X	X	X	X	X	X	X	X	X	X	X
4	X												
5							X						
6													
7		X					X	X					
8	X	X	X*	X	X	X	X	X	X	X	X	X	X
9	X	X		X	X	X	X	X	X		X		X
10 ([1])	X	X	X		X	X	O	X ([2])	X			X ([3])	
11													
— *laissez-passer issued by the apostolic delegation of Jerusalem*		O					X						
— *travel document (brown)*			X ([4])		X ([4])		X ([4])						

([1]) Travel document in lieu of national passport (orange cover).
([2]) With a visa.
([3]) Recognised by Portugal if the document contains a return permit.
([4]) If the requisite return permit is contained in the document in lieu of a passport.

IN — India

	A	B/ NL/ L	D	DK	E	EL	F	FIN	I	IS	NO	P	S
1	X	X	X	X	X	X	X	X	X	X	X	X	X
2	X	X	X	X	X	X	X	X	X	X	X	X	X
3	X	X	X	X	X	X	X	X	X	X	X	X	X
4													
5													
6													
7 (1)		X	O			X	X	X					
8													
9													
10 (2)			O				X (3)						
11													

(1) Continuous certificate of discharge and continuous discharge certificate.
(2) Certificate of identity.
(3) Only recognised if the holder is a Tibetan refugee.

IQ — Iraq

	A	B/ NL/ L	D	DK	E	EL	F	FIN	I	IS	NO	P	S
1	X	X	X	X	X	X	X	X	X	X	X	X	X
2 (1)	X	X	X*	X	X	X	X	X	X	X	X	X	X
3	X	X	X*		X	X	X	X	X		X	X	X
4							X						
5													
6													
7		X	O		X	X	X	X	X			X	
8													
9													
10													
11 — *travel document for Palestinians*			X		X								

(1) Diplomatic passport (green cover) and diplomatic passport for diplomatic carrier (red cover).

IR — Iran

	A	B/ NL/ L	D	DK	E	EL	F	FIN	I	IS	NO	P	S
1	X	X	X	X	X	X	X	X	X	X	X	X	X
2	X	X	X	X	X	X	X	X	X	X	X	X	X
3	X	X	X	X	X	X	X	X	X	X	X	X	X
4													
5													
6													
7		X	X		X	X	X	X	X			X	
8	X	X	X	X	X	X	X	X	X	X	X	X	X
9													
10													
11 — *laissez-passer*			X (1)										

(1) Only for transit and if the document in lieu of passport shows that the person concerned is an Iranian national.

JM — Jamaica

	A	B/ NL/ L	D	DK	E	EL	F	FIN	I	IS	NO	P	S
1	X	X	X*	X	X	X	X	X	X	X	X	X	X
2	X	X	X*	X	X	X	X	X	X	X	X	X	X
3	X	X	X*	X	X	X	X	X	X	X	X	X	X
4													
5													
6													
7		X	X*			X	O	X					X
8	X	X	X*	X	X	X	X	X	X	X	X	X	X
9													
10													
11													

JO — Jordan

	A	B/NL/L	D	DK	E	EL	F	FIN	I	IS	NO	P	S
1	X	X	X	X	X	X	X	X	X	X	X	X	X
2	X	X	X*	X	X	X	X	X	X	X	X	X	X
3	X	X	X	X	X	X	X	X	X	X	X	X	X
4	X	X	X		X	X	X		X			X	
5													
6													
7 (1)							X						
8													
9													
10													
11 — *travel document*			O				O						

(1) Document not issued on 7.5.1998.

JP — Japan

	A	B/NL/L	D	DK	E	EL	F	FIN	I	IS	NO	P	S
1	X	X	X	X	X	X	X	X	X	X	X	X	X
2	X	X	X	X	X	X	X	X	X	X	X	X	X
3	X	X	X	X	X	X	X	X	X	X	X	X	X
4													
5													
6													
7		X					O	X					
8	X	X	X*	X	X	X	X	X	X	X	X	X	X
9													
10 (1)	X		X (2)		O		O		X			X	
11 — *travel for return to Japan*			X (3)										

(1) Re-entry permit to Japan.
(2) Holders are subject to the visa requirement.
(3) Only for the purposes of transit, the holders are subject to the visa requirement.

KE — Kenya

	A	B/NL/L	D	DK	E	EL	F	FIN	I	IS	NO	P	S
1	X	X	X	X	X	X	X	X	X	X	X	X	X
2	X	X	X	X	X	X	X	X	X	X	X	X	X
3													
4													
5													
6													
7													
8	X	X		X	X	X	X	X	X	X	X	X	X
9													
10													
11 — *certificate of identity*							O						

KG — Kyrgyzstan

	A	B/NL/L	D	DK	E	EL	F	FIN	I	IS	NO	P	S
1	X	X	X	X	X	X	X	X	X	X	X	X	X
2	X	X	X*	X	X	X	X	X	X	X	X	X	
3	X	X		X	X		X	X	X	X	X	X	
4													
5													
6													
7					X		O	X				X	
8	X	X	X*	X	X	X	X	X	X	X	X	X	X
9													
10													
11													

KH — Cambodia

	A	B/NL/L	D	DK	E	EL	F	FIN	I	IS	NO	P	S
1	X	X	X	X	X	X	X	X	X	X	X	X	X
2	X	X	X	X	X	X	X	X	X	X	X	X	X
3	X	X	X	X	X	X	X	X	X	X	X	X	X
4													
5													
6													
7		X				O	O	X					
8	X	X	X*	X	X	X	X	X	X	X	X	X	X
9													
10													
11 — *emergency passport for travel to the Kingdom of Cambodia*							X (1)					X (1)	

(1) Recognised for exit or transit for return to Cambodia.

KI — Kiribati

	A	B/NL/L	D	DK	E	EL	F	FIN	I	IS	NO	P	S
1	X	X	X	X	X	X	X	X	X	X	X	X	
2	X	X	X	X	X	X	X	X	X	X	X	X	
3													
4													
5													
6													
7													
8													
9	X	X		X	X	X	X	X	X		X		X
10													
11													
— *emergency certificate*			O				O		O				
— *foreign investor's passport*			O				O		O			O	

KM — The Comoros

	A	B/NL/L	D	DK	E	EL	F	FIN	I	IS	NO	P	S
1	X	X	X	X	X	X	X	X	X	X	X	X	X
2	X	X	X	X	X	X	X	X	X	X	X	X	
3	X	X	X	X	X	X	X	X	X	X	X	X	X
4													
5													
6													
7													
8													
9													
10													
11													

KN — Saint Kitts and Nevis

	A	B/NL/L	D	DK	E	EL	F	FIN	I	IS	NO	P	S
1	X	X	X	X	X	X	X	X	X	X	X	X	X
2	X	X	X	X	X	X	X	X	X	X	X	X	X
3	X						X	X					
4													
5													
6													
7		X				X	O	X					
8													
9													
10													
11													

KP — North Korea

	A	B/NL/L	D	DK	E	EL	F	FIN	I	IS	NO	P	S
1	X	X	X	X	X	O	X	X	X	X	X	X	X
2	X	X	X*	X	X	O	X	X	X	X	X	X	X
3	X	X	X*	X	X	O	X	X	X	X	X	X	X
4													
5													
6													
7						O	X						
8													
9													
10													
11													

KR — South Korea

	A	B/NL/L	D	DK	E	EL	F	FIN	I	IS	NO	P	S
1	X	X	X	X	X	X	X	X	X	X	X	X	X
2	X	X	X	X	X	X	X	X	X	X	X	X	X
3	X	X	X	X	X	X	X	X	X	X	X	X	
4													
5													
6													
7		X	X*			X	O	X				X	
8	X	X	X*	X	X	X	X	X	X	X	X	X	X
9	X	X		X	X	X	X	X	X		X		X
10													
11 — *travel certificate*	X	X	X			X	O		X				

KW — Kuwait

	A	B/NL/L	D	DK	E	EL	F	FIN	I	IS	NO	P	S
1	X	X	X	X	X	X	X	X	X	X	X	X	X
2	X	X	X	X	X	X	X	X	X	X	X	X	X
3			X										
4	X	X		X	X	X	X	X	X	X	X	X	
5													
6													
7							**O**						
8													
9													
10													
11 — *emergency document valid for one trip to Kuwait only*						X	X (1)						
— *laissez-passer*			**O**			**O**							

(1) Recognised for exit or transit to return to Kuwait.

KZ — Kazakhstan

	A	B/NL/L	D	DK	E	EL	F	FIN	I	IS	NO	P	S
1	X	X	X (1)	X	X	X	X	X	X	X	X	X	X
2	X	X	X	X	X	X	X	X	X	X	X	X	X
3	X	X	X	X	X	X	X	X	X	X	X	X	X
4													
5													
6													
7													
8													
9													
10 (2)			X (3)				**O**	X					
11													

(1) Only if the return permit is contained in the passport.
(2) Stateless person certificate.
(3) If the document in lieu of passport contains the exit visa and the requisite return visa.

LA — Laos

	A	B/ NL/ L	D	DK	E	EL	F	FIN	I	IS	NO	P	S
1	X	X	X	X	X	X	X	X	X	X	X	X	X
2	X	X	X	X	X	X	X	X	X	X	X	X	X
3	X	X	X	X	X	X	X	X	X	X	X	X	X
4													
5													
6													
7						O	O					O	
8													
9													
10													
11 — *laissez-passer (replacing passport)*							X [1]						

([1]) Recognised for exit or transit to return to Laos.

LB — Lebanon

	A	B/ NL/ L	D	DK	E	EL	F	FIN	I	IS	NO	P	S
1	X	X	X	X	X	X	X	X	X	X	X	X	X
2	X	X	X	X	X	X	X	X	X	X	X	X	X
3													
4	X	X	X		X	X	X		X			X	
5													
6													
7													
8													
9													
10													
11 — *laissez-passer* — *travel document for Palestinian refugees*	X		O O		X		O X [1]		X			O O	

([1]) Covered if the residence permit is included in the document.

LC — Saint Lucia

	A	B/ NL/ L	D	DK	E	EL	F	FIN	I	IS	NO	P	S
1	X	X	X*	X	X	X	X	X	X	X	X	X	
2	X	X	X*	X	X	X	X	X	X	X	X	X	
3	X	X						X			X		
4													
5 (1)							O						
6													
7		X			X		X	X	X			X	
8													
9													
10													
11													
— *inter-Caribbean travel permit*							O						
— *certificate of identity (loose-leaf)*							O						
— *emergency passport/* passeport provisoire							O						

(1) Collective travel document.

LI — Liechtenstein

	A	B/ NL/ L	D	DK	E	EL	F	FIN	I	IS	NO	P	S
1	X	X	X	X	X	X	X	X	X	X	X	X	X
2	X	X	X*	X	X	X	X	X	X	X	X	X	X
3	X	X	X	X	X	X	X	X	X	X	X	X	X
4													
5	X	X	X*			X	X		X				
6	X	X	X*				X		X				
7													
8	X	X	X*	X	X	X	X	X	X	X	X	X	X
9													
10 (1)			X				O						
11													
— *national identification card*	X	X	X	X	X	X	X	X	X	X	X	X	

(1) *Pass für Ausländer* (passport for foreigners).

LK — Sri Lanka

	A	B/NL/L	D	DK	E	EL	F	FIN	I	IS	NO	P	S
1	X	X	X	X	X	X	X	X	X	X	X	X	X
2	X	X	X	X	X	X	X	X	X	X	X	X	X
3	X						X	X			X	X	X
4													
5													
6													
7		X				X	O	X					
8													
9													
10													
11 — *emergency certificate* — *identity certificate*							 O O						

LR — Liberia

	A	B/NL/L	D	DK	E	EL	F	FIN	I	IS	NO	P	S
1	X	X	X	X	X	X	X	X	X	X	X	X	X
2	X	X	X	X	X	X	X	X	X	X	X	X	X
3	X	X	X	X	X	X	X	X	X	X	X	X	X
4													
5													
6													
7					X	X	X	X	X			X	
8	X	X	X*	X	X	X	X	X	X	X	X	X	X
9	X	X		X	X	X	X	X	X		X		X
10													
11													

LS — Lesotho

	A	B/NL/L	D	DK	E	EL	F	FIN	I	IS	NO	P	S
1	X	X	X	X	X	X	X	X	X	X	X	X	X
2	X	X	X	X	X	X	X	X	X	X	X	X	X
3	X	X	X	X				X	X	X	X	X	
4													
5													
6													
7													
8	X	X	X*	X	X	X	X	X	X	X	X	X	X
9	X	X		X	X	X	X	X	X		X		X
10													
11													

LT — Lithuania

	A	B/NL/L	D	DK	E	EL	F	FIN	I	IS	NO	P	S
1	X	X	X	X	X	X	X	X	X	X	X	X	X
2	X	X	X	X	X	X	X	X	X	X	X	X	X
3													
4													
5													
6 (1)	X		X				**O**	X					X
7		X	X			X	**O**	X					X
8	X	X	X	X	X	X	X	X	X	X	X	X	X
9			X										
10						X							
11 — *repatriation certificate*		X (2)					X (2)	X					

(1) Child's travel document.
(2) Recognised for exit or transit for return to Lithuania.

LV — Latvia

	A	B/ NL/ L	D	DK	E	EL	F	FIN	I	IS	NO	P	S
1	X	X	X	X	X	X	X	X	X	X	X	X	X
2	X	X	X	X	X	X	X	X	X	X	X	X	X
3													
4													
5													
6													
7		X	O		X	X	X	X				X	
8 (1)	X	X	X*	X	X	X	X	X	X	X	X	X	X
9													
10 (2)	X	X	X (4)	X	X	X	X	X	X	X		X	
11 — *certificate of return*		X (3)					X (5)					X	

(1) Not issued on 7.5.1998.
(2) Identification document (Stateless person's travel document)/*personas apliciba* (brown cover) which will expire on 10.4.1999 and alien's passport (purple cover).
(3) If the requisite return permit is contained in the document in lieu of passport (stamp in Lativian and English).
(4) Solely for the purposes of transit to Latvia.
(5) Recognised for exit or transit for return to Latvia.

LY — Libya

	A	B/NL/L	D	DK	E	EL	F	FIN	I	IS	NO	P	S
1	X	X	X (1)	X	X	X	X (1)	X	X	X	X	X	X
2	X	X	X	X	X	X	X (2)	X	X	X	X	X	X
3	X	X	X (2)	X	X	X		X	X	X	X	X	X
4							X (2)						
5													
6													
7		X	X*				X	X	X				
8													
9 (3)	X	X	X*	X	X	X	X	X	X		X		X
10													
11													
— *temporary travel document*			O				O						
— *travel document for Palestinian refugees*	X		O		X		O		O				
— *laissez-passer (32 page booklet, dark green cover)*							O						

(1) Covered if it contains a stamp with a person's identity, date and place of birth, date and place of issue and expiry data translated into French or English.
(2) Covered if the headings contained on pages 2 to 6 on the person and issue of the passport are translated into French or English.
(3) Document not issued on 7.5.1998.

MA — Morocco

	A	B/ NL/ L	D	DK	E	EL	F	FIN	I	IS	NO	P	S
1	X	X	X	X	X	X	X	X	X	X	X	X	X
2	X	X	X*	X	X	X	X	X	X	X	X	X	X
3	X	X	X*	X	X	X	X	X	X	X	X	X	X
4	X		X		X		X					X	
5													
6													
7		X	X		X	X	X		X				
8	X	X	O	X	X	X	X	X	X	X	X	X	X
9													
10													
11													

MC — Monaco

	A	B/ NL/ L	D	DK	E	EL	F	FIN	I	IS	NO	P	S
1	X	X	X	X	X	X	X	X	X	X	X	X	X
2	X	X	X*	X	X	X	X	X	X	X	X	X	X
3	X	X	X*	X	X	X	X	X	X	X	X	X	X
4													
5													
6													
7													
8	X	X	X*	X	X	X	X	X	X	X	X	X	X
9													
10													
11 — *identification card*	X	X	X		X	X	X		X			X	

MD — Moldova

	A	B/ NL/ L	D	DK	E	EL	F	FIN	I	IS	NO	P	S
1	X	X	X	X	X	X	X	X	X	X	X	X	X
2	X	X	X	X	X	X	X	X	X	X	X	X	X
3	X	X	X	X	X	X	X	X	X	X	X	X	X
4													
5													
6													
7													
8													
9													
10 (1)		O				O	O						
11 — *travel document*		X (2)					X (3)						

(1) Passport for Stateless persons.
(2) Only with re-entry visa.
(3) Recognised for exit or transit for return to Moldova.

MG — Madagascar

	A	B/ NL/ L	D	DK	E	EL	F	FIN	I	IS	NO	P	S
1	X	X	X	X	X	X	X	X	X	X	X	X	
2	X	X	X	X	X	X	X	X	X	X	X	X	X
3	X	X	X	X	X	X	X	X	X	X	X	X	X
4													
5													
6													
7		X				X	X	X					
8 (1)	X	X	X*	X	X	X	X	X	X	X	X	X	X
9	X	X		X	X	X	X	X	X		X		X
10													
11 — *safe conduct for people of uncertain nationality*			X (2)				O					O	

(1) Document not issued on 7.5.1998.
(2) If the document in lieu of passport carries a valid re-entry visa.

MH — Marshall Islands

	A	B/NL/L	D	DK	E	EL	F	FIN	I	IS	NO	P	S
1	X	X	X	X	X	X	X	X	X	X	X	X	
2	X	X	X	X	X	X	X	X	X	X	X	X	
3	X	X	X	X	X	X	X	X	X	X	X	X	
4													
5													
6													
7													
8													
9													
10													
11 — *certificate of identity*					O		O						

MK — Former Yugoslav Republic of Macedonia (1)

	A	B/NL/L	D	DK	E	EL	F	FIN	I	IS	NO	P	S
1	X	X	X	X	X	O	X	X	X	X	X	X	X
2	X	X	X	X	X	O	X	X	X	X	X	X	X
3	X	X	X	X	X	O	X	X	X	X	X	X	X
4													
5			X				O						
6													
7													
8	X	X		X		O	(X)	X	X			X	
9							(X)	X	X				
10 (2)			O			O	O					X	
11 — *emergency passport*							X (3)						

(1) Although the name 'Macedonian Republic' appearing on the document is not recognised, the document is recognised as a valid travel document.
(2) Passport for foreigners.
(3) Recognised for exit or transit to the FYROM.

ML — Mali

	A	B/NL/L	D	DK	E	EL	F	FIN	I	IS	NO	P	S
1	X	X	X	X	X	X	X	X	X	X	X	X	X
2	X	X	X	X	X	X	X	X	X	X	X	X	X
3		X			X	X	X	X	X		X	X	X
4													
5													
6													
7													
8	X	X	X*	X	X	X	X	X	X	X	X	X	X
9													
10													
11 — *diplomatic passport (in loose-leaf form* (1)*)* — *official duty passport (loose-leaf form)*			X				O O						

(1) Only issued to former diplomats and their family.

MM — Myanmar

	A	B/NL/L	D	DK	E	EL	F	FIN	I	IS	NO	P	S
1	X	X	X	X	X	X	X	X	X	X	X	X	X
2	X	X	X	X	X	X	X	X	X	X	X	X	X
3	X	X	X*	X	X	X		X	X	X	X	X	X
4							X						
5													
6													
7													
8													
9													
10													
11													

MN — Mongolia

	A	B/NL/L	D	DK	E	EL	F	FIN	I	IS	NO	P	S
1	X	X	X	X	X	X	X	X	X	X	X	X	X
2	X	X	X	X	X	X	X	X	X	X	X	X	X
3	X	X	X	X	X	X	X	X	X	X	X	X	X
4													
5													
6													
7													
8													
9													
10													
11													

MR — Mauritania

	A	B/NL/L	D	DK	E	EL	F	FIN	I	IS	NO	P	S
1	X	X	X	X	X	X	X	X	X	X	X	X	
2	X	X	X*	X	X	X	X	X	X	X	X	X	
3	X	X	X*	X	X	X	X	X	X	X	X	X	
4													
5													
6													
7													
8 (1)	X	X	X*	X	X	X	X	X	X	X	X	X	X
9													
10													
11													

(1) Document not issued on 7.5.1998.

MT — Malta

	A	B/ NL/ L	D	DK	E	EL	F	FIN	I	IS	NO	P	S
1	X	X	X	X	X	X	X	X	X	X	X	X	X
2	X	X	X	X	X	X	X	X	X	X	X	X	X
3	X			X	X	X	X	X	X	X	X	X	
4													
5		X			X	X	X (1)		X			X (1)	
6													
7		X			X	X	X	X	X			X	
8 (2)	X	X	X*	X	X	X	X	X	X	X	X	X	X
9													
10													
11													
— *national identification card*	X	X			X	X	X		X			X	X
— *emergency passport*							X (3)						
— *document of identity issued to an applicant who cannot obtain a national passport*							O						

(1) Only group passports issued in accordance with the European convention of 16 December 1961.
(2) Document not issued on 7.5.1998.
(3) Recognised for exit or transit for return to Malta.

MU — Mauritius

	A	B/ NL/ L	D	DK	E	EL	F	FIN	I	IS	NO	P	S
1	X	X	X	X	X	X	X	X	X	X	X	X	X
2	X	X	X	X	X	X	X	X	X	X	X	X	X
3													
4													
5													
6													
7					X	X	X	X	X			X	
8													
9													
10													
11													

MV — Maldives

	A	B/ NL/ L	D	DK	E	EL	F	FIN	I	IS	NO	P	S
1	X	X	X	X	X	X	X	X	X	X	X	X	X
2	X	X	X	X	X	X	X	X	X	X	X	X	X
3	X	X	X	X	X	X	X	X	X	X	X	X	X
4													
5													
6													
7						X	O						
8													
9													
10													
11 — *temporary travel document*		O					O						X

MW — Malawi

	A	B/ NL/ L	D	DK	E	EL	F	FIN	I	IS	NO	P	S
1	X	X	X	X	X	X	X	X	X	X	X	X	X
2	X	X	X	X	X	X	X	X	X	X	X	X	X
3	X	X	X	X	X	X	X	X	X	X	X	X	X
4													
5													
6													
7													
8	X	X	X	X	X	X	X	X	X	X	X	X	X
9													
10													
11 — *emergency certificate* — *travel document in lieu of a national passport*			X (1) X (2)									X (3)	

(1) Only for transit purposes; holders are subject to the visa requirement.
(2) Only if the Federal Republic of Germany is mentioned as the State of destination in the document in lieu of a passport; holders are subject to the visa requirement.

MX — Mexico

	A	B/NL/L	D	DK	E	EL	F	FIN	I	IS	NO	P	S
1	X	X	X	X	X	X	X	X	X	X	X	X	X
2	X	X	X	X	X	X	X	X	X	X	X	X	X
3	X	X	X	X	X	X	X	X	X	X	X	X	X
4													
5													
6													
7		X			X	X	X	X	X			X	
8													
9													
10													
11 — documento de identidad y viaje							O						

MY — Malaysia

	A	B/NL/L	D	DK	E	EL	F	FIN	I	IS	NO	P	S
1	X	X	X	X	X	X	X	X	X	X	X	X	X
2	X	X	X	X	X	X	X	X	X	X	X	X	X
3	X	X	X	X	X	X	X	X	X	X	X	X	X
4													
5													
6													
7		X						X					
8													
9													
10													
11 — *certificate of identity (booklet with brown cover, 32 pages)*		O	O		O		O		O				
— *emergency certificate*		O	O				X [1]		O				

[1] Recognised for exit or transit for return to Malaysia.

MZ — Mozambique

	A	B/NL/L	D	DK	E	EL	F	FIN	I	IS	NO	P	S
1	X	X	X	X	X	X	X	X	X	X	X	X	X
2	X	X	X	X	X	X	X	X	X	X	X	X	X
3	X	X	X	X	X	X	X	X	X	X	X	X	X
4													
5													
6													
7						X	O					X	
8	X	X	X*	X	X	X	X	X	X	X	X	X	X
9													
10													
11													
— *student's passport*							O						
— *travel document*	O												

NA — Namibia

	A	B/NL/L	D	DK	E	EL	F	FIN	I	IS	NO	P	S
1	X	X	X	X	X	X	X	X	X	X	X	X	X
2	X	X	X*	X	X	X	X	X	X	X	X	X	X
3	X	X	X	X	X	X	X	X	X	X	X	X	X
4													
5													
6													
7													
8	X	X	X*	X	X	X	X	X	X	X	X	X	X
9													
10 (1)	X						O						
11													
— *emergency travel certificate*			X (2)										
— *Council of the United Nations travel document for Namibia*			X (3)										

(1) Document for travel purposes.
(2) Only for transit purposes, provided that the document replacing the passport contains a photo of the holder and is also valid for the Federal Republic of Germany.
(3) Provided that the document contains authorisation to return to the country in which the holder has resided to date or authorisation entitling the holder to enter the territory of another State.

NE — Niger

	A	B/NL/L	D	DK	E	EL	F	FIN	I	IS	NO	P	S
1	X	X	X	X	X	X	X	X	X	X	X	X	X
2	X	X	X	X	X	X	X	X	X	X	X	X	X
3	X	X	X	X	X	X	X	X	X	X	X	X	X
4													
5													
6													
7													
8 (1)	X	X	X*	X	X	X	X	X	X	X	X	X	X
9													
10													
11 — *diplomatic passport (loose-leaf)*							O						

(1) Document not issued on 7.5.1998.

NG — Nigeria

	A	B/NL/L	D	DK	E	EL	F	FIN	I	IS	NO	P	S
1	X	X	X	X	X	X	X	X	X	X	X	X	X
2	X	X	X	X	X	X	X	X	X	X	X	X	X
3	X	X	X	X	X	X	X	X	X	X	X	X	X
4													
5													
6													
7		X	X			X	X	X					
8	X	X	X*	X	X	X	X	X	X	X	X	X	X
9													
10													
11 — *emergency certificate*							X (1)						

(1) Recognised for exit or transit for return to Nigeria.

NI — Nicaragua

	A	B/ NL/ L	D	DK	E	EL	F	FIN	I	IS	NO	P	S
1	X	X	X	X	X	X	X	X	X	X	X	X	X
2	X	X	X	X	X	X	X	X	X	X	X	X	X
3	X	X	X	X	X	X	X	X	X	X	X	X	X
4			X										
5													
6													
7													
8 (1)	X	X	X*	X	X	X	X	X	X	X	X	X	X
9													
10 (2)			X				O		O				
11 — salvo conducto *(loose-leaf)* — pasaporte ordinario provisional — pasaporte provisional			 X (3)		 O		 O X (4)					 O	

(1) Not issued on 7.5.1998.
(2) *Identidad y viaje*
(3) Provided that the document replacing the passport contains a visa for another entry valid for Nicaragua and that the document is valid for the Federal Republic of Germany.
(4) Recognised for exit or transit for return to Nicaragua.

NP — Nepal

	A	B/ NL/ L	D	DK	E	EL	F	FIN	I	IS	NO	P	S
1	X	X	X	X	X	X	X	X	X	X	X	X	X
2	X	X	X*	X	X	X	X	X	X	X	X	X	X
3	X	X	X	X	X	X	X	X	X	X	X	X	X
4													
5													
6													
7													
8													
9													
10													
11 — *travel document (loose-leaf)*							O						

NR — Nauru

	A	B/NL/L	D	DK	E	EL	F	FIN	I	IS	NO	P	S
1	X	X	X	X	X	X	X	X	X	X	X	X	
2	X	X	X*	X	X	X	X	X	X	X	X	X	
3													
4													
5													
6													
7													
8													
9													
10													
11													

NZ — New Zealand

	A	B/NL/L	D	DK	E	EL	F	FIN	I	IS	NO	P	S
1	X	X	X	X	X	X	X	X	X	X	X	X	X
2	X	X	X	X	X	X	X	X	X	X	X	X	X
3	X	X	X	X	X	X	X	X	X	X	X	X	X
4													
5													
6													
7		X				X	X	X					
8	X	X	X*	X	X	X	X	X	X	X	X	X	X
9													
10 (1)			X (2)		O		O		O			X (2)	
11													

(1) Identity certificate.
(2) Recognised if the document contains a return permit.

OM — Oman

	A	B/NL/L	D	DK	E	EL	F	FIN	I	IS	NO	P	S
1	X	X	X	X	X	X	X	X	X	X	X	X	X
2	X	X	X	X	X	X	X	X	X	X	X	X	X
3	X	X	X*	X	X	X	X	X	X	X	X	X	X
4							X		X				
5													
6													
7													
8													
9													
10													
11 — *temporary travel permit* — *travel document (dark green)*			X (1)				 O						

(1) Provided that the document is valid for the Federal Republic of Germany.

PA — Panama

	A	B/NL/L	D	DK	E	EL	F	FIN	I	IS	NO	P	S
1	X	X	X	X	X	X	X	X	X	X	X	X	X
2	X	X	X	X	X	X	X	X	X	X	X	X	X
3	X	X	X	X	X	X	X	X	X	X	X	X	X
4			X				X		O			X	
5													
6													
7		X	O		X	X	X	X	X			X	
8	X	X	X*	X	X	X	X	X	X	X	X	X	X
9													
10													
11 — *consular passport* — *student passport* — salvo conducto *issued by the Ministry of the Interior and of Justice*			 X				X O						

PE — Peru

	A	B/ NL/ L	D	DK	E	EL	F	FIN	I	IS	NO	P	S
1	X	X	X	X	X	X	X	X	X	X	X	X	X
2	X	X	X	X	X	X	X	X	X	X	X	X	X
3	X	X		X	X	X		X		X	X	X	X
4		X	X				X		X				
5													
6													
7		X				X	X	X					
8	X	X	X*	X	X	X	X	X	X	X	X	X	X
9													
10													
11 — *safe-conduct*									O				

PG — Papua New Guinea

	A	B/ NL/ L	D	DK	E	EL	F	FIN	I	IS	NO	P	S
1	X	X	X	X	X	X	X	X	X	X	X	X	X
2	X	X	X	X	X	X	X	X	X	X	X	X	X
3	X	X	X	X	X	X	X	X	X	X	X	X	X
4													
5													
6													
7		X				X	O	X					
8 [1]	X	X	X*	X	X	X	X	X	X	X	X	X	X
9													
10													
11 — *certificate of identity* — *emergency travel document*							O						

[1] Document not issued on 7.5.1998.

PH — Philippines

	A	B/ NL/ L	D	DK	E	EL	F	FIN	I	IS	NO	P	S
1	X	X	X	X	X	X	X	X	X	X	X	X	X
2	X	X	X	X	X	X	X	X	X	X	X	X	X
3	X	X	X	X	X	X	X	X	X	X	X	X	X
4													
5													
6													
7		X	X			X	O	X					
8	X	X	X*	X	X	X	X	X	X	X	X	X	X
9													
10													
11 — *travel document*			X				O						

PK — Pakistan

	A	B/ NL/ L	D	DK	E	EL	F	FIN	I	IS	NO	P	S
1	X	X	X	X	X	X	X	X	X	X	X	X	X
2	X	X	X	X	X	X	X	X	X	X	X	X	X
3	X	X	X	X	X	X	X	X	X	X	X	X	X
4													
5													
6													
7		X				X	O	X					
8													
9													
10													
11													

PL — Poland

	A	B/ NL/ L	D	DK	E	EL	F	FIN	I	IS	NO	P	S
1	X	X	X	X	X	X	X	X	X	X	X	X	X
2	X	X	X	X	X	X	X	X	X	X	X	X	X
3	X	X	X	X	X	X	X	X	X	X	X	X	X
4													
5	X (1)		X (2)				**O**						
6													
7	X	X	X	X	X	X	X	X	X			X	X
8	X	X	X	X	X	X	X	X	X	X	X	X	X
9													
10 (3)	X (4)	**O**			**O**		**O**						
11													
— *consular passport*	X		X (6)										
— *permit for seagoing personnel*	X						**O**						
— *provisional travel document*							**O**						
— *emergency travel document/* Paszport Blankietowy	X (5)		X (7)					X					

(1) Accompanied by an identity card valid for the Republic of Poland.
(2) Provided that the guide has a valid Polish passport and that the members of the group have an identity card with a photo.
(3) Travel document (document *podrozy*).
(4) Solely booklet form recognised.
(5) Recognised for exit and transit for return to Poland.
(6) In booklet form, if the document is valid for the Federal Republic of Germany; in loose-leaf form only for transit purposes.
(7) Solely for transit purposes.

PS — Palestinian Authority

	A	B/NL/L	D	DK	E	EL	F	FIN	I	IS	NO	P	S
1	X	X	X ([1])	X	X	X	X	X	X	X	X	X	X
2													
3													
4 (VIP)	X	X	X ([1])		X	X	X	X	X	X	X	X	X
5													
6													
7													
8													
9													
10													
11													

([1]) Provided that the holder is officially resident in the independent territories.

PW — Palau

	A	B/NL/L	D	DK	E	EL	F	FIN	I	IS	NO	P	S
1	X	X	X	X	X	X	X	X	X	X	X	X	X
2	X	X		X	X		X	X	X	X	X	X	
3	X	X		X	X		X	X	X	X	X	X	
4													
5													
6													
7													
8													
9													
10													
11													

PY — Paraguay

	A	B/NL/L	D	DK	E	EL	F	FIN	I	IS	NO	P	S
1	X	X	X	X	X	X	X	X	X	X	X	X	X
2	X	X	X*	X	X	X	X	X	X	X	X	X	X
3	X	X	X	X	X	X	X	X	X	X	X	X	X
4			X										
5													
6													
7													
8	X	X	X*	X	X	X	X	X	X	X	X	X	X
9													
10													
11													

QA — Qatar

	A	B/NL/L	D	DK	E	EL	F	FIN	I	IS	NO	P	S
1	X	X	X	X	X	X	X	X	X	X	X	X	X
2	X	X	X	X	X	X	X	X	X	X	X	X	X
3	X	X	X	X	X	X	X	X	X	X	X	X	X
4	X		X				X		X				
5													
6													
7													
8													
9													
10													
11 — *travel document* — *travel permit*			O				X ([1]) O						

([1]) Can only be covered if the return permit is contained in the travel document.

RO — Romania

	A	B/ NL/ L	D	DK	E	EL	F	FIN	I	IS	NO	P	S
1	X	X	X	X	X	X	X	X	X	X	X	X	X
2	X	X	X	X	X	X	X	X	X	X	X	X	X
3	X	X	X	X	X	X	X	X	X	X	X	X	X
4													
5			X (1)										
6													
7		X	X		X	X	X	X	X			X	
8	X	X	X	X	X	X	X	X	X	X	X	X	X
9													
10													
11													
— *consular passport*	X		X (2)		O		X (3)					X (3)	
— *Danube boatman's card*	X						O					O	
— *passport for persons without citizenship (also issued to Romanians who have lost their nationality)*		O					O						
— *travel document (issued to illegal aliens)*		O					O					O	
— *certificate of return (simple declaration)*			X (2)										

(1) Provided that the document is valid for the Federal Republic of Germany.
(2) Solely for transit purposes.
(3) Recognised for exit or transit for return to Romania.

RU — Russia

	A	B/ NL/ L	D	DK	E	EL	F	FIN	I	IS	NO	P	S
1	X	X	X	X	X	X	X	X	X	X	X	X	X
2	X	X	X	X	X	X	X	X	X	X	X	X	X
3	X	X	X	X	X	X	X	X	X	X	X	X	X
4													
5													
6													
7		X	X (1)		X	X	X	X	X			X	X
8	X	X	X*	X	X	X	X	X	X	X	X	X	X
9													
10													
11													
— *Danube boatman's card*	X						O					O	
— *repatriation certificate*			X (2)					X					

(1) Provided that it is clear from the seaman's book that the person concerned is of Russian nationality and that there is proof that the person is on the crew list.
(2) Solely for transit purposes.

RW — Rwanda (1)

	A	B/ NL/ L	D	DK	E	EL	F	FIN	I	IS	NO	P	S
1	X	X	X	X	X	X	X	X	X	X	X	X	X
2	X	X	X	X	X	X	X	X	X	X	X	X	X
3	X	X	X	X	X	X	X	X	X	X	X	X	X
4													
5													
6													
7													
8	X	X	X	X	X	X	X	X	X	X	X	X	X
9													
10													
11													
— *laissez-passer replacing the passport*							O						

(1) Passports issued before 30.9.1996 are no longer valid.

SA — Saudi Arabia

	A	B/NL/L	D	DK	E	EL	F	FIN	I	IS	NO	P	S
1	X	X	X	X	X	X	X	X	X	X	X	X	X
2	X	X	X	X	X	X	X	X	X	X	X	X	X
3			X										
4	X	X	X	X	X	X	X	X	X	X	X	X	X
5													
6													
7													
8													
9													
10													
11 — *laissez-passer*			X (1)				O						

(1) If it contains an authorisation of return in the form of an exit/re-entry visa. Otherwise, the passport replacement document and the exit/re-entry visa must be valid for at least six months.

SB — Solomon Islands

	A	B/NL/L	D	DK	E	EL	F	FIN	I	IS	NO	P	S
1	X	X	X*	X	X	X	X	X	X	X	X	X	
2	X	X	X*	X	X	X	X	X	X	X	X	X	
3	X	X	X*	X	X	X	X	X	X	X	X	X	
4													
5													
6													
7		X			X	X		X	X			X	
8	X	X	X*	X	X	X	X	X	X	X	X	X	X
9													
10													
11													

SC — Seychelles

	A	B/NL/L	D	DK	E	EL	F	FIN	I	IS	NO	P	S
1	X	X	X	X	X	X	X	X	X	X	X	X	X
2	X	X	X	X	X	X	X	X	X	X	X	X	X
3	X	X	X	X	X	X	X	X	X	X	X	X	
4													
5													
6													
7		X			X	X	X	X	X			X	
8 (1)	X	X	X*	X	X	X	X	X	X	X	X	X	X
9													
10													
11 — *emergency passport*							O						

(1) Document not issued on 7.5.1998.

SD — Sudan

	A	B/NL/L	D	DK	E	EL	F	FIN	I	IS	NO	P	S
1	X	X	X	X	X	X	X	X	X	X	X	X	X
2	X	X	X	X	X	X	X	X	X	X	X	X	X
3	X	X		X	X		X	X	X	X	X	X	X
4			X										
5													
6													
7		X					O	X					
8	X	X	X (1)	X	X	X	X	X	X	X	X	X	X
9													
10													
11 — *emergency travel document*							O						

(1) Provided that the return permit is contained in the document replacing the passport.

SG — Singapore

	A	B/ NL/ L	D	DK	E	EL	F	FIN	I	IS	NO	P	S
1	X	X	X	X	X	X	X	X	X	X	X	X	X
2	X	X	X	X	X	X	X	X	X	X	X	X	X
3	X	X	X	X	X	X	X	X	X	X	X	X	
4													
5													
6													
7		X				X	X	X					
8													
9													
10	X						O						
11													
— *certificate of identity*			X				O						
— *international certificate of identity with return visa*		X					O						
— *document of identity* (1)	X		X (2)			X	X (3)						

(1) Only for Singapore nationals.
(2) Solely for transit purposes and provided that the route logically passes through the Federal Republic of Germany.
(3) Recognised for exit or transit for return to Singapore.

SI — Slovenia

	A	B/ NL/ L	D	DK	E	EL	F	FIN	I	IS	NO	P	S
1	X	X	X	X	X	X	X	X	X	X	X	X	X
2	X	X	X*	X	X	X	X	X	X	X	X	X	X
3	X	X	X*	X	X	X	X	X	X	X	X	X	X
4	X (1)												
5							O		X				
6													
7		X				X	X		X				
8	X	X	X*	X	X	X	X	X	X	X	X	X	X
9 (2)	X	X		X	X	X	X	X	X		X		X
10 (3)			O				O						
11 — *identity card* — *boatman's card* — *emergency passport*	 X X X						 O O X (4)		 X				

(1) Accompanied by an official pass proving the identity of the holder.
(2) Document not issued on 7.5.1998.
(3) Passport for foreigners.
(4) Recognised for exit or transit for return to Slovenia.

SK — Slovakia

	A	B/ NL/ L	D	DK	E	EL	F	FIN	I	IS	NO	P	S
1	X	X	X	X	X	X	X	X	X	X	X	X	X
2	X	X	X	X	X	X	X	X	X	X	X	X	X
3	X	X	X	X	X	X	X	X	X	X	X	X	X
4													
5													
6	X												
7			X			X	X						
8	X	X	X*	X	X	X	X	X	X	X	X	X	X
9													
10 (1)	X		X		O		O						
11 — *travelling document* (cestovny preukaz)	X		X (2)				X (3)						

(1) *Cestovny preukaz totoznosti*/travel identity card (booklet) and *cestovny preukaz totosnosti* (loose-leaf).
(2) Solely for transit purposes, if in order to return to Slovakia the person has to logically travel through the Federal Republic of Germany.
(3) Recognised for exit or transit to return to Slovakia.

SL — Sierra Leone

	A	B/NL/L	D	DK	E	EL	F	FIN	I	IS	NO	P	S
1	X	X	X	X	X	X	X	X	X	X	X	X	X
2	X	X	X	X	X	X	X	X	X	X	X	X	X
3	X	X	X	X	X	X	X	X	X	X	X	X	X
4													
5													
6													
7		X				X	O	X					
8 (1)	X	X		X	X	X	X	X	X	X	X	X	X
9													
10													
11													

(1) Document not issued on 7.5.1998.

SM — San Marino

	A	B/NL/L	D	DK	E	EL	F	FIN	I	IS	NO	P	S
1	X	X	X	X	X	X	X	X	X	X	X	X	X
2	X	X	X	X	X	X	X	X	X	X	X	X	X
3	X					X	X	X	X		X		X
4													
5													
6													
7													
8													
9													
10													
11													
— *national identity card*	X	X			X	X	X	X	X			X	
— *identity card for State officials*	X								X				
— *children under 15 years of age; photo and confirmation that they are nationals of San Marino*	X								X				

SN — Senegal

	A	B/NL/L	D	DK	E	EL	F	FIN	I	IS	NO	P	S
1	X	X	X	X	X	X	X	X	X	X	X	X	X
2	X	X	X	X	X	X	X	X	X	X	X	X	X
3	X	X	X (1)	X	X	X	X	X	X	X	X	X	X
4													
5													
6													
7		X			X	X	X	X	X			X	
8	X	X	X*	X	X	X	X	X	X	X	X	X	X
9													
10													
11													

(1) In booklet and loose-leaf form.

SO — Somalia

	A (1)	B/NL/L (1)	D (1)	DK (1)	E (1)	EL	F (1)	FIN	I (1)	IS	NO	P (1)	S
1	X	X	X*	X	X	X	X		X			X	O
2	X	X	X*	X	X	X	X		X			X	O
3	X	X	X*	X	X	X	X		X			X	O
4													
5													
6													
7		X				X	O						
8	X	X	X*	X	X	X	X		X	X		X	X
9													
10													
11													

(1) This no longer covers passports or documents replacing passports, issued or extended by a Somalian diplomatic or consular authority or post after 31.1.1991.

SR — Suriname

	A	B/ NL/ L	D	DK	E	EL	F	FIN	I	IS	NO	P	S
1	X	X	X	X	X	X	X	X	X	X	X	X	X
2	X	X	X	X	X	X	X	X	X	X	X	X	
3	X	X	X*	X	X	X	X	X	X	X	X	X	
4													
5													
6													
7							X	X					
8 (1)	X	X	X*	X	X	X	X	X	X	X	X	X	X
9													
10 (2)			X (3)				**O**						
11													
— *ordinary passport for trade*		X					X (4)						
— paspoort *(laissez-passer)*							**O**						

(1) Document not issued on 7.5.1998.
(2) *Paspoort voor vreemdelingen.*
(3) Provided that the document replacing the passport contains a visa for entry valid for Suriname and that it is valid for the territory of the Federal Republic of Germany.
(4) Treated in the same way as an ordinary passport.

ST — São Tomé and Príncipe

	A	B/ NL/ L	D	DK	E	EL	F	FIN	I	IS	NO	P	S
1	X	X	X	X	X	X	X	X	X	X	X	X	
2	X	X	X	X	X	X	X	X	X	X	X	X	X
3	X	X	X	X	X	X	X	X	X	X	X	X	X
4													
5													
6													
7		X				X	**O**	X				X	
8	X	X	X*	X	X	X	X	X	X	X	X	X	X
9													
10													
11													

SV — El Salvador

	A	B/NL/L	D	DK	E	EL	F	FIN	I	IS	NO	P	S
1	X	X	X	X	X	X	X	X	X	X	X	X	X
2	X	X	X	X	X	X	X	X	X	X	X	X	X
3	X	X	X (1)	X	X	X	X	X	X	X	X	X	X
4													
5													
6													
7													
8 (2)	X	X	X*	X	X	X	X	X	X	X	X	X	X
9													
10													
11													

(1) Except for a white service passport. This is not deemed sufficient for crossing the border and staying in the territory of the Federal Republic.
(2) Document not issued on 7.5.1998.

SY — Syria

	A	B/NL/L	D	DK	E	EL	F	FIN	I	IS	NO	P	S
1	X	X	X	X	X	X	X	X	X	X	X	X	X
2	X	X	X*	X	X	X	X	X	X	X	X	X	
3	X	X	O	X	X	X	X	X	X	X	X	X	
4	X	X	X		X	X	X		X			X	
5													
6													
7		X					X	X					
8													
9													
10													
11 — *document for Palestinian refugees*					X		X (1)						

(1) Cannot be covered unless a permanent return permit is contained in the travel document.

SZ — Swaziland

	A	B/NL/L	D	DK	E	EL	F	FIN	I	IS	NO	P	S
1	X	X	X	X	X	X	X	X	X	X	X	X	X
2	X	X	X	X	X	X	X	X	X	X	X	X	X
3													
4													
5													
6													
7													
8	X	X	X*	X	X	X	X	X	X	X	X	X	X
9													
10													
11													

TD — Chad

	A	B/NL/L	D	DK	E	EL	F	FIN	I	IS	NO	P	S
1	X	X	X	X	X	X	X	X	X	X	X	X	X
2	X	X	X	X	X	X	X	X	X	X	X	X	X
3	X	X	X	X	X	X	X	X	X	X	X	X	X
4			X				X						
5													
6													
7													
8	X	X		X	X	X	X	X	X	X	X	X	X
9													
10													
11													
— *travel permit*				O	O		O						
— *laissez-passer*				O	O		O					O	

TG — Togo

	A	B/ NL/ L	D	DK	E	EL	F	FIN	I	IS	NO	P	S
1	X	X	X	X	X	X	X	X	X	X	X	X	X
2	X	X	X	X	X	X	X	X	X	X	X	X	X
3	X	X	X	X	X	X	X	X	X	X	X	X	X
4													
5													
6													
7		X				X	X	X					
8	X	X		X	X	X	X	X	X	X	X	X	X
9													
10													
11													
— *travel permit*			O		O		O						
— *laissez-passer for aliens*			O		O		O						
— *safe conduct*			O				O						
— *identity certificate for the States of the West African Economic and Monetary Union*					O		O					O	

TH — Thailand

	A	B/ NL/ L	D	DK	E	EL	F	FIN	I	IS	NO	P	S
1	X	X	X	X	X	X	X	X	X	X	X	X	X
2	X	X	X	X	X	X	X	X	X	X	X	X	X
3	X	X	X	X	X	X	X	X	X	X	X	X	X
4													
5							O						
6													
7							X						
8													
9													
10 (1)			X (2)				O						
11													
— *free passport*			X				X (3)						
— *certificate of identity (loose-leaf)*							X (4)						
— *emergency certificate*							O						

(1) Travel document for aliens (yellow cover).
(2) The travel document for aliens is recognised provided it is valid for the Federal Republic of Germany and that it contains a return visa.
(3) Issued to officials, Buddhist priests, sportspersons ... dealt with in the same way as an ordinary passport.
(4) Recognised for exit or transit for return to Thailand.

TJ — Tajikistan

	A	B/NL/L	D	DK	E	EL	F	FIN	I	IS	NO	P	S
1	X	X	X	X	X	X	X	X	X	X	X	X	X
2	X	X	X	X	X	X	X	X	X	X	X	X	X
3			X			X	X						X
4													
5													
6													
7					X	X		X				X	
8	X	X		X	X	X	X	X	X	X	X	X	X
9													
10													
11													

TM — Turkmenistan

	A	B/NL/L	D	DK	E	EL	F	FIN	I	IS	NO	P	S
1 [1]	X	X		X	X	X	X	X	X	X	X	X	X
2	X	X	X	X	X	X	X	X	X	X	X	X	X
3	X	X	X	X	X	X	X	X	X	X	X	X	X
4													
5													
6													
7			X				O						
8	X	X		X	X	X	X	X	X	X	X	X	X
9													
10													
11													

[1] Passports from the former USSR are valid until 31.12.2001.

TN — Tunisia

	A	B/NL/L	D	DK	E	EL	F	FIN	I	IS	NO	P	S
1	X	X	X	X	X	X	X	X	X	X	X	X	X
2	X	X	X	X	X	X	X	X	X	X	X	X	X
3	X	X				X		X		X	X		
4	X	X	X		X	X	X		X			X	
5			X										
6													
7		X	X		X	X	X	X	X			X	
8	X	X	X*	X	X	X	X	X	X	X	X	X	X
9	X	X		X	X	X	X	X	X		X		X
10													
11 — *laissez-passer (for exit from Tunisia)*			O				O						

TO — Tonga

	A	B/NL/L	D	DK	E	EL	F	FIN	I	IS	NO	P	S
1	X	X	X*	X	X	X	X	X	X	X	X	X	X
2	X	X	X*	X	X	X	X	X	X	X	X	X	X
3	X	X	X*	X	X	X	X	X	X	X	X	X	X
4													
5													
6													
7		X				X	O						
8													
9													
10							O						
11 — *Tongan protected person passport*		O	O				O		O			O	
— *national Tongan passport (different from the ordinary passport)*									O				
— *certificate of identity*							O						

TR — Turkey

	A	B/NL/L	D	DK	E	EL	F	FIN	I	IS	NO	P	S
1	X	X	X	X	X	X	X	X	X	X	X	X	X
2	X	X	X	X	X	X	X	X	X	X	X	X	X
3	X	X	X	X	X	X	X	X	X	X	X	X	X
4	X	X	X	X		X	X		X		X	X	X
5		X			X	X	X (1)		X	X		X	
6													
7		X	O			O	X						
8	X	X		X	X	X	X	X	X	X	X	X	X
9													
10	X						O						
11 — *travel document valid only for returning to Turkey*	X						X (2)						

(1) Issued in accordance with the European Convention of 16 December 1961 (group passport and group passport for young persons).
(2) Recognised for exit or transit for return to Turkey.

TT — Trinidad and Tobago

	A	B/NL/L	D	DK	E	EL	F	FIN	I	IS	NO	P	S
1	X	X	X	X	X	X	X	X	X	X	X	X	X
2	X	X	X*	X	X	X	X	X	X	X	X	X	X
3	X	X	X*	X	X	X	X	X	X	X	X	X	X
4												X	
5													
6													
7		X				X	X	X					
8													
9	X	X		X	X	X	X	X	X		X		X
10													
11													
— *certificate of identity*			X				O						
— *passport for Members of Parliament*		X					X					X	

TV — Tuvalu

	A	B/ NL/ L	D	DK	E	EL	F	FIN	I	IS	NO	P	S
1	X	X	X	X	X	X	X	X	X	X	X	X	
2	X	X	X	X	X	X	X	X	X	X	X	X	
3													
4													
5													
6													
7			X										
8 (1)	X	X	X	X	X	X	X	X	X	X	X	X	X
9													
10													
11 — *certificate of identity*							O						

(1) Document not issued on 7.5.1998.

TW — Taiwan

	A	B/ NL/ L	D	DK	E	EL	F	FIN	I	IS	NO	P (1)	S
1	X	X	X	X	X	X	X	X	X	X	X	O	X
2	X		X	O		O	O	O (2)	X		X	O	X
3	X		X	O		O	O	O (2)	X		X	O	
4													
5													
6													
7													
8													
9													
10													
11													

(1) Portugal can agree to its partners affixing visas in the passports. Portugal affixes visas on a separate sheet of paper.
(2) Accepted as a normal passport.

TZ — Tanzania

	A	B/ NL/ L	D	DK	E	EL	F	FIN	I	IS	NO	P	S
1	X	X	X	X	X	X	X	X	X	X	X	X	X
2	X	X	X	X	X	X	X	X	X	X	X	X	X
3	X	X	X	X	X	X	X	X	X	X	X	X	X
4													
5													
6													
7					X	X	X	X	X			X	
8	X	X	X	X	X	X	X	X	X	X	X	X	X
9													
10													
11 — *certificate of identity*							**O**						

UA — Ukraine

	A	B/ NL/ L	D	DK	E	EL	F	FIN	I	IS	NO	P	S
1	X	X	X	X	X	X	X	X	X	X	X	X	X
2	X	X	X	X	X	X	X	X	X	X	X	X	X
3	X	X	X	X	X	X	X	X	X	X	X	X	X
4													
5													
6 (1)			X				X	X	X				
7		X	X (2)		X	X	X	X	X				
8													
9													
10 (3)							**O**						
11 — *certificate for returning to Ukraine of a citizen of Ukraine*							X (4)						

(1) Travel document of a child (blue booklet).
(2) Provided that it is clear from the seaman's book that the person concerned is of Ukrainian nationality and that there is proof that the person is on the crew list.
(3) Stateless person's travel document.
(4) Recognised for exit or transit for return to Ukraine.

UG — Uganda

	A	B/ NL/ L	D	DK	E	EL	F	FIN	I	IS	NO	P	S
1	X* (1)	X	X	X	X	X	X	X	X	X	X	X	X
2	X*	X	X	X	X	X	X	X	X	X	X	X	X
3	X*	X	X	X	X	X	X	X	X	X	X	X	X
4													
5													
6													
7													
8	X	X	X*	X	X	X	X	X	X	X	X	X	X
9	X	X		X	X	X	X	X	X		X		X
10													
11													

(1) This asterisk has the same meaning as the asterisk for Germany (see introduction).

US — United States

	A	B/ NL/ L	D	DK	E	EL	F	FIN	I	IS	NO	P	S
1	X	X	X	X	X	X	X	X	X	X	X	X	X
2	X	X	X	X	X	X	X	X	X	X	X	X	X
3	X	X	X	X	X	X	X	X	X	X	X	X	X
4													
5													
6													
7		X					X	X					
8			X										
9													
10 (1)	X	X	X		X	X	X	X	X			X	
11													

(1) Called 'Re-entry permit' or 'Permit to re-enter the United States'.

UY — Uruguay

	A	B/ NL/ L	D	DK	E	EL	F	FIN	I	IS	NO	P	S
1	X	X	X	X	X	X	X	X	X	X	X	X	X
2	X	X	X	X	X	X	X	X	X	X	X	X	X
3	X	X	X	X	X	X	X	X	X	X	X	X	X
4													
5													
6													
7		X			X	X	X	X	X			X	
8	X	X	X*	X	X	X	X	X	X	X	X	X	X
9													
10 (1)		X (2)	X (2)			X (2)	O					X (2)	
11													

(1) *Titulo de identidad de viaje.*
(2) Recognised if the document contains a return permit.

UZ — Uzbekistan

	A	B/ NL/ L	D	DK	E	EL	F	FIN	I	IS	NO	P	S
1	X	X	X	X	X	X	X	X	X	X	X	X	X
2	X	X	X	X	X	X	X	X	X	X	X	X	X
3	X							X			X	X	
4													
5													
6													
7													
8													
9													
10 (1)							O						
11 — *identity card for persons without citizenship*			X				O						

(1) Identity card for foreigners resident in the Republic of Uzbekistan.

VA — Vatican City

	A	B/ NL/ L	D	DK	E	EL	F	FIN	I	IS	NO	P	S
1	X	X	X	X	X	X	X	X	X	X	X	X	
2	X	X	X	X	X	X	X	X	X	X	X	X	
3	X	X	X*	X	X	X	X	X	X	X	X	X	
4													
5													
6													
7													
8 (1)	X	X	X*	X	X	X	X	X	X	X	X	X	X
9 (1)	X	X		X	X	X	X	X	X		X		X
10													
11													

(1) Document not issued on 7.5.1998.

VC — Saint Vincent and the Grenadines

	A	B/ NL/ L	D	DK	E	EL	F	FIN	I	IS	NO	P	S
1	X	X	X	X	X	X	X	X	X	X	X	X	X
2	X	X	X	X	X	X	X	X	X	X	X	X	X
3	X	X	X*	X	X	X	X	X	X	X	X	X	
4													
5													
6													
7		X				X	O	X					
8	X	X	X*	X	X	X	X	X	X	X	X	X	X
9													
10													
11 — *emergency passport*							X (1)						

(1) Recognised for exit or transit to return to Saint Vincent and the Grenadines.

VE — Venezuela

	A	B/NL/L	D	DK	E	EL	F	FIN	I	IS	NO	P	S
1	X	X	X	X	X	X	X	X	X	X	X	X	X
2	X	X	X	X	X	X	X	X	X	X	X	X	X
3	X	X	X	X	X	X	X	X	X	X	X	X	X
4					X							X	
5													
6													
7		X				X	O	X					
8													
9													
10													
11													
— *one-year provisional passport (loose-leaf)*	X		X (1)		X	X	O	X	X			X	
— *emergency passport*		O							O				

(1) The holders are subject to the visa requirement.

VN — Vietnam

	A	B/NL/L	D	DK	E	EL	F	FIN	I	IS	NO	P	S
1	X	X	X	X	X	X	X	X	X	X	X	X	X
2	X	X	X	X	X	X	X	X	X	X	X	X	X
3	X	X	X	X	X	X	X	X	X	X	X	X	X
4													
5													
6													
7 (1)		X				X	O	X					
8													
9													
10													
11													
— *laissez-passer (loose-leaf)*							X (2)						

(1) Seaman's passport (for officers) and seaman's book (for fishermen).
(2) Recognised for exit or transit to return to Vietnam.

VU — Vanuatu

	A	B/ NL/ L	D	DK	E	EL	F	FIN	I	IS	NO	P	S
1	X	X	X	X	X	X	X	X	X	X	X	X	
2	X	X	X	X	X	X	X	X	X	X	X	X	
3	X	X	X	X	X	X	X	X	X	X	X	X	
4													
5													
6													
7													
8													
9													
10													
11													

WS — Western Samoa

	A	B/ NL/ L	D	DK	E	EL	F	FIN	I	IS	NO	P	S
1	X	X	X	X	X	X	X	X	X	X	X	X	
2	X	X	X	X	X	X	X	X	X	X	X	X	
3	X	X	X	X	X	X	X	X	X	X	X	X	
4													
5													
6													
7													
8 (1)	X	X	X*	X	X	X	X	X	X	X	X	X	X
9													
10													
11 — *certificate of identity*							O						

(1) Document not issued on 7.5.1998.

YM —Yemen

	A	B/ NL/ L	D (1)	DK	E	EL	F	FIN	I	IS	NO	P	S
1	X	X	X	X	X	X	X	X	X	X	X	X	
2	X	X	X*	X	X	X	X	X	X	X	X	X	
3	X	X		X	X		X	X	X	X	X	X	
4		X					X					X	
5													
6													
7 (2)							X						
8 (2)	X	X	X*	X	X	X	X	X	X	X	X	X	X
9													
10													
11													

(1) All passports and documents replacing passports issued by the former Arab Republic of Yemen and the former Democratic People's Republic of Yemen are not recognised.
(2) Document not issued on 7.5.1998.

YU — Yugoslavia

	A	B/ NL/ L	D	DK	E	EL	F	FIN	I	IS	NO	P	S
1	X	X	X	X	X	X	X	X	X	X	X	X	X
2	X	X	X	X	X	X	X	X	X	X	X	X	X
3	X	X	X	X	X	X	X	X	X	X	X	X	X
4													
5			O				O		X				
6			X				O					O	
7						X	X	X	X			X	
8	X	X	X	X	X	X	X	X	X	X	X	X	X
9	X	X	X	X	X	X	X	X	X		X		X
10 (1)			O				O						
11 — *Danube boatman's card* — *emergency travel document (laissez-passer)*	X						O X (2)	X				O	

(1) *Putni List Za Strance* (laissez-passer for aliens).
(2) Recognised for exit and transit for return to Yugoslavia.

ZA — South Africa

	A	B/NL/L	D	DK	E	EL	F	FIN	I	IS	NO	P	S
1	X	X	X	X	X	X	X	X	X	X	X	X	X
2	X	X	X	X	X	X	X	X	X	X	X	X	X
3	X	X	X	X	X	X	X	X	X	X	X	X	X
4													
5													
6			X									X	
7		X						X					
8	X	X	X	X	X	X	X	X	X	X	X	X	X
9													
10 ([1])			X ([2])				O					X	
11 — *temporary passport* — *emergency passport*		X ([5])			X ([3])	X ([3])	X ([4]) X ([3])	X				X ([5])	X

([1]) Document for travel purposes.
([2]) If the document contains a guarantee of return (re-entry permit) valid for at least one year.
([3]) Recognised for exit or transit to return to South Africa.
([4]) Only recognised for nationals of South Africa.
([5]) Recognised solely for nationals of South Africa and can only be stamped in the 8 weeks following the date on which it was issued.

ZM — Zambia

	A	B/NL/L	D	DK	E	EL	F	FIN	I	IS	NO	P	S
1	X	X	X	X	X	X	X	X	X	X	X	X	X
2	X	X	X	X	X	X	X	X	X	X	X	X	X
3	X	X			X			X		X	X	X	X
4													
5													
6													
7							X	X					
8	X	X	X	X	X	X	X	X	X	X	X	X	X
9	X	X	X	X	X	X	X	X	X		X		X
10													
11 — *(local) travel document of identity* — *temporary travel document*		O O			O O		O						

ZW — Zimbabwe

	A	B/NL/L	D	DK	E	EL	F	FIN	I	IS	NO	P	S
1	X	X	X	X	X	X	X	X	X	X	X	X	X
2	X	X	X	X	X	X	X	X	X	X	X	X	X
3	X	X	X	X	X	X	X	X	X	X	X	X	X
4													
5													
6													
7													
8	X	X		X	X	X	X	X	X	X	X	X	X
9													
10													
11													
— *emergency travel document*		O			O		O	X					
— *temporary passport*		O			O								
— *passport for business trips*			X										

DECISION OF THE EXECUTIVE COMMITTEE of 28 April 1999 on the compilation of a manual of documents to which a visa may be affixed

(SCH/Com-ex (99) 14)

At its meeting in Berlin on 16 December 1998, the Executive Committee decided to compile a manual of documents to which a visa may be affixed (SCH/Com-ex (98) 56).

The manual will comprise the following sections:

Part I — Travel documents to which a visa may be affixed

Part II — Aliens' passports issued by the Schengen States to which a visa may be affixed

Part III — A list of the travel documents issued by international organisations

Part IV — Gradual compilation of a documentary record containing copies of originals

Part V — Information on known fictitious passports

The Executive Committee takes note of the fact that, in addition to Part I — 'Travel documents to which a visa may be affixed' — which was forwarded to it on 16 December 1998, Parts II, III and V are now also available (see annex ([1])).

This means that the essential components of the manual of documents to which a visa may be affixed are available. The gradual compilation of a documentary record containing copies of originals is being undertaken at European Union level. The manual on authentic documents issued by Interpol can also be used.

([1]) See annex to document SCH/Com-ex (98) 56.

The revised version of Part I as well as Parts II, III and V will be distributed to diplomatic missions and consular posts abroad. They can also be sent to the border authorities and to other bodies dealing with questions relating to the law on aliens.

The existing sections of the manual of documents to which a visa may be affixed should be revised when necessary, for instance every three months, starting on 1 July 1999.

Luxembourg, 28 April 1999

The Chairman

C. H. SCHAPPER

DECISION OF THE EXECUTIVE COMMITTEE of 16 December 1998 on the introduction of a harmonised form providing proof of invitation, sponsorship and accommodation

(SCH/Com-ex (98) 57)

The Executive Committee,

Having regard to Article 132 of the convention implementing the Schengen Agreement,

Having regard to Article 9 of the abovementioned convention,

Whereas it is in the interest of all the Schengen States to apply uniform rules to the issue of visas in the context of their common policy on the movement of persons, with a view to preventing possible negative consequences as regards entry into Schengen territory and internal security,

Wishing to build on hitherto positive experiences of the common consular instructions and to harmonise further the visa-issue procedure,

Guided by the principle of solidarity between the Schengen Partners,

HAS DECIDED AS FOLLOWS:

Point 1.4, Chapter V of the common consular instructions on visas — 'Verification of other documents depending on the application' lays down the use of a harmonised form providing proof of accommodation.

The form attached hereto allows for a high degree of flexibility and for use of the form adapted to the legal situation of each Contracting Party, since the Schengen States currently use very differing forms, for different types of obligation.

These differences have the effect in particular of increasing the risk of misuse and for that reason, the Schengen States are introducing a document incorporating features aimed at preventing counterfeiting and falsification.

Consequently, the standard document is uniform in terms of its:

— layout and structure and;

— security features.

The standard form shall be introduced in 1999 in the States implementing the Schengen Convention in which national law makes provision for this kind of proof.

1. The following sentence shall be added to point 1.4, Chapter V of the common consular instructions

   'Where the national laws of the Schengen States require proof of invitations from private individuals or for business trips, sponsorship declarations or proof of accommodation, a harmonised form shall be used [1].

2. The Schengen Contracting Parties shall complete the harmonised form in accordance with their national laws.

3. The harmonised form to be used by the Schengen Contracting Parties for sponsorship declarations, invitations or proof of accommodation shall be drawn up at a central level, in accordance with the specifications laid down in Annex A (technical description of security features) and in Annexes A1 and A2 (specimen). The obligatory standard elements of the harmonised form are given in Annex B.

4. Specimens of the documents issued by the Contracting Parties shall be added to the common consular instructions in the form of Annex 15.

5. France shall supply the films required for the production of the forms to the other Schengen States. The Contracting Parties shall bear the costs jointly.

6. The security features of the document shall be scrutinised at regular intervals (every two years, if possible) regardless of any general amendments which may prove necessary if the form is falsified by forgers or counterfeiters or if protective measures relating to security features have been revealed.

7. The document shall be produced in at least three languages.

8. This decision shall enter into force when the Schengen States have sent notification that they have implemented the requisite measures.

Berlin, 16 December 1998

The Chairman

C. H. SCHAPPER

[1] Austria, Belgium Denmark, Finland, France, Germany, Greece, Iceland, Italy, Luxembourg, the Netherlands, Norway, Portugal and Sweden apply these principles.

ANNEX A

TECHNICAL DESCRIPTION OF THE FORM

Annex A1

Bundesrepublik Deutschland

Verpflichtungserklärung

Déclaration de prise en charge

Formal obligation

D 00000000

Bundesdruckerei

Artikel-Nr. 10150

Ich, der/die Unterzeichnende Je, soussigné(e) I, the undersigned

Name / Nom / Surname

►

Vorname(n) / Prénom(s) / First name

Geburtstag und -ort / Né(e) le/à / Date and place of birth

Staatsangehörigkeit / Nationalité / Nationality

Identitätsdokument ([1]) / Aufenthaltstitel ([2]) / Document d'identité ([1]) / Titre de séjour ([2])
Identity card ([1]) / Residence title ([2])

wohnhaft in / Adresse / Address

Beruf / Profession / Profession

Zuständige Behörde
Autorité compétente
Competent authority

verpflichte mich gegenüber der Ausländerbehörde/Auslandsvertretung, für

m'engage auprès du service des étrangers/de la représentation diplomatique à héberger

take full responsibility towards the aliens authority/diplomatic representation for accommodating

Name / Nom / Surname

Vorname(n) / Prénom(s) / First name

Geburtstag und -ort / Né(e) le/à / Date and place of birth

Staatsangehörigkeit / Nationalité / Nationality

Reisepaß Nr. / Passeport n° / Passport No.

wohnhaft in / Adresse / Address

Verwandtschaftsbeziehung mit dem Antragsteller / Lien de parenté avec le demandeur /
Family relationship to applicant

und folgende sie/ihn begleitende Personen, nur Ehegatten ([3]) / accompagné(e) de son conjoint ([3]) /
accompanied by his or her spouse ([3])

und Kinder ([3]) / accompagné(e) de ses enfants ([3]) / accompanied by children ([3])

vom ... an bis zum ... / du ... au ... / from ... to ...

nach § 84 des Ausländergesetzes die Kosten für den Lebensunterhalt und nach §§ 82 und 83 des Ausländergesetzes die Kosten für die Ausreise o. g. Ausländers/in zu tragen.

et à prendre en charge le coût de la vie conformément au § 84 de la loi sur les étrangers et les frais de retour de l'étranger ci-dessus conformément aux §§ 82 et 83 de la loi sur les étrangers.

and for bearing the living costs according to § 84 of the Aliens Act and the departure costs of the above foreigner according to §§ 82 and 83 of the Aliens Act.

([1])
Art / type / type
Nummer / numéro / number

([2])
Nur bei Ausländern, Art des Titels / seulement pour les étrangers type de titre / applicable to foreigners only, type of title

([3])
Name / nom / surname
Vorname / prénom / first name
Geburtstag / date de naissance / date of birth
Geschlecht / sexe / sex

Die Verpflichtung umfaßt die Erstattung sämtlicher öffentlicher Mittel, die für den Lebensunterhalt einschließlich der Versorgung mit Wohnraum und der Versorgung im Krankheitsfall und bei Pflegebedürftigkeit aufgewendet werden (z. B. Arztbesuch, Medikamente, Krankenhausaufenthalt). Dies gilt auch, soweit die Aufwendungen auf einem gesetzlichen Anspruch beruhen, im Gegensatz zu Aufwendungen, die auf einer Beitragsleistung beruhen.

Die vorliegende Verpflichtung umfaßt auch die Ausreisekosten (z. B. Flugticket) o. g. Ausländers/in nach §§ 82 und 83 des Ausländergesetzes.

Ich wurde von der Ausländerbehörde hingewiesen auf
- den Umfang und die Dauer der Haftung;
- die Möglichkeit von Versicherungsschutz;
- die zwangsweise Beitreibung der aufgewendeten Kosten im Wege der Vollstreckung, soweit ich meiner Verpflichtung nicht nachkomme, sowie
- die Strafbarkeit z. B. bei vorsätzlichen, unrichtigen oder unvollständigen Angaben (§ 92 des Ausländergesetzes – Freiheitsstrafe bis zu drei Jahren oder Geldstrafe).

Ich bestätige, zu der Verpflichtung aufgrund meiner wirtschaftlichen Verhältnisse in der Lage zu sein.

Behörden-vermerke | Réservé à l'administration | Official remarks

Anschrift der Wohnung, in der die Unterschrift sichergestellt wird, falls abweichend vom gewöhnlichen Wohnsitz des Unterkunftgebers /
Adresse du logement dans lequel l'hébergement sera assuré, au cas où il serait différent du logement habituel de l'hébergeant /
Address of the lodging where accommodation will be provided, if different from the undersigned's normal address

Ich bin / j'en suis / I am

☐ Mieter / locataire / tenant ☐ Eigentümer / propriétaire / owner

Arbeitgeber / Employeur / Employer

Sonstige Angaben zu Wohn-, Einkommens- und Vermögensverhältnissen (Größe der Wohnung, Höhe des Einkommens) /
Renseignements complémentaires concernant le logement, les revenus et la situation financière /
Other details of housing conditions, income and financial situation

Gebühren

Der/die Verpflichtungserklärende

Ich versichere, die vorstehenden Angaben nach bestem Wissen und Gewissen richtig und vollständig gemacht zu haben und gehe eine entsprechende Verpflichtung ein.

Ort Datum

Unterschrift

Bemerkungen

Beglaubigungsvermerk der Ausländerbehörde/Auslandsvertretung

Die Unterschrift der/des Verpflichtungserklärenden ist vor mir vollzogen worden. Die Beglaubigung der Unterschrift dient nur zur Vorlage bei der deutschen Auslandsvertretung.

Behörde:

Ort Datum

Im Auftrag

(Siegel)

Stellungnahme der Ausländerbehörde / Auslandsvertretung

Die finanzielle Leistungsfähigkeit des/der Verpflichtungserklärenden wurde nachgewiesen / glaubhaft gemacht.

Behörde:

Ort Datum

Im Auftrag

(Siegel)

Annex A2

République Française **Attestation d'accueil**
Nachweis der Unterkunft
Proof of accommodation F____________

cerfa
n° 10798*01

Document souscrit en application du décret n° 82-442 du 27 mai 1982 modifié pris pour l'application de l'article 5 de l'ordonnance n° 45-2658 du 2 novembre 1945 modifiée relative aux conditions d'entrée et de séjour des étrangers en France

Je, soussigné(e) **Ich, der/die Unterzeichnende** **I, the undersigned**

nom / Name / name

▶

prénom(s) /Vorname(n) / first name

né(e) le/à / Geburtstag und -ort / date and place of birth

nationalité / Staatsangehörigkeit / nationality

document d'identité ([1]) ou titre de séjour ([1]) /Identitätsdokument ([1]) oder Aufenthaltstitel ([1]) / identity ([1]) or residence document ([1])

adresse complète / wohnhaft in / full address

Département, commune
Zuständige Verwaltung
Competent authority

atteste pouvoir accueillir: **bescheinige, folgende Person(en) unterbringen zu können:** **declare being able to accommodate:**

nom / Name / name

prénom(s) / Vorname(n) / first name

né(e) le/à / geboren am/in / born on/at

nationalité / Staatsangehörigkeit / nationality

passeport n° / Reisepaß-Nr. / passport No.

adresse / wohnhaft in / address

accompagné(e) de son conjoint ([2]) / und folgende sie/ihn begleitende Personen, nur Ehegatten ([2]) / accompanied by spouse ([2])

accompagné(e) de ses enfants ([2]) / und Kinder ([2]) / accompanied by children ([2])

pendant (... jours) entre le ... et le ... / für (... Tage) zwischen dem ... und dem ... / for (... days) from ... to ...

([1])
type / Art / type
numéro / Nummer / number

([2])
nom / Name / name
prénom / Vorname / first name
date de naissance / Geburtstag / date of birth
sexe / Geschlecht / sex

LA LOI N° 78-17 DU 6 JANVIER 1978 RELATIVE A L'INFORMATIQUE, AUX FICHIERS ET AUX LIBERTES **s'applique aux réponses faites sur ce formulaire et garantit un droit d'accès et de rectification pour les données vous concernant auprès de la préfecture.**
ARTICLE 21 DE L'ORDONNANCE DU 2 NOVEMBRE 1945 MODIFIEE: **toute personne française ou étrangère résidant en France ou sur le territoire d'un autre Etat partie à la Convention de Schengen qui aura, par aide directe ou indirecte, facilité ou tenté de faciliter l'entrée, la circulation ou le séjour irrégulier d'un étranger en France ou sur le territoire d'un autre Etat partie de la Convention de Schengen sera punie d'un emprisonnement de 5 ans et d'une amende de 200 000 F.**
ARTICLE 441-5 DU CODE PENAL: **le fait de procurer frauduleusement à autrui un document délivré par une administration publique aux fins de constater un droit, une identité ou d'accorder une autorisation est puni de 5 ans d'emprisonnement et de 500 000 F d'amende. Ces peines peuvent être portées à 7 ans d'emprisonnement et à 700 000 F d'amende dans les cas évoqués au 2ème alinéa du même article.**
ARTICLE 441-6 DU CODE PENAL: **le fait de se faire délivrer indûment, notamment en fournissant une déclaration mensongère, par une administration publique un document destiné à constater un droit, une identité ou une qualité ou à accorder une autorisation est puni de 2 ans d'emprisonnement et de 200 000 F d'amende.**

1°/Cas où l'accueil est assuré au domicile principal de l'hébergeant:	réservé à l'administration
adresse: se reporter à celle mentionnée au recto	**justificatifs du domicile principal de l'hébergeant:**
2°/Cas où l'accueil est assuré au domicile secondaire de l'hébergeant:	réservé à l'administration
adresse complète:	**justificatifs du domicile secondaire de l'hébergeant:**
L'hébergeant	L'autorité publique compétente:
J'atteste sur l'honneur l'exactitude des renseignements portés ci-dessus. **LU ET APPROUVE,**	**Date:**
date et signature	**signature et cachet**
L'autorité consulaire	Les services de contrôle à l'entrée sur le territoire
date et cachet	**date et cachet**

Annex B

Für die Sprachfassung gilt folgendes:

Die Sprache des Ausstellerstaates plus zwei weitere.

Pour la version linguistique:

La langue de l'Etat de délivrance plus deux autres langues. 00000000

The following applies to the languages:

The language of the issuing State plus two others.

Name / Nom / Surname

Vorname(n) / Prénom(s) / First name

Geburtstag und -ort / Né(e) le/à / Date and place of birth

Staatsangehörigkeit / Nationalité / Nationality

Identitätsdokument[(1)]/Aufenthaltstitel[(1)] / Document d'identité[(1)]/Titre de séjour[(1)] / Identity card[(1)]/Résidence title[(1)]

wohnhaft in / Adresse / Address

Beruf / Profession / Profession •

Name / Nom / Surname

Vorname(n) / Prénom(s) / First name

Geburtstag und -ort / Né(e) le/à / Date and place of birth

Staatsangehörigkeit / Nationalité / Nationality

Reisepaß Nr. / Passeport n° / Passport No.

wohnhaft in / Adresse / Address

Verwandtschaftsbeziehung mit dem Antragsteller / Lien de parenté avec le demandeur / Family relationship to applicant *

und folgende sie/ihn begleitende Personen, nur Ehegatten (2)/ accompagné(e) de son conjoint (2) / accompanied by his or her spouse (2)

und Kinder (2) / accompagné(e) de ses enfants (2) / accompanied by children (2)

vom ... an bis zum ... / du ... au ... / from ... to ...**

(1)

Art / type / type
Nummer / numéro / number

(2)

Name / nom / surname
Vorname / prénom / first name
Geburtstag / date de naissance / date of birth
Geschlecht / sexe / sex

* fakultativ / facultatif / optional
** oder eine analoge Formulierung / ou une formulation analogue / or a similar wording

DECISION OF THE EXECUTIVE COMMITTEE of 16 December 1998 on coordinated deployment of document advisers

(SCH/Com-ex (98) 59 rev.)

The Executive Committee,

Having regard to Article 132 of the convention implementing the Schengen Agreement,

Having regard to Articles 12 and 26 of the above convention,

Taking account of its declaration of 16 September 1998 (document SCH/Com-ex (98) decl 3),

HAS DECIDED AS FOLLOWS:

1. The plan for the coordinated deployment of document advisers for air and maritime traffic and at consular representations (document SCH/I-Front (98) 171 rev 4) is hereby approved.

2. The list of locations currently considered suitable in principle for document adviser assignments and the designation of present key locations and regions (document SCH/I-Front (98) 184 rev 3) is hereby noted.

Berlin, 16 December 1998

The Chairman

C. H. SCHAPPER

PRINCIPLES FOR IMPLEMENTATION

SCH/I-Front (98) 171 rev 4

At its meeting on 16 September 1998, the Executive Committee underlined the special importance of document advice in combating illegal immigration into the Schengen area (SCH/Com-ex (98) decl 3).

The Executive Committee also issued a mandate to make practical arrangements, which are set out below.

The coordinated deployment of document advisers for air and maritime traffic consular representations shall proceed according to the following guidelines

1. Arrangements for creating joint document adviser teams

(a) The Schengen States shall, where necessary, hold information seminars, the composition and duration of which shall vary according to the requirements of the individual case, on the following themes:

- the detection of counterfeit and falsified documents;
- modi operandi;
- procurement of equipment for the detection of false and counterfeit documents;
- legal regulations and rules on controls.

These advisory activities shall be provided:

- for airlines or maritime shipping companies;
- to assist the consular representations of one or more Schengen States in third countries;
- to assist border authorities or immigration authorities at airports and seaports of departure in third countries.

The document advisers shall also assist transport companies and the personnel responsible for controls in conducting pre-boarding checks at airports and ports of exit.

The Schengen States shall aim to second advisers for a period of two to three weeks. Individual States reserve the right to take unilateral follow-up measures.

(b) The Schengen States shall designate central contact points via which the need for advice and the capacity to provide support shall be communicated and all organisational aspects arranged and information relating to document advice conveyed. The central contact point of the Schengen State which has proposed the assignment shall be responsible for operational coordination (preparation, implementation and follow-up with regard to specific secondment activities). Both the Presidency and the leading contact point shall take account of parallel activities conducted in the framework of the EU.

(c) The central contact points shall work directly together on a basis of trust.

(d) The central contact points shall regularly determine the need for training material, which it shall supplement where appropriate on the basis of practical experience, and shall inform each other immediately of new modi operandi.

(e) The Presidency in office shall consult the delegations in due time about the need to claim EU funding (Odysseus) and — as concerns practical arrangements for the training courses, support and the production of training materials — shall submit an application for financial assistance from the Odysseus programme to the European Commission via the EU Presidency. The first of these applications together with a definition of the project to be conducted (participating States, coordination of groups, place, financial contribution) shall be submitted at the latest by 31 March 1999 (deadline for submission).

2. Choice of locations suitable for document adviser assignments

The choice of locations with consular representations and (or) transport company offices abroad that are suitable for document adviser assignments given the current situation as it applies in each case shall be made by the subgroup on frontiers in a separate note.

Even if not explicitly mentioned in the above list, the staff of the domestic airline and shipping company transporting people into the Schengen area should also be offered training depending on the capacity available.

Furthermore, if there is sufficient capacity, document advice may also be offered to transport companies which do not directly serve destinations in the Schengen area but operate feeder trips to departure points for connecting air and sea links to the Schengen area.

In all events, once the individual advice projects have been defined, contact should be made immediately with the consular representations and transport companies. In principle, all consular representations of the Schengen States will be informed of the planned secondment of document advisers to the representations at local level.

3. Designation of key places and regions

The deployment of document advisers will be based on a current assessment of the situation. The subgroup on frontiers will determine the key places and regions in a separate note.

4. Document adviser profile

Staff working as document advisers must be professionally and personally suitable. They should have at least five years' experience in an executive capacity.

Document advisers should have sufficient knowledge of the main language used in connection with air and sea traffic at the place where they are deployed and should certainly have a good command of English airline and document terminology (IATA training material). Officials working as document advisers must also have the necessary pedagogical and didactic skills for this activity.

5. Reporting arrangements and plans for further developments

After the mission, the document advisers shall draft a written report on the course of the assignment and the weak points detected, on the modus operandi and the counter-measures already taken. The report shall be forwarded to the leading State and on to the Schengen Secretariat for distribution to all delegations in the subgroup on frontiers.

The Presidency in office shall draw up a summary report to be submitted to Working Group I on Police and Security every half calendar year concerning the activities conducted during that six-month period, including an analysis.

The Presidency shall also devise proposals for further procedures, including the planning of further advisory measures and technical or tactical improvements and submit them for approval to the subgroup on frontiers.

Coordinated deployment of document advisers for air and maritime traffic and at consular representations

(SCH/I-front (98) 184 rev 3)

Choice of locations currently considered suitable in principle for document adviser assignments and designation of current target locations and regions

I. Choice of locations currently considered suitable for document adviser assignments

On the basis of an evaluation of the current situation, consular representations and/or overseas offices of airlines and shipping companies at the following locations are considered suitable in principle for document adviser assignments (the list will be updated where the need arises):

- **Abidjan** (Côte d'Ivoire)
  Airlines
  Representations: France, Portugal

- **Abu Dhabi** (United Arab Emirates)
  Important transit airport for flights to Europe, so advice and training should be of particular benefit to the airlines

- **Accra** (Ghana)
  Airlines

- **Ankara** (Turkey)
  Airlines

- **Bamako** (Mali)
  Airlines
  Representations: France

- **Bangkok** (Thailand)
  Airlines

- **Beijing** (China)
  Airlines
  Representations: France, Spain

- **Bissau** (Guinea-Bissau)
  Airlines
  Representations: Portugal

- **Brazzaville** (Congo)
  Airlines
  Representations: France

- **Casablanca** (Morocco)
  Airlines
  Representations: Spain

- **Colombo** (Sri Lanka)
  Airlines Representations: France

- **Dakar** (Senegal)
  Airlines
  Representations: France, Portugal, Spain

- **Dhaka** (Bangladesh)
  Airlines
  Representations: France

- **Douala** (Cameroon)
  Airlines
  Representations: France

- **Dubai** (United Arab Emirates)
  Important transit airport for flights to Europe, which means that advice and training should be of particular benefit to airlines.

- **Haiti**
  Airlines
  Representations: France

- **Ho Chi Minh City** (Vietnam)
  Airlines
  Representations: France

- **Hong Kong**
  Airlines
  Representations: France

- **Islamabad** (Pakistan)
  Airlines
  Representations: Spain

- **Istanbul** (Turkey)
  Airlines
  Representations: Spain

- **Karachi** (Pakistan)
  Airlines
  Representations: Germany (intensive advice and training desirable)

- **Kiev** (Ukraine)
  Representations: Portugal

- **Kuwait**
  Airlines

- **Lagos** (Nigeria)
  Airlines
  Representations: Germany, France, Spain

- **Lima** (Peru)
  Airlines
  Representations: Spain

- **Luanda** (Angola)
  Airlines
  Representations: Portugal

- **Macao**
  Airlines
  Representations: Portugal

- **Malabo** (Equatorial Guinea)
  Airlines
  Representations: Spain

- **Maputo** (Mozambique)
  Airlines
  Representations: Portugal

- **Moscow** (Russia)
  Airlines

- **Nador** (Morocco)
  Representations: Spain

- **Nairobi** (Kenya)
  Airlines
  Representations: Germany, France

- **Praia** (Cape Verde)
  Airlines
  Representations: Portugal

- **Rabat** (Morocco)
  Airlines
  Representations: Spain

- **Rio de Janeiro** (Brazil)
  Airlines
  Representations: Portugal

- **São Tomé** (São Tomé and Principe)
  Airlines
  Representations: Portugal

- **Sal** (Cape Verde)
  Airlines
  Representations: Portugal

- **San'a** (Yemen)
  Airlines

- **Santo Domingo** (Dominican Republic)
  Airlines
  Representations: Spain

- **Shanghai** (China)
  Airlines
  Representations: France

- **Skopje** (Former Yugoslav Republic of Macedonia)
  Airlines

- **Tangiers** (Morocco)
  Airlines
  Shipping companies
  Representations: Spain

- **Tetuan** (Morocco)
  Representations: Spain

- **Tirana** (Albania)
  Airlines

- **Tunis** (Tunisia)
  Airlines

- **Yaoundé** (Cameroon)
  Airlines
  Representations: France

II. Designation of current key places and regions

Of the locations selected in Section I above, the deployment of document advisers, which will be based on a current assessment of the situation, is seen as a particular priority at the following locations. This list is not final. The list will be updated as needed.

- Abidjan
- Abu Dhabi
- Accra
- Bamako
- Brazzaville
- Casablanca
- Dakar
- Dubai
- Istanbul
- Lagos
- Moscow
- Tirana
- Tunis

Coordinated deployment of document advisers at the above locations immediately should be the aim.

In addition, document advisers should be seconded to the following locations (in the order set out below) as soon as possible:

- Bangkok
- Ankara
- Karachi
- Nairobi
- San'a
- Skopje

DECISION OF THE EXECUTIVE COMMITTEE of 28 April 1999 on the definitive versions of the common manual and the common consular instructions

(SCH/Com-ex (99) 13)

The Executive Committee,

Having regard to Article 132 of the convention implementing the Schengen Agreement,

Having regard also, on one hand, to Articles 3, 5, 6, 7, 8, 11, 12, 17, 18 and 25 of the abovementioned convention, and to Articles 9 and 17 thereof, on the other hand,

Whereas it is in the interest of all the Schengen States to apply uniform rules to the issue of visas in the context of their common policy on the movement of persons, with a view to preventing possible negative consequences as regards entry into Schengen territory and internal security,

Moved by the desire to build on hitherto positive experiences with the common consular instructions and to harmonise further the visa-issue procedure,

Guided by the principle of solidarity between the Schengen States,

HAS DECIDED AS FOLLOWS:

I. 1. The revised version of the common consular instructions (Appendix 1 ([1])) and the annexes thereto, and

2. The revised version of the common manual (Appendix 2 ([2])) and the annexes thereto

are hereby adopted.

The following amendments have been taken into account in drawing up these versions: the amendments to Annexes 1, 2, 3, 5, 7, 10, 12 and 15 to the common consular instructions and the corresponding Annexes 5, 5 A, 14 B, 10, 6 B, 6 C and 14 A to the common manual.

([1]) Annexes 5, 9 and 10 are confidential. See SCH/Com-ex (98) 17.

([2]) Confidential document. See SCH/Com-ex (98) 17.

II. The documents relating to previous versions of the common consular instructions, common manual and the annexes thereto and listed in Appendix 3 shall be repealed once the revised versions are adopted.

III. The document relating to representation in connection with the issue of visas is attached for the purposes of information in Appendix 4 [1].

IV. This decision shall enter into force on the day on which it is adopted.

Luxembourg, 28 April 1999

The Chairman

C. H. SCHAPPER

[1] Document SCH/II (95) 16, rev 19: not published.

Appendix 1

COMMON CONSULAR INSTRUCTIONS FOR THE DIPLOMATIC MISSIONS AND CONSULAR POSTS

Contents

2. Visa applications requiring consultation with the national central authority or the authority of one or more other Contracting Parties, in accordance with Article 17(2)

   2.1. Consultation with the national central authority

   2.2. Consultation with the central authority of one or more Contracting Parties

   2.3. Consultation procedure in the framework of representation

3. Visa applications lodged by non-residents

4. Authorisation to issue uniform visas

III. Initiation of the application procedure

1. Visa application forms — number of application forms

2. Documents to be enclosed

3. Guarantees of means of return and means of subsistence

4. Personal interviews with applicants

IV. Legal basis

V. Examination of applications and decisions taken

Basic criteria for examining applications

1. Examination of visa applications

   1.1. Verification of the visa application

   1.2. Verification of the applicant's identity

   1.3. Verification of the travel document

   1.4. Verification of other documents depending on the application

   — Supporting documents regarding the purpose of the journey

   — Supporting documents regarding means of transport and return

   — Supporting documents regarding means of subsistence

   — Supporting documents regarding accommodation

   — Other documents where necessary

   1.5. Assessment of the applicant's good faith

2. Decision-making procedure for visa applications

   2.1. Choice of type of visa and number of entries

   2.2. The administrative responsibility of the intervening authority

2.3. Procedure to be followed in cases requiring prior consultation with the central authorities of the other Contracting Parties

(a) Procedure

(b) Sending applications to the national central authority

(c) Information sent to the central authority

(d) Sending applications between central authorities

(e) Reply time: extension

(f) Decision based on the outcome of the consultation

(g) Transmission of specific documents

2.4. Refusal to examine an application, to issue a visa

3. Visas with limited territorial validity

VI. How to fill in visa-stickers

1. Common entries section (Section 8)

1.1. 'Valid for' heading

1.2. 'From... to' heading

1.3. 'Number of entries' heading

1.4. 'Duration of visit... days' heading

1.5. 'Issued in... on...' heading

1.6. 'Passport number' heading

1.7. 'Type of visa' heading

2. National entries section (comments) (Section 9)

3. Section on the stamp of the mission or post issuing the visa (Section 4)

4. Section to be electronically scanned (Section 5)

5. Other aspects relating to the issue of visas

5.1. Signing visas

5.2. Invalidating completed visa-stickers

5.3. Affixing visa-stickers to passports

5.4. Passports and travel documents to which uniform visas may be affixed

VII. Administrative management and organisation

1. Organisation of visa sections
2. Filing
3. Visa registers
4. Fees to be charged for the issue of visas

VIII. Consular cooperation at a local level

1. Outline of consular cooperation at a local level
2. How to avoid multiple applications or applications which are lodged after a recent refusal to issue
3. Assessment of the applicant's good faith
4. Exchange of statistics

ANNEXES TO THE COMMON CONSULAR INSTRUCTIONS ON VISAS

1. I. Joint list of States whose citizens are required to have a visa by all the Schengen States.

   II. Updated list of States whose citizens are exempt from the visa requirement by all the Schengen States.

   III. Updated list of States whose citizens are required to have a visa by some Schengen States only.

2. Regulations governing the movement of holders of diplomatic, official and service passports and holders of laissez-passers which certain international intergovernmental organisations issue to their officials.
3. List of States whose citizens are subject to an airport transit visa requirement, where holders of travel documents issued by these States are also subject to this visa requirement.
4. List of documents entitling entry without a visa.
5. List of visa applications requiring prior consultation with the central authorities, in accordance with Article 17(2).
6. List of honorary consuls authorised, in exceptional cases and on a temporary basis, to issue uniform visas.
7. Reference amounts for the crossing of borders fixed annually by the national authorities.
8. Uniform format for visa-stickers and information on their technical specifications and security features.
9. Entries which the Contracting Parties shall write, where necessary, in the 'comments' section.

10. Instructions on writing entries in the section to be electronically scanned.
11. Criteria for travel documents to which a visa may be affixed.
12. Fees, in euro, to be charged when issuing uniform visas.
13. Guidelines on how to fill in visa-stickers.
14. Requirements governing information for the Contracting Parties when issuing visas with limited territorial validity, or when invalidating, repealing or reducing the validity of uniform visas and when issuing national residence permits.
15. Model harmonised forms providing proof of invitation, sponsorship and accommodation drawn up by the Contracting Parties.

COMMON INSTRUCTIONS FOR THE DIPLOMATIC MISSIONS AND CONSULAR POSTS OF THE CONTRACTING PARTIES TO THE SCHENGEN CONVENTION

SUBJECT: Conditions governing the issue of uniform visas, valid for the territory of all the Contracting Parties.

I. General provisions

1. Scope

The following common provisions which are based on the provisions of Chapter 3 (Sections 1 and 2) of the convention implementing the Schengen Agreement of 14 June 1985 between the Governments of the States of the Benelux Economic Union, the Federal Republic of Germany and the French Republic on the gradual abolition of checks at their common borders (hereinafter referred to as 'the convention') signed in Schengen on 19 June 1990, and which Italy, Spain, Portugal, Greece and Austria have since acceded to, apply to the examination of visa applications for a visit not exceeding three months, including transit visas, valid for the territory of all the Contracting Parties ([1]).

Visas for visits exceeding three months shall be national visas, and shall only entitle the holder to reside in that national territory. Nevertheless, such visas shall enable their holders to transit through the territories of the other Contracting Parties in order to reach the territory of the Contracting Party which issued the visa, unless they fail to fulfil the entry conditions referred to in Article 5(1)(a), (d) and (e) or they are on the national list of alerts of the Contracting Party through whose territory they seek to transit.

2. Definition and types of visa

2.1. Uniform visas

These are the authorisation or decision granted in the form of a sticker affixed by a Contracting Party to a passport, travel document or other document which entitles the holder to cross the border. It enables aliens, subject to the visa requirement, to present themselves at the external border of the Contracting Party which issued the visa or that of another Contracting Party and request, depending on the type of visa, transit or residence, provided that the other transit or entry conditions have been met. Mere possession of a uniform visa does not entitle automatic right of entry.

([1]) Pursuant to Article 138 of the convention, these provisions shall only apply to the European territory of the French Republic and the Kingdom of the Netherlands.

2.1.1. Airport transit visas

This visa entitles aliens who are required to have such a visa, to pass through the international transit area of airports, without actually entering the national territory of the country concerned, during a stop-over or transfer between two sections of an international flight. The requirement to have this visa is an exception to the general right to transit without a visa through the abovementioned international transit area.

Nationals from the countries listed in Annex 3 and persons who are not necessarily nationals of those countries but who possess travel documents issued by their authorities, are required to possess this type of visa.

Exemptions from the airport transit visa requirement are laid down in Section III of Annex 3.

2.1.2. Transit visas

This visa entitles aliens who are travelling from one third State to another third State to pass through the territories of the Contracting Parties.

This visa authorises its holder to pass through once, twice or exceptionally several times, provided that no transit shall exceed five days.

2.1.3. Short-stay or travel visas: multiple entry visas

This visa entitles aliens who seek to enter the territories of the Contracting Parties, for reasons other than to immigrate, to carry out a continuous visit or several visits whose duration does not exceed three months in any half-year from the date of first entry. As a general rule, this visa may be issued for one or several entries.

In the case of certain aliens who frequently need to travel to one or several Schengen States, for example on business, short-stay visas may be issued for several visits, provided that the total length of these visits does not exceed three months in any half-year. This multiple entry visa may be valid for one year, and in exceptional cases, for more than a year for certain categories of persons. (see V 2, 2.1)

2.1.4. Group visas

This is a transit visa or a visa limited to a maximum of 30 days, which may be affixed to a group passport — save where national law provides otherwise — issued to a group of aliens formed prior to the decision to travel, provided that the members of the group enter the territory, stay there and leave the territory as a group.

Group visas may be issued to groups of between 5 and 50 people. The person in charge of the group shall possess an individual passport and, where necessary, an individual visa.

2.2. Long-stay visas

Visas for visits exceeding three months shall be national visas issued by one of the Contracting Parties in accordance with its national law.

Nevertheless, such visas shall act as uniform transit visas enabling their holders to travel to the territory of the Contracting Party which issued the visa, provided that the total length of transit does not exceed five days from the date of first entry, and provided that they fulfil the entry conditions and that they are not on the national list of alerts of the Contracting Party or Parties through whose territory they seek to transit (see Annex 4).

2.3. Visas with limited territorial validity

This visa is affixed in exceptional cases to a passport, travel document or other document which entitles the holder to cross the border, where the visit is authorised only in the national territory of one or more Contracting Parties, provided that both entry and exit are through the territory of this or these Contracting Parties (see V 3).

2.4. Visas issued at the border [1]

II. Diplomatic mission or consular post responsible

Aliens who are subject to the visa requirement (see Annex 1), and who seek to enter the territory of a Contracting Party, are obliged to apply to the visa section in the diplomatic mission or consular post responsible.

1. Determining the State responsible

1.1. State responsible for deciding on an application

The following are responsible for examining applications for short-term or transit uniform visas:

(a) The Contracting Party in whose territory the sole or main destination of the visit is found. Under no circumstances shall a transit Contracting Party be considered as the country of main destination.

[1] In exceptional cases, short-stay or transit visas may be issued at the border, pursuant to the conditions defined in part II, point 5 of the common manual on external borders.

The diplomatic mission or consular post with whom the application is lodged shall decide, on a case-by-case basis, which is the Contracting Party of main destination, bearing in mind, in its assessment, all the facts and in particular the purpose behind the visit, the route and length of visit or visits. When looking at these facts, the mission or post shall mainly focus on the supporting documents submitted by the applicant.

It shall specifically focus on the main reason for or the purpose of the visit when one or more destinations are the direct result or complement of another destination.

It shall specifically focus on the longest visit when no destination is the direct result or complement of another destination; where the visits are of equal length, the first destination shall be the determining factor.

(b) The Contracting Party of first entry, when the Contracting Party of main destination cannot be determined.

Contracting Party of first entry shall be the State whose external border the applicant crosses in order to enter the Schengen area after having had his/her documents checked.

When the Contracting Party of first entry does not require a visa, it is not obliged to issue a visa and — unless it issues the visa voluntarily, subject to the consent of the person concerned — the responsibility is transferred to the first Contracting Party of destination or of transit which requires a visa.

The examination of applications and the issue of visas with limited territorial validity (limited to the territory of one Contracting Party or to the territory of the Benelux States) shall be the responsibility of the Contracting Party or Parties concerned.

1.2. State representing the State responsible

(a) If the State responsible has no diplomatic mission or consular post in a given State, the uniform visa may be issued by the mission or post of the Contracting Party which represents the interests of the State responsible. The visa is issued on behalf of the Contracting Party that is being represented, subject to its prior authorisation, and where necessary, consultation between the central authorities. If one of the Benelux States has a mission or post, it shall automatically represent the other Benelux States.

(b) If the State responsible has a diplomatic mission or consular post in the capital city of a country, but not in the area where the application is lodged, and if one or more of the other Contracting Parties does have a mission or post, the visa may, in exceptional cases and only in countries which are geographically very large, be issued by another Contracting Party representing the State responsible, provided that there is a specific agreement on representation between the two Contracting Parties concerned and such action is in accordance with the terms of the said agreement.

(c) In accordance with the provisions contained in (a) and (b), it shall in any event be for the visa applicant to decide whether to contact either the diplomatic mission or the consular post which is representing the State responsible or that of the State responsible.

(d) The subgroup on visas shall draw up an overview of the agreed representation arrangements which it shall update regularly.

(e) The procedure for issuing Schengen visas with reference to article 30(1)(a) of the convention implementing the Schengen Agreement in third States in which not all Schengen States are represented shall be based on the following principles:

The rules on representation shall apply to the processing of applications for uniform airport transit visas, transit visas and short-stay visas issued pursuant to the Schengen Convention and in accordance with the common consular instructions. The representing State is obliged to apply the provisions of the common consular instructions with the same diligence and speed as it issues its own visas of the same category and with the same period of validity.

Except as expressly provided in bilateral agreements, the rules on representation shall not apply to visas issued for the purpose of paid employment or an activity which requires prior permission from the State in which it is to be carried out. The applicant must contact the accredited consular post of the State where the activity is to be performed.

The Schengen States shall not be obliged to ensure that they are represented for visa purposes in every third State. They may decide that in certain third States visa applications or applications for a particular kind of visa must be made at a permanent consular post or diplomatic mission of the State that is the main destination.

The diplomatic missions and consular posts shall have sole responsibility for assessing the risk of illegal immigration posed by a visa application.

The represented State shall assume responsibility for asylum applications made by holders of visas which the visa stamp expressly shows to have been issued by representing States on behalf of represented States.

In exceptional cases, bilateral agreements may stipulate that visa applications from certain categories of alien are either to be submitted by the representing State to the authorities of the represented State in which the main destination is located or forwarded to a permanent consular representation of that State. The categories in question must be laid down in writing (if necessary for each diplomatic mission or consular post). It shall be assumed that the visa has been issued on the authorisation of the represented State pursuant to Article 30(1)(a) of the Schengen Convention.

Bilateral agreements may be amended in the course of time on the basis of decisions made by individual States concerning asylum applications lodged within a set period of time by holders of visas issued in the framework of representation and other information relevant to the issue of visas. Agreement may also be reached on waiving the rules on representation in the case of certain diplomatic missions and consular posts.

Representation shall apply solely in the context of issuing visas. Aliens who are unable to apply for a visa because they cannot furnish sufficient proof that they fulfil the relevant conditions must be informed that they can apply for a visa at a permanent consular post or diplomatic mission of the Schengen State of main destination.

The rules on representation may be refined as a result of further developments in software enabling consular posts and diplomatic missions undertaking representation to consult the central authorities of the represented State without substantial additional effort.

The list containing rules on representation with regard to the issue of Schengen visa in third States in which not all Schengen States are represented is attached to this document. Amendments made to the list by common agreement between the Schengen States concerned shall be submitted to the Central Group for acknowledgement.

2. Visa applications requiring consultation with the national central authority or the authority of one or more other Contracting Parties, in accordance with Article 17(2)

2.1. Consultation with the national central authority

The diplomatic mission or consular post which examines the application, shall seek authorisation from its central authority, consult it or inform it of the decision it plans to take in a case, in accordance with the arrangements and deadlines laid down by national law and practice. Cases requiring national consultation are listed in Annex 5A.

2.2. Consultation with the central authority of one or more Contracting Parties

The diplomatic mission or the consular post with whom an application is lodged shall seek authorisation from its central authority, which, for its part, shall send the application on to the competent central authorities of one or more other Contracting Parties (see Part V, 2, 2.3). Until the final list of cases of mutual consultation has been approved by the Executive Committee, the list annexed to these common consular instructions shall apply (see Annex 5B).

2.3. Consultation procedure in the framework of representation

(a) When visa applications are lodged by nationals of the countries listed in Annex 5C at an embassy or consular representation of a Schengen State, representing another Schengen State, the represented State shall be consulted.

(b) The information exchanged in respect of these visa applications shall be the same as that currently exchanged in the framework of the consultation under Annex 5B. A compulsory heading shall, however, be provided on the form for the references to the territory of the represented State.

(c) The current provisions of the common consular instructions shall apply to the time limits, their extension and the form of the reply.

(d) The consultation provided for in Annex 5B shall be undertaken by the represented State.

3. Visa applications lodged by non-residents

When an application is lodged with a State which is not the applicant's State of residence and there is doubt over the person's intentions (in particular where a risk of illegal immigration has been observed), the visa shall only be issued after consultation with the diplomatic mission or consular post of the applicant's State of residence and/or its central authority.

4. Authorisation to issue uniform visas

Only the diplomatic mission or consular posts of the Contracting Parties shall be entitled to issue uniform visas, with the exception of the cases listed in Annex 6.

III. Initiation of the application procedure

1. Visa application forms — number of application forms

Aliens shall also be required to fill in the uniform visa form.

At least one copy of the application form must be filled in so that it may be used during consultation with the central authorities. The Contracting Parties may, insofar as national administrative procedures so require, request several copies of the application.

2. Documents to be enclosed

— Aliens shall enclose the following documents with the application:

(a) a valid travel document on which a visa may be affixed (see Annex 11);

(b) where necessary, documents supporting the purpose and the conditions of the planned visit.

If the information supplied is sufficient to enable the diplomatic mission or consular post to ascertain that the applicant is acting in good faith, the staff responsible for issuing the visas may exempt the applicant from submitting the abovementioned supporting documents.

3. Guarantees of means of return and means of subsistence

Aliens shall be able to offer the diplomatic mission or consular post with whom they lodge their application, a guarantee that they have adequate means for their subsistence and their return.

4. Personal interviews with applicants

As a general rule, the applicant shall be called on to appear in person in order to verbally justify the grounds for the application, especially where there are doubts over the actual purpose behind the visit or that person's return to the country of departure.

This requirement may be waived in cases where the applicant is well known or where the distance from the diplomatic mission or consular post is too great, provided that there is no doubt as to the good faith of the applicant and where in the case of large groups, a reputable and trustworthy body is able to vouch for the good faith of those persons concerned.

IV. Legal basis

Uniform visas may only be issued once the entry conditions laid down in Articles 15 and 5 of the convention have been met. These articles read as follows:

'Article 15

In principle, the visa referred to in Article 10 may be issued only if an alien fulfils the entry conditions laid down in Article 5(1)(a),(c),(d) and (e).

Article 5

1. For visits not exceeding three months, aliens fulfilling the following conditions may be granted entry into the territories of the Contracting Parties:

(a) the possession of a valid document or documents, as defined by the Executive Committee, authorising them to cross the border;

(b) the possession of a valid visa if required;

(c) if applicable, the aliens shall produce documents substantiating the purpose and the conditions of the planned visit and shall have adequate means of support, both for the period of the planned visit and the return to their country of origin or transit to a third State, where their admission is guaranteed, or shall be in a position to acquire such means legally;

(d) the aliens shall not be persons for whom an alert has been issued for the purposes of refusing entry:

(e) the aliens shall not be considered to be a threat to public policy, national security or the international relations of any of the Contracting Parties.

2. Entry into the territories of the Contracting Parties must be refused to any alien who does not fulfil all the above conditions unless a Contracting Party considers it necessary to derogate from that principle for humanitarian reasons, on grounds of national interest or because of international obligations. In such cases authorisation to enter will be restricted to the territory of the Contracting Party concerned, which must inform the other Contracting Parties accordingly.

These rules shall not preclude the application of special provisions concerning the right to asylum or the provisions laid down in Article 18.'

Visas with limited territorial validity may be issued subject to the conditions laid down in Articles 11(2), 14(1) and 16 in connection with Article 5(2) (see V, 3).

Article 11(2)

2. Paragraph 1 shall not preclude a Contracting Party from issuing a new visa, the validity of which is limited to its own territory, within the half-year in question if necessary.

Article 14(1)

1. No visa may be affixed to a travel document if the travel document is not valid for any of the Contracting Parties. If a travel document is only valid for one Contracting Party or for a number of Contracting Parties the visa to be affixed shall be limited to the Contracting Party or Parties in question.

Article 16

If a Contracting Party considers it necessary to derogate, on one of the grounds listed in Article 5(2) from the principle laid down in Article 15, by issuing a visa to an alien who does not fulfil all the entry conditions referred to in Article 5(1), the validity of this visa shall be restricted to the territory of that Contracting Party, which must inform the other Contracting Parties accordingly.

V. Examination of applications and decisions taken

The diplomatic mission or consular post shall first check the documents submitted (1) and shall then base its decision regarding the visa application on these documents (2):

Basic criteria for examining applications

The main issues to be borne in mind when examining visa applications are: the security of the Contracting Parties and the fight against illegal immigration as well as other aspects relating to international relations. Depending on the country concerned, one of these may take precedence over the other, but at no stage should any of them be forgotten about.

As far as security is concerned, it is advisable to check that the necessary controls have been carried out: a search of the files containing alerts (alerts for the purposes of refusing entry) in the Schengen information system, consultation with the central authorities of the countries subject to this procedure.

The diplomatic mission or consular post shall assume full responsibility in assessing whether there is an immigration risk. The purpose of examining applications is to detect those applicants who are seeking to immigrate to the territory of the Contracting Parties and set themselves up there, using grounds such as tourism, studies, business or family visits as a pretext. Therefore, it is necessary to be particularly vigilant when dealing with 'risk categories', in other words unemployed persons, and those with no regular income, etc. If there is any doubt over the authenticity of the papers and supporting documents submitted, the diplomatic mission or consular post shall refrain from iss*uing the visa.

On the contrary, checks shall be reduced where the applicant is known to be a bona fide person, this information having been exchanged through consular cooperation.

1. Examination of visa applications

1.1. Verification of the visa application

— The length of visit requested shall correspond with the purpose of the visit.

— The replies to the questions on the form shall be complete and coherent. The form shall include an identity photograph of the visa applicant and shall indicate, as far as possible, the main destination of the visit.

1.2. Verification of the applicant's identity and verification as to whether an alert has been issued on the applicant in the Schengen information system (SIS) for the purposes of refusing entry or verification as to whether they pose any other threat (to security) which would constitute grounds for refusal to issue the visa or whether, from an immigration point of view, the applicant poses a risk in that on a previous visit he/she overstayed the authorised length of visit.

1.3. Verification of the travel document

— Verification as to whether the document is in order or not: it should be complete and should be neither amended, falsified or counterfeited.

— Verification of the territorial validity of the travel document: it should be valid for entry into the territory of the Contracting Parties.

— Verification of the period of validity of the travel document: the period of validity of the travel document should exceed that of the visa by three months (Article 13(2) of the convention).

— Nevertheless, for urgent humanitarian reasons, on grounds of national interest or because of international obligations, it shall be possible, in exceptional cases, to affix visas to travel documents whose period of validity is less than that specified in the previous paragraph (three months), provided that the period of validity exceeds that of the visa and that the guarantee of return is not in jeopardy.

— Verification of the length of previous visits to the territory of the Contracting Parties.

1.4. Verification of other documents depending on the application

The number and type of supporting documents required depend on the possible risk of illegal immigration and the local situation (for example whether the currency is convertible) and may vary from one country to another. As concerns assessment of the supporting documents, the diplomatic missions or consular posts of the Contracting Parties may agree on practical arrangements adapted to suit local circumstances.

The supporting documents shall cover the purpose of the journey, means of transport and return, means of subsistence and accommodation:

- supporting documents regarding the purpose of the journey shall mean for example:

  — a letter of invitation,

  — a summons,

  — an organised trip.

- supporting documents regarding means of transport and return shall mean for example:

  — a return ticket,

  — currency for petrol or car insurance.

- supporting documents regarding means of subsistence:

  The following may be accepted as proof of means of subsistence: liquid cash in convertible currency, travellers cheques, cheque books for a foreign currency account, credit cards or any other means that guarantees funds in hard currency.

The level of means of subsistence shall be proportionate to the length of visit and purpose of the visit, and also the cost of living of the Schengen State or States to be visited. To this end, reference amounts shall be fixed each year for the crossing of borders by the national authorities of the Contracting Parties (see Annex 7) ([1]).

- supporting documents regarding accommodation:

The following documents *inter alia* may be accepted as proof of accommodation:

(a) hotel reservation or reservation for a similar establishment;

(b) documents proving the existence of a lease or a property title, in the applicant's name, proving ownership of a property situated in the country to be visited;

(c) Where an alien states that he/she shall stay at a person's home or in an institution, the diplomatic missions and consular posts shall verify whether the alien will actually be accommodated there:

— either by checking with the national authorities, where such checks are necessary;

— or by requiring that a certificate be presented which vouches for the undertaking to accommodate, in the form of a harmonised form filled in by the host and stamped by the competent authority of the Contracting Party, according to the provisions laid down in its national law. A model of the form may be adopted by the Executive Committee;

— or by requiring that a certificate or an official or public document be presented which vouches for the undertaking to accommodate, worded and checked in accordance with the internal law of the Contracting Party concerned.

The presentation of documents relating to the commitment to accommodate referred to in the previous two indents is not a new condition for the issuing of visas. These documents have a practical purpose, aimed at proving that accommodation is available and, where appropriate, the existence of means of subsistence. If a Contracting Party uses this type of document, then it should in any case, specify the identity of the host and of the guest or guests, the address of the accommodation, the length and purpose of the visit, any possible family ties, and indicate whether the host is residing lawfully in the country.

After having issued the visa, the diplomatic mission or consular post shall affix its stamp and write the visa number on the document in order to avoid it being reused.

([1]) These reference amounts shall be fixed according to the arrangements laid down in Part I of the common manual on external borders.

These checks are aimed at avoiding any false/fraudulent invitations or invitations from illegal or possibly illegal aliens.

Before applying for a uniform visa, applicants may be exempted from the requirement to provide supporting documents regarding accommodation if they are able to prove that they have sufficient financial means to cover their subsistence and accommodation costs in the Schengen State or States that they plan to visit.

– Other documents where necessary

Depending on the case in question, other documents may be required, for example:

– proof of place of residence and proof of ties with the country of residence;

– parental authorisation in the case of minors;

– proof of the social and professional status of the applicant.

Where the national laws of the Schengen States require proof of invitations from private individuals or for business trips, sponsorship declarations or proof of accommodation, a harmonised form shall be used.

1.5. Assessment of the applicant's good faith

In order to assess the applicant's good faith, the mission or post shall check whether the applicant is recognised as a person of good faith within the framework of local consular cooperation.

Furthermore, they shall consult the information exchanged, as referred to in Chapter VIII, 3, of these instructions.

2. Decision-making procedure for visa applications

2.1. Choice of type of visa and number of entries

A uniform visa pursuant to Article 11 may be:

– a travel visa valid for one or more entries, provided that neither the length of a continuous visit nor the total length of successive visits exceeds three months in any half-year, from the date of first entry;

– a visa valid for one year, entitling a three month visit during any half-year and several entries; this visa may be issued to persons offering the necessary guarantees and persons whom the Contracting Parties have shown a particular interest in. In exceptional cases, a visa valid for more than one year, but for a maximum of five years, may be issued to certain categories of persons for several entries;

– a transit visa authorising its holder to pass through the territories of the Contracting Parties once, twice or exceptionally several times en route to the territory of a third State, provided that no transit shall exceed five days and provided that the entry of the alien into the territory of the destination third State is guaranteed and that the route being followed normally requires transit through the territories of the Contracting Parties.

2.2. The administrative responsibility of the intervening authority

The diplomatic representative or the head of the consular section shall assume, in accordance with their national powers, full responsibility with regard to the practical arrangements for the issuing of visas by their missions or posts and shall consult each other on this matter.

The diplomatic mission or consular post shall take its decision on the basis of all the information available to it and bearing in mind the specific situation of each applicant.

2.3. Procedure to be followed in cases of prior consultation with the central authorities of the other Contracting Parties

The Contracting Parties have decided to set up a system for the purpose of carrying out consultation with the central authorities.

The following measures may be applied temporarily should the consultation technical system break down and in accordance with the situation:

— limit the number of cases of consultation to those where consultation is deemed essential;

— use the local network of embassies and consulates of the Contracting Parties concerned in order to channel consultation;

— use the network of embassies of the Contracting Parties located (a) in the country carrying out the consultation, (b) in the country which is to be consulted;

— use of conventional means of communication between contact points: fax, telephone, etc.;

— be more vigilant for the benefit of the common interest.

In cases where the applicants come under the categories listed in Annex 5B subject to consultation with a central authority — of the Ministry of Foreign Affairs or of another body — (Article 17(2) of the convention), visas shall be issued according to the procedure outlined below.

The diplomatic mission or consular post with whom an application is lodged by a person from one of these categories shall, in the first instance, check, by carrying out a search in the Schengen information system, whether an alert has been issued on the applicant for the purposes of refusing entry.

It shall then follow the procedure outlined below:

(a) Procedure

The procedure under (b) shall not apply when the visa applicant has been issued an alert in the Schengen information system for the purposes of refusing entry.

(b) Sending applications to the national central authority

The diplomatic mission or consular post with whom an application is lodged by a person from one of the categories subject to consultation shall send this application immediately to the central authority in its country.

– If the central authority decides to refuse an application for which the Contracting Party applied to is responsible, it is not necessary to begin or to continue a consultation procedure with the central authorities of the Contracting Parties which requested to be consulted.

– In the case of an application examined by the representative of the State responsible, the central authority of the Contracting Party with whom the application is lodged shall send it to the central authority of the State responsible. If the central authority of the State being represented — or, the central authority of the representing State, where so provided in the representation agreement — decides to reject the visa application, it is not necessary to begin or to continue a consultation procedure with the central authorities of the Contracting Parties which requested to be consulted.

(c) Information sent to the central authority

As part of consultation with the central authorities, the diplomatic missions or consular posts with whom an application is lodged shall send the following information to their central authority:

1. diplomatic mission or consular post with whom the application was lodged;

2. surname and first names, date and place of birth and, where known, the names of the applicant's parents;

3. nationality of the applicant (s) and, where known, any previous nationalities;

4. type and number of travel document(s) submitted, their date of issue and date of expiry;

5. length and purpose of planned visit;

6. planned dates of travel;

7. residence, profession, employer of the visa applicant;

8. references from the Member States, in particular, any previous applications or visits to the Signatory States;

9. border which the applicant plans to cross in order to enter Schengen territory;

10. any other names (maiden name, or where applicable, married name, in order to complete the identification in accordance with the requirements under the national law of the Contracting Parties and the national law of the State where the applicant is a citizen);

11. any other information deemed necessary by the diplomatic missions or consular posts, concerning for example the spouse or children accompanying the person concerned, any visas previously issued to the applicant and visa applications for the same destination.

This information shall be taken from the visa application form, in the order in which it appears on the aforementioned form.

The above headings shall act as the basis of the information to be sent in consultation between central authorities. The Contracting Party carrying out the consultation shall as a rule be responsible for the way it sends the information, in the understanding that the date and time of transmission and its receipt by the recipient central authorities should be clearly marked.

(d) Sending applications between central authorities

The central authority of the Contracting Party whose mission or post has received an application shall consult, in turn, the central authority or authorities of the Contracting Party or Parties who have asked to be consulted. To this end, the authorities designated by the Contracting Parties shall be considered as central authorities.

After having carried out the necessary checks, these authorities shall send their overall assessment of the visa application to the central authority which consulted them.

(e) Reply time: extension

The maximum deadline which the consulted central authorities have for sending a reply to the central authority which asked for the consultation shall be seven calendar days. The initial reply time is taken from the time at which the application is sent by the central authority which has to carry out the consultation.

If, during the course of these seven days, one of the consulted central authorities asks for the deadline to be extended, this may be increased by seven days.

In exceptional cases, the consulted central authority may submit a justified request for an extension of more than seven days.

The authorities being consulted shall ensure that in cases of urgency, the reply is sent back as quickly as possible.

Where no reply is received by the initial deadline or, where applicable, by the extended deadline it shall be the equivalent of an authorisation and shall mean that there are, as far as the Contracting Party or Parties consulted are concerned, no grounds for objecting to the issue of a visa.

(f) Decision based on the outcome of the consultation

Once the initial or extended deadline has expired, the central authority of the Contracting Party with whom the application is lodged may authorise the diplomatic mission or consular post to issue the uniform visa.

Where there is no clear decision on the part of the central authority, the diplomatic mission or consular post with whom the application is lodged may issue the visa after a period of 14 days, from the time at which the application was sent by the central authority carrying out the consultation. It is up to each central authority to inform its missions and posts at the start of each consultation period.

In cases where the central authority receives a request for an exceptional extension to the deadline, it shall inform the mission or post with whom the application is lodged thereof: it shall not decide on the application before having received clear instructions from its central authority.

(g) Transmission of specific documents

In exceptional cases, the embassy where the visa application is lodged may, at the request of the consular mission of the consulted State, transmit pursuant to Article 17 of the Schengen Convention the visa application form (with a space for a photograph).

This procedure shall only apply in places where there are diplomatic or consular missions of both the consulting State and consulted State and only in respect of the nationalities listed in Annex 5B.

In no circumstances may the reply to the consultation or the request to extend the time limit for consultation be undertaken locally, with the exception of consultation at local level in accordance with the current provisions of Annex 5B of the common consular instructions; the consultation network shall always be used for exchanges between the central authorities.

2.4. Refusal to examine an application, to issue a visa

The procedure and the possible channels of appeal in cases where the diplomatic mission or consular post of a Contracting Party refuses to examine an application or issue a visa, are governed by the law of that Contracting Party.

If a visa is refused and national law provides for the grounds for such a refusal to be given, this must be done on the basis of the following text:

'Your request for a visa has been refused pursuant to Article 15 in conjunction with Article 5 of the convention implementing the Schengen Agreement of 19 June 1990 because you do not satisfy the conditions under (a), (c), (d), (e), (indicate relevant condition(s)) of Article 5(1) of the said convention, which stipulates......................... (quote relevant condition(s)).'

If necessary, the above grounds may be supplemented with more detailed information or contain other information in accordance with the requirements in this area laid down in the national law of the Schengen States.

When an embassy or consular post which is representing another Schengen State is forced to discontinue its examination of a visa application, the applicant should be notified thereof and informed that he/she may go to the nearest diplomatic or consular mission of the State competent to examine the visa application.

3. Visas with limited territorial validity

A visa whose validity is limited to the national territory of one or several Contracting Parties may be issued:

1. In cases where a diplomatic mission or consular post considers it necessary to derogate from the principle laid down in Article 15 of the convention (Article 16) on one of the grounds listed in Article 5(2) (for humanitarian reasons, on grounds of national interest or because of international obligations);

2. In cases provided for in Article 14 of the convention, according to which:

   '1. No visa may be affixed to a travel document if that travel document is not valid for any of the Contracting Parties. If a travel document is only valid for one Contracting Party or for a number of Contracting Parties the visa to be affixed shall be limited to the Contracting Party or Parties in question.

   2. If a travel document is not recognised as valid by one or more of the Contracting Parties an authorisation may be issued in place of a visa.'

3. In cases where, due to extreme urgency, (for humanitarian reasons, on grounds of national interest or because of international obligations), a mission or post does not consult the central authorities or where this procedure gives rise to protest;

4. In cases where a mission or post issues, as an absolute necessity, a new visa for a visit to be carried out during the same half-year to an applicant who, over a six-month period, has already used a visa with a validity of three months.

The validity is limited to the territory of one Contracting Party, the Benelux or two Benelux States for scenarios 1, 3 and 4 above, and to the territory of one or several Contracting Parties, the Benelux or two Benelux States for Scenario 2.

The missions or posts of the other Contracting Parties shall be informed of cases where these visas are issued.

VI. How to fill in visa-stickers

Annexes 8 and 13 contain the following: 8 — a description of the sticker's security features; 13 — examples of specimen visa-stickers that have already been filled in.

1. Common entries section (Section 8)

1.1. 'Valid for' heading

This heading indicates the territory in which the visa holder is entitled to travel.

This heading may only be completed in one of the following three ways:

(a) Schengen States;

(b) Schengen State or Schengen States to whose territory the validity of the visa is limited (in this case the following abbreviations are used: F for France, D for Germany, E for Spain, GR for Greece, P for Portugal, I for Italy, L for Luxembourg, N for the Netherlands, B for Belgium);

(c) Benelux.

— When the sticker is used to issue the uniform visa pursuant to Articles 10 and 11 of the convention, or to issue a visa whose validity is not limited to the territory of the Contracting Party which issued the visa, the heading 'valid for' is filled in using the words 'Schengen States', in the language of the Contracting Party which issued the visa.

— When the sticker is used to issue visas which restrict entry, stay and exit to just one territory, this heading shall be filled in, in the national language, with the name of the Contracting Party to which the visa holder's entry, stay and exit are limited.

— Pursuant to Article 14 of the convention, limited territorial validity may cover the territory of several Contracting Parties; in such cases, the name of the Contracting Parties concerned shall be written under this heading.

— Limited territorial validity may not apply to a territory smaller than that of a Contracting Party.

1.2. 'From... to' heading

This heading shows the period during which the holder may carry out the visit authorised by the visa.

The date from which the visa holder may enter the territory for which the visa is valid, is written as below, following the word 'From':

— the day is written using two figures, the first of which is a zero if the day in question is a single figure;

— horizontal dash;

- the month is written using two figures, the first of which is a zero if the month in question is a single figure;

- horizontal dash;

- the year is written using two figures, which correspond with the last two figures of the year;

- for example: 15-04-94 = 15 April 1994.

The last date on which the visa holder may carry out the visit authorised by the visa is written following the word 'TO'. The visa holder must have left the territory for which the visa is valid by midnight on this date.

This date is written in the same way as the first date above.

1.3. 'Number of entries' heading

This heading shows the number of times the visa holder may enter the territory for which the visa is valid; in other words, this shall mean the number of periods of stay which may be divided over the entire period of validity, see 1.4.

The number of entries may be one, two or more. This number is written to the right hand-side of the pre-printed part, using '01', '02' or the abbreviation 'MULT', where the visa authorises more than two entries.

For a transit visa, only one or two entries may be authorised ('01' or '02' shall be written). More than two entries ('MULT') shall only be authorised in exceptional cases.

The visa shall expire when the total number of exits made by the holder equals the number of authorised entries, even if the holder has not used up the number of days authorised by the visa.

1.4. 'Duration of visit... days' heading

This heading indicates the number of days during which the holder may stay in the territory for which the visa is valid [1]. This visit may be a continuous one or divided up, depending on the number of days authorised, over several periods between the dates mentioned under 1.2, bearing in mind the number of entries authorised under 1.3.

The number of days authorised is written in the blank space between 'Duration of visit' and 'Days', in the form of two figures, the first of which is a zero if the number of days is less than 10.

The maximum number of days that can be included under this heading is 90 per any half-year.

---

[1] In the case of transit visas, the length of transit shall not exceed five days.

1.5. 'Issued in... on...' heading

This heading shows, in the language of the Contracting Party issuing the visa, the name of the town in which the diplomatic mission or consular post which is issuing the visa is found, this name is written between 'IN' and 'ON'. The date of issue is indicated after 'ON'.

The date of issue is written in the same way as the date referred to in 1.2.

The authority which issued the visa may be identified by way of the entry which appears in the stamp affixed to Section 4.

1.6. 'Passport number' heading

This heading indicates the number of the passport to which the visa-sticker is affixed. This number shall be followed by reference to any children and to the spouse if these appear in the passport, who are accompanying the holder (a letter 'X' for children preceded by the number thereof (for example 3X = three children) and a letter 'Y' for the spouse).

The passport number is the series number which is pre-printed or perforated on all or almost all of the pages of the passport.

1.7. 'Type of visa' heading

In order to facilitate matters for the control authorities, this heading specifies the type of visa using the letters A, B, C and D as follows:

A: airport transit visa

B: transit visa

C: short-term visa

D: long-term national visa

For visas with limited territorial validity and group visas the letters A, B or C shall be used depending on the case in question.

2. National entries section ('COMMENTS'). Section 9

Contrary to Section 8 (joint and obligatory entries), this section is reserved for any comments relating to national provisions. Although the Contracting Parties shall be free to include any comments which they deem relevant, they shall be obliged to inform their partners thereof in order that these comments may be interpreted (see Annex 9).

3. Section on the stamp of the mission or post issuing the visa. Section 4

The stamp of the mission or post issuing the visa is affixed in the rectangle between the left-hand side of the sticker and the section 'COMMENTS' and the rotogravure section and the section to be electronically scanned.

The size and content of the stamp and the ink to be used shall be determined by the national provisions of the Contracting Parties.

4. Section to be electronically scanned. Section 5

Both the format of the visa-sticker and that of the electronically scanned section have been decided by the ICAO on the basis of a proposal put forward by the Schengen States. This section is made up of two lines of 36 characters (OCR B-10 cpi). Annex 10 explains how this section is to be filled in.

5. Other aspects relating to the issue of visas

5.1. Signing visas

In cases where the law or practice of a Contracting Party requires a hand-written signature, the sticker affixed to the page of the passport shall be signed by the official responsible in this regard.

The signature is placed at the right-hand side of the heading 'Comments'; part of the signature should extend onto the page of the passport or the travel document, but it must not cover the section to be electronically scanned.

5.2. Invalidating completed visa-stickers

No changes shall be made to the visa-sticker. If there is a mistake made when the visa is issued then the sticker shall be invalidated.

— If the mistake is detected on a sticker which has not yet been affixed to the passport, the sticker shall be destroyed or cut diagonally in half.

— If the mistake is detected after the sticker has been affixed to the passport, the sticker shall have a red cross drawn on it and a new sticker shall be affixed.

5.3. Affixing visa-stickers to passports

The sticker shall be filled in before being affixed to the passport. The stamp and the signature shall be placed on the sticker once it has been affixed to the passport or travel document.

Once the visa-sticker has been correctly filled in, it shall be affixed to the first page of the passport that is free from any other entries or stamps — other than the identification stamp of the application. Passports which do not have space free for affixing the sticker, passports which have expired and passports which do not authorise exit from the territory before the visa expires, or the alien's return to his/her country of origin or entry into a third country (see Article 13 of the convention), shall be refused.

5.4. Passports and travel documents to which uniform visas may be affixed

The criteria for deciding which travel documents may bear a visa, in accordance with the provision of Article 17(3)(a) of the convention, are listed in Annex 11.

In accordance with Article 14, no visa may be affixed to a travel document if that travel document is not valid for any of the Contracting Parties. If a travel document is only valid for one Contracting Party or for a number of Contracting Parties the visa to be affixed shall be limited to the Contracting Party or Parties in question.

If a travel document is not recognised as valid by one or more of the Contracting Parties an authorisation may be issued in place of the visa. This authorisation shall be written on a separate sheet of paper and shall only have the effect of a visa with limited territorial validity.

VII. Administrative management and organisation

1. Organisation of visa sections

Each Contracting Party shall be responsible for organising its visa sections.

The heads of the missions or posts shall ensure that the section responsible for issuing visas is organised in such a way as to avoid any type of negligent behaviour which could facilitate theft and falsifications.

- The staff responsible for issuing visas shall in no way be exposed to local pressure.
- In order to avoid 'habits' being formed which could lead to a decline in the level of vigilance, the officers responsible shall be rotated on a regular basis.
- The storage and use of visa-stickers shall be the subject of security measures similar to those applied to other documents which require protection.

2. Filing

Each Contracting Party shall be responsible for filing visa applications, and photographs of applicants in cases where visas are subject to central consultation.

Visa applications shall be kept for at least one year where the visa has been issued and at least five years where the visa has been refused.

In order to make it easier to locate an application, the file and archive references shall be mentioned during consultation and in replies to consultation.

3. Visa registers

Each Contracting Party shall register visas which have been issued in accordance with national practice. Visa-stickers shall be registered as such.

4. Fees to be charged for the issue of visas

The fees to be charged for the issue of visas are listed in Annex 12.

VIII. Consular cooperation at a local level

1. Outline of consular cooperation at a local level

On the spot consular cooperation shall, generally speaking, focus on assessing immigration risks. It shall mainly be aimed at determining common criteria for examining files, exchanging information on the use of false documents, on possible illegal immigration routes and on refusing visas where applications are clearly ill-founded or fraudulent. It should also enable the exchange of information on bona fide applicants and on the joint development of information for the general public on the conditions governing Schengen visa applications.

Consular cooperation shall also take account of the local administrative situation and social and economic structure.

The missions and posts shall organise meetings on a regular basis depending on circumstances and as often as they deem suitable: they shall submit reports on these meetings to the central authorities. At the request of the Presidency they shall submit a general half-yearly report.

2. How to avoid multiple applications or applications which are lodged after a recent refusal to issue

The exchange of information between missions and posts and the identification of applications by means of a stamp or by other means are aimed at preventing the presentation, by the same person, of multiple or successive visa applications, either whilst an application is being examined, or after an application had been refused, by the same mission or post or by a different mission or post.

Without prejudice to the consultation which may take place between the missions and posts and the exchanges of information which they may carry out, the mission or post with whom an application is lodged, shall affix a stamp to each applicant's passport stipulating 'Visa applied for on... at...'. The space following 'on' shall be filled in with six figures (two figures for the day, two for the month and two for the year): the second space shall be reserved for the diplomatic mission or consular post concerned. The code for the visa that has been applied for must be added.

The mission or post which receives the application shall decide whether or not to affix a stamp to diplomatic and service passports.

The stamp may also be affixed in the case of applications for long-stay visas.

When a Schengen State is representing another Schengen State, the stamp shall show, after the code of the type of visa requested, the indication 'R' followed by the code of the represented State.

Where the visa is issued, the sticker shall, as far as possible, be affixed on top of the identification stamp.

In exceptional circumstances when it is impracticable to affix a stamp, the mission or post of the Presidency in office shall inform the relevant Schengen group and submit for the group's approval an alternative proposal, for instance involving the exchange of photocopies of passports or lists of rejected visa applications giving grounds for the refusal.

The heads of the diplomatic missions or posts shall adopt at a local level, and at the initiative of the Presidency, alternative or additional preventative measures, where such measures prove necessary.

3. Assessment of the applicant's good faith

In order to facilitate the assessment of the applicant's good faith, the diplomatic missions or consular posts may, in accordance with national legislation, carry out an exchange of information on the basis of arrangements concluded at a local level as part of their cooperation, and pursuant to point 1 of this chapter.

Information on the following may be exchanged from time to time: persons whose applications have been refused due to the fact that stolen, lost or falsified documents have been used, or that the date of exit on the previous visa was not respected or that there is a risk to security and in particular there is reason to believe that an attempt is being made to illegally immigrate to the territory of the Contracting Parties.

The information which is jointly exchanged and produced shall serve as a working instrument for assessing visa applications. It shall not, however, replace the actual examination of the visa application nor the search in the Schengen information system, nor consultation with the requesting central authorities.

4. Exchange of statistics

4.1. Statistics on short-stay visas, transit visas and airport transit visas that have been issued and on applications for such visas that have been formally rejected shall be exchanged every three months.

4.2. Without prejudice to the obligations laid down in Article 16 of the convention, which are clearly set out in Annex 14 to the common consular instructions and which require the Schengen States to forward within 72 hours details concerning the issue of visas with limited territorial validity, the diplomatic missions and consular posts of the Schengen States are obliged to exchange their statistics on visas with limited territorial validity issued the previous month and transmit them to their respective national central authorities.

ANNEX 1

I. Joint list of States whose citizens are required to have a visa by all the Schengen States

II. Updated list of States whose citizens are exempt from the visa requirement by all the Schengen States

III. Updated list of States whose citizens are required to have a visa by some Schengen States only

The lists below show the decisions adopted by the Executive Committee of Schengen up to 1 May 1999. Information on any amendments made after 1 May 1999 may be obtained from the relevant departments of the Commission or of the General Secretariat of the Council.

I. Joint list of States (1) whose citizens are required to have a visa by all the Schengen States

AFGHANISTAN (2)
ALBANIA (2)
ALGERIA (2)
ANGOLA (2)
ANTIGUA AND BARBUDA
ARMENIA (2)
AZERBAIJAN (2)
BAHAMAS
BAHRAIN (2)
BANGLADESH (2)
BARBADOS
BELARUS (2)
BELIZE
BENIN (2)
BHUTAN (2)
BOSNIA-HERZEGOVINA
BOTSWANA
BULGARIA (2)
BURKINA FASO (2)
BURMA/MYANMAR (2)
BURUNDI (2)
CAMBODIA (2)
CAMEROON (2)
CAPE VERDE (2)
CENTRAL AFRICAN REPUBLIC (2)
CHAD (2)
CHINA (2)
COMOROS (2)

(1) This list shall be without prejudice to the position of each of the Schengen States with regard to the international status of the countries mentioned, and without prejudice to the relations they might have with the latter.

(2) Referred to in the annex to Council Regulation (EC) No 574/1999 of 12 March 1999 determining the third countries whose nationals must be in possession of visas when crossing the external borders of the Member States.

CONGO BRAZZAVILLE ([1])
CONGO (DEMOCRATIC REPUBLIC OF) ([1])
COTE D'IVOIRE ([1])
CUBA ([1])
DJIBOUTI ([1])
DOMINICA
DOMINICAN REPUBLIC ([1])
EGYPT ([1])
EQUATORIAL GUINEA ([1])
ERITREA ([1])
ETHIOPIA ([1])
FIJI ([1])
FEDERAL REPUBLIC OF YUGOSLAVIA (SERBIA AND MONTENEGRO) ([1])
FORMER YUGOSLAV REPUBLIC OF MACEDONIA ([1])
GABON ([1])
GAMBIA ([1])
GEORGIA ([1])
GHANA ([1])
GRENADA
GUINEA ([1])
GUINEA-BISSAU ([1])
GUYANA ([1])
HAITI ([1])
INDIA ([1])
INDONESIA ([1])
IRAN ([1])
IRAQ ([1])
JAMAICA
JORDAN ([1])
KAZAKHSTAN ([1])
KENYA
KIRIBATI
KUWAIT ([1])
KYRGYZSTAN ([1])
LAOS ([1])
LEBANON ([1])
LESOTHO
LIBERIA ([1])
LIBYA ([1])
MADAGASCAR ([1])
MALAWI
MALDIVES ([1])
MALI ([1])
MARSHALL ISLANDS
MAURITANIA ([1])
MAURITIUS ([1])
MICRONESIA
MOLDOVA ([1])
MONGOLIA ([1])
MOROCCO ([1])
MOZAMBIQUE ([1])
NAMIBIA
NAURU
NEPAL ([1])
NIGER ([1])
NIGERIA ([1])
NORTH KOREA ([1])
NORTHERN MARIANAS (ISLANDS)
OMAN ([1])
PAKISTAN ([1])
PALAU
PAPUA NEW GUINEA ([1])
PERU ([1])
PHILIPPINES ([1])
QATAR ([1])
ROMANIA ([1])
RUSSIA ([1])
RWANDA ([1])
SAINT CHRISTOPHER AND NEVIS
SAINT LUCIA
SAINT VINCENT AND THE GRENADINES
SAMOA (WESTERN)
SÃO TOMÉ AND PRINCIPE ([1])
SAUDI ARABIA ([1])
SENEGAL ([1])
SEYCHELLES
SIERRA LEONE ([1])
SOLOMON ISLANDS
SOMALIA ([1])
SOUTH AFRICA
SRI LANKA ([1])
SUDAN ([1])
SURINAME ([1])
SWAZILAND
SYRIA ([1])
TAIWAN ([1])
TAJIKISTAN ([1])
TANZANIA ([1])
THAILAND ([1])
TOGO ([1])
TONGA
TRINIDAD AND TOBAGO

([1]) Referred to in the annex to Council Regulation (EC) No 574/1999 of 12 March 1999 determining the third countries whose nationals must be in possession of visas when crossing the external borders of the Member States.

TUNISIA [1]
TURKEY [1]
TURKMENISTAN [1]
TUVALU
UGANDA [1]
UKRAINE [1]
UNITED ARAB EMIRATES [1]
UZBEKISTAN [1]
VANUATU
VIETNAM [1]
YEMEN [1]
ZAMBIA [1]
ZIMBABWE

[1] Referred to in the annex to Council Regulation (EC) No 574/1999 of 12 March 1999 determining the third countries whose nationals must be in possession of visas when crossing the external borders of the Member States.

II. Updated schedule of States whose citizens are exempt from the visa requirement by all the Schengen States

ANDORRA
ARGENTINA
AUSTRALIA
BOLIVIA
BRAZIL [1]
BRUNEI
CANADA
CHILE
COSTA RICA
CROATIA
CYPRUS
CZECH REPUBLIC
ECUADOR
ESTONIA
GUATEMALA
HONDURAS
HUNGARY
ICELAND
ISRAEL [2]
JAPAN
LATVIA
LIECHTENSTEIN
LITHUANIA
MALAYSIA
MALTA
MEXICO
MONACO
NEW ZEALAND
NICARAGUA
NORWAY
PANAMA
PARAGUAY
POLAND [1]
SALVADOR
SAN MARINO
SINGAPORE
SLOVAKIA
SLOVENIA
SOUTH KOREA
SWITZERLAND
UNITED STATES [3]
URUGUAY
VATICAN CITY STATE
VENEZUELA

(1) Greece requires visas for seamen who are nationals of this State.

(2) France shall continue to require short-term visas from vessel and aircraft crew members carrying out their duties.

(3) France requires visas for the following categories of nationals of the United States:
- students;
- journalists on assignment;
- ship or flight crews in the exercise of their duties.

III. Updated schedule of States whose citizens are required to have a visa by one or more Schengen States

COLOMBIA

LIST OF STATES WHOSE CITIZENS ARE REQUIRED TO HAVE A VISA BY SOME SCHENGEN STATES ONLY								
	Austria	Germany	Benelux	Spain	France	Greece	Italy	Portugal
Colombia			V		V	V		V

ANNEX 2

Regulations governing the movement of holders of diplomatic, official and service passports, and holders of laissez-passers which certain international intergovernmental organisations issue to their officials

I. Regulations governing movements at external borders

1. Movements of holders of diplomatic, official and service passports is not governed by the common list of visa requirements. The Contracting States undertake, however, to keep their partners informed, in advance of any changes that they intend to make to the regulations governing the movements of holders of the abovementioned passports and to take into account the interests of their partners.

2. Given the aim of an increase in flexibility being adopted in the approach to harmonising the rules applied to holders of the abovementioned passports, a schedule of countries whose nationals are not subject to a visa requirement since they hold the abovementioned passports, although this visa requirement applies to ordinary passport holders of the same nationality, is annexed to the common visa instructions, for information purposes. The reverse situation shall also be compiled in a schedule, should this be necessary. The Executive Committee shall assume responsibility for updating these lists.

3. The regulations governing movements mentioned in this document shall not apply to holders of ordinary passports carrying out public affairs nor holders of service, official, or special passports, etc. for which the issue by third countries is not in line with the international practice applied by the Schengen States. Accordingly, the Executive Committee, acting on a proposal of a group of experts, could draw up a list of passports other than the ordinary passports for holders, which the Schengen States do not plan to accord preferential treatment.

4. Pursuant to the provisions of Article 18 of the implementing convention, persons to whom a visa is issued so that they may reach the territory of the Schengen State for the purposes of their accreditation may, at least, pass through the other States on their way to the State which issued the visa.

5. Persons who have already been accredited by a diplomatic or consular representation and their family members who hold an identity card issued by the Ministry of Foreign Affairs may cross the external border with the Schengen area on production of the said identity card, and, where necessary, the travel document.

6. In general, the holders of diplomatic, official or service passports, even though they remain subject to a visa requirement, when this requirement exists, do not have to prove that they have sufficient means of subsistence at their disposal. However, if they are travelling in a personal capacity, they may, where necessary, be asked to produce the same supporting documents as are required from ordinary passport holders applying for visas.

7. A *note verbale* from the Ministry of Foreign Affairs or from a diplomatic mission (if the visa application is lodged in a third country) should accompany each application for a visa for a diplomatic, official or service passport when the applicant is on official duty. Where the journey is for private purposes, a *note verbale* may also be required.

8.1. The arrangement for prior consultation with the central authorities of the other Contracting States shall apply to applications for visas made by holders of diplomatic, official and service passports. Prior consultation shall not be made with the State which concluded an agreement removing the visa requirement for holders of diplomatic and/or service passports with the country whose nationals are concerned by the consultation (in the cases contained in Annex 5 to this instruction).

Should one of the Contracting States raise objections, the Schengen State which should decide on the application for a visa can issue a visa of limited territorial validity.

8.2. The Schengen States undertake not to conclude at a future date, without prior agreement with the other Member States, agreements in the area of removing visa requirements for holders of diplomatic, official and service passports with States whose nationals are subject to prior consultation for a visa to be issued by another Schengen State.

8.3. If it involves a visa being issued for accrediting a foreigner who is listed as not to be granted entry and the arrangement for prior consultation applies, the consultation should be carried out in accordance with the provisions of Article 25 of the implementing convention.

9. If a Contracting State invokes the exceptions provided for under Article 5(2) of the implementing convention, granting entry to holders of diplomatic, official or service passports would also be limited to the national territory of the State in question, which should inform the other Member States.

II. Regulations governing movements at internal borders

In general, the arrangement under Articles 19 et seq. shall apply, except for the issue of a visa of limited territorial validity.

The holders of diplomatic, official and service passports may move within the territory of the Contracting States for three months from the date of entry (if they are not subject to the visa requirements) or for the duration provided for by the visa.

Persons accredited by a diplomatic or consular post and their family members, holders of the card issued by the Ministry for Foreign Affairs may move within the territory of the Contracting States for a maximum duration of three months upon production of this card and, if required, the travel document.

Regulations governing movements outlined in this document shall apply to laissez-passers issued by the intergovernmental international organisations which all the Schengen States are members of, to their officials, who pursuant to the Treaty constituting these organisations, are exempt from registering with the Immigration Office and from holding a residence permit (see page 47 of the common manual).

III. Regulations governing movement of holders of diplomatic, official and service passports

Schedule A

Countries whose nationals are not subject to a visa requirement in one or more Schengen States when they are holders of diplomatic, official and service passports, but which are subject to this requirement when they are holders of ordinary passports.

	A	B/NL/L	D	EL	E	F	I	P
Albania				DS			D	
Algeria							DS	
Angola								DS
Antigua and Barbados				DS				
Bahamas	DS							
Barbados	DS						DS	
Benin							DS	
Bosnia Herzegovina	D			D				
Botswana							DS	
Bulgaria	D		D	DS	D	D		D
Burkina Faso							DS	
Cape Verde								DS
Chad		D	DS					
Côte d'Ivoire	DS	DS				DS	DS	
Dominica							DS	
Dominican Republic							DS	
Egypt							DS	
Federal Republic of Yugoslavia				DS			DS	
Fiji							DS	
Former Yugoslav Republic of Macedonia	D					D	DS	
Gabon						D		
Gambia							DS	
Ghana			DS					
Guyana							DS	

	A	B/NL/L	D	EL	E	F	I	P
India			D					
Jamaica		DS						
Kuwait							DS	
Lesotho							DS	
Malawi		DS						
Maldives	DS							
Morocco	DS	DS	D	DS	D	D	DS	DS
Mauritania							DS	
Mozambique								DS
Niger							DS	
Uganda							DS	
Pakistan	DS	DS	DS					
Peru	DS			DS			DS	
Philippines	DS		DS	DS	DS		DS	
Romania	D	D		D	D	D	D	D
Western Samoa							DS	
São Tomé and Príncipe								DS
Senegal	DS	DS	DS			D	DS	
Seychelles	D							
South Africa	DS							
Swaziland							DS	
Thailand	DS	DS	DS				DS	
Togo							DS	
Trinidad and Tobago	DS							
Tunisia	DS	DS		DS	D	D	DS	DS
Turkey	DS	DS	DS	DS	DS	DS	DS	
Uganda							DS	
Venezuela								D
Zimbabwe				DS				

DS: The holders of diplomatic and service passports are exempt from visa requirements.
D: Only holders of diplomatic passports are exempted from a visa requirement.

Schedule B

Countries whose nationals are subject to visas in one or more Schengen States, when they are holders of diplomatic, official, or service passports, but which are not subject to this requirement when they are holders of ordinary passports.

	A	B/NL/L	D	EL	E	F	I	P
Australia								X
Chile						X		
Israel						X		
Mexico	X							
Paraguay								X
United States				X		X (1)		

(1) If travelling on official business.

ANNEX 3

List of States whose nationals are subject to an airport transit visa requirement, where holders of travel documents issued by these States are also subject to this visa requirement (1)

The Schengen States undertake not to amend Part I of Annex 3 without the prior consent of the other Member States.

If a Member State intends to amend Part II of this annex, it undertakes to inform its partners and to take account of its interests.

Part I: Joint list of States whose nationals are subject to airport visa requirements (ATV) by all Schengen States, holders of travel documents issued by these States also being subject to this requirement (2) (3)

AFGHANISTAN
BANGLADESH
CONGO (Democratic Republic) (4)
ERITREA (4)
ETHIOPIA
GHANA
IRAQ
IRAN
NIGERIA
PAKISTAN
SOMALIA
SRI LANKA

These persons shall not be subject to the visa requirement if they hold one of the residence permits of an EEA Member State listed in Part III (A) of this annex or one of the residence permits of Andorra, Japan, Canada, Monaco, San Marino, Switzerland or the United

(1) It is not necessary to consult the central authorities for the issue of an airport transit visa (ATV).

(2) For all the Schengen States
The following persons shall be exempt from the ATV requirement:
— airplane crew members who are nationals of a Contracting Party to the convention of Chicago.

(3) For the Benelux countries, Spain and France
The following persons shall be exempt from the ATV requirement:
— holders of diplomatic and service passports.

(4) For Germany
The visa requirement will only take effect when the national initiated procedures have been completed.

States indicated below which guarantees an unqualified right of return, referred to in Part III (B).

The list of residence permits shall be completed by mutual agreement in the framework of Working Group II subgroup on visas and subjected to regular scrutiny. Should problems arise, the Schengen States may suspend the application of these measures until such time as the problems in question have been resolved by mutual agreement. The Contracting States may exclude certain residence permits from the exemption where indicated in Section III.

Exemptions from the airport transit visa requirement for holders of diplomatic, service or other official passports shall be decided by each Member State individually.

Part II: List of States whose nationals are subject to an airport transit visa requirement by some Schengen States only, with holders of travel documents issued by these States also being subject to this requirement

	A (1)	B / NL / L (2)	D	EL	E (3)	F(4)	I(5)	P
Albania						x		
Angola		x	x	x	x	x		
Bulgaria			x					
Côte d'Ivoire					x			
Gambia			x					
Guinea Bissau					x			
Haiti						x		
India		x	x(6)	x	x		x	
Indonesia								x
Jordan			x					
Lebanon		x	x					
Liberia	x				x	x		x
Libya	x					x		
Mali					x			
Romania			x					
Senegal					x		x	x
Sierra Leone					x	x		
Sudan	x		x	x				
Syria		x	x	x				
Togo					x			
Turkey		x	x(6)	x				

(1) Aliens subject to transit visa obligations no longer require an airport transit visa for transit (ATV) via an Austrian airport provided they hold one of the following documents that is valid for the length of the stay necessary for the transit:
— a residence permit issued by Andorra, Japan, Canada, Monaco, San Marino, Switzerland, the Holy See or the US which guarantees an unqualified right to return;
— a visa or residence permit issued by a Schengen State for which the accession agreement has been brought into force;
— a residence permit issued by a Member State of the EEA.

(2) Only when nationals are not in possession of a valid residence permit for the Member States of the EEA, the United States or Canada. Holders of diplomatic and service passports are also exempt.

(3) Holders of diplomatic, official and service passports are not subject to the ATV requirement. The same applies to holders of ordinary passports residing in a Member State of the EEA, the United States, or holding a valid entry visa for one of those countries.

(4) The following persons shall be exempt from the ATV requirement:
— holders of diplomatic and service passports;
— holders of one of the residence permits listed in Part III;
— aeroplane crew members who are nationals of a Contracting Party to the convention of Chicago.

(5) Only when nationals are not in possession of a valid residence permit for the Member States of the EEA, the United States or Canada.

(6) Only when nationals are not in possession of a valid visa for the Member States of the EEA, Switzerland, Canada or the United States.

Part III:

A. List of residence permits of EEA States for which the holders are exempt from the airport transit visa requirement on presentation of the document

DENMARK

- *Opholdstilladelse* (residence permit in the form of a card marked C, D, E, F, G, H, J, K or L)
- *Opholdstilladelse* (residence permit in the form of a pink and white sticker affixed to the passport and marked B, C or H)
- *Tilbagerejsetilladelse* (re-entry permit in the form of a stamp affixed to the passport and marked I, II or III)

FINLAND

- *Oleskelulupa uppehållstillstånd* (residence permit in card form for EU nationals or EEA nationals and their family members residing in Finland)
- Residence permit in the form of a sticker filled out in English and clearly showing the type and length of validity of the permit: bears the inscription 'Suomi Finland', 'visa' and 'permit'
- Residence permit in the form of a sticker modelled on a visa sticker with the entry in Finnish '*Oleskelulupa Ja Työlupa*' (residence and work permit)
- *Oleskelulupa uppehållstillstånd* (uniform EU residence permit filled out in Finnish/ Swedish)

ICELAND

- Alien's passport (brown cover) in conjunction with a re-entry permit in the form of a stamp in the passport [1]
- Temporary residence permit (red card) in conjunction with a re-entry permit in the form of a stamp in the passport
- Permanent residence permit (yellow card with a green stripe)
- Permanent work and residence permit (green card)

[1] This residence permit does not exempt the holder from the airport transit visa requirement in Germany.

IRELAND

- Residence permit only in conjunction with a re-entry visa

LIECHTENSTEIN

- *Livret pour étranger B* (residence permit, sufficient within the period of validity of one year) ([1])
- *Livret pour étranger C* (settlement permit, sufficient within the period of validity of 5 or 10 years)

NORWAY

- *Oppholdstillatelse* (temporary residence permit)
- *Arbeidstillatelse* (temporary work permit)
- *Bosettingstillatelse* (permanent residence and work permit)

SWEDEN

- Permanent residence permit in the form of a sticker affixed to the passport and marked '*SVERIGE Bevis om permanent uppehållstillstånd*; Sweden: certificate of permanent residence permit'
- Residence and work permit in the form of a visa sticker affixed to the passport and marked '*SVERIGE Uppehålls och arbetstillstånd*; Sweden: residence and work permit'

UNITED KINGDOM

- Leave to remain in the United Kingdom for an indefinite period (this document is only sufficient when the holder has not been away for more than two years)
- Certificate of entitlement to the right of abode

B. List of residence permits with unlimited right of return on presentation of which the holders are exempt from the airport transit visa requirement:

ANDORRA

- *Tarjeta provisional de estancia y de trabajo* (provisional residence and work permit) (white). These are issued to seasonal workers; the period of validity depends on the duration of employment, but never exceeds six months. This permit is not renewable ([1]).

- *Tarjeta de estancia y de trabajo* (residence and work permit) (white). This permit is issued for six months and may be renewed for another year ([1]).

([1]) This residence permit does not exempt the holder from the airport transit visa requirement in Germany.

- *Tarjeta de estancia (*residence permit) (white). This permit is issued for six months and may be renewed for another year ([1]).

- *Tarjeta temporal de residencia* (temporary residence permit) (pink). This permit is issued for one year and may be renewed twice, each time for another year ([1]).

- *Tarjeta ordinaria de residencia* (ordinary residence permit) (yellow). This permit is issued for three years and may be renewed for another three years ([1]).

- *Tarjeta privilegiada de residencia* (special residence permit) (green). This permit is issued for five years and is renewable, each time for another five years.

- *Autorización de residencia* (residence authorisation) (green). This permit is issued for one year and is renewable, each time for another three years ([1]).

- *Autorización temporal de residencia y de trabajo* (temporary residence and work authorisation) (pink). This permit is issued for two years and may be renewed for another two years ([1]).

- *Autorización ordinaria de residencia y de trabajo* (ordinary residence and work authorisation) (yellow). This permit is issued for five years.

- *Autorización privilegiada de residencia y de trabajo* (special residence and work authorisation) (green). This permit is issued for 10 years and is renewable, each time for another 10 years.

CANADA

- Returning resident permit (loose-leaf in passport)

JAPAN

- Re-entry permit to Japan ([1])

MONACO

- *Carte de séjour de résident temporaire de Monaco* (temporary resident's permit) ([1])

- *Carte de séjour de résident ordinaire de Monaco* (ordinary resident's permit)

- *Carte de séjour de résident privilégié* (privileged resident's permit)

- *Carte de séjour de conjoint de ressortissant monégasque* (residence permit for the spouse of a person of Monegasque nationality)

([1]) This residence permit does not exempt the holder from the airport transit visa requirement in Germany.

SAN MARINO

- *Permesso di soggiorno ordinario (validità illimitata)* (ordinary residence permit (no expiry date))
- *Permesso di soggiorno continuativo speciale (validità illimitata)* (special permanent residence permit (no expiry date))
- *Carta d'identità de San Marino (validità illimitata)* (San Marino identity card (no expiry date))

SWITZERLAND

- *Livret pour étranger B* (residence permit, guaranteeing return of holder within the period of validity of one year) ([1])
- *Livret pour étranger C* (settlement permit, guaranteeing return of holder within the period of validity of 5 or 10 years)

UNITED STATES OF AMERICA

- Form I-551 permanent resident card (valid for 2 ([1]) to 10 years)
- Form I-551 Alien registration receipt card (valid for 2 ([1]) to 10 years)
- Form I-551 Alien registration receipt card (no expiry date)
- Form I-327 Re-entry document (valid for two years — issued to holders of an I-551) ([1])
- Resident alien card (valid for 2 ([1]) or 10 years or no expiry date. This document is only sufficient when the holder was absent from the US for not longer than one year.)
- Permit to re-enter (valid for two years. This document is only sufficient when the holder was absent from the US for not longer than two years.) ([1])
- Valid temporary residence stamp in a valid passport (valid for one year from the date of issue) ([1])

([1]) This residence permit does not exempt the holder from the airport transit visa requirement in Germany.

ANNEX 4

List of documents entitling entry without a visa

BELGIUM

- *Carte d'identité d'étranger*
  Identiteitskaart voor vreemdelingen
  Personalausweis für Ausländer
  (Identity card for foreigners)
- *Certificat d'inscription au régistre des étrangers*
  Bewijs van inschrijving in het vreemdelingenregister
  Bescheinigung der Eintragung im Ausländer-register
  (Certificate attesting to entry in foreigners' register)
- Special residence permits issued by the Ministry of Foreign Affairs:
  - *Carte d'identité diplomatique*
    Diplomatieke identiteitskaart
    Diplomatischer Personalausweis
    (Diplomat's identity card)
  - *Carte d'identité consulaire*
    Consular identiteitskaart
    Konsularer Personalausweis
    (Consular identity card)
  - *Carte d'identité spéciale — couleur bleue*
    Bijzondere identiteitskaart — blauw
    Besonderer Personalausweis — blau
    (Special identity card — blue in colour)
  - *Carte d'identité spéciale — couleur rouge*
    Bijzondere identiteitskaart — rood
    Besonderer Personalausweis — rot
    (Special identity card — red in colour)
  - *Certificat d'identité pour les enfants âgés de moins de cinq ans des étrangers privilégiés titulaires d'une carte d'identité diplomatique, d'une carte d'identité consulaire, d'une carte d'identité spéciale — couleur bleue ou d'une carte d'identité — couleur rouge*
    Identiteitsbewijs voor kinderen, die de leeftijd van vijf jaar nog niet hebben bereikt, van een bevoorrecht vreemdeling dewelke houder is van een diplomatieke identiteitskaart, consulaire identiteitskaart, bijzondere identiteitskaart — blauw of bijzondere identiteitskaart — rood
    Identitätsnachweis für Kinder unter fünf Jahren von privilegierten Ausländer, die Inhaber eines diplomatischen Personalausweises sind, eines konsularen Personalausweis, eines besonderen Personalausweis — rot oder eines besonderen Personalausweis — blau

(Identity card for children, under the age of five, of aliens who are holders of diplomatic identity cards, consular identity cards, blue special identity cards or red special identity cards)

- *Certificat d'identité avec photographie délivré par une administration communale belge à un enfant de moins de douze years*
  Door een Belgisch gemeentebestuur aan een kind beneden de 12 jaar afgegeven identiteitsbewijs met foto
  Von einer belgischen Gemeindeverwaltung einem Kind unter dem 12. Lebensjahr ausgestellter Personalausweis mit Lichtbild
  (Certificate of identity with photograph issued by Belgian communes to children under 12)
- List of persons participating in a school trip within the European Union

GERMANY

- *Aufenthaltserlaubnis für die Bundesrepublik Deutschland*
  (Residence permit for the Federal Republic of Germany)
- *Aufenthaltserlaubnis für Angehörige eines Mitgliedstaates der EWG*
  (Residence permit for EC nationals)
- *Aufenthaltsberechtigung für die Bundesrepublik Deutschland*
  (Residence permit for the Federal Republic of Germany)
- *Aufenthaltsbewilligung für die Bundesrepublik Deutschland*
  (Residence authorisation for the Federal Republic of Germany)
- *Aufenthaltsbefugnis für die Bundesrepublik Deutschland*
  (Residence permit for the Federal Republic of Germany)

  These residence permits only entitle entry without a visa when they are inserted in a passport or issued in connection with a passport as an authorisation replacing a visa. They do not entitle entry without a visa if they are issued instead of a national identity document.

  The document for a deferred expulsion measure '*Aussetzung der Abschiebung (Duldung)*' and the temporary residence authorisation for asylum-seekers '*Aufenthaltsgestattung für Asylbewerber*' does not entitle entry without a visa either.
- Special residence permits issued by the Ministry of Foreign Affairs
  - *Diplomatenausweis*
    (Diplomat's pass) (red in colour)
  - *Ausweis für bevorrechtigte Personen*
    (VIP pass) (blue in colour)
  - *Ausweis*
    (Pass) (yellow in colour)
  - *Personalausweis*
    (Identity card) (green in colour)
- Special residence permits issued by the *Länder*:
  - *Ausweis für Mitglieder des Konsularkorps*
    (Pass for members of the consular corps) (white in colour)
  - *Ausweis*
    (Pass) (grey in colour)

- *Ausweis für Mitglieder des Konsularkorps*
  (Pass for members of the consular corps) (white with green stripes)
- *Ausweis*
  (Pass) (yellow in colour)
- *Ausweis*
  (Pass) (green in colour)

— List of persons participating in a school trip within the European Union.

GREECE

— *Αδεια παραμονής αλλοδαπού για εργασία*
(Work permit)

— *Αδεια παραμονής μελών οικογενείας αλλοδαπού*
(Residence permit issued for family reunion)

— *Αδεια παραμονής αλλοδαπού για σπουδές*
(Residence permit for study purposes)

— *Αδεια παραμονής αλλοδαπού (χρώμα λευκό)*
(Alien's residence permit) (white)
(This document is issued to aliens who are married to Greek nationals; it is valid for one year and can be extended for as long as the marriage lasts.)

— *Δελτίο ταυτότητας αλλοδαπού (χρώμα πράσινο)*
(Alien's identity card) (green)
(This document is issued only to aliens of Greek origin; it is valid for two to five years.)

— *Ειδικό Δελτίο Ταυτότητας Ομογενούς (χρώμα μπέζ)*
(Special identity card for persons of Greek origin) (beige)
(This document is issued to Albanian nationals of Greek origin; it is valid for three years. This card is also issued to their spouses and descendants of Greek origin, regardless of nationality, provided there is official documentation of some kind to prove their family ties.)

— List of persons participating in a school trip within the European Union.

SPAIN

Holders of a valid re-entry authorisation will be allowed entry without a visa.

Residence permits entitling aliens who for reasons of nationality, would normally be subject to a visa requirement to enter Spanish territory without a visa are as follows:

— *Permiso de Residencia Inicial*
(Initial residence permit)

— *Permiso de Residencia Ordinario*
(Ordinary residence permit)

— *Permiso de Residencia Especial*
(Special residence permit)

— *Tarjeta de Estudiante*
(Student card)

— *Permiso de Residencia tipo A*
(Type A residence permit)

— *Permiso de Residencia tipo b*
(Type b residence permit)

— *Permiso de Trabajo y de Residencia tipo B*
(Type B work and residence permit)

— *Permiso de Trabajo y de Residencia tipo C*
(Type C work and residence permit)

— *Permiso de Trabajo y de Residencia tipo d*
(Type d work and residence permit)

— *Permiso de Trabajo y de Residencia tipo D*
(Type D work and residence permit)

— *Permiso de Trabajo y de Residencia tipo E*
(Type E work and residence permit)

— *Permisa de Trabajo fronterizo tipo F*
(Type F border work permit)

— *Permisa de Trabajo y Residencia tipo P*
(Type P work and residence permit)

— *Permisa de Trabajo y Residencia tipo Ex*
(Type Ex work and residence permit)

— *Tarjeta de Reconocimiento de la excepción a la necesidad de obtener Permi-so de Trabajo y Permiso de Residencia (art. Ley 7/85)*
(Pass recognising exemption from the need to obtain a work and residence permit — Article 16 Law 7/85)

— *Permiso de Residencia para Refugiados*
(Residence permit for refugees)

— *Lista de personas que participan en un viaje excolar dentro de la Unión Europea*
(List of persons participating in a school trip within the European Union)

— *Tarjeta de Familiar Residente Comunitario*
(Pass for relatives of a Community resident)

— *Tarjeta temporal de Familiar de Residente Comunitario*
(Temporary pass for relatives of a Community resident)

The holders of the following valid accreditation cards issued by the Ministry of Foreign Affairs may enter without a visa:

— *Tarjeta especial* (Special pass, red in colour), on the cover it reads '*Cuerpo Diplomático. Embajador. Documento de Identidad*' (Diplomatic corps. Ambassador. Identity document), issued to accredited ambassadors;

— *Tarjeta especial* (Special pass, red in colour), on the cover it reads '*Cuerpo Diplomático. Documento de Identidad*' (Diplomatic corps. Identity document), issued to staff accredited to diplomatic missions who have diplomatic status. An F is added to the document when issued to spouses or children;

— *Tarjeta especial* (Special pass, yellow in colour), on the cover it reads '*Misiones Diplomáticas. Personal Administrativo y Técnico. Documento de Identidad*' (Diplomatic missions. Administrative and technical staff. Identity document), issued to administrative officials at accredited diplomatic missions. An F is added to the document when issued to spouses or children;

— *Tarjeta especial* (Special pass, red in colour), on the cover it reads '*Tarjeta Diplomática de Identidad*' (Diplomatic identity card), issued to staff with diplomatic status at the office of the League of Arab Nations and to staff accredited to the office of the Palestinian General Mission (*Oficina de la Delegación General*). An F is added to the document when issued to spouses or children;

— *Tarjeta especial* (Special pass, red in colour), on the cover it reads '*Organismos Internacionales. Estatuto Diplomático. Documento de Identidad*' (International organisations. Diplomatic status. Identity document), issued to staff with diplomatic status accredited to International Organisations. An F is added to the document when issued to spouses or children;

— *Tarjeta especial* (Special pass, blue in colour), on the cover it reads '*Organismos Internacionales. Personal Administrativo y Técnico. Documento de Identidad*' (International organisations. Administrative and technical staff. Identity document), issued to administrative officials accredited to international organisations. An F is added to the document when issued to spouses or children;

— *Tarjeta especial* (Special pass, green in colour), on the cover it reads '*Funcionario Consular de Carrera. Documento de Identidad*' (Career consular official. Identity document), issued to career consular officials accredited in Spain. An F is added to the document when issued to spouses or children;

— *Tarjeta especial* (Special pass, green in colour), entitled '*Empleado Consular. Emitido a.... Documento de Identidad*' (Consular employee. Issued on behalf of... Identity document), issued to consular administrative officials accredited in Spain. An F is added to the document when issued to spouses or children;

– *Tarjeta especial* (Special pass,grey in colour), entitled *'Personal de Servicio. Missiones Diplomáticas, Oficinas Consulares y Organismos Internacionales. Emitido a.... Documento de Identidad'* (Service duty staff. Diplomatic missions, consular posts and international organisations. Issued on behalf of... Identity document). This is issued to staff working in the domestic service of diplomatic missions, consular posts and international organisations (service duty staff) and staff with career diplomatic or consular status (special servants). An F is added to the document when issued to spouses or children.

FRANCE

1. Adult aliens should be in possession of the following documents:

– *Carte de séjour temporaire comportant une mention particulière qui varie selon le motif du séjour autorisé*
(A temporary residence permit containing particular details which will vary in accordance with the grounds for the authorised stay)

– *Carte de résident*
(Resident's card)

– *Certificat de résidence d'Algérien comportant une mention particulière qui varie selon le motif du séjour autorisé (1 an, 10 ans)*
(Algerian residence certificate marked according to the grounds for the authorised stay) (1 year, 10 years)

– *Certificat de résidence d'Algérien portant la mention 'membre d'un organisme officiel' (2 ans)*
(Algerian residence certificate marked 'member of an official organisation') (2 years)

– *Carte de séjour des Communautés européennes (1 an, 5 ans, 10 ans)*
(European Communities residence permit) (1 year, 5/10 years)

– *Carte de séjour de l'Espace Economique Européen*
(European Economic Area residence permit)

– *Cartes officielles valant de titre de séjour, délivrées par le Ministère des Affaires Etrangères*
(Official permits with the same status as residence permits issued by the Ministry of Foreign Affairs)

(a) *Cartes diplomatiques* (diplomatic permits)

- *Carte portant la mention 'corps diplomatique' délivrée aux chefs de mission diplomatique (couleur blanche)*
(Permit with the heading 'diplomatic corps' issued to heads of diplomatic missions) (white)

- *Carte portant la mention 'corps diplomatique' délivrée au personnel des représentations diplomatiques accréditées en France (couleur orange)*
(Permit with the heading 'diplomatic corps' issued to staff at accredited diplomatic missions in France) (orange)

- *Carte portant la mention 'organisations internationales' et en deuxième page 'assimilé à un chef de mission diplomatique' (couleur blanche)*
(Permit with the heading 'international organisations' and on the second page 'comparable to a head of a diplomatic mission') (white)

- *Carte portant la mention 'organisations internationales' et en deuxième page 'assimilé à un membre de mission diplomatique' (couleur bleue)*
(Permit with the heading 'international organisations' and on the second page 'comparable to a member of a diplomatic mission') (blue).

(b) *Cartes spéciales* (special permits)

- *Carte spéciale portant la mention 'carte consulaire' délivrée aux fonctionnaires des postes consulaires (couleur verte)*
(Special permit with the heading 'consular permit' issued to officials at consular posts) (green)

- *Carte spéciale portant la mention 'organisations internationales' délivrée aux fonctionnaires internationaux des organisations situées en France (couleur verte)*
(Special permit with the heading 'international organisations' issued to foreign officials of international organisations based in France) (green)

- *Carte spéciale portant la mention 'carte spéciale' délivrée au personnel administratif et technique, de nationalité étrangère, des missions diplomatiques et consulaires et des organisations internationales (couleur beige)*
(Special permit with the heading 'special permit' issued to foreign administrative and technical staff working in diplomatic missions, consular posts or international organisations) (beige)

- *Carte spéciale portant la mention 'carte spéciale délivrée au personnel de service, de nationalité étrangère, des missions diplomatiques et des postes consulaires, et des organisations internationales (couleur grise)*
(Special permit with the heading 'special permit' issued to foreign service staff working in diplomatic missions, consular posts or international organisations) (grey)

- *Carte spéciale portant la mention 'carte spéciale' délivrée au personnel privé, de nationalité étrangère, au service des agents diplomatiques ou assimilés, des fonctionnaires consulaires, et des fonctionnaires internationaux (couleur grise)*
(Special permit with the heading 'special permit' issued to foreign private staff working for diplomatic officials or comparable officials, consular officials and international officials) (grey)

- *Carte spéciale portant la mention 'carte spéciale' délivrée au personnel étranger en mission officielle et de statut particulier (couleur bleu-gris)*
  Special permit with the heading 'special permit' issued to foreign staff on an official mission or with special status) (blue-grey)

2. Aliens who are minors should be in possession of the following documents:

— *Document de circulation pour étrangers mineurs*
(Travel document for alien minors)

— *Visa de retour (sans condition de nationalité et sans présentation du titre de séjour, auquel ne sont pas soumis les enfants mineurs)*
(Return visas) (alien minors are not subject to nationality conditions or to production of residence permits)

— *Passeport diplomatique/de service/ordinaire des enfants mineurs des titulaires d'une carte spéciale du Ministère des Affaires étrangères revêtu d'un visa de circulation*
(Diplomatic/service/ordinary passposts for minors who are children of holders of a special pass issued by the Ministry of Foreign Affairs to which a travel visa is affixed)

NB: It should be noted that acknowledgements of first-time applications for residence permits are not valid. In contrast, acknowledgements of requests to renew residence permits, or to amend permits are considered valid, when these are accompanied by the old permit.

The 'certificate of duty' issued at the discretion of the Ministry of Foreign Affairs, does not constitute a replacement for a residence permit. Holders must also be in possession of one of the ordinary law residence permits (1 — 6 in the list).

3. List of persons participating in a school trip within the European Union.

ITALY

— *Carta di soggiorno (validità illimitata)*
(Residence permit) (unlimited validity)

— *Permesso di soggiorno con esclusione delle sottoelencate tipologie:*
(Residence permit with the exception of the following:)

1. *Permesso di soggiorno provvisorio per richiesta asilo politico ai sensi della Convenzione di Dublino*
   (Provisional residence permit for political asylum seekers pursuant to the Dublin Convention)

2. *Permesso di soggiorno per cure mediche*
   (Residence permit for medical treatment)

3. *Permeso di soggiorno per motivi di giustizia*
(Residence permit for legal reasons)

- *Carta d'identità M.A.E. — Corpo diplomatico*
(Identity card issued by the Ministry of Foreign Affairs — Diplomatic corps)

- *Carta d'identità — Organizzazioni internazionali e Missioni Estere Speciali*
(Identity card — International organisations and special foreign missions)

- *Carta d'identità — Rappresentanze Diplomatiche*
(Identity card — Diplomatic representations)

- *Carta d'identità — Corpo Consolare*
(Identity card — Consular corps)

- *Carta d'identità — Uffici Consolari*
(Identity card — Consulates)

- *Carta d'identità — Rappresentanze Diplomatiche (personale amministrativo e tecnico)*
(Identity card — Diplomatic representations (administrative and technical staff))

- *Carta d'identità — Rappresentanze Diplomatiche e Consolari (personale di servizio)*
(Identity card — Diplomatic and consular representations (official duty staff))

- List of persons participating in a school trip within the European Union.

LUXEMBOURG

- *Carte d'identité d'étranger*
(Alien's identity card)

- *Autorisation de séjour provisoire apposée dans le passeport national*
(Provisional residence authorisation affixed in national passports)

- *Carte diplomatique délivrée par le Ministère des Affaires étrangères*
(Diplomat's pass issued by the Ministry of Foreign Affairs)

- *Titre de légitimation délivré par le Ministère des Affaires étrangères au personnel administratif et technique des Ambassades*
(Certificate issued by the Ministry of Foreign Affairs to the Embassy's administrative and technical staff)

— *Titre de légitimation délivré par le Ministère de la Justice au personnel des institutions et organisations internationales établies au Luxembourg*
(Certificate issued by the Ministry for Justice to the staff of institutions and international organisations based in Luxembourg)

— List of persons participating in a school trip within the European Union.

THE NETHERLANDS

— Documents take the following forms:

- *Vergunning tot vestiging (Model 'A')*
(Authorisation to settle)

- *Toelating als vluchteling (Model 'B')*
(Admission document for refugees)

- *Verblijf voor onbepaalde duur (Model 'C')*
(Residence permit for an indefinite period)

- *Vergunning tot verblijf (Model 'D')*
(Residence authorisation)

- *Voorwaardelijke vergunning tot verblijf (Model 'D' bearing the mark 'voorwaardelijk' (conditional))*
(Conditional residence authorisation)

- *Verblijfskaart van een onderdaan van een Lid-Staat der E.E.G. (Model 'E')*
(Residence permit for EC nationals)

— *Vergunning tot verblijf (in de vorm van een stempel in het paspoort)*
(Residence authorisation (in the form of a stamp in a passport))

— *Vreemdelingendocument with the code 'A', 'B', 'C', 'D', 'E', F1', 'F2' or 'F3'*
(Document for aliens)

— *Legitimatiebewijs voor leden van diplomatieke of consular posten*
(Identity document for members of diplomatic missions and consular posts)

— *Legitimatiebewijs voor ambtenaren met een bijzondere status*
(Identity document for officials with a special status)

— *Legitimatiebewijs voor ambtenaren van internationale organisaties*
(Identity document for officials of international organisations)

— *Identiteitskaart voor leden van internationale organisaties waarvan de zetel. in Nederland is gevestigd*
(Identity card for members of international organisations with which the Netherlands has concluded a headquarters agreement)

— *Visum voor terugkeer*
(Return visas)

— List of persons participating in a school trip within the European Union.

Comment on indents 1 and 2

The issue of residence documents mentioned under indents 1 and 2 has stopped since 1 March 1994 (the issue of Model 'D' and the affixing of stamps in passports came to an end on 1 June 1994). Documents already in circulation will remain valid until 1 January 1997 at the latest.

Comment on indent 3

Issue of the document for aliens has been effective since 1 March 1994. This document in the form of a credit card will gradually replace the residence authorisations mentioned in indents 1 and 2. The code corresponding to the category of residence will be retained.

The document for aliens marked with the code E will be issued both to EC nationals and to nationals of Contracting States to the European Economic Area Agreement.

Conditional Residence Authorisations are marked with codes F1, F2 or F3.

Comment on indent 7

List of international organisations with office in the Netherlands whose members (including family members) hold identity papers not issued by the Ministry for Foreign Affairs

1. European Space Agency (ESA)

2. European Patent Office (EPO)

3. International Tea Promotion Association (ITPA)

4. International Service for National Agricultural Research (ISNAR)

5. Technical Centre for Agricultural and Rural Cooperation (ACP)

6. United Nations University Institute for New Technologies (UNU-Intech)

7. African Management Services Company (AMSCO)

AUSTRIA

- *Aufenthaltstitel in Form der Vignette entsprechend der Gemeinsamen Maßnahme der Europäischen Union vom 16. Dezember 1996 zur einheitlichen Gestaltung der Auftenthaltstitel*
  (Residence permit in the form of a sticker in accordance with the EU joint action of 16 December 1996 concerning a uniform format for residence permits)

  (As from 1 January 1998 residence permits will be issued and extended in this form only. The following will be entered under 'Type of permit': *Niederlassungsbewilligung* (Permanent residence permit); *Aufenthaltserlaubnis* (Residence permit) *'Befr. Aufenthaltsrecht'* (Temporary residence permit).
- *Vor dem 1. Jänner 1998 erteilte Aufenthaltstitel im Rahmen der — auch 'unbefristet' eingetragenen — Gültigkeitsdauer:*
  Residence permits issued before 1 January 1998 on the basis of the validity indicated, including unlimited validity:
  ('Wiedereinreise — Sichtvermerk' oder 'Einreise — Sichtvermerk'; wurden bis 31.12.1992 von Inlandsbehörden, aber auch von Vertretungsbehörden in Form eines Stempels ausgestellt;
  Re-entry visas or entry visas issued by the Austrian authorities until 31 December 1992, but also in the form of a stamp by the representing authorities;
  'Gewöhnlicher Sichtvermerk'; wurde vom 1.1.1993 bis 31.12.1997 in Form einer Vignette — ab 1.9.1996 entsprechend der VO(EG) 1683/95 — ausgestellt;
  (Ordinary visa: issued between 1 January 1993 and 31 December 1997 in the form of a sticker — as from 1 September 1996 in accordance with EU Regulation (EC) No 1683/95)
  'Aufenthaltsbewilligung'; wurde vom 1.1.1993 bis 31.12.1997 in Form einer speziellen Vignette ausgestellt.)
  (Residence permit: issued between 1 January 1993 and 31 December 1997, in the form of a special sticker)
- *Konventionsreisepaß ausgestellt ab 1.1.1993*
  (Travel document, issued as of 1 January 1993)
- *Legitimationskarte für Träger von Privilegien und Immunitäten in den Farben rot, gelb und blau, ausgestellt vom Bundesministerium für auswärtige Angelegenheiten*
  (Accreditation pass for the bearers of privileges and immunities in red, yellow and blue issued by the Ministry for Foreign Affairs)
- List of pupils participating in school trips within the European Union

The following are not valid as residence permits and therefore do not entitle the holder to visa-free entry into Austria:

- *Lichtbildausweis für Fremde gemäß § 85 Fremdengesetz 1997*
  (Alien's identity card with photograph pursuant to § 85 of 1997 Aliens Act)
- *Durchsetzungsaufschub und Abschiebungsaufschub nach Aufenthaltsverbot oder Ausweisung*
  (Stay of execution and stay of deportation following an exclusion order or expulsion order)
- *Bewilligung zur Wiedereinreise trotz bestehenden Aufenthaltsverbotes, in Form eines Visums erteilt, jedoch als eine solche Bewilligung gekennzeichnet*
  (Authorisation of re-entry, despite existing exclusion order, issued in the form of a visa indicating that it is an authorisation of this kind)

— *Vorläufige Aufenthaltsberechtigung gemäß § 19 Asylgesetz 1997, bzw. § 7 AsylG 1991*
(Provisional residence permit pursuant to § 19 of the 1997 Asylum Act or § 7 of the 1991 Asylum Act)

— *Befristete Aufenthaltsberechtigung gemäß § 15 Asylgesetz 1997, bzw. § 8 AsylG 1991, als Duldung des Aufenthaltes trotz abgelehntem Asylantrag*
(Temporary residence permit pursuant to § 15 of 1997 Asylum Act or § 8 of the 1991 Asylum Act, tolerating the stay despite the rejection of the application for asylum)

PORTUGAL

— *Cartão de Identidade (emitido pelo Ministério dos Negócios Estrangeiros)*
(Identity card issued by the Ministry of Foreign Affairs)
Corpo Consular, Chefe de Missão
(Consular corps, Head of mission)

— *Cartão de Identidade (emitido pelo Ministério dos Negócios Estrangeiros)*
(Identity card issued by the Ministry of Foreign Affairs)
Corpo Consular, Funcionário de Missão
(Consular corps, mission official)

— *Cartão de Identidade (emitido pelo Ministério dos Negócios Estrangeiros)*
(Identity card issued by the Ministry of Foreign Affairs)
Pessoal Auxiliar de Missão Estrangeira
(Auxiliary staff working in a foreign mission)

— *Cartão de Identidade (emitido pelo Ministério dos Negócios Estrangeiros)*
(Identity card issued by the Ministry of Foreign Affairs)
Funcionário Admnistrativo de Missão Estrangeira
(Administrative officer working in a foreign mission)

— *Cartão de Identidade (emitido pelo Ministério dos Negócios Estrangeiros)*
(Identity card issued by the Ministry of Foreign Affairs)
Corpo Diplomático, Chefe de Missão
(Diplomatic corps, Head of mission)

— *Cartão de Identidade (emitido pelo Ministério dos Negócios Estrangeiros)*
(Identity card issued by the Ministry of Foreign Affairs)
Corpo Diplomático, Funcionário de Missão
(Diplomatic corps, mission official)

— *Título de Residência (1 Ano)*
(Residence permit — one year)

— *Título de Residência Anual (1 Ano)*
(Annual residence permit — one year)

— *Título de Residência Anual (cor de laranja)*
(Annual residence permit — orange in colour)
Título de Residência Temporário (5 Anos)
(Temporary residence permit — five years)

— *Título de Residência Vitalício*
(Residence permit valid for life)

— *Cartão de Residência de Nacional de Um Estado Membro da Comunidade Europeia*
(National residence permit of an EC Member State)

— *Cartão de Residência Temporário*
(Temporary residence permit)

— *Cartão de Residência*
(Residence permit)

— *Autorização de Residência Provisória*
(Provisional residence authorisation)

— *Título de Identidade de Refugiado*
(Refugee identity document)

CONFIDENTIAL

ANNEX 5

List of visa applications requiring prior consultation with the central authorities, in accordance with Article 17(2)

ANNEX 6

List of honorary consuls authorised, in exceptional cases and on a temporary basis, to issue uniform visas

In accordance with the decision taken by the ministers and secretaries of State at the meeting of 15 December 1992, all the Schengen States accepted that the following honorary consuls would be authorised to issue uniform visas for the period specified below.

The current Honorary Consul of the Netherlands:

— in Nassau (Bahamas) until one of the Schengen States sets up a representation with career diplomats;

— in Manama (Bahrain), for five years until the entry into force of the convention implementing the Schengen Agreement.

ANNEX 7

Reference amounts required for crossing borders fixed annually by the national authorities

BELGIUM

Belgian law lays down general provisions for the verification of adequate means of subsistence, without stipulating any mandatory rules.

The administrative practice is as follows:

— Aliens staying with a private person

Proof of means of subsistence may be furnished by means of a sponsorship undertaking signed by the person accommodating the alien in Belgium and authenticated by the local administrative authority of his place of residence.

The sponsorship undertaking covers the costs of the alien's stay, health care, accommodation and repatriation, should the alien be unable to pay, so as to rule out payment by the public authorities. The undertaking must be signed by a person who is solvent and, if this person is an alien, is in possession of a residence permit or establishment permit.

If necessary, the alien may also be required to furnish proof of personal resources.

If he has no financial credit whatsoever, he must be able to access at least BEF 1 500 for each day of the planned stay.

— Aliens staying at a hotel

If the alien is unable to furnish proof of any credit whatsoever, he must be able to access at least approximately BEF 2 000 for each day of the planned stay.

Furthermore, in most cases, the person concerned must produce a ticket (air ticket) enabling him to return to his country of origin or residence.

GERMANY

Pursuant to Article 60(2) of the aliens act of 9 July 1990 (AuslG), an alien may be refused entry at the border if there are grounds for expulsion.

This is the case if an alien is forced to claim or claims social welfare benefit from the German State for himself, for members of his family staying on German territory or for his dependants (Article 46(6) of the Aliens Act).

Reference amounts have not been fixed for the attention of border control officials. In practice, an amount of DEM 50 per day is generally used as a basic reference. The alien must also have a return ticket or equivalent financial means.

Nevertheless, before the decision not to admit the alien is made, he must be granted the opportunity to produce, in good time and by legal means, the financial means necessary to secure his stay on German territory, namely by presenting:

— a legal guarantee from a German bank,

— a letter of guarantee from the host,

— a telegraphic money order,

— a guarantee deposited with the immigration authorities responsible for the stay.

GREECE

Ministerial Decree No 3011/2/1f of 11 January 1992 fixes the amount of the means of subsistence which foreign nationals — with the exception of nationals of the Member States of the European Community — must have at their disposal if they wish to enter Greek territory.

Pursuant to the abovementioned ministerial decree, the amount of foreign currency enabling foreign nationals of non-Member States of the European Community to enter Greece is fixed at the equivalent of GRD 5 000 in foreign currency per person per day, and a minimum total amount of GRD 35 000.

The amount of foreign currency required per day is reduced by 50 % for minors who are members of the alien's family.

Nationals of non-Community countries which oblige Greek nationals to change currency at the borders are also subject to this obligation on the principle of reciprocity.

SPAIN

Aliens must prove that they have adequate means of subsistence. The minimum amount is given below:

(a) for the costs of their stay in Spain: ESP 5 000, or the equivalent in foreign currency, multiplied by the planned number of days of the stay in Spain and by the number of family members travelling with the person concerned. Regardless of the planned duration of the stay, the minimum amount for which he must provide proof must always be ESP 50 000 per person.

(b) for their return to the State of provenance or for transit via third States: the personal, untransferable and fixed-date ticket or tickets for the planned means of transport.

Aliens must prove that they have the above means of subsistence either by producing them if they are in cash, or by producing certified cheques, traveller's cheques, receipts, letters of credit or a bank certificate confirming the existence of these means. Failing these documents, any other supporting documents recognised by the Spanish border police authorities may be produced.

FRANCE

The reference amount for the adequate means of subsistence for the planned duration of an alien's stay or for his transit via France to a destination in a third State is equal to the amount of the guaranteed minimum wage in France (SMIC) calculated daily on the basis of the rate fixed on 1 January of the current year.

This amount is regularly reassessed on the basis of the French cost of living index:

— automatically whenever the retail price index rises more than 2 %,

— by a governmental decision — after consultation with the national commission for collective bargaining — to grant a rise higher than the rise in the retail price index.

As of 1 July 1998, the daily amount of the SMIC (minimum wage) is FRF 302.

Holders of an accommodation certificate must possess a minimum amount of money, equivalent to half the SMIC, in order to stay in France. This amount is therefore FRF 151 per day.

ITALY

A precise amount has never been fixed for the means of subsistence of which non-Community nationals wishing to stay in Italy must provide proof to the border control authorities, despite the fact that these means of subsistence are given a general mention in Article 3(5) of Law No 39 of 28 February 1990 on the 'Urgent standards for matters of political asylum, entry and stay for non-Community nationals and for matters governing the stay of non-Community nationals and stateless persons already on national territory'.

In fact, it is at the discretion of border control officials to assess whether the alien has adequate financial means. This assessment is based on the duration of and reason for the stay, on the alien's nationality (so as to determine whether the alien belongs to a State which is sensitive in terms of immigration), on the alien's personal circumstances and on the mode of transport used.

The alien may prove that he has the necessary financial means by producing cash, credit cards or other evidence of credit (e.g. traveller's cheques).

Pursuant to Article 3(6) of the abovementioned law, the alien is not deemed to be without means of subsistence if he is able to submit documents certifying that he has property in Italy or that he has an occupation with a regular income there (e.g. work permit) or that an institution, company or private person has promised to guarantee his accommodation or subsistence and his return home.

Failing any of the above, the alien must always have a return ticket or, at least, equivalent funds (including the money necessary to return home plus the amount considered necessary to cover his expenses during his stay).

LUXEMBOURG

The law of Luxembourg does not provide for any reference amount for border controls. The official carrying out the control decides on a case-by-case basis whether an alien approaching the border has adequate means of subsistence. To this end, the official takes into account the purpose of the stay and the type of accommodation.

THE NETHERLANDS

The amount which border control officials take as a basis when verifying means of subsistence is currently NLG 75 per person per day.

The application of this criterion is flexible since the required amount of the means of subsistence is determined on the basis of the planned duration of the stay, the reason for the visit and the personal circumstances of the person concerned.

AUSTRIA

Pursuant to § 32(2) Z 3 of the law on aliens, aliens shall be turned away at the border if they have no place of residence in Austria and do not have sufficient means of subsistence to meet the costs of their stay and return.

However, there are no reference amounts for the above. Decisions are made on a case-by-case basis depending on the purpose, type and duration of the stay. Cash and — depending on the circumstances of the individual case — traveller's cheques, credit cards, bank guarantees or letters of guarantee from solvent persons living in Austria may be accepted as proof.

PORTUGAL

Aliens must be in possession of the following amounts if they wish to enter or stay in Portugal:

— PTE 15 000 — for each entry;

— PTE 8 000 — for each day spent on the territory.

Aliens who are able to prove that their board and lodging are guaranteed for the duration of their stay may be exempted from paying the above amounts.

ANNEX 8

UNIFORM FORMAT FOR VISA-STICKERS AND INFORMATION ON THEIR TECHNICAL SPECIFICATIONS AND SECURITY FEATURES

The technical specifications and security features contained in Council Regulation (EC) No 1683/95 laying down a uniform format for visas have been in force since 7 September 1996.

COUNCIL REGULATION (EC) No 1683/95 of 29 May 1995 laying down a uniform format for visas

THE COUNCIL OF THE EUROPEAN UNION,

Having regard to the Treaty establishing the European Community, in particular Article 100c(3) thereof,

Having regard to the proposal from the Commission,

Having regard to the opinion of the European Parliament,

Whereas Article 100c(3) of the Treaty requires the Council to adopt measures relating to a uniform format for visas before 1 January 1996;

Whereas the introduction of a uniform format for visas is an important step towards the harmonisation of visa policy; whereas Article 7a of the Treaty stipulates that the internal market shall comprise an area without internal frontiers in which the free movement of persons is ensured in accordance with the provisions of the Treaty; whereas this step is also to be regarded as forming a coherent whole with measures falling within Title VI of the Treaty on European Union;

Whereas it is essential that the uniform format for visas should contain all the necessary information and meet very high technical standards, notably as regards safeguards against counterfeiting and falsification; whereas it must also be suited to use by all the Member States and bear universally recognisable security features which are clearly visible to the naked eye;

Whereas this regulation only lays down such specifications as are not secret; whereas these specifications need to be supplemented by further specifications which must remain secret in order to prevent counterfeiting and falsification and which may not include personal data or references to such data; whereas powers to adopt further specifications should be conferred on the Commission;

Whereas, to ensure that the information referred to is not made available to more persons than necessary, it is also essential that each Member State should designate not more than one body having responsibility for printing the uniform format for visas, with Member States remaining free to change the body, if need be; whereas, for security reasons, each Member State must communicate the name of the competent body to the Commission and the other Member States;

Whereas, to be effective, this regulation should apply to all visas covered by Article 5; whereas Member States should be free also to use the uniform visa format for visas which can be used for purposes other than those covered by Article 5 provided differences visible to the naked eye are incorporated to make confusion with the uniform visa impossible;

Whereas, with regard to the personal data to be entered on the uniform format for visas in accordance with the annex hereto, compliance should be ensured with Member States' data-protection provisions as well as with the relevant Community legislation,

HAS ADOPTED THIS REGULATION:

Article 1

Visas issued by the Member States in conformity with Article 5 shall be produced in the form of a uniform format (sticker). They shall conform to the specifications set out in the annex.

Article 2

Further technical specifications which render the visa difficult to counterfeit or falsify shall be laid down in accordance with the procedure set out in Article 6.

Article 3

1. The specifications referred to in Article 2 shall be secret and not be published. They shall be made available only to bodies designated by the Member States as responsible for printing and to persons duly authorised by a Member State or the Commission.

2. Each Member State shall designate one body having responsibility for printing visas. It shall communicate the name of that body to the Commission and the other Member States. The same body may be designated by two or more Member States for this purpose. Each Member State shall be entitled to change its designated body. It shall inform the Commission and the other Member States accordingly.

Article 4

1. Without prejudice to the relevant more extensive provisions concerning data protection, an individual to whom a visa is issued shall have the right to verify the personal particulars entered on the visa and, where appropriate, to ask for any corrections or deletions to be made.

2. No information in machine-readable form shall be given on the uniform format for visas unless it also appears in the boxes described in points 6 to 12 of the annex, or unless it is mentioned in the relevant travel document.

Article 5

For the purposes of this regulation a 'visa' shall mean an authorisation given by or a decision taken by a Member State which is required for entry into its territory with a view to:

— an intended stay in that Member State or in several Member States of no more than three months in all;

— transit through the territory or airport transit zone of that Member State or several Member States.

Article 6

1. Where reference is made to the procedure defined in this article, the following provisions shall apply.

2. The Commission shall be assisted by a committee composed of the representatives of the Member States and chaired by the representative of the Commission.

The representative of the Commission shall submit to the committee a draft of the measures to be taken. The committee shall deliver its opinion on the draft within a time limit which the chairman may lay down according to the urgency of the matter. The opinion shall be delivered by the majority laid down in Article 148(2) of the Treaty in the case of decisions which the Council is required to adopt on a proposal from the Commission. The votes of the representatives of the Member States within the committee shall be weighted in the manner set out in that article. The chairman shall not vote.

3. (a) The Commission shall adopt the measures envisaged if they are in accordance with the opinion of the committee.

(b) If the measures envisaged are not in accordance with the opinion of the committee, or if no opinion is delivered, the Commission shall, without delay, submit to the Council a proposal relating to the measures to be taken. The Council shall act by a qualified majority.

If, on the expiry of a period of two months, the Council has not acted, the proposed measures shall be adopted by the Commission, save where the Council has decided against the said measures by a simple majority.

Article 7

Where Member States use the uniform visa format for purposes other than those covered by Article 5, appropriate measures must be taken to ensure that confusion with the visa referred to in Article 5 is not possible.

Article 8

This regulation shall enter into force on the twentieth day following that of its publication in the *Official Journal of the European Communities.*

Article 1 shall become applicable six months after the adoption of the measures referred to in Article 2.

This regulation shall be binding in its entirety and directly applicable in all Member States.

Done at Brussels, 29 May 1995.

For the Council

The President

H. de CHARETTE

ANNEX

Security features

1. A sign consisting of nine ellipses in a fan-shape shall appear in this space.

2. An optically variable mark ('kinegram' or equivalent) shall appear in this space. Depending on the angle of view, 12 stars, the letter 'E' and a globe become visible in various sizes and colours.

3. The logo consisting of a letter or letters indicating the issuing Member State (or 'BNL' in the case of the Benelux countries, namely Belgium, Luxembourg and the Netherlands) with a latent image effect shall appear in this space. This logo shall appear light when held flat and dark when turned by 90'. The following logos shall be used: A for Austria, BNL for Benelux, D for Germany, DK for Denmark, E for Spain, F for France, FIN for Finland, GR for Greece, I for Italy, IRL for Ireland, P for Portugal, S for Sweden, UK for the United Kingdom.

4. The word 'visa' in capital letters shall appear in the middle of this space in optically variable colouring. Depending on the angle of view, it shall appear green or red.

5. This box shall contain the number of the visa, which shall be pre-printed and shall begin with the letter or letters indicating the issuing country as described in point 3 above. A special type shall be used.

Sections to be completed

6. This box shall begin with the words 'valid for'. The issuing authority shall indicate the territory or territories for which the visa is valid.
7. This box shall begin with the word 'from' and the word 'until' shall appear further along the line. The issuing authority shall indicate here the period of validity of the visa.
8. This box shall begin with the words number of entries' and further along the line the words 'duration of stay' (i.e. duration of applicants' intended stay) and again 'days' shall appear.
9. This box shall begin with the words 'issued in' and shall be used to indicate the place of issue.
10. This box shall begin with the word 'on' (after which the date of issue shall be filled in by the issuing authority) and further along the line the words 'number of passport' shall appear (after which the holder's passport number shall appear).
11. This box shall begin with the words 'type of visa'. The issuing authority shall indicate the category of visa in conformity with Articles 5 and 7 of this regulation.
12. This box shall begin with the word 'remarks'. It shall be used by the issuing authority to indicate any further information which is considered necessary, provided that it complies with Article 4 of this regulation. The following two and a half lines shall be left empty for such remarks.
13. This box shall contain the relevant machine-readable information to facilitate external border controls.

The paper shall be pastel green with red and blue markings.

The words designating the boxes shall appear in English and French. The issuing State may add a third official Community language. However, the word 'visa' in the top line may appear in any one official language of the Community.

CONFIDENTIAL

ANNEX 9

Entries which the Contracting Parties shall write, where necessary, in the 'comments' section

CONFIDENTIAL

ANNEX 10

Instructions on writing entries in the section to be electronically scanned

ANNEX 11

Criteria for travel documents to which a visa may be affixed.

The travel documents outlined below shall be considered valid for the purposes of Article 17(3)(a) of the convention implementing the Schengen Agreement, provided that they attest to the holder's identity and, in the cases mentioned under (a) and (b) below, the holder's nationality or citizenship and provided that they fulfil the conditions under Articles 13 and 14.

(a) Travel documents issued in accordance with international rules applied by countries or regional and local bodies recognised by all Member States.

(b) The passports or travel documents which, although issued by the countries or international bodies not recognised by all Member States, guarantee that the alien will return and provided that the Executive Committee recognises these as valid documents on which to affix the uniform visa (alternatively affixed on a separate sheet) of a joint visa. The unanimous approval of the Executive Committee shall be required for:

- the list of these passports or travel documents.
- the list of countries or entities that are not recognised, which have issued documents:

The possible compilation of these lists, which shall only apply to the requirements for implementing the Schengen Convention, shall not prejudice Member State' recognition of countries or regional and local entities that are not recognised.

(c) Travel documents for refugees, issued in accordance with the convention of 1951 on the Status of Refugees.

(d) Travel documents for Stateless persons issued in accordance with the convention of 1954 on the Status of Stateless Persons [1]

[1] Portugal and Austria, although not Contracting Parties to this convention, accept that travel documents issued in accordance with this convention may bear the uniform visa issued by the Schengen States.

ANNEX 12

Fees, in euro, to be charged when issuing uniform visas

A.	Airport transit visas	EUR10
B.	Transit visas (one, two or multiple entries)	EUR 10
C1.	Very short-stay visas (maximum 30 days)	EUR 15—25
C2.	Short-stay visas (maximum 90 days)	EUR 30 + EUR 5 from the second entry, when there are multiple entries
C3.	Multiple entry visas, valid for one year	EUR 50
C4.	Multiple entry visas, valid for max. five years	EUR 50 + EUR 30 for each additional year
D.	National long-stay visas	The amount shall be fixed by the Contracting Parties, who may decide to issue these visas free of charge.
—	Visa with limited territorial validity	The amount shall be at least equal to 50 % of the amount fixed for Category A, B and C visas
—	Visas issued at the border	The amount shall be double that of the category of visa issued. These visas may be issued free of charge.
—	Group visas, Categories A and B (5—50 persons)	EUR 10 + EUR 1 per person
—	Group visas, Category C1 (30 days), one or two entries (5—50 persons)	EUR 30 + EUR 1 per person
—	Group visas, Category C1 (30 days), more than two entries (5—50 persons)	EUR 30 + EUR 3 per person

Rules:

I. These fees shall be paid in a convertible currency or in the national currency on the basis of the official exchange rates in force.

II. In individual cases, the amount of fees to be charged may be reduced or may be waived in accordance with national law when this protects cultural interests, in the field of foreign policy, development policy or other areas of vital public interest.

III. Group visas are issued in accordance with national law, for a maximum of 30 days.

ANNEX 13

Guidelines on how to fill in visa-stickers

Please note: in general, visas can be issued at the earliest three months before they are first used.

AIRPORT TRANSIT VISAS (ATVs)

It is pointed out that only nationals of certain 'sensitive' countries (see Annex 3) are subject to an ATV. ATV holders may not leave the international section of the airport through which they travel in transit.

Example 1

72/VI

SINGLE-ENTRY AIRPORT TRANSIT VISAS

— Type of visa: ATVs bear the identification code A.

— The single-entry ATV gives access to one country only (France in this example).

— The duration of validity is calculated from the date of departure (e.g. 1.2.2000); the term is established by adding a period of grace of seven days in case the visa holder postpones departure.

— ATVs do not give right to residence, the heading 'residence' should be crossed out with XXX.

Example 2(a)

DUAL-ENTRY (RETURN) ATVs (valid in one country only)

— The return ATV authorises airport transit for both outward and return journeys.

— The duration of the visa's validity is calculated as follows: date of the return journeys + seven days (in the example shown: Return date 15.2.2000).

— If transit is envisaged through one airport only, the name of the country concerned is filled in under the heading 'valid for' (Example 2a). If transit is made exceptionally via two different Schengen countries on the outward and return journeys, the visa is marked 'Schengen States' (see Example 2b below).

Example 2(b)

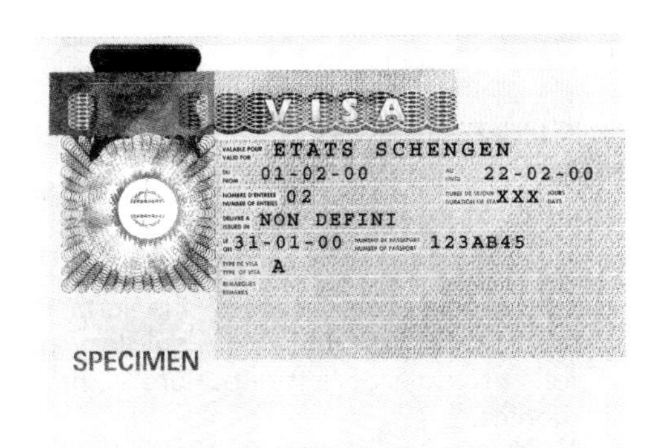

DUAL-ENTRY ATVs (valid in several countries)

— 'Schengen States' should be filled in under the heading 'valid for' to enable transit via two airports situated in two different countries.

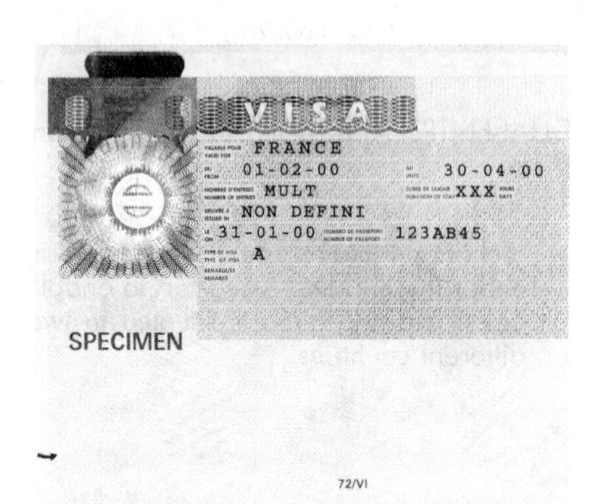

Example 3

MULTIPLE-ENTRY ATVs (should only be issued in exceptional cases)

— In the case of multiple-entry ATVs (enabling several transits) the term of the visa's validity is calculated as follows: date of first departure + three months.

— For filling in the heading 'valid for', the same rule applies as to dual-entry ATVs.

TRANSIT VISAS

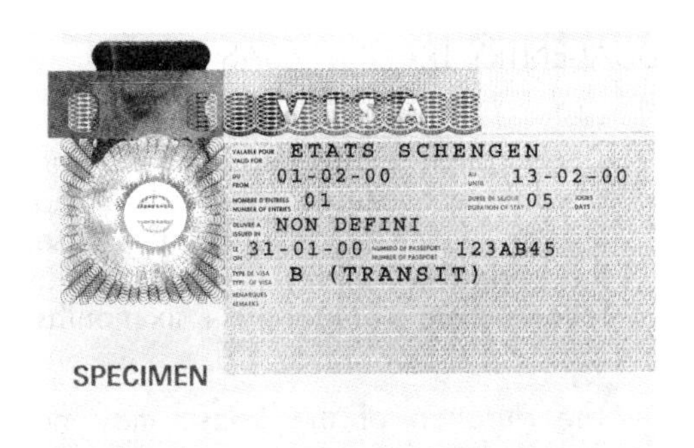

Example 4

SINGLE-ENTRY TRANSIT VISAS

— Type of visa: the transit visa bears the identification code B. It is recommended to add the word 'TRANSIT'.

— The duration of validity is calculated from the date of departure (e.g. 1.2.2000). The term is fixed as follows: date of departure + (five days maximum) + seven days (period of grace in case the visa holder postpones departure).

— The duration of the transit may not exceed five days.

Example 5

DUAL-ENTRY TRANSIT VISAS

— The duration of validity: when the date of different transit journeys is not known, which is generally the case, the period of validity is calculated as follows: date of departure + six months.

— The duration of the transit may not exceed five days.

Example 6

72/VI

MULTIPLE-ENTRY TRANSIT VISAS

— The duration of validity is calculated in the same way as for dual-entry transit visas (see Example 5).

— The duration of the stay may not exceed five days in transit.

SHORT-STAY VISAS

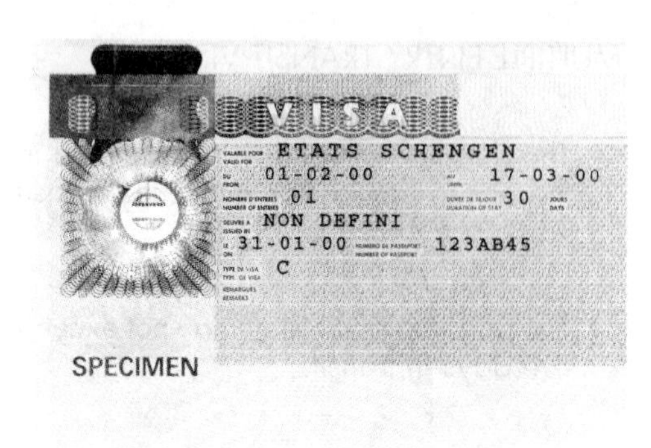

Example 7

SINGLE-ENTRY SHORT-STAY VISAS

— Type of visa: the short-stay visa bears the identification code C.

— The duration of the visa's validity is calculated as follows: from the date of departure (e.g. 1.2.2000). The period is fixed as follows: date of departure + duration of stay + period of grace – 15 days.

— The duration of the stay may not exceed 90 days in any six-month period (30 days in the example shown here).

Example 8

72/VI

MULTIPLE-ENTRY SHORT-STAY VISA

— The duration of validity is calculated from the date of departure + six months maximum on the basis of the documentary evidence provided.

— The duration of the stay may not exceed 90 days in any six-month period (in the example shown here, but the duration may also be less). The duration of the stay is that of the cumulative total of successive stays. This is also based on the documentary evidence provided.

Example 9

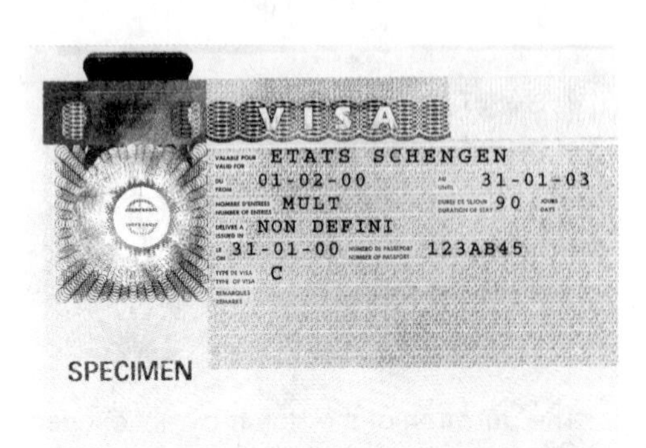

SHORT-STAY TRAVEL VISA

— This is a multiple-entry short-stay visa which is valid for over six months or one, two, three years, five years in exceptional cases (e.g. VIPs).

  In the example shown here the validity is three years.

— Same rules apply to the duration of the stay as in Example 8 (90 days maximum).

VISAS WITH LIMITED TERRITORIAL VALIDITY (LTV visas)

The LTV visa can be either a short-stay visa or a transit visa.

The limitation of validity may apply to one or to several States.

Example 10

SHORT-STAY LTV visas, ONE COUNTRY ONLY.

- In this example, the territorial validity is limited to one country only, i.e. France.
- The short-stay LTV visa bears the identification code C (in the same way as Example 7)

Example 11

72/VI

SHORT-STAY LTV visas, VALIDITY LIMITED TO SEVERAL COUNTRIES

— In this case, the following country codes indicating the countries for which the visa is valid are filled in under the heading 'valid for': (Austria: A, Belgium: B, France: F, Germany: D, Greece: GR, Italy: I, Luxembourg: L, The Netherlands: NL, Portugal: P, Spain: E. In the case of the Benelux countries: BNL).

— In the example shown, the territorial validity is limited to France and Spain.

Example 12

72/VI

TRANSIT LTV visas, ONE COUNTRY

— The transit visa bears the identification code B under the heading for the type of visa.

— In the example shown, the visa is limited to French territory.

ACCOMPANYING PERSONS

Example 13

— In this case, one or more children and in exceptional circumstances, a spouse travel on one passport.

— If one or more children travelling on the travel document are covered by a visa, under the heading 'passport number', after the passport number, + nX is added, indicating the number of children, and if a spouse is travelling on the passport + Y is added. In the example shown here (single-entry, short-stay visa, with a duration of stay 30 days) the visa is issued for the passport holder, three children and the passport holder's spouse.

VISA ISSUED BY REPRESENTATION

Example 14

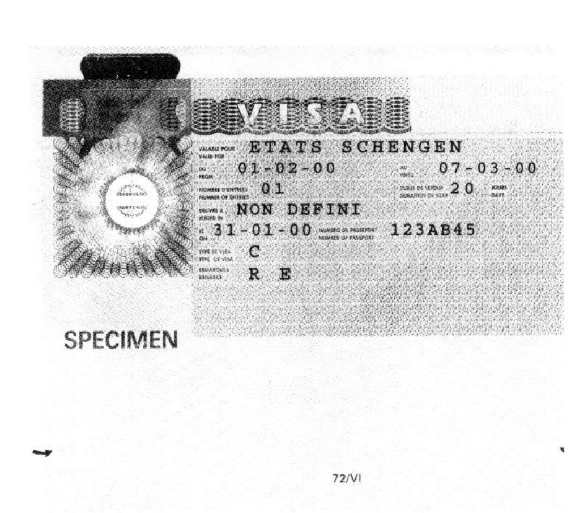

The above visa was issued by a consular post of a Schengen State representing another Schengen State.

In this case, under the heading 'Observations', the letter 'R' must be filled in, followed by the country code of the country on whose behalf the visa was issued.

The country codes to be used are as follows:

Austria: A
Belgium: B
France: F
Germany: D
Greece: GR
Italy: I
Luxembourg: L
The Netherlands: NL
Portugal: P
Spain: E

In the above example, the Belgian embassy in Brazzaville issued a visa on behalf of Spain.

SUMMARY

	'VALID FOR'	'TYPE'	'NUMBER OF ENTRIES'	'FROM' ... 'TO'		'MAXIMUM DURATION OF VISIT' (in days)
Airport transit visas (ATVs)	FRANCE (for example) or SCHENGEN STATES	A	01	Departure date	Departure date + seven days	XXX
			02	Departure date	Date of return + seven days	
			MULT ([1])	First departure date	First departure date + number of months authorised (maximum three months)	
Transit visas	SCHENGEN STATES or FRANCE (for example)	B	01	Departure date	Departure date + duration of visit + seven days	XXX or from 1 to 5
			02	First departure date	First departure date + number of months authorised (maximum six months)	
			MULT ([1])	First departure date		
Short-stay visas	SCHENGEN STATES or FRANCE (for example)	C	01	Departure date	Departure date + duration of visit + 15 days	from 1 to 90
			MULT ([2])	First departure date	First departure date + number of months authorised (maximum five years)	

([1]) MULT means several trips, thus more than two entries.
([2]) MULT means several trips, thus more than one entry.

ANNEX 14

Rules and procedures governing information to be sent by Contracting Parties when issuing visas with limited territorial validity, when cancelling, revoking and reducing the duration of a uniform visa's validity and when issuing national residence permits

1. Information when issuing visas with limited territorial validity

1.1. General conditions

In order that authorisation to enter the national territory of Schengen Contracting Parties can be granted, nationals from a third country should generally fulfil the conditions laid down in Article 5(1) of the convention implementing the Schengen Agreement.

If a national from a third country does not fulfil all these conditions, entry or the issue of a visa shall be refused except if a Contracting Party considers it necessary to derogate from this rule for humanitarian reasons, on grounds of national interest, or due to international obligations. In such cases, the Contracting Party concerned may only issue a visa with limited territorial validity (LTV) and must inform the other Contracting Parties (Articles 5(2) and 16 of the Schengen Convention).

The issue of short-stay LTVs is in accordance with the Schengen Convention and the common consular instructions on visas (SCH/II-Visa (93) 11, 6 Rev., 4 corr., Chapter V, point 3) generally subject to the following conditions:

(a) LTVs are issued by way of exception. The conditions under which this type of visa is issued shall be carefully examined on a case-by-case basis.

(b) This does not mean that the Schengen Contracting Parties will use and abuse the possibility to issue LTVs; this would not be in keeping with the principles and objectives of Schengen. Given that the number of LTVs being issued will most probably be small, it is not necessary to envisage an automated procedure for informing the other Contracting Parties.

1.2. Rules of procedure

When defining rules of procedure governing the information to be sent by Contracting Parties when issuing LTVs, a distinction shall be made between visas issued by diplomatic and consular representations and visas issued by the border authorities. The rules of procedure in use are as follows:

1.2.1. Issue of visas by diplomatic and consular representations

In general, the rules laid down for the provisional arrangements for consultation with the central authorities (Article 17(2) of the Schengen Convention shall apply *mutatis mutandis* to the information procedure used by the other Contracting Parties (see Doc. SCH/II-Visa (94) 7). Where different rules are used, these shall be notified by the Contracting Parties concerned. In general, information shall be sent within 72 hours.

1.2.2. Issue of visas by the border authorities

In this case, information shall be sent within 72 hours to the central authorities of the other Contracting Parties.

1.2.3. The Contracting Parties must designate which contact points should receive this information.

1.2.4. When setting up an automated procedure to enable consultation between the central authorities (Article 17(2), of the Schengen Convention), this shall include a provision ensuring that other Contracting Parties are informed of the issue of an LTV where the LTV is issued as a result of an objection to the issue of a Schengen visa on the part of one (or more) Contracting Party/Parties), in the framework of consultation. Where LTVs are issued in other circumstances, this procedure cannot be used for sending information between States.

1.2.5. The following information shall be sent to the Contracting Parties:

- Surname, first name, and date of birth of visa holder;
- Nationality of visa holder;
- Date and place of issue of LTV;
- Reasons for issuing visas with limited territorial validity;
  - humanitarian reasons,
  - reasons of national interest,
  - international obligations,
  - travel document which is not valid in all Contracting Parties,
  - second issue of a visa within a six-month period,

- in emergencies, there was no consultation with the central authorities,

- the central authorities of a Contracting Party raised objections during consultation.

2. Cancelling, revoking and reducing the duration of validity of a uniform visa

In accordance with the principles adopted by the Committee Executive when cancelling, revoking and reducing the duration of a uniform visa's validity (SCH/Com-ex (93) 24), the following information must be sent to the other Contracting Parties.

2.1. Cancelling visas

Cancelling a Schengen visa aims to prevent persons entering the territory of the Contracting Parties when it transpires after a visa has been issued that these persons do not fulfil the conditions warranting the issue of a visa.

Contracting Parties who cancel a visa issued by another Contracting Party shall generally inform the central authorities of the issuing State within 72 hours.

This notification shall contain the following information:

— Surname, first name, and date of birth of visa holder;

— Nationality of visa holder;

— Type and number of travel document;

— Number of the sticker-visa;

— Category of visa;

— Date and place of visa issue;

— Date and reasons for cancellation.

2.2. Revoking visas

Revoking a visa permits cancellation, even after entry to the territory, of the remaining duration of a visa's validity.

A Contracting Party who revokes a uniform visa shall generally inform the issuing Contracting Party within 72 hours. This notification shall contain the same information as mentioned under point 2.1.

2.3. Reducing the duration of a visa's validity

When a Schengen State reduces the duration of validity of a visa issued by another Contracting Party, it shall generally inform this Contracting Party's central authorities within 72 hours. This notification shall contain the same information as mentioned under point 2.1.

2.4. Procedure

The information sent to the Contracting Party who issued the visa when the duration of a visa's validity is cancelled, revoked or reduced shall generally be sent to the central authority designated by this Contracting Party.

3. Information on national residence permits (Article 25)

Article 25(1) lays down that where a Contracting Party considers issuing a residence permit to an alien for whom an alert has been issued for the purposes of refusing entry, it shall first consult the issuing Contracting Party and shall take account of its interests: the residence permit shall be issued only for serious reasons, in particular of a humanitarian nature or arising from international obligations.

The second subparagraph in Article 25(1) provides that the Contracting Party issuing the alert shall withdraw the alert, but may still put the alien concerned on its national list of alerts.

The application of the provisions mentioned above involves two instances of information transmission between the Contracting Party intending to issue the residence permit and the Contracting Party issuing the alert:

— prior consultation with the Contracting Party issuing the alert to take account of its interests;

— information about the issue of the residence permit, so that the Contracting Party issuing the alert can withdraw it.

In accordance with the provisions of Article 25(2) of the Schengen Convention, the issuing Contracting Party issuing the alert must also undertake consultation if it only transpires *a posteriori*, i.e. after the residence permit has been issued, that an alert has been issued for the purposes of refusing entry to the holder of the residence permit.

In view of the underlying principles of the Schengen Convention, the issue of a residence permit to nationals from a third country for whom an alert has been issued for the purposes of refusing entry by one of the Contracting Parties shall also be limited to exceptional circumstances.

With regard to the consultation referred to in Article 25 of the convention, this action is highly dependent on the functioning of the Schengen information system (SIS). It should be examined if this information could be sent via the forthcoming Sirene procedure.

The rules of procedure outlined in this note shall be re-examined from the point of view of their practical applicability at the latest 12 months after the convention implementing the Schengen Agreement has been brought into force.

ANNEX 15

Model harmonised forms providing proof of invitation, sponsorship and accommodation drawn up by the Contracting Parties

Bundesrepublik Deutschland

VERPFLICHTUNGSERKLÄRUNG
DÉCLARATION DE PRISE EN CHARGE
FORMAL OBLIGATION

D 00000000

Bundesdruckerei
Artikel-Nr. 10150

Ich, der/die Unterzeichnende Je, soussigné(e) I, the undersigned

Name / Nom / Surname

▶

Vorname(n) / Prénom(s) / First name

Geburtstag und -ort / Né(e) le/à / Date and place of birth

Staatsangehörigkeit / Nationalité / Nationality

Identitätsdokument ([1]) / Aufenthaltstitel ([2]) / Document d'identité ([1]) / Titre de séjour ([2]) / Identity card ([1]) / Residence title ([2])

wohnhaft in / Adresse / Address

Beruf / Profession / Profession

Zuständige Behörde
Autorité compétente
Competent authority

verpflichte mich gegenüber der Ausländerbehörde/Auslandsvertretung, für

m' engage auprès du service des étrangers/de la représentation diplomatique à héberger

take full responsibility towards the aliens authority / diplomatic representation for accommodating

Name / Nom / Surname

Vorname(n) / Prénom(s) / First name

Geburtstag und -ort / Né(e) le/à / Date and place of birth

Staatsangehörigkeit / Nationalité / Nationality

Reisepaß Nr. / Passeport n° / Passport No.

wohnhaft in / Adresse / Address

Verwandtschaftsbeziehung mit dem Antragsteller / Lien de parenté avec le demandeur / Family relationship to applicant

und folgende sie/ihn begleitende Personen, nur Ehegatten ([3]) / accompagné(e) de son conjoint ([3]) / accompanied by his or her spouse ([3])

und Kinder ([3]) / accompagné(e) de ses enfants ([3]) / accompanied by children ([3])

vom ... an bis zum ... / du ... au ... / from ... to ...

nach § 84 des Ausländergesetzes die Kosten für den Lebensunterhalt und nach §§ 82 und 83 des Ausländergesetzes die Kosten für die Ausreise o. g. Ausländers/in zu tragen.

et à prendre en charge le coût de la vie conformément au § 84 de la loi sur les étrangers et les frais de retour de l'étranger ci-dessus conformément aux §§ 82 et 83 de la loi sur les étrangers.

and for bearing the living costs according to § 84 of the Aliens Act and and the departure costs of the above foreigner according to §§ 82 and 83 of the Aliens Act.

([1])
Art / type / type
Nummer / numéro / number

([2])

Nur bei	seulement	applicable
Ausländern,	pour les	to foreigners
Art des	étrangers	only,
Titels	type de titre	type of title

([3])
Name / nom / surname
Vorname / prénom / first name
Geburtstag / date de naissance / date of birth
Geschlecht / sexe / sex

Die Verpflichtung umfaßt die Erstattung sämtlicher öffentlicher Mittel, die für den Lebensunterhalt einschließlich der Versorgung mit Wohnraum und der Versorgung im Krankheitsfall und bei Pflegebedürftigkeit aufgewendet werden (z. B. Arztbesuch, Medikamente, Krankenhausaufenthalt). Dies gilt auch, soweit die Aufwendungen auf einem gesetzlichen Anspruch beruhen, im Gegensatz zu Aufwendungen, die auf einer Beitragsleistung beruhen.

Die vorliegende Verpflichtung umfaßt auch die Ausreisekosten (z. B. Flugticket) o. g. Ausländers/in nach §§ 82 und 83 des Ausländergesetzes.

Ich wurde von der Ausländerbehörde hingewiesen auf
- den Umfang und die Dauer der Haftung;
- die Möglichkeit von Versicherungsschutz;
- die zwangsweise Beitreibung der aufgewendeten Kosten im Wege der Vollstreckung, soweit ich meiner Verpflichtung nicht nachkomme, sowie
- die Strafbarkeit z. B. bei vorsätzlichen, unrichtigen oder unvollständigen Angaben (§ 92 des Ausländergesetzes – Freiheitsstrafe bis zu drei Jahren oder Geldstrafe).

Ich bestätige, zu der Verpflichtung aufgrund meiner wirtschaftlichen Verhältnisse in der Lage zu sein.

Behörden-vermerke | Réservé à l'administration | Official remarks

Anschrift der Wohnung, in der die Unterschrift sichergestellt wird, falls abweichend vom gewöhnlichen Wohnsitz des Unterkunftgebers /
Adresse du logement dans lequel l'hébergement sera assuré, au cas où il serait différent du logement habituel de l'hébergeant /
Address of the lodging where accommodation will be provided, if different from the undersigned's normal address

Ich bin / j'en suis / I am

☐ Mieter / locataire / tenant ☐ Eigentümer / propriétaire / owner

Arbeitgeber / Employeur / Employer

Sonstige Angaben zu Wohn-, Einkommens- und Vermögensverhältnissen (Größe der Wohnung, Höhe des Einkommens) /
Renseignements complémentaires concernant le logement, les revenus et la situation financière /
Other details of housing conditions, income and financial situation

Gebühren

Der/die Verpflichtungserklärende

Ich versichere, die vorstehenden Angaben nach bestem Wissen und Gewissen richtig und vollständig gemacht zu haben und gehe eine entsprechende Verpflichtung ein.

Ort Datum

Unterschrift

Bemerkungen

Beglaubigungsvermerk der Ausländerbehörde/Auslandsvertretung

Die Unterschrift der/des Verpflichtungserklärenden ist vor mir vollzogen worden. Die Beglaubigung der Unterschrift dient nur zur Vorlage bei der deutschen Auslandsvertretung.

Behörde:

Ort Datum

Im Auftrag

(Siegel)

Stellungnahme der Ausländerbehörde/Auslandsvertretung

Die finanzielle Leistungsfähigkeit des/der Verpflichtungserklärenden wurde nachgewiesen / glaubhaft gemacht.

Behörde:

Ort Datum

Im Auftrag

(Siegel)

République Française

ATTESTATION D'ACCUEIL
NACHWEIS DER UNTERKUNFT
PROOF OF ACCOMMODATION

F____________

cerfa

n° 10798*01

Document souscrit en application du décret n° 82-442 du 27 mai 1982 modifié pris pour l'application de l'article 5 de l'ordonnance n° 45-2658 du 2 novembre 1945 modifiée relative aux conditions d'entrée et de séjour des étrangers en France

Je, soussigné(e) Ich, der/die Unterzeichnende I, the undersigned

nom / Name / name

▶

prénom(s) /Vorname(n) / first name

né(e) le/à / Geburtstag und -ort / date and place of birth

nationalité / Staatsangehörigkeit / nationality

document d'identité ([1]) ou titre de séjour ([1]) / Identitätsdokument ([1]) / Aufenthaltstitel ([1]) / identity ([1]) or residence document ([1])

adresse complète / wohnhaft in / full address

Département, commune
Zuständige Verwaltung
Competent authority

atteste pouvoir accueillir: **bescheinige, folgende Person(en) unterbringen zu können:** **declare being able to accommodate:**

nom / Name / name

prénom(s) / Vorname(n) / first name

né(e) le/à /geboren am/in / born on/at

nationalité / Staatsangehörigkeit / nationality

passeport n° / Reisepaß-Nr. / passport No.

adresse / wohnhaft in / address

accompagné(e) de son conjoint ([2]) / und folgende sie/ihn begleitende Personen, nur Ehegatten ([2]) / accompanied by spouse ([2])

accompagné(e) de ses enfants ([2]) / und Kinder ([2]) / accompanied by children ([2])

pendant (... jours) entre le ... et le ... / für (... Tage) zwischen dem ... und dem ... / for (... days) from ... to ... Reisepaß

([1])
type / Art / type
numéro / Nummer / number

([2])
nom / Name / name
prénom / Vorname / first name
date de naissance / Geburtstag / date of birth
sexe / Geschlecht / sex

LA LOI N° 78-17 DU 6 JANVIER 1978 RELATIVE A L'INFORMATIQUE, AUX FICHIERS ET AUX LIBERTES s'applique aux réponses faites sur ce formulaire et garantit un droit d'accès et de rectification pour les données vous concernant auprès de la préfecture.
ARTICLE 21 DE L'ORDONNANCE DU 2 NOVEMBRE 1945 MODIFIEE: **toute personne française ou étrangère résidant en France ou sur le territoire d'un autre Etat partie à la Convention de Schengen qui aura, par aide directe ou indirecte, facilité ou tenté de faciliter l'entrée, la circulation ou le séjour irrégulier d'un étranger en France ou sur le territoire d'un autre Etat partie de la Convention de Schengen sera punie d'un emprisonnement de 5 ans et d'une amende de 200 000 F.**
ARTICLE 441-5 DU CODE PENAL: **le fait de procurer frauduleusement à autrui un document délivré par une administration publique aux fins de constater un droit, une identité ou d'accorder une autorisation est puni de 5 ans d'emprisonnement et de 500 000 F d'amende. Ces peines peuvent être portées à 7 ans d'emprisonnement et à 700 000 F d'amende dans les cas évoqués au 2ième alinéa du même article.**
ARTICLE 441-6 DU CODE PENAL: **le fait de se faire délivrer indûment, notamment en fournissant une déclaration mensongère, par une administration publique un document destiné à constater un droit, une identité ou une qualité ou à accorder une autorisation est puni de 2 ans d'emprisonnement et de 200 000 F d'amende.**

1°/Cas où l'accueil est assuré au domicile principal de l'hébergeant:

adresse: se reporter à celle mentionnée au recto

réservé à l'administration

justificatifs du domicile principal de l'hébergeant:

2°/Cas où l'accueil est assuré au domicile secondaire de l'hébergeant:

adresse complète:

réservé à l'administration

justificatifs du domicile secondaire de l'hébergeant:

L'hébergeant

J'atteste sur l'honneur l'exactitude des renseignements portés ci-dessus.
LU ET APPROUVE,

date et signature

L'autorité publique compétente:

Date:

signature et cachet

L'autorité consulaire

date et cachet

Les services de contrôle à l'entrée sur le territoire

date et cachet

Appendix 2

CONFIDENTIAL

COMMON MANUAL

CONFIDENTIAL

Appendix 3

The following Executive Committee and Central Group decisions are repealed:

(a) Executive Committee decisions

SCH/Com-ex (93) 4 rev 2 of 14 December 1993
SCH/Com-ex (93) 5 rev of 14 December 1993
SCH/Com-ex (94) 5 of 27 June 1994
SCH/Com-ex (94) 6 of 27 June 1994
SCH/Com-ex (94) 7 of 27 June 1994
SCH/Com-ex (94) 12 of 27 June 1994
SCH/Com-ex (94) 20 rev of 21 November 1994
SCH/Com-ex (94) 23 rev of 22 December 1994
SCH/Com-ex (94) 24 rev of 22 December 1994
SCH/Com-ex (95) 1 of 28 April 1995
SCH/Com-ex (95) 4 of 28 April 1995
SCH/Com-ex (95) 15 rev 2 of 29 June 1995
SCH/Com-ex (95) 22 rev of 20 December 1995
SCH/Com-ex (96) 14 rev of 27 June 1996
SCH/Com-ex (96) 24 of 19 December 1996
SCH/Com-ex (97) 13 of 24 June 1997
SCH/Com-ex (97) 21 of 7 October 1997
SCH/Com-ex (97) 36 of 15 December 1997
SCH/Com-ex (97) 41 of 15 December 1997
SCH/Com-ex (98) 13 of 21 April 1998
SCH/Com-ex (98) 36 of 16 September 1998
SCH/Com-ex (98) 38 corr. of 16 September 1998
SCH/Com-ex (98) 54 of 16 December 1998
SCH/Com-ex (98) 55 of 16 December 1998

(b) Central Group decisions

SCH/C (96) 16 of 12 March 1996
SCH/C (96) 32 of 26 April 1996
SCH/C (96) 40 of 28 May 1996
SCH/C (96) 41 of 23 May 1996
SCH/C (96) 96 of 11 May 1996
SCH/SG (97) 9 of 17 January 1997
SCH/C (97) 95 of 7 July 1997
SCH/SG (97) 79 of 7 October 1997
SCH/Pers (98) 9 rev of 30 March 1998
SCH/SG (98) 25 rev 2 of 31 March 1998
SCH/C (98) 135 of 15 December 1998

2.3. POLICE COOPERATION

DECISION OF THE EXECUTIVE COMMITTEE of 24 June 1997 on the Schengen manual on police cooperation in the field of public order and security

(SCH/Com-ex (97) 6 rev 2)

The Executive Committee,

Having regard to Article 132 of the convention implementing the Schengen Agreement,

Having regard to Article 46 of the abovementioned convention,

HAS DECIDED AS FOLLOWS:

1. The Schengen manual on police cooperation in the field of public order and security (SCH/I (97) 36 rev 5 ([1])), the purpose of which is to foster cooperation between the Schengen States with regard to the maintenance of public order and security and which is geared towards averting threats to disturbances of public order and security which may concern one or more Schengen States, is hereby approved.

2. The Schengen States may incorporate the contents of the abovementioned manual into their national handbooks and manuals.

Lisbon, 24 June 1997

The Chairman

F. SEIXAS DA COSTA

([1]) Correct version SCH/Com-ex (98) 52.

DECISION OF THE EXECUTIVE COMMITTEE of 16 September 1998 on forwarding the common manual to EU applicant States

(SCH/Com-ex (98) 35 rev 2)

The Executive Committee,

Having regard to Article 132 of the convention implementing the Schengen Agreement,

Whereas the Schengen *acquis* is to be integrated into the framework of the European Union pursuant to the relevant protocol to the Amsterdam Treaty,

Whereas pursuant to Article 8 of the said protocol, the Schengen *acquis* must be accepted in full by all applicant States and whereas the latter must be adequately prepared to that end,

Whereas the common manual on checks at the external borders, in particular, is an important component of the Schengen *acquis* and the States with which specific accession negotiations are being conducted must be informed thereof now so that they may prepare to accept the *acquis*,

Whereas, to that end, the common manual on checks at the external borders, with the exception of certain annexes, and other documents should be forwarded to the States, despite the fact that they are confidential documents,

Whereas the forwarding of public decisions and declarations of the Executive Committee may also be necessary,

HAS DECIDED AS FOLLOWS:

1. The Presidency-in-office may forward the common manual on checks at the external borders, without Annexes 6b, 6c and 14b, to the applicant States with which specific negotiations on their accession to the European Union are being conducted.

2. The Central Group is empowered to decide on a case-by-case basis on forwarding other confidential documents to those States.

3. Upon forwarding as referred to in points 1 and 2, it must be pointed out that this document is confidential. The State receiving the common manual on checks at the external borders or any other confidential document must undertake to treat such document as confidential.

4. Moreover, the Presidency-in-office may forward public decisions and declarations of the Executive Committee and other non-confidential documents to States and other services for internal use where a warranted interest is demonstrated.

Königswinter, 16 September 1998

The Chairman

M. KANTHER

DECISION OF THE EXECUTIVE COMMITTEE of 16 December 1998 on cross-border police cooperation in the area of crime prevention and detection

(SCH/Com-ex (98) 51 rev 3)

The Executive Committee,

Having regard to Articles 39 and 132 of the agreement implementing the Schengen Convention,

— stressing the need for the Schengen States further to improve crime prevention and detection by means of closer cooperation,

— confirming the importance of mutual police assistance pursuant to Article 39 of the Schengen Convention for the attainment of this objective,

— convinced that in certain cases in which no coercive measures are required police cooperation — under the executive authority of the judicial authorities — may be immediately necessary in order to ensure that delay in processing a request does not thwart the outcome of an investigation,

— whereas it is necessary for reasons of operational security and legal certainty to draw up a common list defining the scope of such police cooperation and to determine appropriate channels for the transmission of police requests,

HAS DECIDED AS FOLLOWS:

1. In accordance with the objectives set out in Article 39 of the Schengen Convention, the Schengen States shall endeavour to bring police cooperation in the fight against crime up to a level meeting the needs for rapid and effective action against criminals operating internationally. To this end it is particularly important to draw up a common list of activities which may be requested and undertaken under the law of the Schengen States in cases in which the prior consent of the judicial and/or administrative authorities is not mandatory and without prejudice to the control exercised in such matters by the judicial authorities. If agreement on such a list is reached, the definitive decision will be taken by the Central Group.

2. Without prejudice to the common list to be adopted pursuant to point 1 above, the Schengen States shall list, for the purpose of inclusion in the national fact sheets of the Handbook on Crossborder Police Cooperation, the activities within the meaning of Article

39(1) of the convention that may be requested and undertaken in accordance with national law by their police authorities subject to the conditions pursuant to paragraph 1.

3. National legal order permitting, the Schengen States may increase police cooperation in the area of crime prevention and detection by concluding bilateral agreements and specify what activities in addition to the measures in the list referred to in point 1 may come within the scope of mutual police assistance without the intervention of the judicial and/or administrative authorities. These bilateral agreements should also specify how police requests are to be transmitted to the competent authorities and how the use as evidence in criminal proceedings of the information transmitted can be simplified.

4. Working Group I shall, by agreement with Working Group III, submit to the Central Group an annual report based on the experiences of the Contracting Parties concerning the progress made in improving police cooperation in preventing and detecting crime.

Berlin, 16 December 1998

The Chairman

C. H. SCHAPPER

DECISION OF THE EXECUTIVE COMMITTEE of 16 December 1998 on the handbook on cross-border police cooperation

(SCH/Com-ex (98) 52)

The Executive Committee,

Having regard to Article 132 of the convention implementing the Schengen Agreement,

Having regard to Articles 2(3), 3, 7, 39, 40, 41, 46, 47 and 92 of the abovementioned convention,

HAS DECIDED AS FOLLOWS:

1. The Schengen handbook on cross-border police cooperation (document SCH/I (98) 90 ([1])), annexed hereto, is hereby adopted. At the same time the Executive Committee declaration of 29 June 1995 (document SCH/Com-ex (95) decl 2) is hereby repealed.

2. The Schengen manual on police cooperation in maintaining public order and security (document SCH/I (97) 36 rev 5) has been incorporated into the handbook on cross-border police cooperation. The Executive Committee decision of 24 June 1997 (document SCH/Com-ex (97) 6 rev 2) is hereby repealed.

3. The Contracting States shall incorporate the handbook on cross-border police cooperation into their national orders and forward the handbook to their police services for implementation.

4. The Schengen Secretariat shall be responsible for constantly updating the Handbook in the form of a loose-leaf binder. To this end the Contracting States shall keep the General Secretariat abreast of any amendments to be made to their national fact sheets.

5. Every six months the Presidency-in-office shall consult the States on the need to update the General Part and shall update the handbook.

6. The Presidency will forward the handbook to the European Union for information purposes.

Berlin, 16 December 1998

The Chairman

C. H. SCHAPPER

([1]) Restricted document.

DECISION OF THE EXECUTIVE COMMITTEE of 28 April 1999 on the Schengen *acquis* relating to telecommunications

(SCH/Com-ex (99) 6)

The Executive Committee,

Having regard to Article 132 of the convention implementing the Schengen Agreement,

Having regard to Article 44 of the abovementioned convention,

HAS DECIDED AS FOLLOWS:

The tactical and operational requirements for a future cross-border digital radio system for the police and customs services in the Schengen States defined in accordance with the mandate pursuant to Article 44, the rules for manufacturing and administering uniform encryption algorithms, and other agreements established within the remit of the subgroup on telecommunications, as set out in the following nine documents, are hereby approved.

1. SCH/I-Telecom (92) 21 rev 2 ([1]) of 12 June 1992
   'Definition of the Telecommunications Equipment Needs of Police and Customs Services'

2. SCH/I-Telecom (95) 18 ([1]) of 8 June 1995 'Digital Radiocommunications Systems for Security Organisations (tactical and operational requirements)'

3. SCH/I-Telecom (96) 44 rev 5 ([1]) of 14 November 1997 'Requirements for terminals and their user interfaces in the Schengen States' future digital trunk radio systems'

4. SCH/I-Telecom (95) 33 rev 2 ([1]) of 6 December 1995
   'Request to ETSI for a study of the European norms meeting Schengen functional requirements'

5. SCH/I-Telecom (95) 35 ([1]) of 21 November 1995
   'Schengen communication requirements and the TETRA standard'

6. SCH/I-Telecom-Crypto (95) 37 rev 4 ([1]) of 8 July 1996
   'Digital Radio Communications Network for Security Organisations (Security Requirements'

([1]) Restricted document.

7. SCH/I-Telecom-Crypto (97) 7 rev 5 [1] of 24 February 1998
   'Agreement for the use and custody of Schengen Algorithms'

8. SCH/I-Telecom-Crypto (97) 10 rev 2 [1] of 24 February 1998
   'Criteria for manufacturing Schengen specific algorithms'

9. SCH/I (98) 17 rev 4 [1] of 26 May 1998
   'Amendment to the mandate of the subgroup on telecommunications to examine the interoperability aspects of different digital radio communications systems'

Luxembourg, 28 April 1999

The Chairman

C. H. SCHAPPER

(1) Restricted document.

DECISION OF THE EXECUTIVE COMMITTEE of 28 April 1999 on liaison officers

(SCH/Com-ex (99) 7 rev 2)

The Executive Committee,

Having regard to Article 132 of the convention implementing the Schengen Agreement,

Having regard to Articles 7 and 47 of the abovementioned convention,

Taking account of its declaration of 16 September 1998 (doc. SCH/Com-ex (98) decl 2 rev);

HAS DECIDED AS FOLLOWS:

1. The plan for the reciprocal secondment of liaison officers to advise and assist in the performance of tasks of security and checking at the external borders (document SCH/I-Front (98) 170 rev 5) is hereby approved.

2. It is recommended that the States Parties second liaison officers to the locations of their choice included in the list in document SCH/I-Front (99) 9 rev 3 forthwith and that, where appropriate, the bilateral agreements still required be concluded. This indicative list is not binding and shall be updated in line with the situation as it develops.

Luxembourg, 28 April 1999

The Chairman

C. H. SCHAPPER

Reciprocal secondment of liaison officers to advise and assist in the performance of tasks of security and checking at the external borders

SCH/I-Front (98) 170 rev 5

At its meeting on 16 September 1998, the Executive Committee adopted declaration SCH/Com-ex (98) decl 2 rev 2 entrusting the Central Group with the task of examining whether advice and assistance by employees of one of the Contracting Parties whilst checks were being carried out at the external borders of the other Contracting Party could improve border security.

Following thorough discussion of the possibilities for advice and assistance by liaison officers seconded to the external borders at its meeting on 28 September 1998, the subgroup on frontiers decided unreservedly that this was the case.

To fulfil the remaining part of the mandate from the Executive Committee, the subgroup hereby submits the following plan for the reciprocal secondment of liaison officers to advise and assist in the performance of tasks of security and checking at the external borders.

1. General

1.1. Legal framework

The secondment and activities of liaison officers shall be governed by Article 47(1) to (3) of the Schengen Convention and Article 7, third sentence of the Schengen Convention. These provisions allow liaison officers to be seconded permanently or temporarily with the aim of furthering and accelerating cooperation between the Contracting Parties. This also applies expressly to mutual assistance between the cross-border authorities at the external borders.

Furthermore, this secondment at operational level will always be based on the bilateral agreements between the Partner States which may, if necessary, be supplemented by more specific arrangements between the relevant administrative authorities. Arrangements that derogate from the following rules may thus be made bilaterally between the States exchanging liaison officers. However, the conclusion of bilateral agreements shall not in any way impede mutual consultation and notification.

1.2. Areas of operation

The liaison officers may be posted to executive border police agencies working at the maritime and land borders and corresponding airports, as well as the coast guard. They shall advise and support the regular members of the executive agencies of the Schengen States in the surveillance and checking measures at the external Schengen borders at their request and in agreement with the host authority and in accordance with their instructions. In so doing they may observe and gather evidence to establish a presumption relation to illegal immigration and cross-border crime. They should not, however, carry out any tasks relating to the sovereignty of States. These officers must be posted principally on border crossing points and stretches of the border which are of particular interest in terms of illegal immigration into the Schengen area.

The liaison officers' activities shall be without prejudice to the sovereignty of the assisted State; its domestic law and administrative regulations should not be affected by the performance of their tasks.

The liaison officers' tasks listed below by way of example shall be performed solely in the context of providing advice and support to the host State's authorities responsible for border police duties.

In each case the tasks shall be fulfilled:

— in accordance with national law;

— in strict compliance with the specific regulations contained in the various bilateral agreements which may, if necessary, be supplemented by more specific arrangements;

— in agreement with the host State authorities and in accordance with their instructions.

These tasks may include:

Information exchange

— regular collection and exchange of information on specific cases;

— forging of links between competent authorities, in particular pursuant to Articles 39 and 46 of the Schengen Convention;

— informing the authorities in the host State on matters regarding entry and exit in relation to the State of origin of the seconded officers.

Advice and assistance to the officers of the host State

— advice and assistance to the host State's officers in:

- interviewing travellers,
- verifying the authenticity of documents issued by the State of origin of the seconded officers;

— advice and assistance to the host State's officers in border police follow-ups, such as:

- making reports,
- recording statements,
- conducting interviews,
- compiling statistics;

— advice and assistance to the host State's officers in:

- evaluating documents about which the liaison officers are knowledgeable,
- planning border surveillance measures,
- the evaluation of border police operations;

— advice and assistance to the host State's officers in updating the situation report;

— accompanying the host State's officers carrying out border patrols.

Moreover, the following tasks may also be performed at airports and maritime ports:

— advice/information to authorities for repatriation measures by the State of origin of the seconded officers bearing in mind existing readmission agreements;

— advice to contact persons for travellers or carriers of the State of origin of the seconded officers.

1.3. Profile of liaison officers

The officers to be seconded must also be suitable in professional and personal terms for possible long-term foreign assignments. They must have cross-border experience. Where possible, they should have a thorough knowledge of the host country's language and at least master the working language mostly used at the assignment location.

In principle, the secondment of highly professionally qualified officers is to be given preference.

1.4. Logistics

The host State shall provide the seconding State with logistical support with due regard for the sovereignty of both States and pursuant to the relevant bilateral agreement.

— The liaison officers should, in as far as local conditions so permit, be provided with their own office by the host authority or at least be able to share an office. The liaison officer should be able to share all logistical facilities in the host authority.

— The liaison officer's accommodation shall be paid for by the seconding State. The host State must assist in obtaining accommodation.

— The official involvement of liaison officers in the host State (embassy of the seconding State or Ministry/authorities of the host State) shall be defined in the bilateral agreements.

— Medical treatment
The seconding State shall ensure that sufficient health insurance cover is available in the host State for the liaison officer in case of illness. Supplementary insurance should be taken out if necessary.

2. Assignment locations

The selection of locations recommended to the Schengen States for the deployment of liaison officers shall be laid down separately by the subgroup on frontiers. This indicative list will not be in any way binding and will be updated in line with the evolving situation.

3. Evaluation/follow-up

The Schengen States will exchange their experiences on the secondment of liaison officers where necessary in the subgroup on frontiers [1].

[1] After Schengen has been integrated into the European Union, the work of the subgroup on frontiers will be continued in the Council body competent for matters relating to external borders.

Reciprocal secondment of liaison officers to advise and assist in the performance of tasks of security and checking at the external borders

SCH/I-Front (99) 9 rev 3

Indicative list of locations currently recommended to the Schengen States for the secondment of liaison officers

Below is a list of the locations which the subgroup on frontiers currently recommends to the Schengen States for the secondment of liaison officers.

This indicative list is not in any way binding and will be updated by the subgroup on frontiers in line with the current situation (1).

1. Belgium

— Brussels (Zaventem Airport)

2. Germany

— Frankfurt/Main Airport
— Munich (Franz-Joseph-Strauß Airport)
— Frankfurt/Oder (land border with Poland)
— Ludwigsdorf (land border with Poland)
— Zinnwald (land border with the Czech Republic)
— Waidhaus (land border with the Czech Republic)
— Hamburg (port)

3. Greece

— Athens (Airport)
— Thessaloniki (Airport)
— Kakabia (land border with Albania)
— Kastanies (land border with Turkey)
— Samos
— Corfu

(1) After Schengen has been integrated into the European Union, the work of the subgroup on frontiers will be continued in the Council body responsible for matters relating to external borders.

4. Spain

— Algeciras (port)
— Madrid (Barajas Airport)

5. France

— Marseille (port)
— Paris (Charles de Gaulle Airport)

6. Italy

— Rome — Fiumicino (Airport)
— Brindisi (maritime border)
— Trapani
— Trieste (land border with Slovenia)
— Milan (Malpensa Airport)

7. The Netherlands

— Amsterdam (Schiphol Airport)

8. Austria

— Vienna-Schwechat (Airport)
— Nickelsdorf motorway (land border with Hungary)
— Spielfeld (land border with Slovenia)
— Berg (land border with the Slovakia)
— Drasenhofen (land border with the Czech Republic)

DECISION OF THE EXECUTIVE COMMITTEE of 28 April 1999 on general principles governing the payment of informers

(SCH/Com-ex (99) 8 rev 2)

The Executive Committee,

— Having regard to Article 132 of the agreement implementing the Schengen Convention,

— Having regard to Articles 70 to 76 of the abovementioned convention,

HAS DECIDED AS FOLLOWS:

The Executive Committee hereby approves the decision of the Central Group of 22 March 1999 on the general principles governing payment of informers (SCH/C (99) 25, SCH/Stup (98) 72 rev).

Luxembourg, 28 April 1999

The Chairman

C. H. SCHAPPER

Subject: General principles governing payment of informers

SCH/Stup (98) 72 rev 2

1. Introduction

International drug-related crime, other forms of serious crime and organised crime are a growing phenomenon which also affects the Schengen States.

Criminals, particularly those involved in illicit trafficking in drugs, are adopting an increasingly professional approach and adapting flexibly to new geopolitical, legal, economic and technological circumstances, using entrepreneurial structures and interweaving illegal business dealings with legitimate commercial activities. They are also prepared to act ruthlessly to achieve their objectives, threatening or resorting to violence against people and property and seeking to manipulate politicians, businessmen and public officials, their main motivation being the maximisation of profits and the pursuit of power.

The modus operandi of criminal networks involved in drugs is characterised by specialisation, division of labour and compartmentalisation. Illegal profits are 'reinvested' in new criminal activities or injected into legitimate commercial activities in order to gain influence and create a criminal monopoly.

Even special investigative methods are becoming increasingly ineffective. Actively obtaining information undercover and using operational investigative methods such as systematic evaluation have therefore become an increasingly important technique for identifying and fighting organised crime in the field of drugs. In this regard particular attention should be focused on the systematic, coordinated and targeted use of informers.

Informers must gain the trust of the criminals so that they are in a position to shed light on the structure of criminal organisations and structures.

That is why the Presidency carried out a survey in the Schengen States (see document SCH/Stup (98) 25). Document SCH/Stup (98) 60 rev was subsequently distributed outlining the results. The survey showed that the law and, also in part, legal practice with regard to the payment of informers in the Schengen States differed widely. At its meeting of 21 October 1998 the Working Group on Drugs therefore agreed to draw up common non-binding guidelines for paying informers and guaranteeing them non-material benefits.

The general principles governing payment of informers are to be used as non-mandatory guidelines within the Schengen area and are intended to contribute to the further improvement of customs and police cooperation in this sensitive sphere. They should also serve as benchmarks for those Schengen States currently engaged in drafting or amplifying similar regulations.

2. General

Informers' motives for cooperating with police and customs authorities are frequently financial. They should therefore be provided with financial incentives that take market realities into account and correspond to their personal circumstances, reflect the skills required for the operation and are commensurate with the risk involved and the outcome of the investigation. Economic considerations are also a factor, since using informers often works out cheaper.

Ensuring that the following guidelines are observed throughout the Schengen area would in particular permit compliance with tactical and legal requirements that apply to drugs investigations while also taking account of specific bilateral and regional features and the particular nature of the offence. This would also prevent incidentally the emergence of 'informer tourism', with police forces and customs authorities which run informers competing with each other on a bilateral level or with other services throughout Schengen.

3. Principles

These principles shall be without prejudice to national provisions.

Payments made to informers should be in reasonable proportion to the outcome of the investigation achieved as a result of criminal prosecution and/or the danger that is averted by the use of an informer on the one hand and the involvement of and personal risk incurred by the informer on the other. The financial incentive must not incite the informer to commit an offence.

Particular criteria are as follows:

— The quantity of information and the results it produces, e.g. the value and the importance of the drugs that are seized, the number and calibre of the criminals arrested and/or the value of the assets confiscated.

— The quality of the information, e.g. strategically or tactically useful information about methods, logistical approach used by the criminals, aims of the criminal organisation, the way in which it responds to measures taken by the criminal justice authorities.

– The personal characteristics of the informer, e.g. degree of involvement in the operation, particular difficulties, risks and dangers, trustworthiness and motivation.

– The importance of the criminal hierarchy/organisation, or investigating the criminal activity of the members, their influence within the criminal milieu, degree of infiltration into public life, actual or potential damage caused, social relevance of the case and the degree to which it is rooted in the local criminal environment, the information also being used for strategic purposes.

Payment for cooperating is generally case-specific. No attempt should be made to provide the informer with living expenses for an indefinite period.

Informers may also benefit from special protective or post-operation measures (so-called witness protection) and arrangements may be made to provide social protection.

Costs incurred by an informer (expenses) may be refunded in specific cases.

Payment is made after completion of the assignment. Part payments may be made after parts of the assignment have been completed. Advances should not be paid.

An informer's earnings are still subject to national tax and social security regulations.

Generally speaking, the costs of using an informer are borne by the police or customs authority. If an investigation is to be conducted jointly by several Schengen bodies, agreement should be reached at an early stage on how the costs are to be shared. Contributions from third parties should not as a rule be included in the payment made to the informer.

Non-material benefits may also be provided subject to the provisions of national law in force in the various Schengen States and counted as material contributions. The nature of the benefit, its importance to the informer and the cost to the State in providing it are the factors to be taken into account in this regard. Protecting the informer in dangerous situations, an easing of the detention regime and full or partial remission of sentence in accordance with national law also come into the category of non-material benefit.

If an informer acts improperly e.g. by not keeping to the agreement, committing a criminal offence in a particular case, knowingly or recklessly giving false information, culpably failing to follow received instructions or wilfully departing from tactical directives, payments may be reduced, withheld or recovered in their totality depending on the seriousness of the informer's misconduct. If two or more Schengen States are affected or might be affected in such a situation, the relevant national agencies should give notification ('warning') as soon as possible.

The competent central authorities should exchange information on current criteria for payments in the different States.

DECISION OF THE CENTRAL GROUP of 22 March 1999 on general principles governing the payment of informers

(SCH/C (99) 25)

Informers play a valuable role in the fight against serious cross-border crime, and drug-related crime in particular, since they usually enjoy the trust of the offenders and thus use of such persons affords an opportunity to gain a general picture of the activities of clandestine criminal organisations and structures.

The Working Group on Drugs has addressed this issue under the German Presidency and examined the laws and practices relating to the payment of informers in each Schengen State. Based on the results of this analysis, the Working Group on Drugs has devised common guiding principles for the payment of informers in the form of money or non-material benefits. These general principles are to be regarded as non-binding guidelines in the Schengen area and are intended to contribute to the further enhancement of police and customs cooperation in this sensitive sphere. They are also to serve as a possible guide for those Schengen States currently engaged in drafting or amplifying similar regulations.

The Central Group acknowledges and endorses the — non-binding — 'general principles governing the payment of informers' (document SCH/Stup (98) 72 rev 2), subject to approval by the Executive Committee.

DECISION OF THE EXECUTIVE COMMITTEE of 28 April 1999 on the improvement of police cooperation in preventing and detecting criminal offences

(SCH/Com-ex (99) 18)

The Executive Committee,

Having regard to Article 132 of the agreement implementing the Schengen Convention,

Having regard to Article 39 of the abovementioned convention,

Desiring to continue efforts to improve the conditions for cross-border police cooperation,

Taking account of the Executive Committee decision of 16 December 1998 (doc. SCH/Com-ex (98) 51 rev 3),

HAS DECIDED AS FOLLOWS:

The principles governing police cooperation in preventing and investigating criminal offences as set out in the Presidency's note (doc. SCH/I (98) 75 rev 5) of 28 April 1999 are hereby approved.

Luxembourg, 28 April 1999

The Chairman

C. H. SCHAPPER

Subject: application of article 39 of the convention: improving police cooperation in preventing and investigating criminal offences

SCH/I (98) 75 rev 5

The German Presidency is striving to improve police cooperation between the Contracting States in investigating criminal offences. At Group I's meeting on 14 September 1998, the Presidency submitted a note setting out the problems and possible solutions (SCH/I (98) 55 rev).

All delegations agreed that much could be done to alleviate the shortcomings in police cooperation in the area of investigating criminal offences if the provisions of the Schengen Convention were given a uniform interpretation and applied on the basis of its objectives.

The Contracting States agree that improved police cooperation in criminal investigation must not prejudice the powers of the judicial authorities.

The following solutions are feasible in the short-term:

1. List

For the purpose of applying Article 39 of the Schengen Convention and improving the investigation and prevention of criminal offences, the police forces of the Schengen States may exchange information provided that

— information exchange does not require the use of coercive measures

— information exchange is admissible under the domestic law of the requested Contracting State and the activities to be carried out are not solely the preserve of the judicial authorities or require their consent.

Improvements in investigating and preventing crime will be achieved by means of cooperation between the police forces of the Schengen States without the involvement of the judicial authorities when grounds for suspicion or concrete dangers arise, notably via steps such as those listed below. This list is not exhaustive and the implementation of the steps mentioned is subject to their admissibility under the national law of the requested and requesting State:

— identification of vehicle owners and drivers;

— driver's licence enquiries;

— tracing whereabouts and residence;

— identification of telecommunications subscribers (telephone, fax and Internet), provided this information is publicly available;

— obtaining information from the persons concerned by the police on a voluntary basis [1];

— identification of persons;

— transmission of police intelligence from police databases or files, subject to compliance with the relevant legal provisions governing data protection;

— preparation of plans and coordination of search measures and the initiation of emergency searches (independently of SIS searches);

— tracing the origins of goods, particularly weapons and vehicles (tracing sales channels);

— examination of evidence (such as vehicle damage after hit and run accidents, erasures in documents, etc.).

Schengen States may in accordance with Article 39 of the Schengen Convention agree with individual or all Contracting Parties to lay down additional areas in which the police can provide mutual assistance without involving the judicial authorities.

2. Application of the judicial consent proviso (Article 39(2))

The prompt use of information as evidence in criminal proceedings is only possible if the requested Contracting State does not require formal letters rogatory in addition to the police request. The scant resources of the authorities responsible for criminal prosecution must be deployed to deal with the urgent problems of crime prevention and not unnecessarily constrained by the consent requirement.

[1] Under the national law of Austria, Germany and the Netherlands, the principle of voluntary police interviews applies.

At no point does Article 39(2) stipulate that authorisation must be obtained from the judicial authorities in order to introduce documents as evidence. The procedure for obtaining authorisation is therefore a matter for the Contracting States to determine.

The Schengen States agree that the police forces and judicial authorities may transmit requests for authorisation and the documents resulting from dealing with such requests by any means that allow swift transmission, provided the transmission provides a written trace of the document's author (e.g. telefax, e-mail).

3. Simplification of procedures

Criminal investigations, particularly in emergencies, can also be accelerated by simplifying procedures. This is exemplified in the bilateral arrangements between two Schengen States whereby, at the instigation of the judicial authorities, the police authorities cooperate directly by assisting each other with police interviews, searches and the seizure of objects when a delay would be dangerous.

The Contracting States will look at the experiences gained with this or similar agreements to determine whether appropriate Schengen-wide procedures can be devised.

2.4. JUDICIAL COOPERATION

DECISION OF THE EXECUTIVE COMMITTEE of 14 December 1993 on improving practical judicial cooperation for combating drug trafficking

(SCH/Com-ex (93) 14)

The Executive Committee,

Having regard to Article 132 of the convention implementing the Schengen Agreement, hereinafter 'the Schengen Convention',

Having regard to Articles 48 to 53 and 70 to 76 of the abovementioned convention,

HAS DECIDED AS FOLLOWS:

So as to improve practical judicial cooperation in combating drug trafficking, the Contracting Parties undertake that should the requested party not intend to enforce a request for mutual assistance, or intend to enforce it only in part, it will inform the requesting party of the reasons for its refusal and, where possible, of the conditions to be met before such a request can be enforced.

This decision shall enter into force once all the States party to the Schengen Convention have notified that the procedures required by their legal system for these decisions to be binding on their territory have been completed.

Paris, 14 December 1993

The Chairman

A. LAMASSOURE

DECISION OF THE EXECUTIVE COMMITTEE of 28 April 1999 on the Agreement on Cooperation in Proceedings for Road Traffic Offences

(SCH/Com-ex (99) 11 rev 2)

The Executive Committee,

Having regard to Article 132 of the convention implementing the Schengen Agreement,

Having regard to the joint declaration made by the ministers and State-secretaries meeting in Schengen on 19 June 1990,

HAS DECIDED AS FOLLOWS:

The Agreement on Cooperation in Proceedings for Road Traffic Offences and the Enforcement of Financial Penalties imposed in respect thereof (SCH/III (96) 25 rev.18) is hereby adopted.

The delegations' representatives are requested to draw up an explanatory report to the agreement, dealing in particular with the points outlined in the annex to this decision.

Luxembourg, 28 April 1999

The Chairman

C. H. SCHAPPER

AGREEMENT ON COOPERATION IN PROCEEDINGS FOR ROAD TRAFFIC OFFENCES AND THE ENFORCEMENT OF FINANCIAL PENALTIES IMPOSED IN RESPECT THEREOF

SCH/III (96) 25 rev 18

The Governments of the Kingdom of Belgium, the Federal Republic of Germany, the French Republic, the Grand Duchy of Luxembourg and the Kingdom of the Netherlands, Parties to the convention implementing the Schengen Agreement of 14 June 1985 between the Governments of the States of the Benelux Economic Union, the Federal Republic of Germany and the French Republic on the gradual abolition of checks at their common borders signed in Schengen on 19 June 1990, hereinafter referred to as the '1990 Convention', as well as the Governments of the Italian Republic, the Kingdom of Spain and the Portuguese Republic, the Hellenic Republic, the Republic of Austria, the Kingdom of Denmark, the Kingdom of Sweden and the Republic of Finland which acceded to the 1990 Convention by the agreements signed on 27 November 1990, 25 June 1991, 6 November 1992, 28 April 1995 and 19 December 1996 respectively, and the Governments of the Kingdom of Norway and the Republic of Iceland, which signed a cooperation agreement with the former on 19 December 1996, hereinafter referred to as the 'Contracting Parties',

Whereas the free movement of persons referred to in the 1990 Convention furthers the travel of citizens across the internal borders;

Whereas it is common knowledge that citizens of the Schengen States also commit road traffic offences when staying on the territory of a Contracting Party other than that on whose territory they habitually reside;

Whereas it has been shown that it is not always possible, in spite of sustained efforts to clamp down on road traffic offences, to establish the identity of the perpetrators before they return to the territory of the Contracting Party where they habitually reside and to enforce financial penalties in respect of the offences committed;

Convinced that cooperation between the Contracting Parties in this field is necessary and that the fact that different authorities are responsible for enforcement of the Highway Code should not become an obstacle to such cooperation,

Implementing the joint declaration of the ministers and secretaries of State of 19 June 1990, which lays down that discussions should be held to improve cooperation in prosecuting road traffic offences and to examine the scope for the mutual enforcement of financial penalties,

HAVE AGREED AS FOLLOWS:

CHAPTER I

DEFINITIONS

Article 1

For the purposes of this agreement:

'Road traffic offence' shall mean conduct which infringes road traffic regulations and which is considered a criminal or administrative offence, including breaches of regulations pertaining to driving hours and rest periods and regulations on hazardous goods;

'Financial penalty' shall mean the obligation to pay a sum of money in respect of a road traffic offence, the amount of which is assessed by the judicial or administrative authorities of the Contracting Parties;

'Competent Authority' shall mean the judicial or administrative authority of the Contracting Parties responsible for proceedings for road traffic offences and enforcing financial penalties in respect thereof;

'Decision' shall mean an act by the competent authorities of one of the Contracting Parties establishing a road traffic offence in respect of which a financial penalty has been imposed on a person, against which an appeal may be or could have been lodged;

'Requesting Authority' shall mean the competent authority of the Contracting Party in whose territory the road traffic offence was committed;

'Requested Authority' shall mean the competent authority of the Contracting Party in whose territory the person suspected of having committed a road traffic offence or upon whom a financial penalty has been imposed in respect thereof either resides or has his habitual residence;

'Requesting Contracting Party' shall mean the Contracting Party in whose territory a decision has been delivered in respect of a person who either resides or has his habitual residence in the territory of another Contracting Party;

'Requested Contracting Party' shall mean the Contracting Party in whose territory a person in respect of whom a decision has been delivered in the territory of another Contracting Party either resides or has his habitual residence.

CHAPTER II

PRINCIPLES

Article 2

1. The Contracting Parties undertake to accord each other the widest possible cooperation in proceedings for road traffic offences and the enforcement of decisions in respect thereof in accordance with the provisions of this agreement.

2. Paragraph 1 shall be without prejudice to the application of broader provisions of bilateral or multilateral agreements in force between the Contracting Parties.

3. Chapter IV of this agreement shall not apply:

(a) to the enforcement of a decision which includes a penalty involving deprivation of liberty as the main penalty;

(b) to road traffic offences which coincide with offences that are not related to road traffic only, unless the road traffic offence is prosecuted exclusively or separately.

CHAPTER III

COOPERATION IN PROCEEDINGS FOR ROAD TRAFFIC OFFENCES

Article 3

1. The competent authorities may, by communicating a vehicle registration number through their national vehicle registration authorities, request information from the national vehicle registration authorities of the other Contracting Parties concerning the type and make of the corresponding motor vehicle as well as the identity and address of the person or persons with whom the motor vehicle in question was registered when the road traffic offence was committed.

2. The vehicle registration authorities of the Contracting Parties shall directly send each other the information referred to in paragraph 1 with a view to transmission to the competent authority. They shall also send the name and address of the requested authority if it is a different authority.

3. A Contracting Party may designate another central authority for the exchange of the information referred to in paragraph 2.

4. The relevant provisions of the 1990 Convention and, in particular, Articles 126 to 128 thereof shall apply to the transmission of personal data in accordance with paragraph 1.

Article 4

1. The requesting authority may send all communications concerning the consequences and decisions relating to the road traffic offence directly to the persons suspected of having committed a road traffic offence. The provisions of Article 52 of the 1990 Convention shall apply by analogy.

2. The communications and decisions referred to in paragraph 1 shall contain or be accompanied by all information which the recipient requires in order to react, in particular regarding:

(a) the nature of the road traffic offence, the place, date and time at which it was committed and the manner in which it was established;

(b) the registration number and, where possible, the type and make of the motor vehicle with which the road traffic offence was committed or, in the absence of this information, any means of identifying the vehicle;

(c) the amount of the financial penalty which may be imposed, or, where appropriate, the financial penalty which has been imposed, the deadline within which it has to be paid and the method of payment;

(d) the possibility of invoking exonerating circumstances, as well as the deadlines and procedures for presenting these circumstances;

(e) the possible channels of appeal against the decisions, the procedures and deadlines for lodging an appeal, as well as the contact details of the authority with which an appeal should be lodged.

Article 5

1. If the addressee does not respond to communications or decisions pursuant to Article 4 within the stipulated period or if the requesting authority considers further information necessary to apply this agreement, the latter may directly seek assistance from the requested authority. A translation into the official language or one of the official languages of the requested Contracting Party shall be attached to such requests for assistance.

2. The provisions of Title III, Chapter 2 of the 1990 Convention shall apply to the requests referred to in paragraph 1.

CHAPTER IV

ENFORCEMENT OF DECISIONS

Article 6

1. The transfer of the enforcement of decisions may only be requested under this agreement where:

(a) all channels of appeal against the decision have been exhausted and the decision is enforceable in the territory of the requesting Contracting Party;

(b) the competent authorities have, in particular in accordance with Article 4, requested the person concerned to pay the financial penalty imposed but to no avail;

(c) the financial penalty is not statute-barred by limitation under the law of the requesting Contracting Party;

(d) the decision concerns a person who resides or who has his habitual residence in the territory of the requested Contracting Party;

(e) the amount of the fine or financial penalty imposed is at least EUR 40.

2. The Contracting Parties may bilaterally alter the scope of the provisions under paragraph 1(e).

Article 7

1. The transfer of the enforcement of a decision may not be refused unless the requested Contracting Party deems that:

(a) the road traffic offence giving rise to the decision is not provided for under the law of the requested Contracting Party;

(b) enforcement of the request runs counter to the principle of *ne bis in idem* pursuant to Articles 54 to 58 of the 1990 Convention;

(a) the financial penalty is statute-barred by limitation under the law of the requested Contracting Party;

(b) the person concerned would have been granted an amnesty or a pardon by the requested Contracting Party if the road traffic offence had been committed on the territory of the requested Contracting Party.

2. The requested Contracting Party shall inform the requesting Contracting Party as soon as possible of a refusal to execute the request, giving the reasons for the refusal.

Article 8

1. The decision shall be enforced without delay by the competent authorities of the requested Contracting Party.

2. The financial penalty shall be payable in the currency of the requested Contracting Party. The amount shall be calculated on the basis of the official exchange rate obtaining when the decision mentioned in paragraph 1 is taken.

3. Should it transpire upon conversion that the amount of the financial penalty imposed by the decision exceeds the maximum amount of the financial penalty prescribed in respect of the same type of road traffic offence by the law of the requested Contracting Party, the enforcement of the decision shall not exceed this maximum amount.

4. At the time of depositing its instrument of ratification, acceptance or approval, each State may, for reasons of a constitutional order or of equal importance, declare that it intends to derogate from the application of paragraph 1 by making a declaration defining the cases in which the financial penalty to be enforced must be declared enforceable by a judicial decision of the requested Contracting Party before enforcement. This judicial decision shall not, however, concern the contents and the amount of the decision of the requesting Contracting Party which is to be enforced.

Article 9

1. The enforcement of the decision shall be governed by the law of the requested Contracting Party.

2. Any part of the financial penalty already enforced in the requesting Contracting Party shall be deducted in full from the penalty to be enforced in the requested Contracting Party.

3. Where a financial penalty cannot be enforced, either totally or in part, an alternative penalty involving deprivation of liberty or coercive detention may be applied by the requested Contracting Party if provided for in both Contracting States, unless expressly excluded by the requesting Contracting Party.

Article 10

The requesting Contracting Party may no longer proceed with the enforcement of the decision once it has requested the transfer of enforcement. The right of enforcement shall revert to the requesting Contracting Party upon its being informed by the requested Contracting Party of the latter's refusal or inability to enforce.

Article 11

The requested Contracting Party shall terminate enforcement of the decision as soon as it (the requested Contracting Party) is informed by the requesting Contracting Party of any decision, measure or any other circumstance as a result of which enforcement of the decision is suspended or the decision ceases to be enforceable.

Article 12

1. Requests for the transfer of the enforcement of a decision and all communications relating thereto shall be made in writing. They may be transmitted through any appropriate channels leaving a written record, including a fax.

2. Documents shall be transmitted directly between the competent authorities of the Contracting Parties, the contact details of which shall be furnished by the vehicle registration authorities (Article 3(2)). These documents shall be transmitted via the designated central authorities of the Contracting Party if the contact details of the competent authority cannot be inferred from the information referred to in the first sentence.

Article 13

1. The request for the transfer of enforcement of a decision shall be accompanied by a copy of the decision and a declaration by the competent authority of the requesting Contracting Party certifying that the conditions laid down in subparagraphs a, b and c of Article 6(1) have been fulfilled.

2. Where appropriate, the requesting Contracting Party shall accompany its request by other information relevant to the transfer of the enforcement of a decision, in particular information regarding the special circumstances of the offence which were taken into consideration when assessing the financial penalty and, where possible, the text of the legal provisions applied.

3. If the requested Contracting Party considers that the information supplied by the requesting Contracting Party is inadequate to enable it to apply this agreement, it shall ask for the additional information required.

4. The translation of the relevant documents into the official language or one of the official languages of the requested Contracting Party shall be attached.

Article 14

The competent authorities of the requested Contracting Party shall inform the competent authorities of the requesting Contracting Party of the enforcement of the financial penalty or, where appropriate, of inability to enforce the decision.

Article 15

The financial penalty and the cost of proceedings incurred by the requesting Contracting Party shall be enforced. Monies obtained from the enforcement of decisions shall accrue to the requested Contracting Party.

Article 16

Contracting Parties shall not claim from each other the refund of costs resulting from application of this agreement.

CHAPTER V

FINAL PROVISIONS

Article 17

1. The Executive Committee established by the 1990 Convention shall have the general task of monitoring the proper application of this agreement. The provisions of Article 132 of the 1990 Convention shall apply.

2. The Joint Supervisory Authority established by the 1990 Convention shall be responsible, in matters relating to the protection of personal data, for delivering an opinion on the common aspects resulting from the implementation of this agreement.

3. At the proposal of a Contracting Party, the Executive Committee may decide to alter the amount provided for under paragraph (e) of Article 6(1).

Article 18

This Agreement shall apply to the territory of the Contracting Parties. However, pursuant to Article 138 of the 1990 Convention, as regards the French Republic this agreement shall apply only to the European territory of the French Republic, and as regards the Kingdom of the Netherlands this agreement shall apply only to the European territory of the Kingdom of the Netherlands. Pursuant to Article 5(1) of the agreement on the accession of the Kingdom of Denmark to the 1990 Convention, this agreement shall not apply to the Faeroe Islands and Greenland.

Article 19

1. This agreement shall also be applicable to traffic offences committed before its entry into force.

2. When depositing its instrument of ratification, acceptance or approval, each State may declare that, as far as it is concerned and in its relations with those Contracting Parties which have made a similar declaration, this agreement shall only apply to road traffic offences committed after its entry into force or after it has become applicable.

Article 20

1. This agreement is subject to ratification, acceptance or approval. The instruments of ratification, acceptance or approval shall be deposited with the Government of the Grand Duchy of Luxembourg, which shall notify all the Contracting Parties thereof.

2. This agreement shall enter into force on the first day of the second month following the date of deposit of the last instrument of ratification, acceptance or approval by the States for which the 1990 Convention has been brought into force as pursuant to paragraph 1, second subparagraph, of the final act of the abovementioned convention.

The Government of the Grand Duchy of Luxembourg shall notify all the Contracting Parties of the date of entry into force.

In respect of the other States, this agreement shall enter into force on the first day of the second month following the date of deposit of the instruments of ratification, acceptance or approval, at the earliest, however, on the date of bringing into force an accession agreement for these States to the 1990 Convention or to the 1996 Cooperation Agreement.

3. Pending the entry into force of this agreement, each State in which the 1990 Convention has been brought into force at the time of deposit of its instrument of ratification, acceptance or approval may, when depositing this instrument or at any later stage, declare this agreement applicable in its relations with those States which make a similar declaration. This declaration shall take effect as of the first day of the second month following the date of deposit.

Article 21

1. Each Contracting Party may submit a proposal for an amendment to this agreement to the depositary. The depositary shall inform the other Contracting Parties of this proposal.

2. The Contracting Parties shall adopt any amendments to this agreement by common assent.

3. The amendments shall enter into force on the first day of the second month following the date of deposit of the last instrument of ratification, acceptance or approval.

Article 22

1. At the latest when depositing its instrument of ratification, acceptance or approval, each State shall notify the depositary of the names and addresses of the authorities within the meaning of Articles 1, 3 and 11(2).

2. The lists of authorities pursuant to paragraph 1 may, by way of derogation from Article 19(1), be subsequently changed at any time by notification to the depositary.

3. The depositary shall inform each Contracting Party of the designated authorities and subsequent changes.

Article 23

This agreement shall be open to accession by all States which become Parties to the 1990 Convention.

In witness whereof, the undersigned, duly authorised to that end, have signed this agreement.

Done at Luxembourg, on 28 April 1999, in a single original in the Dutch, English, French, German, Greek Italian, Portuguese and Spanish languages, all eight texts being equally authentic. The texts in the Danish, Finnish, Icelandic, Norwegian and Swedish languages, to be submitted at a date after the signing, shall be equally authentic.

DECLARATION OF THE EXECUTIVE COMMITTEE of 26 June 1996 on extradition

(SCH/Com-ex (96) decl 6 rev 2)

Whereas the free movement of persons provided for in the Schengen Agreement and the convention implementing the Schengen Agreement is accompanied by compensatory measures aiming to guarantee security within the territory of the Schengen States;

Whereas judicial cooperation in criminal matters is an important aspect of these measures;

Whereas the convention implementing the Schengen Agreement contains provisions aiming to simplify judicial cooperation in criminal matters, in particular extradition;

Having regard to the experience gained in the field of extradition, in particular for terrorist offences, since the convention was brought into force;

Taking into account the importance that the Contracting Parties attach to effectively combating terrorism within their common territory;

Taking into account the declaration on the fight against terrorism adopted by the Executive Committee at The Hague on 21 February 1996;

Welcoming the agreement reached on 26 June 1996 between the Member States of the European Union on a convention on the improvement of extradition, which represents a positive step forward in cooperation between the Member States;

The Contracting Parties hereby declare that:

1. When examining a request for extradition, each requested State shall take into account the need to safeguard the Schengen area of free movement and security;

2. Each requested State shall take the necessary steps to ensure that when a decision is taken to suspend detention pending extradition, appropriate measures may be adopted so that the person sought does not have the opportunity to escape extradition following the decision, and where the law of the requested State does not provide a sufficient legal

basis for the measures in question, the requested State shall undertake to initiate, in accordance with constitutional requirements, the legal measures to achieve the aforementioned objective;

3. Each requested State shall inform the requesting State without delay when detention of the person sought pending extradition is suspended;

4. Pending agreement on a legal basis as provided for under point 2, the parties concerned shall take all necessary measures bilaterally to prevent any act which might jeopardise law and order in a Schengen Member State.

DECLARATION OF THE EXECUTIVE COMMITTEE of 9 February 1998 on the abduction of minors

(SCH/Com-ex (97) decl. 13 rev 2)

The Executive Committee

Whereas the abduction of minors or the unlawful removal of a minor by one of the parents from the person to whom the right of custody has been attributed is a matter of real concern for the Contracting Parties to the convention implementing the Schengen Agreement,

Taking into account Article 93 of the abovementioned convention, which declares that the purpose of the Schengen information system shall be to maintain public policy and public security and to apply the provisions of this convention relating to the movement of persons,

Whereas it is up to the State concerned to decide in accordance with national provisions whether an alert may be entered into the Schengen information system on the abductor or the parent unlawfully removing the minor from the person awarded legal custody;

Whereas it is not possible to include the necessary information in the alert on the minor pursuant to Article 97 of the said convention;

Whereas a uniform solution should be found so that a minor who has been abducted or unlawfully removed by one of the parents from the person awarded legal custody can be located and returned to that person as quickly as possible;

RECOMMENDS AS FOLLOWS:

1. Where a minor is unlawfully removed by one of the parents or by a third party from the care of the persons awarded custody it is advisable, in any event, to enter an alert on the minor pursuant to Article 97.

2. This alert shall be accompanied by an M form which shall be sent to all Sirene bureaux and shall contain full details of the circumstances surrounding the disappearance as well as information for the identification of the abductor and the person(s) or institution legally accorded the right of education or the right of custody.

3. In the event that this information, for reasons appertaining to national procedures, cannot be sent as provided for under point 2, in the event of a hit it should be forwarded as soon as possible to the Sirene bureau of the State which obtained the hit.

4. That the authorities entering the alerts into the Schengen information system follow this procedure and send the relevant Sirene bureau all the necessary information so that this may then be diffused via an M form.

5. That it is equally imperative that the authorities responsible for border control at the external borders systematically check the identity papers and the travel documents of minors. This is particularly important if minors are travelling in the company of just one adult.

6. That, as far as possible, documents should also be checked in the course of controls or similar procedures within the territory.

2.5. SIS

DECISION OF THE EXECUTIVE COMMITTEE of 14 December 1993 on the financial regulation on the costs of installing and operating the Schengen information system (C.SIS)

(SCH/Com-ex (93) 16)

The Executive Committee,

— Having regard to Article 132 of the convention implementing the Schengen Agreement,

— Having regard to Articles 92 and 119 of the abovementioned convention,

HAS DECIDED AS FOLLOWS:

The financial regulation on the installation costs and the technical support function costs of the Schengen information system (C.SIS), attached hereto is hereby adopted ([1]).

Paris, 14 December 1993

The Chairman

A. LAMASSOURE

([1]) Updated version: see SCH/Com-ex (97) 35.

DECISION OF THE EXECUTIVE COMMITTEE of 25 April 1997 on awarding the contract for the SIS II Preliminary Study

(SCH/Com-ex (97) 2 rev 2)

The Executive Committee,

Having regard to Article 132 of the convention implementing the Schengen Agreement,

Having regard to the decision adopted at the meeting held in Luxembourg on 19 December 1996 to create a second generation SIS, SIS II, which should not just permit the integration of all Schengen States but should also comprise new functions,

Whereas the creation of SIS II involves conducting a preliminary study to define the architecture of the new system and whereas, to this end, a procedure must be initiated in accordance with Directive 92/50/EEC of 18 June 1992 relating to the coordination of procedures for the award of public service contracts,

HAS DECIDED AS FOLLOWS:

1. Portugal is hereby instructed to work closely with the other Schengen States to award the contract for the preliminary study for SIS II by initiating a procedure in accordance with Directive 92/50/EEC of 18 June 1992 relating to the coordination of procedures for the award of public service contracts and in accordance with applicable Portuguese law.

2. Portugal is hereby entrusted with the coordination and budgetary management of this project, whilst working closely with the other Schengen States.

3. A financial regulation shall be drawn up to regulate all the budgetary questions related to the preliminary study for SIS II; this regulation should provide Portugal with all the legal and financial guarantees.

4. An administrative regulation shall also be drawn up to define clearly the powers and obligations of all parties involved, namely the contracting authority, the Schengen States and the Schengen Secretariat.

5. The Schengen Secretariat shall coordinate the project, including administrative management and coordination between the various Schengen working groups, in close collaboration with the project manager and the head of budgetary management.

6. The Executive Committee hereby awards a mandate to the Central Group to supervise the procedure, more specifically with regard to:

(a) the specifications for the preliminary study for SIS II and the notice of call for tenders;

(b) the financial regulation and the administrative regulation.

Lisbon, 25 April 1997

The Chairman

F. SEIXAS DA COSTA

DECISION OF THE EXECUTIVE COMMITTEE of 7 October 1997 on contributions from Iceland and Norway to the costs of installing and operating of the C.SIS

(SCH/Com-ex (97) 18)

The Executive Committee,

Having regard to Article 132 of the convention implementing the Schengen Agreement,

Having regard to Articles 92 and 119 of the abovementioned convention,

Having regard to Articles 2 and 3 of the Cooperation Agreement between the Contracting Parties to the Schengen Agreement and the Schengen Convention and the Republic of Iceland and the Kingdom of Norway,

HAS DECIDED AS FOLLOWS:

1. The contributions of Iceland and Norway, hereinafter referred to as the States of the Cooperation Agreement, to the costs of installing and operating the C.SIS:

— The contributions of the States of the Cooperation Agreement shall correspond to their share in the total of the gross domestic products of the Contracting Parties and the States of the Cooperation Agreement.

— The contributions of the Contracting Parties shall be calculated pursuant to Article 119(1) of the Schengen Convention.

2. Method of calculation:

— The contributions from Iceland and Norway shall be calculated by means of a comparison of the gross domestic products of all Contracting Parties and the States of the Cooperation Agreement.

— The contributions from the Contracting Parties which are Member States of the EU shall be calculated on the basis of the value-added tax assessment base pursuant to Article 119(1), sentence 2, of the Schengen Convention after deducting the contributions from Iceland and Norway.

3. The deadline for payment of contributions by the Nordic States shall be fixed for 1 January 1997.

Vienna, 7 October 1997

The Chairman

K. SCHLÖGL

DECISION OF THE EXECUTIVE COMMITTEE of 7 October 1997 on the development of the SIS

(SCH/Com-ex (97) 24)

The Executive Committee,

Having regard to Article 132 of the convention implementing the Schengen Agreement,

Having regard to Article 92(3) of the abovementioned convention,

Whereas the SIS Steering Committee has conducted an analysis (doc. SCH/OR.SIS (97) 146 rev. 2),

HAS DECIDED AS FOLLOWS:

Work carried out on SIS II will run concurrently with measures to renew the current C.SIS for 10 States. However, preparations will be made to run it for 15 States to enable the Nordic States to be integrated immediately after the SIS has been stabilised for 10 States on the new platform.

The Nordic States should be integrated as quickly as possible during the year 2000.

During implementation the following guidelines should be observed:

1. The parallel development of SIS I and SIS II will in no way affect the development of SIS II as a strategic goal. Only the SIS II will be able to meet a certain number of essential operational demands.

2. This objective should be achieved by a restricted tender procedure organised by France, as the contracting authority.

3. The parallel development of SIS I and SIS II entails all the States deciding to provide the necessary resources in terms of funding and manpower.

Vienna, 7 October 1997

The Chairman

K. SCHLÖGL

SCH/OR.SIS (97) 146 rev 2

Subject: Development of the SIS

1. The note drafted by the PWP and the Steering Committee regarding the further development of the SIS (SCH/OR.SIS (97) 105 rev.) was presented at the meeting of the Central Group on 23 June 1997. No consensus as to how to proceed was reached at this meeting.

2. At the meeting on 8 July 1997, the Steering Committee granted the PWP a mandate to analyse the preferred scenarios again from a technical point of view and to prepare an overview of the requirements and costs.

3. Intensive work by the PWP over the summer months has resulted in note SCH/OR.SIS-SIS (97) 425 rev., attached as annex, on the possibility for further technical development of the existing system, taking into account the participation of the Nordic States in the SIS (SCH/OR.SIS (97) 425 rev.).

During this work, and particularly during discussions with the consortium, it transpired that a decision on the further development of the SIS must be taken quickly. Unless the system is upgraded by exchanging the hardware and software, it will probably not be able to cope with the change of date for the millennium.

According to official statements by the consortium, no guarantee can be given that the problems in the current system can be solved. Moreover, the consortium is of the opinion that the modifications would not be covered by the existing maintenance contracts.

4. Technical factors make it impossible to integrate the Nordic States into the SIS before the new millennium.

After studying the PWP's research, the Steering Committee recommends that the Central Group proceed as follows:

Take a decision immediately on the procedure outlined below and — in the light of the prevailing situation regarding decisions at Executive Committee level — submit this matter to the Executive Committee with a view to taking a further decision.

Work carried out on SIS II will run concurrently with measures to renew the current C.SIS for 10 States. However, preparations will be made to run it for 15 States to enable the Nordic States to be integrated immediately after the stabilisation of the 10-State SIS on the new platform.

The Nordic States should be integrated as quickly as possible during the year 2000. The project aimed at renewing and extending the SIS will therefore consist of two phases. The first phase will involve preparation of the hardware and the technical specifications for a system that operates with 15 States and implementation for 10 States. The second phase comprises the integration of the Nordic States.

During implementation account should be taken of the following guidelines:

1. The parallel development of SIS.I and SIS.II will in no way affect the development of SIS.II as a strategic goal. Only the SIS.II will be able to meet essential operational demands placed on the SIS. (The functional scope for SIS I will remain the same after renewal).

2. The Steering Committee considers that the only way of ensuring that this scenario is realised is via a restricted procedure for calls for tender. The procedure must be undertaken by France in accordance with Article 92, paragraph 3 of the Schengen Convention.

3. The parallel development of SIS.I and SIS.II requires all States to demonstrate the readiness and the will to provide the necessary resources in terms of funding and manpower. The cost of updating SIS.I is estimated at approximately FRF 16 million (excluding the cost of adapting the national Schengen information systems).

The Steering Committee emphasises that any delay in decision-making will jeopardise the operation of the system after 1 January 2000.

DECISION OF THE EXECUTIVE COMMITTEE of 15 December 1997 amending the Financial Regulation on C.SIS

(SCH/Com-ex (97) 35)

The Executive Committee,

Having regard to Article 132 of the convention implementing the Schengen Agreement,

Having regard to Articles 92 and 119 of the abovementioned convention,

Having regard to Articles 2 and 3 of the Cooperation Agreement between the Contracting Parties to the Schengen Agreement and the Schengen Convention of the one part and the Republic of Iceland and the Kingdom of Norway of the other,

HAS DECIDED AS FOLLOWS:

The version of the financial regulation on the costs of installing and operating the Schengen C.SIS (SCH/Com-ex (93) 16 rev), dated 20 December 1996, is hereby amended as follows.

Vienna, 15 December 1997

The Chairman

K. SCHLÖGL

SCH/Com-ex (93) 16 rev 2

The Executive Committee,

Having regard to Article 132 of the convention implementing the Schengen Agreement,

Having regard to Articles 92 and 119 of the abovementioned convention,

Having regard to Articles 2 and 3 of the Cooperation Agreement between the Contracting Parties to the Schengen Agreement and the Schengen Convention of the one part and the Republic of Iceland and the Kingdom of Norway of the other,

HAS DECIDED AS FOLLOWS:

The financial regulation for the costs of installing and operating for the technical support function for the Schengen information system (C.SIS), attached hereto, is hereby adopted.

FINANCIAL REGULATION FOR THE INSTALLATION AND OPERATION OF THE SCHENGEN C.SIS

TITLE I

GENERAL PROVISIONS

The budget for the technical support function of the Schengen information system in Strasbourg provided for in Articles 92 and 119 of the Schengen Agreement of 14 June 1985, hereinafter 'the C.SIS', shall be made up of:

— the installation budget for the central information system, for which expenditure shall be approved by the Executive Committee, after receiving the Central Group's opinion;

— the operating budget, for which the annual amount of expenditure shall be approved by the Executive Committee, after receiving the Central Group's opinion;

The installation and operating budgets for the C.SIS shall as far as possible take into account the multiannual table for the SIS installation and operating budgets.

The multiannual table for the SIS installation and operating budgets, covering at least three years, shall contain an estimate of predicted expenditure.

The multiannual table for the SIS installation and operating budgets shall be updated each year by the SIS Steering Committee and approved by the Central Group during the first quarter of the calendar year.

1. C.SIS own resources

C.SIS own resources for both the installation and operating budgets shall be composed of the contributions of the Contracting Parties and the States of the Cooperation Agreement, hereinafter 'the Cooperating States'. The Cooperating States' contributions shall be determined on the basis of their share in the GDP aggregate of all the Contracting Parties and Cooperating States. The Contracting Parties' contributions shall be determined on the basis of each Contracting Party's share in the uniform VAT assessment base within the meaning of Article 2(1)(c) of the Council decision of 24 June 1988 on the system of the Communities' own resources.

The breakdown of contributions among the Contracting Parties of the one part and the Cooperating States of the other shall be determined on the basis of the share of each Contracting Party and Cooperating State in the GDP aggregate of all the Contracting Parties and Cooperating States for the preceding year. The breakdown of contributions among the Contracting Parties shall be determined each year, taking into account the Cooperating States' contributions, on the basis of each Contracting Party's share of own resources in the European Communities' VAT resources, as established by the last amendment to the Community budget for the preceding financial year.

The contributions of the Contracting Parties and Cooperating States to each budget shall be calculated and laid down in French francs by the French Contracting Party.

2. Payment of contributions

Each Contracting Party and Cooperating State shall transfer its contributions to the following account:

COMPTE TRESOR PUBLIC
Banque de France
No 9000-3
(agence centrale comptable du trésor)

Each payment shall be lodged in a support fund set up under the French Republic's budget (*fonds de concours* No 09.1.4.782) with the Ministry of the Interior as beneficiary.

3. Accession of new States

If a new Contracting Party accedes, the following shall apply as of the date of accession:

— the contributions of the Contracting Parties and the Cooperating States shall be adjusted pursuant to Title I.1 of this financial regulation;

— the contributions of the Contracting Parties and the Cooperating States shall be adjusted with a view to fixing the new Contracting Party's contribution to C.SIS operating costs as of the year of accession;

— the contributions of the Contracting Parties and the Cooperating States shall be adjusted with a view to allocating to the new Contracting Party a proportion of the costs previously incurred for the installation of the C.SIS. This amount shall be calculated according to the share of the new Contracting Party's VAT resources in the total European Communities' VAT resources for the years in which costs were incurred for the installation of the C.SIS prior to the new Contracting Party's accession. This amount shall be reimbursed to the other States in proportion to their contribution, calculated pursuant to Title I.1 of this regulation.

TITLE II

INSTALLATION BUDGET

The French Republic shall bear all the advance costs of C.SIS installation in accordance with the rules of law governing French public finances. The amounts fixed as the contribution of each Member State and Cooperating State shall be calculated and laid down in French francs by the French Contracting Party pursuant to Title I.1 of this financial regulation.

1. Forecast expenditure

During the year before the budget is due to be implemented, the French Contracting Party shall draw up an annual draft budget for C.SIS installation expenditure taking into account as far as possible the provisional multiannual table for SIS installation and operations. This draft budget shall be submitted to the Central Group for its opinion and to the Executive Committee for adoption at least six months before the beginning of the financial year.

If the draft budget is rejected, the French Contracting Party shall prepare a new draft within one month which, following the Central Group's opinion, shall be submitted immediately to the Executive Committee for adoption.

At the end of each quarter of the financial year, the Central Group shall, after receiving the SIS Steering Committee's opinion, authorise C.SIS installation expenditure as well as any unforeseen expenditure, which shall be justified in a supporting document.

In the six months following the closure of the financial year, the French Contracting Party shall draw up a multiannual table of the C.SIS installation expenditure that is authorised by the Central Group until the end of the financial year.

This table shall be submitted to the Executive Committee for approval at the same time as the annual draft budget for C.SIS installation expenditure.

The contributions of the respective States shall fall due for payment upon the Executive Committee's approval of expenditure and shall be paid pursuant to the procedure laid down in Title II.2.

The Contracting Parties and Cooperating States undertake to cover all installation expenditure up to the amount approved by the Executive Committee.

The Contracting Parties and Cooperating States may choose to pay their contributions for C.SIS installation in the form of an advance covering part or all of their forecast contribution.

2. Method of payment

As a rule, the contributions of the Contracting Parties and the Cooperating States shall fall due on the date on which the French Contracting Party makes the payments.

Nevertheless, and with a view to restricting the number of calls for payment, the French Contracting Party shall send calls for payment to the States twice a year, on 30 April and 31 October, to take into account the States' deadlines for operating expenditure commitments.

The French Contracting Party shall send a letter containing a call for payment to the States via the designated administrative authorities, details of which have been given to it.

This letter shall state:

- the legal bases for the call for payment;

- the amount of the C.SIS installation budget approved;

- the amount to be paid for the period in question;

- the necessary information for payment of the contribution, as stipulated under Title I.2 of this financial regulation.

The following documents shall be attached to this letter:

- a table showing the shares of the Cooperating States, calculated on the basis of GDP, and a table showing each State's share of the C.SIS operating budget for the expenditure incurred during the given period, calculated on the basis of its VAT share in the SIS;

- copies of documents warranting the amount to be transferred.

To ensure the smooth transfer of payments, each State should attach to its transfer a note containing the following information:

OBJET: versement de la quote-part 199... de l'Etat... au budget d'installation du système informatique SCHENGEN

MONTANT: ...... francs

BENEFICIAIRE: Ministère de l'Intérieur, Direction des transmissions et de l'informatique

(**SUBJECT:** payment of the 199... contribution from..... (State) to the installation budget of the Schengen information system

AMOUNT: ... francs

BENEFICIARY: Ministry of the Interior, Department of data transmission and informatics)

3. Financing by a State other than the French Republic

If, in agreement with the other Contracting Parties and the Cooperating States, a Contracting Party or Cooperating State directly bears part of the C.SIS installation costs, this expenditure shall be apportioned to the Contracting States in accordance with the distribution key laid down by the French Contracting Party for the financial year in which the expenditure is made.

The Contracting Party or Cooperating State having directly borne this expenditure shall inform the French Contracting Party, which shall call in the contributions of the Contracting Parties and the Cooperating States, calculated pursuant to this financial regulation.

The French Contracting Party shall reimburse the payment made as soon as the contributions owing have been received from the other Contracting Parties and Cooperating States.

TITLE III

OPERATING BUDGET

The French Republic shall bear the advance costs of C.SIS operations in accordance with the rules of law governing French public finances. The amounts fixed as the contribution of each Contracting Party and Cooperating State shall be calculated and laid down in French francs by the French Contracting Party pursuant to Title I.1 of this financial regulation.

1. Draft operating budget

During the year before the budget is due to be implemented, the French Contracting Party shall draw up the draft budget for C.SIS operating expenditure. The draft budget shall be submitted to the Central Group for its opinion and to the Executive Committee for adoption at least six months before the beginning of the financial year.

This draft budget shall take into account as far as possible the multiannual table on SIS installation and operations.

Documents on forecast expenditure shall be annexed to the draft budget.

The budget shall be adopted unanimously by the Contracting Parties.

If the draft budget is rejected, the French Contracting Party shall prepare a new draft within one month which, following the Central Group's opinion, shall be immediately submitted to the Executive Committee for adoption.

During the period between the two consultations or failing adoption of the draft budget, the French Contracting Party may call in the contributions of the Contracting Parties and the Cooperating States and initiate the implementation of the budget by provisional twelfths until such time as the budget for the current financial year is adopted.

The French Contracting Party may submit an amending draft budget to the Executive Committee. This shall be submitted to the latter for adoption following the Central Group's opinion.

Any deficit or surplus arising during the financial year must be cleared the following year in the course of the budget's implementation.

2. Method of payment

The Executive Committee decision adopting the budget shall be duly notified to all the Contracting Parties and Cooperating States by the Presidency-in-office; the contributions of the Contracting Parties and Cooperating States shall fall due for payment immediately thereafter.

To this end, the French Contracting Party shall send each Contracting Party and Cooperating State a call for payment of contributions owing and shall forward the Presidency a copy thereof.

The Contracting Parties and the Cooperating States shall pay their contributions in full by 30 April of the current financial year.

If a Contracting Party does not honour its financial obligations by that date, the Community regulations in force governing the interest to be paid in default in payment of contributions to the Community budget shall apply. These regulations shall apply *mutatis mutandis* in cases where a Cooperating State does not honour its financial obligations in due time.

The French Contracting Party shall send a letter containing a call for payment to the States via the designated administrative authorities, details of which have been given to it, at the beginning of the financial year in which the adopted operating budget is to be implemented.

The letter shall state:

— the legal bases for the call for payment;

— the amount of the operating budget adopted by the Executive Committee for the year in question.

A table showing the contributions of the Cooperating States, calculated on the basis of GDP, and a table showing each Contracting Party's contribution to the C.SIS operating budget calculated on the basis of its VAT share in the SIS, shall be attached to this letter. A table showing the calculation of the GDP share and the VAT share in the SIS for the year in which the expenditure is to be made shall also be annexed.

To ensure the smooth transfer of payments, each State should attach to its transfer a note containing the following information:

OBJET: versement de la quote-part 199... de l'Etat... au budget de fonctionnement du système informatique SCHENGEN

MONTANT: ...... francs

BENEFICIAIRE: Ministère de l'Intérieur, Direction des transmissions et de l'informatique

(**SUBJECT:** payment of the 199... contribution from... (State) to the operating budget of the Schengen information system

AMOUNT: ... francs

BENEFICIARY: Ministry of the Interior, Department of data transmission and informatics)

The Contracting Parties and Cooperating States may choose to advance an amount to cover their estimated contributions for a number of financial years.

TITLE IV

APPROVAL OF ACCOUNTS

At the beginning of each financial year, the French Contracting Party shall send the States a document, drawn up on the basis of the provisions of this financial regulation, required for the Executive Committee to give final discharge for the preceding financial year following the Central Group's opinion.

The document shall contain:

1. For the installation budget

— a statement of the expenditure made by the French Contracting Party and, where appropriate, by the other Contracting Parties or the Cooperating States pursuant to the provisions of Title II.3 of this financial regulation;

– the amount and breakdown of the contributions paid into the support fund (*fonds de concours)* by each State and, where appropriate, any outstanding amounts to be recovered.

2. For the operating budget

– a statement of expenditure made during the preceding financial year. This table shall indicate the deficit or surplus as compared with the adopted budget pursuant to Title III.1 of this financial regulation, so that the States may be charged or reimbursed the appropriate amounts;

– the amount and breakdown of the contributions paid into the support fund and, where appropriate, any amounts owing by the States.

The document shall be certified by a financial controller of the French Ministry of the Interior and sent to all the Contracting Parties and Cooperating States by the Presidency-in-office.

The Executive Committee's approval of the said document shall constitute the final discharge of the accounts presented by the French Republic for the financial year in question. Approval shall be given during the first quarter of the year following the budgetary year in question.

A table showing the contributions of each State for the following financial year, calculated pursuant to Title I.1 of this financial regulation, shall be attached to the document.

If a State decides to pay its contributions partly or wholly in the form of an advance, the document shall indicate the outstanding balance following deduction of amounts owing for the budgetary year in question.

This decision shall enter into force once all the Contracting Parties to the Schengen Convention have given notification that the procedures required by their legal system for these decisions to be binding on their territory have been completed.

DECISION OF THE EXECUTIVE COMMITTEE of 21 April 1998 on C.SIS with 15/18 connections

(SCH/Com-ex (98) 11)

The Executive Committee,

Having regard to Article 132 of the convention implementing the Schengen Agreement,

Having regard to Article (92)3 of the abovementioned convention,

Having regard to the decision of the Executive Committee on the revision and extension of the C.SIS (SCH/Com-ex (97) 24),

Having regard to the opinions of the technical groups, approved by the Central Group at its meeting on 30 March 1998,

HAS DECIDED AS FOLLOWS:

The revised C.SIS shall provide 18 connections — 15 connections for the Signatory States and 3 reserve technical connections.

Brussels, 21 April 1998

The Chairman

J. VANDE LANOTTE

DECISION OF THE EXECUTIVE COMMITTEE of 28 April 1999 on the Help Desk budget for 1999

(SCH/Com-ex (99) 3)

The Executive Committee,

Having regard to Article 132 of the convention implementing the Schengen Agreement, hereinafter 'the Schengen Convention'

Having regard to Article 119 of the abovementioned convention,

HAS DECIDED AS FOLLOWS:

1. The draft budget for 1999 for the Help Desk shall be fixed at BEF 1 880 000 for 1999.

2. The contributions from the Parties shall be calculated according to the distribution key laid down in Article 119 of the Schengen Convention and pursuant to the Executive Committee decision of 7 October 1997 (document SCH/Com-ex (97) 18).

3. This decision shall constitute as a mandate for the Benelux Economic Union, which is a party to this contract, to launch the call for contributions from the Parties.

Luxembourg, 28 April 1999

The Chairman

C. H. SCHAPPER

DECISION OF THE EXECUTIVE COMMITTEE of 28 April 1999 on C.SIS installation expenditure

(SCH/Com-ex (99) 4)

The Executive Committee,

Having regard to Article 132 of the convention implementing the Schengen Agreement,

Having regard to Articles 92 and 119 of the abovementioned convention,

Taking note of and approving document SCH/OR.SIS (99) 3 rev,

HAS DECIDED AS FOLLOWS:

The new expenditure added to the C.SIS installation budget is hereby approved and the share attributable to each of the Schengen States shall thus fall due in accordance with the written procedure under Title II, No 2 of the financial regulation for the costs of installing and operating the Schengen information system (C.SIS) (SCH/Com-ex (93) 16 rev 2 of 15 December 1997).

Luxembourg, 28 April 1999

The Chairman

C. H. SCHAPPER

Subject: Multiannual table of authorised C.SIS installation expenditure.

SCH/OR.SIS (99) 3 rev

Situation as of 31 December 1998.

In accordance with the financial regulations on the costs of installing and operating the C.SIS (SCH/Com-ex (93) 16 rev 2), the French delegation presents overleaf the table summarising the new C.SIS installation expenditure authorised at the end of the 1998 financial year.

As requested by the Steering Committee meeting of 14 January 1999, the figure quoted in this document for the second quarter is not the same as the figure given in the second quarterly report (doc. SCH/OR.SIS (98) 118) as approved by the Central Group on 8 September 1998.

In fact, that document quoted the amount earmarked for the C.SIS revision contract, namely of 41 million French francs. After the contract was signed with Atos, the actual amount turned out to be less than the estimate, ie FRF 38 577 191.

The Steering Committee has been able to charge the difference to the third and fourth quarters for C.SIS revision expenses under the same budgetary heading, without overshooting the amount initially authorised (FRF 41 million).

This substantial difference called for the table of authorised expenditure for 1998 to be amended, without waiting for the C.SIS management report for 1998 to be published, which will give the details of actual expenditure.

This table should be submitted to the Executive Committee for approval.

MULTIANNUAL TABLE OF AUTHORISED INSTALLATION EXPENDITURE for the technical support function of the C.SIS as at 31 December 1998

Breakdown of expenditure	Amount in FRF	Total
C.SIS I		
Budget approved from 18.12.1991 (first budget) to 31.12.1997	54 828 609	
Sub-total		**54 828 609**
New expenditure approved: Expenditure approved during the first quarter of 1998 Expenditure approved during the second quarter of 1998 Expenditure approved during the third quarter of 1998 Expenditure approved during the fourth quarter of 1998	 662 094 39 520 727 1 705 332 1 734 221	
Sub-total		**43 622 374**
Total C.SIS I		**98 450 983**
SIS II		
Budget approved up to 31.12.1997	2 400 000	
I. Sub-total		**2 400 000**
New expenditure approved: Expenditure approved during the first quarter of 1998 Expenditure approved during the second quarter of 1998 Expenditure approved during the third quarter of 1998 Expenditure approved during the fourth quarter of 1998	 600 000 0 13 000 0	
Sub-total		**613 000**
Total SIS II		**3 301 300**
Overall total		**101 463 983**

DECISION OF THE EXECUTIVE COMMITTEE of 28 April 1999 on updating the Sirene manual

(SCH/Com-ex (99) 5)

The Executive Committee,

— Having regard to Article 132 of the convention implementing the Schengen Agreement,

— Having regard to Article 108 of the abovementioned convention,

HAS DECIDED AS FOLLOWS:

The Sirene manual has been updated; the new version (SCH/OR.SIS-SIRENE (99) 64) is attached to this decision [1].

Luxembourg, 28 April 1999

The Chairman

C. H. SCHAPPER

(1) See SCH/Com-ex (98) 17.

DECLARATION OF THE EXECUTIVE COMMITTEE of 18 April 1996 defining the concept of alien

(SCH/Com-ex (96) decl 5)

Having regard to the Schengen Convention of 19 June 1990, in particular Article 134 thereof,

Having regard to the progress made within the European Union on placing persons, who are covered by Community law, on the joint list,

In the context of Article 96 of the aforementioned convention,

Persons who are covered by Community law should not in principle be placed on the joint list of persons to be refused entry.

However, the following categories of persons who are covered by Community law may be placed on the joint list if the conditions governing such placing are compatible with Community law:

(a) family members of European Union citizens who have third-country nationality and are entitled to enter and reside in a Member State, pursuant to a decision made in accordance with the Treaty establishing the European Community;

(b) nationals of Iceland, Liechtenstein and Norway and members of their families who fall within the scope of the provisions of Community law on entry and residence.

If it emerges that Community law covers a person included on the joint list of persons to be refused entry, that person may only remain on the list if it is compatible with Community law. If this is not the case, the Member State which placed the person on the list shall take the necessary steps to delete his or her name from the list.

DECLARATION OF THE EXECUTIVE COMMITTEE of 28 April 1999 on the structure of SIS

(SCH/Com-ex (99) decl. 2 rev)

Pursuant to Article 108(1) of the convention implementing the Schengen Agreement, each Contracting Party shall designate an authority which shall have central responsibility for the national section of the Schengen information system.

The Executive Committee takes note of the lists submitted which have already been incorporated into the joint list (see annex, document SCH/OR.SIS (99) 1 rev.3 ([1])).

Luxembourg, 28 April 1999

The Chairman

C. H. SCHAPPER

([1]) Restricted documents.

2.6. DIVERS

DECISION OF THE EXECUTIVE COMMITTEE of 22 December 1994 on the certificate provided for in Article 75 to carry narcotic drugs and psychotropic substances

(SCH/Com-ex (94) 28 rev)

The Executive Committee,

Having regard to Article 132 of the convention implementing the Schengen Agreement,

Having regard to Article 75 of the abovementioned convention,

HAS DECIDED AS FOLLOWS:

Document SCH/Stup (94) 21 rev 2 annexed hereto, setting out the certificate to carry narcotic drugs and/or psychotropic substances for the purposes of medical treatment, is hereby approved.

Bonn, 22 December 1994

The Chairman

B. SCHMIDBAUER

Certificate to carry narcotic drugs and/or psychotropic substances for the purpose of medical treatment pursuant to Article 75 of the implementing convention

(SCH/Stup (94) 21 rev 2)

1. The Schengen States have adopted the certificate set out in Annex 1, in accordance with Article 75 of the implementing convention. The form shall be used uniformly in all the Schengen States and shall be drawn up in the respective national languages. English and French translations of the form's preprinted headings are provided on the reverse side of the certificate.

2. The competent authorities of the Schengen State shall issue this certificate to persons resident on their territory who want to travel to another Schengen State and who, owing to a medical prescription, need to take narcotic drugs and/or psychotropic substances during this period. The certificate shall be valid for a maximum period of 30 days.

3. The certificate shall be issued or authenticated by the competent authorities on the basis of a medical prescription. A separate certificate shall be required for each narcotic drug/ psychotropic substance prescribed. The competent authorities shall keep a copy of the certificate.

4. Doctors may prescribe narcotic drugs for travel needs of up to 30 days. The travel period may be shorter than this.

5. Each Member State has designated a central office responsible for answering any questions that arise in this connection (see Annex 2). The designated central office is also the authority with responsibility for issuing or authenticating certificates in Belgium, Luxembourg and the Netherlands only.

Annex 1

Annex 1

______ (Country) ______ (Town) ______ (Date) — (1)

A. Prescribing doctor

______ (Name) ______ (First name) ______ (Tel.) (2)

______ (Address) (3)

where issued by a doctor:

______ (Doctor's stamp) ______ (Doctor's signature)(4) (4)

B. Patient

______ (Name) (First name) (5)

______ (No of passport or other identity document) (6)

______ (Place of birth) (7)

______ (Date of birth) (8)

______ (Nationality) (9)

______ (Sex) (10)

______ (Address) (11)

______ (No of travel days) (12)

______ (Validity of authorisation — max. 30 days) (13)

C. Prescribed drug

______ (Trade name or special preparation) (14)

______ (Dosage form) (15)

______ (International name of active substance) (16)

______ (Concentration of active substance) (17)

______ (Instructions for use) (18)

______ (Total quantity of active substance) (19)

______ (Duration of prescription in days — max. 30 days) (20)

______ (Remarks) (21)

D. Issuing/accrediting authority (Delete where not applicable)

______ (Name) (22)

______ (Address) (Tel.) (23)

______ (Authority's stamp) ______ **(Authority's signature)** **(24)**

Reverse side of the certificate

	Certificate to carry drugs and/or psychotropic substances for the purpose of medical treatment — Article 75 of the Schengen Convention	Certificat pour le transport de stupéfiants et/ou de substances psychotropes à des fins thérapeutiques — Article 75 de la Convention d'application de l'Accord de Schengen
(1)	country, town, date	pays, délivré à, date
A	**Prescribing doctor**	**Médecin prescripteur**
(2)	name, first name, tel.	nom, prénom, téléphone
(3)	address	adresse
(4)	where issued by a doctor: doctor's stamp and signature	en cas de délivrance par un médecin: cachet, signature du médecin
B	**Patient**	**Patient**
(5)	name, first name	nom, prénom
(6)	No of passport or other identity document	n° du passeport ou du document d'identité
(7)	place of birth	lieu de naissance
(8)	date of birth	date de naissance
(9)	nationality	nationalité
(10)	sex	sexe
(11)	address	adresse
(12)	duration of travel in days	durée du voyage en jours
(13)	validity of authorisation from/to — max. 30 days	durée de validité de l'autorisation du/au — max. 30 jours
C	**Prescribed drug**	**Médicament prescrit**
(14)	trade name or special preparation	nom commercial ou préparation spéciale
(15)	dosage form	forme pharmaceutique
(16)	international name of active substance	dénomination internationale de la substance active
(17)	concentration of active substance	concentration de la substance active
(18)	instructions for use	mode d'emploi
(19)	total quantity of active substance	quantité totale de la substance active
(20)	duration of prescription in days — max. 30 days	durée de la prescription, en jours — max. 30 jours
(21)	remarks	remarques
D	**Issuing/accrediting authority (delete where not applicable)**	**Autorité qui délivre/authentifie (biffer ce qui ne convient pas)**
(22)	name	désignation
(23)	address, tel.	adresse, téléphone
(24)	authority's stamp and signature	sceau, signature de l'autorité

Annex 2

CENTRAL AUTHORITY TO BE CONTACTED IN THE EVENT OF PROBLEMS (Article 75 of the convention)

Belgium

Ministère de la Santé Publique
Inspection générale de la Pharmacie
Quartier Vésale — Cité administrative de l'Etat
B-1010 Bruxelles
Tel. (32-2) 210 49 28
Fax (32-2) 210 63 70

Germany

Ministerium für Arbeit, Gesundheit und Soziales des Landes Nordrhein-Westfalen
Pharmaziedezernat
Horionplatz 1 — Landeshaus
D-40213 Düsseldorf
Tel. (49-211) 837 35 91
Fax (49-211) 837 36 62

Spain

Servicio de Restricción de Estupefacientes
Dirección Gral. de Farmacia y Productos Sanitarios
Ministerio de Sanidad y Consumo
Calle Principe de Vergara, 54
E-28006 Madrid
Chef du service: D. Luis Dominguez Arques
Tel. (34) 15 75 27 63
Fax (34) 15 78 12 31

France

Ministère de la Santé
Direction Générale de la Santé
1, place de Fontenoy
F-75350 Paris Cedex 07 SP
Tel. (33) 140 56 47 16 or 40 56 43 41
Fax (33) 140 56 40 54

Greece

Ministry of Health
Medicines Department
Narcotic Drugs Division
Aristotelous Street 17
GR-10433 Athens
Tel. (30-1) 522 53 01

Italy

Ministero della Sanità
Direzione Generale Servizio Farmaceutico
Ufficio centrale Stupefacenti
Via della Civiltà Romana 7
I-00144 Roma
Tel. (39) 06 59 94 31 77
Fax. (39) 06 59 94 33 65

Luxembourg

Ministère de la Santé
Direction de la Santé
L-2935 Luxembourg
Tel. (352) 478 55 50
Fax (352) 48 49 03

The Netherlands

Hoofdinspectie voor de geneesmiddelen
van het Staatstoezicht op de Volksgezondheid
PO Box 5406
NL-2280 HK Rijswijk
Tel. (31-70) 340 64 23

Portugal

Instituto Nacional da Farmacia e do Medicamento (Infarmed)
Parque de Saúde
Av. do Brazil, 53
P-1700 Lisboa
Fax (351-1) 795 91 16 [1]

Austria

Bundesministerium für Gesundheit, Sport und Konsumentenschutz
Abteilung II/C/18
Radetzkysstraße 2
A-1030 Wien
Tel. (43-1) 711 72 47 34
Fax (43-1) 713 86 14

(1) Subject to approval by a higher authority.

DECISION OF THE EXECUTIVE COMMITTEE of 28 April 1999 on the illegal trade in firearms

(SCH/Com-ex (99) 10)

The Executive Committee,

Having regard to Article 132 of the convention implementing the Schengen Agreement,

Having regard to Article 9 of the abovementioned convention,

HAS DECIDED AS FOLLOWS:

Henceforth, the Contracting Parties shall submit each year by 31 July their national annual data for the preceding year on illegal trade in firearms, on the basis of the joint table for compiling statistics annexed to document SCH/I-ar (98) 32.

Luxembourg, 28 April 1999

The Chairman

C. H. SCHAPPER

SCH/I-Ar (98) 32

1. Total number of firearms seized (1) during the period (2) from ... to (*)

		Reference period	Comparative period
Category (3) A			
Category B	B 1 Handguns (4)		
	B 2 Long firearms (5)		
	Total		
Category C			
Category D			
Total			
Category X (6)			

(1) Includes the illegal trade, possession, illegal import and illegal carrying of firearms.
(2) If possible, should be defined on the basis of a calendar year — e.g. 1996.
(3) Firearms category pursuant to Directive 91/477/EEC.
(4) Handguns up to 60 cm total length.
(5) Long firearms.
(6) Includes firearms which cannot be subsumed under categories A-C, such as arms used as a warning, arms containing irritants or self-defence sprays.
(*) Noteworthy factors effecting the data should be given separately, not in the table (such as 1 000 firearms seized in one single operation, particularly frequent seizures of one specific type of firearm).

2. Country of origin ([1]) of the firearms seized during the period from ... to ... (*)

		Schengen States	Non-Schengen States
Category A			
Category B	B 1 Handguns		
	B 2 Long firearms		
	Total		
Category C			
Category D			
Total			
Category X			

([1]) County of origin = Country of manufacture
(*) Noteworthy factors effecting the data should be given separately, not in the table (such as 1 000 firearms seized in one single operation, particularly frequent seizures of one specific type of firearm).

3. Means of transport used for the firearms seized during the period from ... to ... (*) (expressed in %)

		Train	Bus	HGV	Car	Aero-plane	Ship	Parcel post
Category A								
Category B	B 1 Hand-guns							
	B 2 Long firearms							
Category C								
Category D								
Category X								

(*) Noteworthy factors effecting the data should be given separately, not in the table (such as 1 000 firearms seized in one single operation, particularly frequent seizures of one specific type of firearm).

4. Main smuggling routes for firearms seized during the period from ... to ... (*)

(please indicate the three most frequently used routes per category)

			Country of origin [1]	Country of transit	Country of seizure
Category A		1			
		2			
		3			
Category B	B 1 Hand-guns	1			
		2			
		3			
	B 2 Long firearms	1			
		2			
		3			
Category C		1			
		2			
		3			
Category D		1			
		2			
		3			
Category X		1			
		2			
		3			

[1] Country of origin = Country of manufacture.
(*) Noteworthy factors effecting the data should be given separately, not in the table (such as 1 000 firearms seized in one single operation, particularly frequent seizures of one specific type of firearm).

Council of the European Union

The Schengen *acquis* integrated into the European Union

Luxembourg: Office for Official Publications of the European Communities

2001 — 577 pp. — 17.6 x 25 cm

ISBN 92-824-1776-X

Price (excluding VAT) in Luxembourg: EUR 66